Ways of Writing

Ways of Writing

Critical Essays on Zakes Mda

Edited by

DAVID BELL AND J.U. JACOBS

UNIVERSITY OF KwaZulu-Natal Press

Published in 2009 by University of KwaZulu-Natal Press
Private Bag X01
Scottsville 3209
South Africa
E-mail: books@ukzn.ac.za
Website: www.ukznpress.co.za

ISBN: 978-1-86914-151-6

Managing editor: Sally Hines
Editor: Alison Lockhart
Typesetter: Patricia Comrie
Indexer: Catherine Dubbeld
Cover design: M Design

The editors and publishers acknowledge permission from the Missionary Oblates of Mary
Immaculate for the use of the cover image (*Married Couple*) and Figures 1, 3, 5, 11, 12 and 14.
These paintings were originally published in Frans Claerhout, *Catcher of the Sun* (Cape Town:
Tafelberg, 1983). The publishers also give due thanks to the Johannes Stegmann Art Gallery
at the University of the Free State, Bloemfontein, where the Catcher of the Sun/Sonnevanger
series by Frans Claerhout is housed in a permanent collection. The editors and publishers
would also like to thank Dirk Schwager for permission to use Figures 2, 4, 6, 7, 8, 9, 10 and
13. These paintings were originally published in Dirk and Dominique Schwager, *Claerhout:
Artist and Priest* (Maseru: Visual Publications, 1994).

Printed and bound by Interpak Books, Pietermaritzburg

Contents

Acknowledgements

Thanks are due to the Nordic Africa Institute, Uppsala, Sweden for accepting David Bell as a Nordic Guest Researcher and for giving him the opportunity to carry out valuable research at their institute. The following Swedish organisations have generously provided him with travel grants for research in South Africa and for participation in international conferences: Birgit and Gad Rausing Foundation, The Swedish Institute and Sparbanksstiftelsen Jämtlands Län (the Jämtland County Savings Bank Foundation).

David would also like to thank the members of the Department of English at Lund University, Sweden, and in particular their research seminar in English literature, for their support and critical stimulation during a vital stage in his research.

J.U. Jacobs is grateful to the National Research Foundation, South Africa, for a grant that enabled him to conduct research into Zakes Mda's sources, and to Dr Arie Kuijers of the Johannes Stegmann Art Gallery of the University of the Free State for having provided him with access to the collection of paintings by Frans Claerhout.

Finally, both editors would also like to express their sincere appreciation for all the assistance provided by the staff – and especially by Thomas Jeffery – of the National English Literary Museum in Grahamstown in the compilation of the critical bibliographies and with obtaining access to critical material.

Zakes Mda

Ways of Writing

DAVID BELL AND J.U. JACOBS

ZAKES MDA IS RECOGNISED as an important African and significant South African writer. Like Chinua Achebe, he has engaged with the colonial, post-colonial and also neo-colonial history of his country. As in the case of Wole Soyinka's work, Mda's oeuvre encompasses both drama and fiction, which draw on Western and indigenous performance traditions. Mda's career, like that of Ngugi wa Thiong'o, has followed a double trajectory and he has distinguished himself not only as a creative writer, but also as a cultural theorist and activist. Furthermore, in common with fellow African authors, Mda has written from a position of exile, as well as from within his native country.

In the South African context, Mda's writings may be compared with those of Nadine Gordimer, in so far as they depict the history of South Africa during and after apartheid 'from the inside', to use Stephen Clingman's well-known phrase about Gordimer (1986: 1). To the extent that Mda has made his mark as a literary and social theorist, as well as a playwright and novelist, he also invites comparison with a writer such as André P. Brink, or, for that matter, Njabulo S. Ndebele. The degree of self-reflexivity in Mda's novels positions them in the same category as the metafictional discourse of J.M. Coetzee, just as their imaginative inventiveness is matched perhaps only in the fictional works of Ivan Vladislavić or Etienne van Heerden. And like Antjie Krog – indeed, all of these contemporary South African writers – Mda is concerned with examining the lives and experiences of ordinary people in democratic

1

South Africa, and the ways in which they are coming to terms with the apartheid past, without their being overwhelmed by it or constrained by its categories. Mda's is a significant voice among the many in contemporary South Africa that are exploiting innovative forms to explore and scrutinise a culture in transition, voices that demand attention and critical appraisal.

For all that he shares with this company of African and South African writers, Mda's works are nevertheless distinguished by their striking originality, by an experimental quality that is as varied as it is extraordinary, and that contributes, as this collection demonstrates, to the richness of what has by now become a major, coherent body of writing by a writer who is in mature command of his narrative craft.

Although the eighteen essays in this volume have been organised chronologically in terms of Mda's prolific output of more than thirty plays and six novels over the last three decades, there emerges an overarching critical narrative that is suggested by the recurrent and intriguing motif of closely paired siblings or of actual twinning in Mda's works, especially in his novels. A homeboy and homegirl from the same mountain village in *Ways of Dying*; a brother and sister who are born in the same year to a woman who consequently becomes known as Mother of Twins in *She Plays with the Darkness*; twin brothers who are descended from ancestral twin brothers, named Twin and Twin-Twin, in *The Heart of Redness*; a white man and a black man whose worlds are brought into close and conflicting relation with each other through their common half-sister in *The Madonna of Excelsior*; destructive twin children in *The Whale Caller*; and two slave half-brothers to whose histories the complex commingling of races and cultures is traced back in *Cion* – all these are metonymic of a fundamental duality in Mda's art of writing.

*   *   *

Since Mda's life has been contiguous with the rise and fall of the apartheid state and its subsequent transition to democracy – he was born in 1948, the son of A.P. Mda, an African National Congress (ANC) and later Pan-Africanist Congress (PAC) activist – it seems inevitable that his political persona would develop alongside his artistic one. Throughout his career, Mda has willingly

shared his views on literature and on political and social issues in South Africa with a wider audience in newspaper articles, contributions to journals and in several published interviews. Over the years, he has taken many opportunities to underscore and elaborate on his political and social commitment in his work. In so doing, he has provided a greater insight into the relationship he perceives between art and politics and into the nature of and changes in his own writing. He explained his attitude to his work and the role of the artist in an extensive interview in 1988, before he began writing novels:

> I do not believe that art necessarily distracts from social relevance. I also do not see how social relevance makes a work inartistic . . . [T]he role that I hope to play as an artist, and the role I hope my work plays is that of social commentator and social commentary. I am against art for art's sake – in African aesthetics that is a strange concept because the artist was actually a social commentator . . . I want [my art] to rally people to action. (Holloway 1988: 83)

These remarks introduce a strand of thought that has been a persistent feature of Mda's work: that the social function of his art and its obligation to provide social commentary are grounded in an African aesthetics.

Mda clearly sees his early plays as being highly political, but in recent interviews he has provided a context within which this political perspective is to be judged by pointing to a symbiotic relationship between the artist and society and arguing that the work of any artist is a response to his/her world and the changes it undergoes (Austen 2005; Wark 2005). In this respect, Mda's early, anti-apartheid plays can be seen as belonging to a period in which cultural contributions in South Africa were overtly political, driven by the need – at times, the demand – for artists to use their work as a weapon in the struggle against apartheid (Mbele 1989: 62–63; Kachuba 2005; Weber 2004; Austen 2005). This focus, in turn, had an influence on what was written, on the choice of subject matter and genre (Weber 2004; Wark 2005). In this context, literature (in particular, poetry, theatre and the short story) provided modes of performance that had immediate impact and, as Mda argued, could provide 'social commentary' and 'rally the people to action' (Holloway 1988: 83).

It is this duality in Mda's work as playwright and as an activist that David Bell explores in Chapter 1. Bell argues that Mda's dramaturgy underwent a paradigmatic shift after 1990: what was formerly essentially a theatre of resistance against apartheid became a theatre for development and a literary practice for democracy, as realised in the plays themselves and also articulated more fully by Mda in his book, *When People Play People: Development Communication through Theatre* (1993). Bell shows how Mda not only acted as a theatre practitioner, but also developed a theoretical framework, shaped by the ideas of Paulo Freire and Augusto Boal, which can be applied to all of his theatre. In her discussion of Mda's early plays in Chapter 2, Carolyn Duggan similarly foregrounds the social and political concerns and traces the theme of betrayal – personal, social and political – throughout these works and analyses the ways in which Mda's characters become empowered in a context of poverty and struggle. From the first play, *Dead End* (1979), to *Joys of War* (1989), Duggan outlines the ways in which Mda mirrors the social and political context of apartheid and the struggles of ordinary people to retain some freedom and humanity under an oppressive regime. In the third chapter on Mda's dramatic works in this collection, Shane Graham argues that one of Mda's later plays, *The Bells of Amersfoort*, is an example of 'theatre of reconciliation' – an extension of Mda's idea of 'theatre for development' – with its emphasis on healing and nation-building through memory and South Africans' renegotiation of their relationship to the land. Graham draws attention to the way in which Mda's innovative techniques involving space and time integrate performance and meaning, so that performance *is* meaning.

With the ending of apartheid, Mda experienced a sense of liberation. No longer under pressure to produce theatre to mobilise against an oppressive regime, he found the time to work on long pieces of prose and moved from being a political playwright to a critical novelist. He explained his position to Benjamin Austen in an interview published in December 2005:

I am free now. And the end of apartheid has freed the imagination of the artist. I tell stories now. But these stories come from an environment that is highly politically charged . . . But my main mission is to tell a story, rather than to propagate a political message. During apartheid, it was the other way around. It was part of my political commitment, I wrote plays. I only started novels after the political changes. (Austen 2005)

Mda's freedom has not meant a diminishing of his concern for current social and political issues or his critical commentary – he still has a 'political commitment' – but he has shifted emphasis to cope with the diverse voices that have emerged in contemporary South Africa and which have become represented in its fiction.

Mda's willingness to adapt to the changes taking place in South Africa has influenced his approach to his work. While his pre-1994 work and his commentaries on it were characterised by a clear anti-apartheid and anti-neo-colonial stance, in post-1994 South Africa, he sees himself as a novelist writing works that are critical of events in South Africa, but which treat the issues in an even-handed manner (Mbele 1989: 62–63; Kachuba 2005), as he has explicitly illustrated in his discussions of *The Madonna of Excelsior*, which he sees as 'a balanced kind of portrayal of the situation in South Africa today' (Kachuba 2005).

*   *   *

In addition to the general twinning of Mda's political and artistic personae, as discussed earlier, there is a further duality in his art, especially his fiction, which combines a faithfulness to history and authenticity on the one hand, with a markedly performative character, on the other hand.

The underlying factual basis of Mda's work was made apparent even in an early interview concerning his plays where he pointed out that the prison labour on farms referred to in *Dark Voices Ring* was based on information he had acquired through the press, in particular Henry Nxumalo's investigations published in *Drum* in the 1950s (Holloway 1988: 84). This desire to be factually accurate is especially apparent in Mda's novels. The deaths in *Ways of Dying*, for instance, had been reported in *The Sunday Times* and *City Press* newspapers at the time that he was writing the novel (Naidoo 1997: 253; Bell 2004). Similarly, the nineteenth-century events depicted in *The Heart of Redness* are

closely aligned to the historical account of the Xhosa cattle killings by J.B.
Peires to ensure the authenticity of the interactions between fictional and
historical characters in the novel (Bell 2004). In the case of *The Madonna of
Excelsior*, once Mda had fixed on his subject, he researched the case in magazines
and newspapers in Johannesburg and Bloemfontein (Bell 2004; Kachuba 2005;
Weber 2004). At times, Mda has used his own experience to provide a
background to the characters in his novels. In *She Plays with the Darkness*,
Radisene is based, to some extent, on Mda's experiences as an article clerk in
Lesotho, and Camagu in *The Heart of Redness* experiences the kind of reception
Mda himself met when returning to South Africa after a long period of exile
abroad (Naidoo 1997: 255; Kachuba 2005; Wark 2005; Bell 2004).

A concern for authenticity is reflected in Mda's emphasis on the importance
of actual place in his choice of story and narrative: 'Place is key. To me place is
not just background for my cast of characters. The place is so important that
many of my novels are suggested by the place.' (Weber 2004) But this is a more
complex process than this quote suggests. In *Ways of Dying*, for example, the
main character was developed first and was then introduced, at an early stage,
into a story about the deaths taking place in South Africa in the early 1990s
(Weber 2004; Bell 2004). *The Heart of Redness* was inspired in part by the
place, Qolorha-by-Sea, and in part by an enthusiasm for the history associated
with the legend of Nongqawuse (Bell 2004). *The Madonna of Excelsior* came
about after a drive through the Free State and the memory of past events in
the small town of Excelsior in the 1970s. In addition, the naive paintings of
madonnas by Father Frans Claerhout had inspired the narrative style of the
novel (Weber 2004; Bell 2004; Kachuba 2005). Finally, *The Whale Caller* was
inspired by a television programme on the whale caller of Hermanus and the
great disappointment Mda experienced when he discovered that the whale
caller did not call the whales, but called people to come and see them (Kachuba
2005).

Whatever the basis of his writing, Mda has consistently drawn attention to
the creative process in and innovative nature of his work. As Mda puts it, he is
in the 'God Business' and can make things happen the way he wants them to,
'however much that might contradict what you might call objective reality'
(Naidoo 1997: 250; Kachuba 2005). This attitude has its origins in his early

work as a dramatist living in either Lesotho or the United States, where, unlike writers in South Africa who were able to 'get their characters and stories from what they saw around them', he was 'far away from the situation itself . . . [and] was forced to use [his] imagination' (Naidoo 1997: 251; see also Galgut 2005). Mda has argued that this has been to his advantage, as he is now able to use his imagination in writing novels at a time when the easy 'slice of life' absurdity of apartheid is no longer there to provide a source of material and stories (Wark 2005).

Given his earlier work as a playwright, it is perhaps understandable that there is a strong performative element in Mda's novels, as well as a historical dimension. Performance is most obviously foregrounded in his fictional narratives in the form of social ceremonies or festivals – the various funeral rituals in *Ways of Dying*; the customary social gatherings of the Basotho people, with their traditional dances in *She Plays with the Darkness*; the Xhosa tradition of split-tone singing in *The Heart of Redness*; the Ficksburg Cherry Festival in *The Madonna of Excelsior*; the Kalfiefees in Hermanus when the Southern Right Whales arrive annually to give birth in *The Whale Caller*; and the Court Street Halloween parade that frames the narrative in *Cion*.

At a deeper narrative level, however, Mda's fictional works are performative in ways that go to the essence of his art and its roots in African narrative forms and ontology. Mda has consistently drawn attention to the African origins of his art. While in various interviews he has mentioned representatives of the Western dramatic tradition as influences on his playwriting, he has placed greater emphasis on the influence of Athol Fugard, Gibson Kente, Wole Soyinka and other West African playwrights (Holloway 1988: 83; Naidoo 1997: 249; Wark 2005). And while, as a novelist, Mda has recognised the influences of Gabriel García Márquez and Yvonne Vera (Naidoo 1997: 250; Kachuba 2005), he has always maintained that the distinguishing characteristics of his style – a minimalist theatre of the absurd and magical realist elements in both his plays and novels – have arisen from an African (and particularly South African) narrative context and only later has he consciously become aware of and explored the theatre of the absurd, Brechtian drama and magical realism (Holloway 1988: 83; Naidoo 1997: 249–50; Wark 2005).

Mda has given increasing prominence to the importance of an African storytelling tradition in his mode of writing. By 2005, he was making a strong case for the African oral tradition in his work: 'Mine also draws from that oral tradition. It draws from it very strongly. My work will always have that intertextuality . . . with "orature", as it is called, in other words, oral literature' (Kachuba 2005). In an interview in 2004, Mda also affirmed that he drew his inspiration 'from the African oral tradition and not only inspiration, but the actual mode of storytelling, the participatory mode of storytelling' (Wark 2005). Mda thus sees his work as deriving from and as part of a dynamic, African tradition of oral storytelling in which participatory, performative modes are paramount.

This appreciation of the African storytelling tradition focuses on two elements: 'magic', as Mda refers to Western perceptions of the irrational, and the use of a collective/communal narrator. In this respect, Mda has referred to his own work as drawing on 'the sources that are having this constant conversation between the living and the fourth dimension', a formulation derived from Ayi Kwei Armah who, Mda points out, was 'referring to both the dead and the unborn' (Kachuba 2005). For Mda, this has certainly not been an abstract phenomenon. In a 1997 interview, he put forward the perspective that 'we Africans always live with magic . . . Here in Africa there is magic happening all the time. There are many belief systems and in fact a lot of the things that the Western world refers to as superstition. For me such things actually happen and I portray them as such in my writings'; and the elements of 'magic' that critics comment on in *She Plays with the Darkness*, he considers to be part of 'the way people live in Lesotho' (Naidoo 1997: 250, 254).

Mda's complex relation to magic realism has been extensively explored. He has pointed to the presence of this mode in his writing before he had become aware of magic realism as a distinctive form: 'I had not heard of magic realism when I started writing those plays. It is something that I have always done in my writing. I make things happen the way I want things to happen, however much that might contradict what you might call objective reality' (Naidoo 1997: 250). Here a natural explanation has been allied to the power of the writer to decide over his own text. But later in the same interview, Mda develops a more conscious argument that incorporates both a 'natural' African origin of his style and a deliberate attempt at understanding and using the style developed by writers such as Márquez. When asked about the magic realist elements in his first two novels, Mda replied: 'When I started my first novel, *Ways of Dying*, I was conscious of a movement called magic realism and that I was writing a magic realist novel. But basically, I was doing what I had done much earlier' (250). He later elaborates on his position by referring to his attempts to define the term and the relationship of his work to it. Mda mentions two key elements he discerns in magic realism: 'the supernatural is not presented as problematical' and 'an absurd metamorphosis is described as if it did not contradict our laws of reason' (255). Both of these elements, Mda argues, are characteristic of his work: 'the unreal happens as part of reality' (255). In later interviews, Mda has emphasised the African origins of his use of what critics label magic realism:

> I draw from the same sources as creators of magical realism . . . the world from which my fiction draws has not got that line of demarcation between the supernatural on one hand and what you would call objective reality on the other hand. The two merge and live side by side. Those who live in that world cannot separate the two. Magic is part of their real world, their realism. (Kachuba 2005)

It is in this context of Mda's claims that his novels are performative of an African epistemology that Christopher Warnes's wide-ranging, theoretical discussion in Chapter 4 of the question of magical realism in South African literature, and especially in Mda's work, needs to be read. In this chapter, which also serves to introduce the other chapters that deal with Mda's novels, Warnes considers the various meanings of the term 'magic realism' and its manifestations in African writing, and concludes that Mda's magic realism is not quite of the same order, but is rather more restrained and more ironic in nature.

The second strand of Mda's African narrative tradition, and one which highlights the shared nature of creative experience, is his use of a third person, communal narrator. This, he has argued, is part of the oral tradition and in relation to his first two novels, it comes 'very much from orature, because the story can be told in the plural form. This is how African people tell stories' (Naidoo 1997: 254). In *The Madonna of Excelsior*, the communal narrator has meant that: 'the reader then becomes part of the community. This is something you do find a lot in the oral tradition. We talk in terms of "we", we the community. The community is everywhere. Niki has been there, the lawyer has been. We have a common story to tell. We have experienced this story together' (Kachuba 2005).

In their analysis in Chapter 5 of the ways in which community history and community memory are given life and substance in *Ways of Dying*, Rogier Courau and Sally-Ann Murray argue that the performance of funeral rites, combined with Toloki's innovative performances as a professional mourner, provide a source of vital continuity in a complex and curious cultural dynamic. Nokuthula Mazibuko similarly engages with the idea of community in her discussion of *Ways of Dying* in Chapter 6, but approaches it from a feminist perspective, showing how Mda draws from and innovatively adapts a range of symbolic African constructions of womanhood to present a number of 'wayward' women in his novel. These women, marginalised by a male-dominated and materialist discourse, while also the custodians of creativity and healing, are seen by the author as central to the rebuilding of a post-colonial and post-apartheid South Africa. In Chapter 7, T. Spreelin MacDonald explores Mda's recurrent trope of a bonded pair of characters in relation to the African concept of *ubuntu*, or humanism, in his discussion of Mda's second novel, *She Plays with the Darkness*. Twinship, MacDonald argues, is a humanistic concept, a perception of brotherhood and sisterhood as a fundamental and inescapable bond, which Mda shows as being 'of continued relevance in a post-colonial age which is otherwise fractured by identity politics'. MacDonald's argument is premised on the fact that Radisene and Dikosha are doubly 'twinned', not only to each other, but each of them also to their community.

The critical attention paid to Mda's third novel, *The Heart of Redness*, indicates that it has achieved something of the status of a contemporary classic. The richness and complexity of the work are evidenced by the range of theoretical perspectives from which it has been approached by the authors of the six chapters dealing with this text. In Chapter 8, Mike Kissack and Michael Titlestad provide a compelling analysis of the protagonist, Camagu, in terms of what Edward Said refers to as the 'secular intellectual', a figure through whom Mda can explore and mediate the complexities of the post-apartheid social revolution, enacting through the persona of Camagu his own engagement in debates about traditional African values and social development. Hilary P. Dannenberg shows in Chapter 9 how *The Heart of Redness* dramatises culture as a complex and dynamic process, and she demonstrates how in the course of the narrative, interactive processes are played out, whereby cultures coming into contact with other hegemonic cultures undergo change and cultural hybridisation results. In Chapter 10, Gail Fincham juxtaposes *The Heart of Redness* with Joseph Conrad's novella, *Heart of Darkness*, establishing an intertextual dialogue between the works. She compares and contrasts the ways in which Mda deconstructs the tropes of empire from a post-colonial perspective with Conrad's insights into the processes and consequences of colonial domination.

If the previous three chapters demonstrate how the narrative of *The Heart of Redness* enacts debates about social revolution and development, cultural hybridisation, and colonialism and post-colonialism, Harry Sewlall's approach to the novel from an ecocritical perspective in Chapter 11 shows how Mda's text performs and preserves in its magical way the worldview of the amaXhosa in which humans interact symbiotically with animals, and animals exist in an interpersonal relationship with humans. Meg Samuelson provides a feminist reading of *The Heart of Redness* that is both appreciative and corrective in Chapter 12. Focusing on Nongqawuse's story and the Xhosa cattle killings, Samuelson offers not only a fine assessment of the success of the novel in providing a counterpoint to the linear model of history and in challenging development ideologies, she also points to a significant difference between what the novel professes and what it performs in terms of its gendered conception of authorship, as well as in its conception and presentation of female characters. Finally, in Chapter 13, Grant Farred subjects *The Heart of Redness* to a philosophical critique in terms of the concept of the theocratic, which, according to Farred, is also the space of the politically dissensual. In his analysis of Nongqawuse's prophecy and its acceptance and dismissal by the Believers and the Non-Believers as represented in the novel, Farred exposes what he sees as the inability of Mda's novel to understand and appreciate the extent of the complexity of the discourse of Christianity and its dialogical relationship to the prophetic tradition.

In Chapter 14, the first of the three chapters dealing with *The Madonna of Excelsior*, J.U. Jacobs also takes the dual nature of Mda's fictional discourse as a point of departure. In an analysis of the newspaper reports on which Mda based his narrative, he shows, on the one hand, Mda's fidelity to his historical sources; on the other hand, in an analysis of Mda's ecphrasis, Jacobs also shows the performative character of Mda's text, in so far as it creates an African narrative equivalent of the expressionist paintings of the Flemish priest Father Frans Claerhout. In Chapter 15, Ralph Goodman discusses a different kind of performativity in Mda's narrative: he explores how the novel satirically exposes apartheid and its notorious Immorality Act and 'sets in motion a process of open-ended dialogue between the indignant patriarchalism of the South African state towards the existence of so-called mixed-race people on the one hand, and the subversive delight in creolisation taken by so many post-colonial texts on the other'. In his discussion in Chapter 16 of how Mda narrates transformative possibilities in *The Madonna of Excelsior*, N.S. Zulu focuses on the nature and operation of the communal narrative voice, which, he concludes, is omniscient, complex and multiple, self-mocking, ironic and satirical, one that subverts notions of racial and political homogeneity and dismantles past social and ideological categories.

Mda's fifth novel, *The Whale Caller* distinguishes itself from his previous novels by addressing more fully ecological issues and the relationship of humans to animals, in this case, the Southern Right Whale. In Chapter 17, Wendy Woodward provides an extensively theorised, comparative ecocritical reading of Mda's novel and Jane Rosenthal's *Souvenir*. Both works represent, Woodward argues, a major development away from post-apartheid literature in that they foreground, in the context of the global ecological predicament, the interactions and interconnections between humans and 'earth-others', and between human culture and the material environment. Woodward's chapter opens the field of critical studies on Mda to a wider field of comparative readings and contemporary concerns for humankind's future on this planet.

In conclusion, in Chapter 18, J.U. Jacobs and David Bell return to Mda's characteristic discursive doubling of history and performance in his sixth and most recent novel, *Cion*, where his art of fiction can be seen to have come full circle. As in Mda's previous novels, *Cion* engages with various forms of artistic expression as metaphors for different ways of writing, the most important being the ever-developing performances of Toloki, his professional mourner from *Ways of Dying*, who is made to accompany Mda to Athens, Ohio. The novel also explores the art of quilt-making as a parallel to the art of writing by drawing attention to its metaphors of meaning and important traditions, while demonstrating a concern that these traditions should not inhibit genuine imaginative creativity. *Cion* self-reflexively performs and flaunts its fictionality to an unprecedented degree, as well as the relative status of its author and its protagonist. Whereas in earlier novels, Mda experiments with various ways of writing fiction, *Cion* is his most overtly *meta*fictional novel to date, and it returns him to the roots of his writing. The novel concludes with Toloki's realisation that Greek tragedy developed out of ritual mourning, and that out of this ancient dramatic tradition developed also Mda's own theatre pieces and his works of fiction – and that, as a professional mourner, Toloki has his being at the very beginnings and also at the self-reflexive conclusion of a long history of very many ways of writing.

This first collection of critical essays on Zakes Mda addresses the extensive body of his drama and fiction from the earliest plays in the 1970s to the most recent novel in 2007. The wide critical range of the essays presented here reinforces the impression of Mda as an innovative and important writer whose use of creative skills draws attention to the plight of underprivileged people in South Africa and elsewhere. The content of the volume is intended to provide challenging reading to anyone with an interest in South African writing and it is hoped it will stimulate further research on Zakes Mda.

Works cited

Austen, Benjamin. 2005. 'An interview with Zakes Mda'. *nat creole* magazine. http://www.natcreole.com/features.htm#title1, Part i, accessed 16 December 2005; Part ii, accessed 19 January 2006.

Bell, David. 2004. Conversation with Zakes Mda. Market Theatre, Johannesburg. 16 July.

Clingman, Stephen R. 1986. *The Novels of Nadine Gordimer: History from the Inside*. Johannesburg: Ravan Press.

Galgut, Damon. 2005. 'In conversation with Zakes Mda'. The Absa/LitNet Chain Interview. LitNet, 19 July. http://www.litnet.co.za/chain/damon_galgut_vs_zakes_mda.asp, accessed 19 January 2006.

Holloway, Myles. 1988. 'An interview with Zakes Mda' (7 February 1987). *South African Theatre Journal* 2(2): 81–88.

Horn, Andrew. 1980. 'Arts and Africa: An interview with Zakes Mda'. BBC Broadcast No. 316: 1–5.

———. 1990. 'People are being murdered here: An introduction to the theatre of Zakes Mda'. In: Mda, Zakes. *The Plays of Zakes Mda*. Johannesburg: Ravan Press: vii–liv.

Kachuba, John B. 2005. 'An interview with Zakes Mda'. *Tin House* 20. http://www.tinhouse.com/issues/issue_20/interview.html, accessed 14 September 2005.

Mbele, Maggie. 1989. 'Putting people first: Interview with Zakes Mda'. *Tribute*, 13 November: 62–64.

Mda, Zakes. 1993. *When People Play People: Development Communication through Theatre*. Johannesburg: Wits University Press; London: Zed Books.

Naidoo, Venu. 1997. 'An interview with Zakes Mda'. *Alternation* 4(1): 247–61.

Wark, Julie. 2005. 'Interview with Zakes Mda'. *Studia africana: revista interuniversitària d'estudis africans* (Barcelona) 16: 109–23. Online version originally available as 'An interview with Zakes Mda'. 15–16 October 2004. http://www.zakesmda.com/pages/JWarkinterview.html, accessed 10 October 2005.

Weber, Rebceca L. 2004. 'Q&A: Zakes Mda'. *The Africana*, http://www.africana.com, 25 May, accessed 14 September 2005.

A Theatre for Democracy

DAVID BELL

THE FOUR YEARS FROM 1990 to 1994 marked a turning point in the history of the state of South Africa, bringing to an end the almost century-long system of racial rule that began with the Union of South Africa in 1910 and ended with the brutally repressive state of emergency in the Republic of South Africa in the late 1980s. This shift in the political configuration also occasioned a paradigmatic shift in the ideological discourse in the region. Throughout the period of white, minority rule, culture had played a significant role in articulating grievances and bringing the injustices that prevailed in South Africa to the notice of both international and national publics. With the unbanning of the African National Congress (ANC) in 1990, followed by the first democratic elections in 1994, the prevailing binary discourse of apartheid/resistance to apartheid changed to one of reconciliation, reconstruction and the legitimate demands of a democratic society. Given the nature of the history of South Africa, changes in the political agenda have also influenced developments in and perceptions of culture.[1]

That there would be a need for a shift in perceptions in the field of culture had already been foreshadowed by Njabulo S. Ndebele's 1984 essay, 'Rediscovery of the Ordinary' and Albie Sachs's in-house paper for the ANC of 1989, 'Preparing Ourselves for Freedom', both of which dealt with the need for a change in cultural direction and content.[2] The result in South African literature and its critical appraisal has been a shift from a dominant, binary discourse determined by apartheid to a much more problematical discourse that concerns itself with the uncertain interactions of history and memory, and with present and future aspirations. In the process, such political and ideological notions as 'the Rainbow Nation' and 'the African Renaissance'[3] have been promulgated by leading figures in the political and cultural arenas and incorporated into the everyday discourse of the nation.

Among the many writers whose works span this major shift in the cultural life in South Africa, Zakes Mda is of particular interest as a prolific writer, for both stage and television, a practitioner of theatre for development, a novelist and a newspaper columnist. In this chapter, the focus is on exploring Mda's plays in relation to the paradigmatic shift in South African culture and to argue for his dramaturgy as a theatre for democracy. As those acquainted with his work will know, a concern with the ordinary and with the marginalised people of South Africa is one of its distinguishing features. In many respects, Mda's work can be seen to fit neatly into the paradigmatic shift indicated above; in other respects, it does not. In such a schema, the plays written and performed mainly between 1979 and 1989 constitute a theatre of resistance and are formulated in and arise out of the binary discourse of apartheid. Mda's writing on theatre for development in the early 1990s, based on his work in Lesotho from 1985 and later in South Africa, represents what can be considered as a shift away from a literature of resistance to a literary practice for democracy. Finally, his later plays focus on the critical issues of reconciliation, the condition of contemporary South Africa and democratic legitimacy.

The first part of this chapter constitutes my reading of and reflection on Mda's writing on theatre for development and other references to theatre in South Africa, from which I explicate a theoretical and conceptual framework of theatre. In the second part of the chapter, this framework is applied to a selection of Mda's published plays from 1979 to 2002. It is not my intention to engage in a study of the practice of forum theatre modes, but rather to engage in a discussion of how crucial concepts in Mda's theatre for development, such as conscientisation and the use of popular indigenous modes of performance and central values and ideas, such as the meaning of democracy and the practices of corruption, are embodied in these plays.

A theory of theatre

Discernible within Mda's work is a consistency of approach, which bridges the shift from a theatrical practice defined by resistance to apartheid to a theatre that engages with democracy in the new South African nation. Given this consistency, there are good reasons for taking Mda's ideas on theatre for development as a starting point for a discussion of his work, for it is here that an explicit theory of theatre for development is articulated and key ideas governing his work are expressed. It is my contention that the consistency I see in Mda's work is indicative of an underlying sense of values, both aesthetic and social, deriving from his work in theatre for development, which constitute the basis of his perspective on the shifts in the paradigm of political rhetoric. My argument is essentially that Mda's work is informed both by the dominant discourses of anti-apartheid and the new, democratic South Africa (including ideas such as 'the African Renaissance') and the democratic values expressed in his thinking on theatre for development.

Mda's ideas about theatre for development derive, in part, from his experience with the Marotholi Travelling Theatre, a theatre-for-development group he began working with in Lesotho in 1985. His ideas have been expressed in a number of publications, of which *When People Play People: Development Communication through Theatre* is the most extensive, and to which a number of other articles provide a useful complement.[4] From his writing, it is clear that Mda has been influenced by the works of both Paulo Freire and Augusto Boal, who have been active in encouraging democratic processes in Latin America, by African practitioners such as David Kerr, Kidd Ross and Christopher Kamlongera, and not least by his own experiences as director of the Theatre for Development Project at the University of Lesotho, where traditional indigenous modes of performance have been employed to ensure effective communication (see Mda 1993b).

Mda has defined the two crucial concepts of theatre and development as follows: Theatre is defined as 'the production and communication of meaning in the performance itself, in other words a transaction or negotiation of meaning in a performer-spectator situation' (Mda 1990b: 352; see also 1993b: 45–46). Development, he argues, is a means by which 'a society should achieve a greater control of its social, economic and political destiny ... [which] means that individual members of the community should have increased control of their institutions' (1990b: 354; see also 1993b: 39–42). As Mda points out, this is a dangerous concept in many Third World countries, as development implies liberation – 'a freeing from all forms of domination, of dependence and oppression' (1990b: 354; see also 1993b: 42).

A vital aspect of Mda's formulation of theatre for development is the need for critical awareness arising from an analysis of the context and leading ultimately to a solution. As he puts it, theatre for development should 'arouse the people's capacity to participate and decide things for themselves' (Mda 1990b: 354). Theatre should be seen as 'a vehicle for critical analysis which will result in critical awareness or "conscientization"' (1998: 259) and thereby act as a means of empowerment. Essential to this process is the intervention of catalysts, whom Mda describes as 'outsiders with specialist skills' and who are able to 'raise the consciousness of their target audience' – in effect the members of or actors in a theatre-for-development group (Mda 1993: 19, 20).

In the practical execution of theatre for development, Mda sees this as a three-stage process of naming, reflection and action (1993b: 101). This, he argues, involves 'an active participation of the people in transforming themselves by engaging in a dialogue to identify problems, reflect on them and take action to solve them' (1998: 260). His early experience with the Marotholi Travelling Theatre project, where the limited success of a top-down, agitprop approach, which, though it acted as a rallying force, eventually encouraged dependency and not agency, gave rise to two alternative methods of theatre for development. Mda defines these modes as 'Participatory Theatre' and 'Theatre for Conscientization' (1990b: 354; 1993b: 49–51). They involve a theatre of 'self-education [in which . . .] consciousness is raised from the inside by group analysis of social reality and power relations' (1990b: 355), the ultimate aim being to subvert the culture of silence (1993b: 45). In this context, theatre practitioners create a theatre *with* the people, not *for* the people (1994: 142). Mda further suggests that in contrast to conventional theatre in South Africa, which he argues is informed by Western models of drama, theatre for development relies on indigenous modes of festival and performance that enable communication with the marginalised in the rural areas and urban slums where the majority of the black population live (1998: 259).

In his study on theatre for development, *When People Play People*, Mda provides a number of case studies that exemplify the practice underlying his theoretical approach to the use of theatre as a means of stimulating development, but also theatre as a means of communication. What emerges from his discussion of various projects is a dramaturgical practice that rejects the kind of theatre based on conventional Western modes. In such a practice, outside actors and experts provide the supposed beneficiaries of development with both the problem and the solution, pre-packaged and ready for consumption by the audience. In the analytical evaluation of four theatre-for-development performances covered in his study, Mda exhibits a teleological line of argument that demonstrates a progressive shift from an 'agitprop', top-down, theatre to a 'forum', bottom-up, theatre (Mda 1993b: 98). The latter is seen as an ideal mode of theatre that can communicate effectively with its target audience, the rural poor and the urban slum dwellers. The four plays chosen are presented chronologically and are given titles, though only the first play actually had one. They are classified according to their placing on a scale of agitprop/forum theatre: '*Kopano ke Matla*' (Unity is Strength), an agitprop play about co-operatives; 'The Rural Sanitation Play', participatory agitprop; 'The Agro-Action Play', simultaneous dramaturgy, and 'The Trade Union Play', forum theatre (98).

Mda's most negative critique is directed at the first play, which he admits was an excellent theatrical production in the traditional literary sense, but was not effective in terms of communication or as a means of democratisation in the context of encouraging development among the communities for which it was performed (Mda 1993b: 98–114). The information on which the subject of the play was based and from which the problem was formulated had been gathered from experts and officials, the play was rehearsed and performed using Western conventions of the separation of actors or catalysts (see Mda 1993: 19) and audience and, with problem and solution given, the play resulted in closure. The villagers for whom the play was intended became, in this way, the objects of discussion, rather than the subjects of their own story. Mda quotes a comment made by Dr Victor Mtubani of the University of Botswana at a conference on theatre for development to highlight the key issue involving this mode of theatrical performance in the cause of development: 'The whole thing has to begin from the inside . . . It would be more profitable if this encouragement involved the local people. The base must be the villagers, so that the institutions we establish must remain, even when we have gone back to the comforts of our middle-class homes' (105). Effective communication, Mda argues, cannot be achieved using a theatrical mode in which the audience is not literate, is not able to read the codes and so to decipher the messages. It is essential that the audience has a 'functional level of literacy' in the medium used (114).

Following this play, Marotholi shifted by degrees to more democratic forms that made use of popular, indigenous modes of performance. 'The Rural Sanitation Play' used theatre in the round, *lifela*[5] and participation during the performance to engage with the audience, though even here the problem and the solution were part of a primarily 'official eye technique'[6] (Mda 1993b: 115–26). Once again, ready technical solutions were provided for perceived problems, rather than encouraging the villagers to develop insights into their own reality and to formulate their own problems and find suitable solutions.

The next two plays moved much closer to Mda's ideal. 'The Agro-Action Project' in the Mafeteng District concerned a project for the development of agricultural products run by a German non-governmental organisation (NGO) that had run into a number of difficulties (126–43). Here, Marotholi discovered a number of problems that needed to be addressed and gathered information using the 'official eye technique', as well as formal and informal interviews. Members of Marotholi went to the village and discussed the concept of 'theatre for development' and also the matters that the villagers saw as important. This resulted in a play consisting of three sketches, all open-ended, and spectators could discuss the issues and various courses of action during the performance. In Mda's words: 'The play [became] a democratic vehicle for community dialogue and community decision' (135). Using this approach to theatre, the problems were explored from the perspective of the villagers and historical, economic and political factors were examined in explaining the current problems (139). Mda argues that this type of theatre gives rise to a multiplication of communicational factors involving both spectators and actors/catalysts, as the villagers intervene and direct the course of the play. With the breaching of the boundaries between audience and performers, there occurs an interaction between the real world and the fictional world of the performance, which is perhaps the most valuable consequence of this mode of representation.

The fourth play, 'The Trade Union Play', was one that came about expressly at the wish of the villagers (Mda 1993b: 143–56). This was a simple performance on a Saturday where the actors/catalysts arrived at the village and, together with some of the villagers, prepared two sketches. The play was held in the afternoon in a festive atmosphere created to help people to relax and to build confidence. This performance succeeded in achieving the aims of forum theatre whereby the spectators gradually became the actors, as they did not simply comment and debate from the sidelines but actually participated as actors in the dramatic context. They encoded the information and were involved at all stages of performance. This ensured a high level of community participation, as the villagers themselves decided on the subject matter and content of the play. Naming, reflection and action, the key processes in conscientisation, were achieved in the performance, as critical analysis led to critical awareness. The play resulted in a greater awareness of the nature and role of trade unions, particularly in the mining industry in South Africa, and of the structural aspects involved at local, national and international levels. Not least, attention was drawn to the negative attitude of the Lesotho government to the involvement of the migrant workers in South Africa in the National Union of Miners, one of the more radical trade unions. A spin-off from this play was the decision to produce another play on the problems of wheat production in the village. When it was performed, this play revealed a high level of corruption in the village, which involved the headman and brought with it a demand for change (1993b: 151; 1990b: 357; 1994: 210).

The teleological historiography that emerges out of a reading of Mda's work on theatre for development also colours Mda's comments on the history of political theatre in South Africa. In three published pieces where he has addressed this matter, Mda describes a three-phase process from a theatre of protest via a theatre of resistance to a theatre of reconciliation (Mda 1995; 1996a; 1998). In this final phase, he sees the theory and practice of theatre for development as making a vital contribution. In this historiography, the 1960s are characterised by a theatre of protest based on Western models, both traditional and experimental, largely with white practitioners and audiences and designed to appeal to the consciences of the oppressor. In these plays, the oppressed, the black majority, suffer in silence and display none of the spirit of defiance that existed at the time. Congruent with this elite theatre, there was a popular, formulaic, musical theatre, often with strong moral themes, being performed in the black townships. In the 1970s, the Black Consciousness Movement brought about a new kind of oppositional theatre, theatre for resistance. The practitioners of this form of theatre argued that theatre for protest placed the onus on black people to prove their humanity and was addressed to the oppressor. Theatre for resistance, on the other hand, addressed the oppressed with the aim of mobilising them in the struggle. It was an agitprop theatre that was performed in public places, such as at weddings, funerals and political rallies. Mda argues that later this, too, moved into city venues and ultimately became a theatre for export, aiming largely at overseas audiences to gain support in the struggle against apartheid in South Africa. The third phase is seen as theatre for reconciliation, but once again, it is a theatre of Western modes with priorities chosen by the elite. Here, Mda argues, the practices of theatre for development can and should play an important role:

> Theatre for development has the potential to be the most relevant theatre
> in a democratic South Africa, since it can be rooted with the people in
> the marginalized rural areas and slums. It utilizes modes of communica-
> tion and entertainment that already exist in these areas. It is the theatre
> of the illiterate since, in its most progressive form, it has no dramatic
> text that acts as a referent for the performance text. (1998: 264)

As Mda points out, workers and peasants together form the vast majority of the population of South Africa, so this is a theatre not for the few, but for the many (Mda 1995; 1996a; 1998).

A recurring theme in Mda's discussion of theatre for development is an emphasis on the use of popular indigenous modes of performance and he lists a number of traditional modes in Lesotho, such as *lifela, mohobelo, mokhibo* and *lipina*,[7] some of which were used by the Marotholi Travelling Theatre (Mda 1993b: 63). One argument for this emphasis on traditional and popular modes is that the audience has a functional level of literacy in the medium used (114), which makes them ideal as effective carriers of political and social messages (48; 1995: 39). Equally importantly, popular and traditional modes facilitate horizontal communication and, with their characteristics of participation, they enable the poor and the disadvantaged to formulate and spread their own messages: 'The disadvantaged must initiate the process of communication, and distribute their own messages both among themselves and to the ruling classes. Only then will self-reliance and self-development be achieved' (1994: 143). In propagating indigenous modes of performance, Mda sees participation as being a natural element of African culture and this is embodied in a process in which traditional modes are constantly modified and utilised to focus on current problems and issues (144–45). As co-creators, theatre practitioners and audiences 'create new meaning from the ancient wisdom of orature', which becomes a process of empowerment as new messages are distributed through a medium familiar to the people (147).

To Mda's literary theory and practice must be added other aspects of his concern with current developments in South Africa. In the context of the African Renaissance, Mda has described himself as 'a Pan-Africanist', a position he defines as 'the outlook that recognises the common history of the African people in Africa and the Diaspora and this should not be seen as a racial term' (Naidoo 1997: 258). However, a word of warning on the discourse of African Renaissance is contained in his comments on popular theatre, where he argues that a discussion of popular performance, for example, should 'not [be] an attempt at retrieving and reconstructing pre-colonial modes that have no relevance in present-day Africa'. Rather, it should be a case of '[a]dopting and enriching the people's own forms of expression' and 'not, as it may be mistakenly thought, the revival of the great African myths and long-forgotten rituals' (Mda 1993b: 47).

I would summarise Mda's position on theatre for development as involving the key concepts of the transaction or negotiation of meaning, critical analysis, critical awareness or conscientisation, participation and empowerment through dialogue, as initiated by the intervention of catalysts. It is, I would suggest, a model for a theatre for democracy. It is also a theatre that seeks to incorporate and apply indigenous performance techniques.

Theory and practice

Mda has recognised the effect of the theatre of the absurd on his plays, although he has denied any direct influence of the work of Samuel Beckett and Bertolt Brecht, rather seeing the absurd as part of his subject matter and theatrical objective, i.e. the absurdity of apartheid in South Africa and the need to provide flexible dramatic productions for an easily accessible theatre of resistance. In addition, Mda has referred to the African tradition of storytelling as part of his practice of narration. The use of only a few actors and little scenery adheres to both traditions, as Mda focuses on showing the issues involved and engaging in a dialogue and in argumentation to educate the characters and the audience on the ideological message contained in each work.[8] In stressing an African mode of writing, Mda has drawn attention to his use of magic realism, arguing that it derives from a natural process of being African and writing in a South African context. As he explains: 'In magic realism the supernatural is not presented as problematic', but '[a]n absurd metamorphosis is described as if it did not contradict our laws of reason' (Naidoo 1997: 256). Rob Amato has coined the terms 'Mdada' or 'Mdada-ism' to refer to what he calls an 'an elusive black theatrical satire in the old and new Southern Africa' and argues that 'Mda's theatricality is both African and modern' and it 'works through forcing an improbable set of assumptions on the audience' (Amato 2002: v).

In terms of a metadiscourse of resistance, Mda's early plays, from 1976 to 1990, can be grouped into anti-apartheid plays and neo-colonial plays.[9] The first group consists of plays that are specifically concerned with raising consciousness against apartheid in South Africa and include *Dead End* (1979), *Dark Voices Ring* (1976), *Banned* (1982) and *Joys of War* (1989), all of which demonstrate a close affinity with political developments as the anti-apartheid struggle intensified from an awareness of the iniquities of the system to active, military resistance against it. To this group must also be added *The Road* (1982), where Mda specifically addresses the ideology and hypocrisy of the apartheid system. The second group consists of *The Hill* (1977–78) and *And the Girls in Their Sunday Dresses?* (1993), which reveal the destabilising influence of apartheid South Africa on neighbouring countries and communities. This group also includes an early play, *We Shall Sing for the Fatherland* (1976–77), which is a study of post-independence betrayal and neo-colonialism in an unnamed African state. An argument can be seen developing through these plays of a transition from stasis to action and the achievement of salvation through human community (*ubuntu*) gained through political action.

As with all of Mda's plays, *Dead End* is concerned with how individual lives are distorted by the demands of the apartheid system and the apartheid mentality. Prostitution, pimping, abortion and murder provide the context for demonstrating the injustice of the white/black binary society, in which a 'causal series of betrayals' (Horn 1990: ix) leaves the two main characters isolated in incarceration and death. The growing awareness of the protagonist, Charley, is achieved in jail in a dialogue with God concerning a recollection of recent past events where, in keeping with much of Mda's work, past and present are inextricably mixed. However, Charley's perceptions are limited to an awareness of the injustices of a system that automatically privileges white over black and stop short of a critical awareness that progresses to 'coherent analysis or insight' (xi) and seeing a solution to the problem.

In contrast, *Dark Voices Ring* is the first play in which Mda endorses violent resistance to apartheid as a solution to the problem. Its main characters are an old couple, Woman and Old Man, who have become isolated in their community, as a result of the man's over-enthusiastic collaboration as a *baasboy* (literally, 'boss boy', a black overseer/supervisor) with his white employers in the treatment of convict labourers.[10] He is beaten by members of the community and his daughter, Nontobeko, is killed in an arson attack on their home.

The role of catalyst in this drama is assigned to a young man,[11] their son-in-law, the Man, who in a duologue with the old woman forces her to recapitulate the true nature of past events and thereby recognise her and her husband's true situation. Through enacting and re-enacting the past, the young man leads her to a 'therapeutic resolution by confronting her illusion with reality' (Horn 1990: xxv). In this process of the 'didactic application of re-enactment and imaginative projection' (xxvi), the story that unfolds exposes the barbaric nature of the convict labour system under apartheid and illustrates the way in which it perverts individual lives. The solution, for which the young man seeks and obtains the old couple's blessing, is to leave to join the anti-government forces outside the country. This decision releases both the old *baasboy* and his wife from their self-imposed apathy. By joining the resistance, the son-in-law atones for the old couple's sin of the 'fracturing of human community' (xxiii) and redeems the child lost in the burning of their house.

Banned and *Joys of War* are both overtly concerned with the active struggle against apartheid. *Banned* deals with the political growth of both its protagonists: Cynthia, a social worker, and her former case, Bra Zet, a one-time gangster, now forced to use a wheelchair. The house arrest Cynthia is placed under for her activities in helping people in squatter camps and shantytowns reduces her voice to a monologue, which, while mediating her current isolated and absurd position, paradoxically gives voice to the silenced voices of the oppressed. As Mda fuses 'past and present into an evocative suggestion of the potency of experience and memory as political weapons' (Peterson 1993: xiii) in the interaction of Cynthia's monologue of the present with the enactment/re-enactment of the past, her progress from protest to critical awareness and conscientisation is shown in her decision to join the anti-apartheid movement abroad. Cynthia's process is initiated by her involvement with the community – her catalyst – while she acts as the catalyst to Bra Zet's transition to a greater awareness of his place in the apartheid system, thus initiating a willingness to act. It is his tragic destiny to make a suicidal charge on the police who are shooting at a demonstration of schoolchildren, while Cynthia remains to embody hope for the future.

Joys of War explores the paradoxes and legitimacy of violence in resistance to the apartheid state. The play focuses on two members of a military organisation, Soldiers One and Two, who are on a sabotage assignment in South Africa. In a parallel action, the mother and daughter of Soldier One are seen on a journey. In unfolding the stories of these four characters in a series of reminiscences, time and location shifts, and in their roles as both audiences and performers, Mda examines the legitimacy of either humanity or atonement as reasons for joining the army of liberation. The decision taken by Soldier One, a leading member of his squatter community and active in his resistance to authority, to secretly abandon his family and community in order to pursue the struggle by joining an army of resistance is questioned by the members of his community and initiates the quest by his mother and daughter to clear his name. The heroic status of Soldier Two is undermined by the revelation that he has joined the anti-apartheid forces because his false accusations against a rival for the love of a woman resulted in the man's death at the hands of the South African police. Faced with the possibility of disgrace, Soldier Two commits suicide. Into this dialogue of moral responsibility are also projected the struggles, doubts and hopes of Soldier One's mother and his child. When they ultimately achieve their objective of finding Soldier One, the daughter has matured and replaces Soldier Two in the liberation struggle. As Bhekizizwe Peterson points out, this play challenges the rhetoric of cleansing souls through violence, which can be seen to undermine other forms of resistance: 'Mda's concern with the ordinary is a check on the elevation of violence as the only means of struggle' (Peterson 1993: xvii).

The final play in this group, *The Road*, is clearly distinguished from the others, in that it gives a face and presence to apartheid, which is embodied in the character of an Afrikaner farmer, and it contains the main themes of Mda's work of this decade (1979–89): the immorality of apartheid and its practitioners, the traumatic and tragic effects of the system on ordinary people and the influence of apartheid South Africa on neighbouring states. Central to the play is the exposition of the ideology of apartheid. In the middle of an open road two men, a white Afrikaner farmer and a migrant labourer from Lesotho, meet under the shade of the only tree. Mda makes use of non-communicating dialogue, absurd situations and historical re-enactment to present the central concepts of apartheid policy and its counter-discourse, as well as to expose the hypocrisy of apartheid in practice. The perversion of individual lives and modes of thinking that are caused by the system are shown to inhibit mutual understanding and result in violence, which has tragic consequences.

The manner in which the economy of South Africa influences Lesotho is a central theme of *The Hill*, which deals with migrant workers waiting for an opportunity to be employed in the gold mines of the Witwatersrand, near Johannesburg. The voice of experience, caution and age is countered by the voices of youthful expectation, and voices of exploitation, deceit, theft, bribery and prostitution. Though providing a clear exposure of the cash nexus that dominates the lives of these ordinary people (the men sell their blood – literally – and labour to get money for food and survival and the women sell their bodies), the play ascribes causality and effect, but does not progress to conscientisation and agency for change.

In contrast, *And the Girls in Their Sunday Dresses?*, which explores the fates of two women, an ageing prostitute, The Lady, and an ordinary working mother, The Woman, who have both been cheated by the same white man, does move to conscientisation. The two women discuss their lives and values as they wait in line for the distribution of cheap grain, given as aid to the government of their country, Lesotho. The indignity of queuing for food, the clear divisions in the distribution of wealth and the corruption associated with aid allowances are raised as the two women eventually discover their 'sisterhood'. With the strength of The Woman's experience of labour organisation and working with a community they move from passivity to action.

In an earlier play, *We Shall Sing for the Fatherland*, Mda exposes the betrayal of former freedom-fighters in a newly independent African state. The two ex-soldiers eke out a living in a park in the centre of a city. They are unable to see the reality of their lives or to believe that they have been betrayed by a neo-colonial system after fighting for independence. Eventually the two freedom-fighters are released from their poverty by freezing to death and are free to wander the world, as only the rich go to heaven.

The plays Mda has written since 1990 continue some of the themes visible in his earlier work, but with the ending of apartheid, new issues of reconciliation and democracy replace the themes of resistance and struggle. The four plays focused on here are *The Mother of All Eating* (1992), *You Fool, How Can the Sky Fall?* (1995), *The Nun's Romantic Story* (1995) and *The Bells of Amersfoort* (2002).[12] The first two of these plays continue key and related themes in Mda's earlier plays, such as corruption and the post-independence betrayal of the struggle against colonialism. The second two plays contain tangential references to these themes, but also raise the new and vital matters of revenge, justice, restitution and reconciliation that were at the core of South African politics in the mid-1990s.

In *The Mother of All Eating*, The Man, a corrupt government official in Lesotho, gives an account, mostly in monologue, of his nefarious activities. His litany of corrupt practices is interrupted by two elements: one is a concern for his pregnant wife and a close friend, both of whom are inexplicably not at their homes, and the second is the intrusion of The Man's accomplices into his home to complain about their share of the rewards from corrupt deals.

These intrusions act very much as spectators would act in a forum theatre performance, raising issues that comment on or counter the monologue of justification for his corrupt deeds that The Man gives. As each intrusion occurs, the plot moves forward, either deepening and expanding his account of the extent of corruption in the state system, as exemplified by the accomplices, or raising questions of honesty, domesticity and betrayal in the case of The Man's concern for his wife and his best friend. While this process of naming, reflecting and acting is performed, the audience is not allowed to sit in passive observance. At various points, The Man addresses himself directly to the audience, demanding and expecting their compliance in and validation of his corruption: 'I hear whispers and your snide remarks. Who of you here can claim to have clean hands? Now, tell me! Did you buy those BMs and Benzes that you drive with your meagre salaries? I am no different from any one of you. The word that we use here at home is that we eat! Our culture today is that of eating. Everybody eats' (Mda 2002: 10).

The denouement of the play sees The Man punished for his corruption in two respects: firstly, by hearing of the severe injury to his wife and the deaths of his newly born child and his best friend in a car accident caused by potholes in one of the roads for which he has cheated on the contract for repairs; and secondly, by being almost beaten to death by his accomplices in revenge for his cheating on them. While the ending does not involve closure – The Man may still be alive and he may live to 'eat' again – there is clearly a moralistic and didactic element in the play that impresses some kind of censure of The Man's behaviour onto the audience. In contrast, the audience is also forced to reflect on its own compliance in these practices.

The second play in this group, *You Fool, How Can the Sky Fall?*, explores the betrayal of the 'revolution' by ministers in a post-independence government. The surrealistic setting in what appears to be a prison cell, reinforced by a grotesque series of incidents where members of the cabinet are taken away by shadowy figures for torture, is used to explore a situation in which a cabinet of ministers appears to be divorced from its people and subject to the dictates of some unknown outside force. In this claustrophobic environment, the leaders of the nation are seen to be petty and conspiratorial in their relationships with each other, prone to the cult of personality and utterly divorced from the reality of the world outside. Into this menagerie, Mda puts a young man, whose function is to act as the catalyst that brings elements of the real world into the imaginary one of the cabinet ministers and thereby exposes the unscrupulous and manipulative nature of the president himself. The Young Man draws attention to the temper of the people and, in particular, relates the story of the Daughters of the Revolution, from whom the ministers have stolen power and who march through the square in the nude, demanding restitution.[13] The warning directed at the newly democratic state of South Africa is perspicuously apparent.

The final two plays, *The Nun's Romantic Story* and *The Bells of Amersfoort*, both touch on themes that are consistent throughout Mda's work – corruption and the betrayal of the revolution – but more importantly, they address equally vital issues relevant to the situation in South Africa in the mid-1990s – revenge, retribution and reconciliation. Both plays show striking similarities in the use of scenography by utilising three areas that indicate spatial and temporal shifts, in the manner initiated in *Joys of War*, and they both make use of African-based music and dance in a manner reminiscent of the performance modes that Mda espouses for theatre for development. In *The Nun's Romantic Story*, there are directions that invite the audience to participate in musical performances and thereby become one with the play (Mda 1996b: 110). With regard to *The Bells of Amersfoort*, Mda stated in a note to the publishers:

> The story in this play is told in the manner of the Xhosa traditional theatre known as Intsomi. Scene 12 [the final scene], especially, uses the Intsomi storytelling devices, with the woman asking grotesque figures questions about her lover, and the figures punctuating their responses with an Intsomi song in the same manner as it would be told by storytellers around the fire in the evening. (quoted in Amato 2002: xviii)

Of the two plays, indeed of the four later plays discussed here, *The Bells of Amersfoort* adheres most fully to Mda's concept of ideal theatre for development in its use of indigenous modes of performance and in nurturing all intelligences – multiple intelligences – to encourage a vibrant process of conscientisation (Mda 1994: 147).

The issues at the forefront of *The Nun's Romantic Story* are revenge, justice and retribution.[14] A young Catholic nun, Anna-Maria, sees in church the General who commanded the soldiers responsible for the rape of her mother and the murder of her family twenty years previously in a foreign-backed, military coup following a democratic election that would have given power to a radical political party. The nun decides to kill the General and, as he is about to take communion, she shoots him with a gun stolen from the local priest. The play builds on the discussions concerning the nun's defence by exploring retrospectively the events of the past twenty years: the overthrow of democracy, the interference of Western powers in Third World politics of the Cold War period, and the involvement of the Catholic Church in support of the coup – a litany of violence, corruption, deceit and betrayal. While these national and international aspects frame the tale, the key issue lies on the personal level, the right of the nun to avenge her family:

> ANNA-MARIA: We are taught to forgive those who have wronged us. I prayed very hard to the Blessed Virgin, to give me strength, and I forgave. Then I saw the man. Although I never really understood the political struggles that led to my family's death, I realised that I never forgave the people who brought it about. The Blessed Virgin never really wanted me to forgive them. (Mda 1996b: 106)

The play does not resolve the dilemma of a personal conviction of the right to kill, albeit couched in terms of divine right, versus the dictates of morality and the law on the sanctity of human life. Instead, in an ironic twist, Anna-Maria is spirited away from her prison cell, called by the Virgin Mary, taking her guitar with her, but leaving behind her nun's raiment. The audience is left to ponder this dilemma.

In keeping with much of Mda's work, *The Nun's Romantic Story* exploits the potential of the elusive satire contained in Amato's concept of Mdada-ism which employs magic-realist elements to confront the audience with its own sense of logic and reason, thereby engaging in a process of reflection and assessment. There is no given answer or solution in an Mda play, instead actors and audience alike are encouraged to create their own, to participate, to be involved and ultimately to perform.

While in *The Nun's Romantic Story* the proposition of the right to exact revenge is posed, in *The Bells of Amersfoort*, this option is transferred to the process of reconciliation. Again, while the background to the story involves national and international aspects of the struggle against apartheid and its aftermath, the key issues are played out on a personal level. Tami Walaza, in exile in the Netherlands, struggles to escape the demons of the past – memories of torture and interrogation – and alcoholism, an escape from loneliness and betrayal at home, in order to return to South Africa to 'heal the land'. Tami's recovery comes partly as a result of her involvement in a multicultural band in which she performs African music and dance and tells stories, and partly as a result of meeting, in the Netherlands, her former interrogator, Johan van der Bijl, who, after having confessed to the Truth and Reconciliation Commission (TRC), has become a *dominee* (minister of the church). Mda explores the moral issues involved in reconciliation in a series of exchanges:

> JOHAN: I do not have to explain myself to you. In my country I went before the Truth and Reconciliation Commission. I revealed all I knew. I confessed to what I did. What is most important to me is that the Commission granted me an amnesty. My conscience is now clear . . .
> MARTIJN [Tami's drummer accompanist]: You confessed to your Truth Commission and they forgave you. But did the person you did all these filthy things to forgive you? (Mda 2002: 149)

The question of personal forgiveness is shown to be much more complex and problematic than institutionalised forgiveness:

> JOHAN: I want to make peace, Tami Walaza.
> TAMI: And will that bring my life back? Will that restore the life that you stole in its prime? (150)

Tami quite rightly raises the question of justice as she shouts at an imagined TRC hearing, 'You cannot absolve him on my behalf. I want justice!' (151) and pinpoints the problem when she argues for the victims of apartheid: 'And what did they get in return? You got something. You got amnesty. Even if I wanted to sue you for what you did to me it would be impossible, because you got amnesty. What did I get? What did the victims get for their stories?' (151).

On an earlier occasion, Mda argued:

> A true theater of reconciliation will not shy away from addressing the past. But it will not address the past for its own sake, nor for the sake of feeding the victim syndrome . . . It will address the past solely for the purpose of understanding the present, of understanding why it is absolutely necessary for us to have reconciliation . . . It is important that the past is not only addressed – it must be redressed as well. (1995: 44)

Though *The Bells of Amersfoort* raises the issue of restitution for the victims, the culmination of the play is a plea for reconciliation. On her return to South Africa, Tami discovers that her fiancé has betrayed not only her, but his ideals as well and he has become just another young man on the make in a corrupt society. Tami is once again a victim of the 'twin diseases of the democratic South Africa: instant gratification and conspicuous consumption' (Mda 2002: 160). However, the play ends on a joyful note and a fortuitous meeting between Tami and Johan as they both ride their bicycles in a South African village. The moment of reconciliation is achieved as Tami appeals to Johan: 'Help me do what . . . I had vowed to do: rebuild the scarred land. Heal the wounds that still ache, that history has imposed on my people.' Johan replies in the affirmative: 'I will be with you. It is not an easy task to heal the wounded earth' (160). In this meeting and throughout the course of the play, both Tami and Johan have been able to confront and name their demons, reflect on their situations and establish a course of action. Conscientisation is achieved on a personal level, but it also strikes a relevant chord for society as a whole.

A theatre for democracy
At the core of the argument in this chapter is an interpretation of Mda's theatre based on the ideas and ideals he espouses in his work on theatre for development. Mda has not only acted as a practitioner, but has also developed a theoretical framework that can be applied to all his theatre. At the heart of

this approach is a belief that theatre can help people change their lives through a process of conscientisation, naming, reflecting and acting, that leads to critical awareness and self-reliance. In theatre for development, this involves breaking down the barriers between actors and audience to encourage participation in both the formulation of the issue and in the dramatic performance, thereby achieving an interaction between the real world and the fictional world of the plays. Furthermore, it is clear that Mda sees indigenous, popular and traditional African modes of performance as vital to effective communication.

By its very nature, theatre for development is concerned with democratic processes and egalitarian values. However, the past 30 years in the history of southern Africa have also dictated the subject matter of Mda's plays, as he playfully, satirically and ruthlessly exposes the system of apartheid, post-independence betrayal, neo-colonial practices and corruption at work in Lesotho, South Africa and other Third World countries. Such concerns with current issues are characteristic of all of Mda's work.

It would be wrong to assume that there is a simple transfer between the practices of theatre for development and a theatre essentially designed for stage performance. Nevertheless, within the performance and in the limited degree of actor-audience interaction that is attainable in each play, it is possible to discern the key issues of the process of conscientisation that constitute the theoretical foundation of Mda's thinking in this area. In the early plays, this process becomes more and more apparent as the struggle against apartheid intensified. In the later plays, it is part of the covert didacticism that forces the members of the audience to explore their consciences in relation to the reality of the world around them, the need for reconciliation and the dangers of corruption and the lack of democracy.

Notes

1. To the outside world at least, the work of Nobel Prize winner, Nadine Gordimer, to name but one example, is respected as much for its critique of apartheid ideology as for its artistic quality (see The Swedish Academy press release and Nobel presentation speech at http://nobelprize.org/literature/laureates/1991/press.html, accessed 11 November 2001). Since 1990, the political rhetoric has encompassed the ideas of 'the Rainbow

Nation' (Archbishop Desmond Tutu and Nelson Mandela) – with multiculturalism within one nation as its theme and possibly its greatest achievements being the successful elections of 1994 and the work of the Truth and Reconciliation Commission (TRC) – and 'the African Renaissance' (Thabo Mbeki) – with the reassertion of an African dynamic in the political, economic and cultural fields – as South Africa and its new regime have sought to establish their position on the southern African, African and global stages.

2. Ndebele's essay was originally presented at a conference on 'New Writing Africa: Continuity and Change' at the Commonwealth Institute, London, November 1984 and published in Njabulo S. Ndebele, *South African Literature and Culture* (1994). Sachs's paper was published in Ingrid de Kok and Karen Press (eds.), *Spring is Rebellious: Arguments about Cultural Freedom by Albie Sachs and Respondents* (1990).

3. The significant feature of this latest cultural discourse is the use of the prefix 're', which demands the assertion and elevation of a previous state of cultural development in Africa in place of a divisive discourse and practice resulting from colonialism, imperialism and apartheid. The implication of this is the initiation of a process towards a changed ontology and epistemology from a predominantly Western secular and rational conceptual framework to one incorporating an African cosmology.

4. See, for example: 'The Marotholi Travelling Theatre: Towards an alternative perspective of development' in the *Journal of Southern African Studies* (1990), reprinted in Liz Gunner (ed.), *Politics and Performance: Theatre, Poetry and Song in Southern Africa* (1994); his keynote address to the Conference of the Association of Drama Departments of South Africa in conjunction with the South African Association for Drama and Youth Theatre, University of Natal, Pietermaritzburg: 13 July 1994, 'Learning from the ancient wisdom of Africa: In the creation and distribution of messages', published in *Current Writing* 6(2) (1994); 'Theater and reconciliation in South Africa' in *Theater* 25(3) (1995), and 'Current trends in theatre for development in South Africa,' in Derek Attridge and Rosemary Jolly (eds.), *Writing in South Africa: Literature, Apartheid and Democracy, 1970–1995* (1998).

5. In *When People Play People*, Mda refers to *lifela* (singular, *sefela*) as performances of songs primarily by migrant workers in the South African mines. The songs have a storyline and sometimes act as a vehicle of protest. As Mda points out, *lifela* are 'poetic self-definition created from traditional sources to express class consciousness and resistance to the controls of the migrant labour system' (1993b: 73, 74).

6. The 'official eye technique' is simply a method of gathering information from official sources when preparing theatre for development. The term is taken from the report of a workshop held in Kumba, Cameroon. Mda quotes from Hansel Ndumbe Eyoh, 'Theatre, Adult Education and Development, A Workshop at Kumba (Cameroon)', in *Ifda Dossier* 60, July/August (1987): 8 (Mda 1993b: 68).

7. In *When People Play People*, Mda refers to *mohobelo* as a 'graceful stamping dance for men performed at ceremonial occasions and for recreation. The song is led by a soloist and the other men respond in a chorus while they stamp their feet in a slow rhythmic movement.' *Mokhibo* is referred to the 'most popular form of dance performed by troupes of girls or women who bounce gently to the rhythm of a single drum. The music is led by

a soloist whose lyrics reflect the experiences and concerns of the villagers.' *Lipina* means songs, but Mda specifically refers to *lipina-tsa-mokopu* (songs of the pumpkin) 'a song-dance mode performed by girls . . . Although the function of *pina-tsa-mokopu* is primarily to entertain, they are also a reflection of the world the girls live in, and the social relations in the village' (Mda1993b: 78, 76).

8. In some respects, the plays can be considered allegorical, particularly as they make use of characters as types, as the use of general attributes or occupation for the names of the black African characters suggests. (Duggan 1997: 28–29).

9. The dates given here are those of the first performances of the plays.

10. Andrew Horn describes them as follows: 'He is catatonic and she a nearly paranoid recluse, fugitives from social censure' (1990: xx).

11. The term 'catalyst' is essentially used in the context of theatre for development. My argument here is that even in Mda's published stage plays, the role of catalyst is contained within the performance, as the plays themselves enact a process of conscientisation. This is similar to the 'transplantation' of Mda's theories on theatre for development to his novel *Ways of Dying* that Margaret Mervis analyses in her article, 'Fiction for development: Zakes Mda's *Ways of Dying*', published in *Current Writing* (see Mervis 1998: 40).

12. Again, the dates given here are those of the first performances. *The Nun's Romantic Story* was first broadcast on the BBC in 1992 and first performed on stage in Johannesburg in 1995.

13. Rob Amato points out in his introduction to the published play that '[i]n 2001 many large South African black women . . . did indeed sing their protest songs in the nude . . . [I]t made very surreal cover photos for *The Sowetan*, a Johannesburg newspaper with a largely black readership.' (Amato 2002: xiii) This shows, in a very real sense, the real world entering the fictional world of the stage.

14. The play has no specific location, but in his introduction to the published version, Mda states: 'It is not set in South Africa, but in an unspecified "Third World" country. In fact, the play was influenced by events in Lesotho when the state of emergency was declared in 1970.' (Mda 1996a: xxiii)

Works cited

Amato, Rob. 2002. 'Introduction'. In: Mda, Zakes. *Fools, Bells, and the Habit of Eating: Three Satires*. Johannesburg: Wits University Press, v–xxi.

De Kok, Ingrid and Karen Press (eds.). 1990. *Spring is Rebellious: Arguments about Cultural Freedom by Albie Sachs and Respondents*. Cape Town: Buchu Books.

Duggan, Carolyn. 1997. 'Things of darkness: Character construction in the earlier plays of Zakes Mda'. *Alternation* 4(1): 27–44.

Horn, Andrew. 1990. 'People are being murdered here: An introduction to the theatre of Zakes Mda'. In: Mda, Zakes. *The Plays of Zakes Mda*. Johannesburg: Ravan Press, vii–liv.

Mda, Zakes. 1990a. *The Plays of Zakes Mda*. Johannesburg: Ravan Press.

———. 1990b. 'The Marotholi Travelling Theatre: Towards an alternative perspective of development'. *Journal of Southern African Studies* (June) 16(2): 352–58. Academic Search Elite, http://ehostvgw10.epnet.com, accessed 14 January 2002. Reprinted in: Gunner, Liz (ed.). *Politics and Performance: Theatre, Poetry and Song in Southern Africa*. Johannesburg: Wits University Press, 1994, 203–10.

———. 1993a. *And the Girls in Their Sunday Dresses?: Four Works*. Johannesburg: Wits University Press.

———. 1993b. *When People Play People: Development Communication through Theatre*. Johannesburg: Wits University Press; London and New Jersey: Zed Books.

———. 1994. 'Learning from the ancient wisdom of Africa: In the creation and distribution of messages'. *Current Writing* 6(2): 139–50.

———.1995. 'Theater and reconciliation in South Africa'. *Theater* 25(3): 38–45.

———. 1996a. 'Introduction'. In: Mda, Zakes. *Four Plays Compiled and Introduced by Zakes Mda*. Florida Hills: Vivlia, i–xxvi.

———. 1996b. *The Nun's Romantic Story*. In: Mda, Zakes. *Four Plays Compiled and Introduced by Zakes Mda*. Florida Hills: Vivlia, 78–123.

———. 1998. 'Current trends in theatre for development in South Africa'. In: Attridge, Derek and Rosemary Jolly (eds.). *Writing in South Africa: Literature, Apartheid and Democracy, 1970–1995*. Cambridge: Cambridge University Press, 257–64.

———. 2002. *Fools, Bells, and the Habit of Eating: Three Satires*. Johannesburg: Wits University Press.

Mervis, Margaret. 1998. 'Fiction for development: Zakes Mda's *Ways of Dying*'. *Current Writing* 10(1): 39–56.

Naidoo, Venu. 1997. 'Interview with Zakes Mda'. *Alternation* 4(1): 247–61.

Ndebele, Njabulo S. 1994. *South African Literature and Culture: Rediscovery of the Ordinary*. Manchester: Manchester University Press.

Peterson, Bhekizizwe. 1993. 'Introduction'. In: Mda, Zakes. *And the Girls in Their Sunday Dresses?: Four Works*. Johannesburg: Wits University Press, vii–xxviii.

2

Betrayal and the Search for Empowerment in the Early Plays

CAROLYN DUGGAN

DISCRIMINATION, MOST NOTABLY APARTHEID, forms an underlying pattern in Zakes Mda's early plays (1979–89), along with an exploration of the quandaries of human existence. He treats these issues with sophistication, using a deceptively simple mode of presentation. Mda's philosophical concerns apply to all humankind but, in particular, he iterates the plight of the colonised and the struggles and pitfalls of post-colonial society.

The earliest of the plays, *Dead End*, was written in the 1960s, but not performed until 1979. The dominant theme of this play is betrayal; all the characters betray and/or are betrayed. In the opening scene, the protagonist, Charley, telling the story in a flashback from prison, asserts, in relation to his girlfriend and the heroine of the play, Tseli: 'I dare not desert her now' (Mda 1990: 5). Yet he has already betrayed Tseli doubly: she was a virgin when she fell in love with him and not only did he refuse to marry her when she became pregnant, he also pushed her into having an abortion at the hands of an unqualified doctor whose reputation rests on his ministrations to Charley's prostitutes. Despite his protestations to Frikkie that '[t]his is my girl, Frikkie . . . This is Tseli. She is a decent type' (19), Charley's actions illustrate his exploitative and disparaging attitudes towards Tseli and women in general, and provide a clear sense of his defining characteristics as an individual. Charley has been betrayed by apartheid society, which does not recognise or reward his education, but relegates him to menial positions because he is black. However, through dubious morality and by displaying no loyalty to others, he improves his lot.

Charley's ambivalent moral position mirrors his societal one: he is not yet clear who he is. Here lies also the beginning of Mda's ontological theme, which is only touched on in this play. Charley's dilemma is secondary, in his eyes, to his state of being. His conversation with God in his prison cell is largely an attempt to come to terms with his embryonic conscience, but he and Tseli also discuss the possibility that either or both of them could be dead, but have no way of proving it. Charley resolves this conundrum in an open-ended manner that is later to become typical of Mda: 'Look Tseli, maybe we are dead . . . maybe not. We are not sure, you can't be sure of anything these days. So let's forget it' (Mda 1990: 15–16).

Apartheid forms the background to the play: the social positions of the protagonists are defined and circumscribed by it. Tseli is almost as much at the mercy of her white, male employer as Charley and Frikkie's girls are to their pimps. Her subservient position as a black domestic worker allows her no recourse to defence; if she objects to any of his commands or requests, she will surely lose her job. Individual disempowerment becomes a collective matter, as the reaction of the crowd to Tseli's collapse testifies. Although they offer suggestions as to how to help her, the main concern is to keep on the right side of the law at all costs and not to become involved – 'Want to be witness in court?' (Mda 1990: 19) is the most potent injunction against interference. There is a general deference then to Frikkie, the white male's assumption of rights. He is challenged by no one and Charley assures God in his final conversation that 'he was in the right' (20) because of his whiteness. Almost as an after-thought, he asks God: 'Say, what is your colour?' The issue remains unresolved, but it has been raised.

Dark Voices Ring, also produced in 1979, employs three characters, Woman, Old Man and Man, and is ostensibly about the contract and convict farm labour system that was practised widely in South Africa from about the mid-nineteenth century. However, what also emerges is a far more cogent analysis of cognitive dissonance, so that the play is both didactic and cathartic, suggesting that the role of victim is not inevitable, but that it is possible to assume agency over one's own existence.

Apartheid is obviously central to the subject of forced labour, but Mda also investigates individual complicity with the system. At the beginning of the play, the Woman focuses on the elevated position that her husband (the Old Man) has enjoyed as an *induna* (headman), but she fails to see the anomaly or the precariousness of his compromised position. One of the methods of manipulation used directly or indirectly by elites is to create in individuals a bourgeois appetite for personal success. The emergence of populism as a style of political action thus coincides with the emergence of the oppressed. The populist leader who rises from this process is an ambiguous being who, shuttling back and forth between the people and the dominant oligarchies, bears the marks of both groups (see Weffert in Freire 1972: 119). The old couple are well aware of the fact that they are envied, but they seem not to recognise that they are also despised. Mda's critique of the role of the collaborator is fully articulated when the Man (their son-in-law) finally breaks out into a forceful diatribe against the 'black officials of the regime . . . civil servants who carry out the repressive laws . . . chiefs . . . policemen . . . in Soweto . . . Langa . . . New Brighton . . . throughout the land . . . They are doing their duty' (Mda 1990: 64).

In *Dark Voices Ring*, Mda implies that apartheid can really only be countered by armed rebellion: whenever the Man raises the subject, he is not challenged by the Woman. She is more concerned with her own subjective state and never objects to his declared intentions of joining the armed rebellion. Furthermore, there is no contradictory authorial voice when he iterates his intention of going north, 'where people are translating [their dreams] into reality . . . with their guns' (Mda 1990: 57). The denouement comes when the Man informs the Old Man (in the Woman's absence) of his intentions, which jolts the Old Man out of his catatonic state and he smiles his blessing on the 'just war' (64), which will vindicate the sufferings of all the oppressed of South Africa. Thus the Old Man's only action in the play, the smile, is symbolic of 'the rejection of an earlier servility and, more importantly, the move to a reconstructed life as a consequence of militant black nationalism' (Holloway 1989: 33).[1]

The ontological discourse in *Dark Voices Ring* incorporates themes of isolation and sexuality. The fiction of Nontobeko's death must be maintained at all costs if the Woman is to maintain her precarious sanity, while the Old Man has already retreated into a half-life. Their paranoid behaviour at the start of the play is enough to convince the audience that their lives are decidedly in the balance, but as the play progresses, we are reminded of just how tenuous their situation is. The Woman has built her fragile sanity through a fiction of dreams, both familial and sexual, which obtrudes on her sense of order with disquieting regularity.

We Shall Sing for the Fatherland completes the trilogy of plays produced in 1979 and widens the discussion of the political issues raised. The setting could be anywhere in post-colonial Africa. Mda's political concerns in this play centre on the figure of the idealist or 'true believer', as defined by Eric Hoffer (1952), as well as looking at neo-colonialism and the relative merits of socialism versus capitalism. Armed rebellion is a fait accompli and although the two veteran soldiers affirm the link between independence and armed struggle with their worn army uniforms and militarist rhetoric, militarism is not an issue explored here. Rather, Mda investigates the lot of the impoverished ex-freedom-fighter in post-colonial society and tests his idealism.

The idealist or 'true believer' is exemplified by Sergeant. Sergeant, it seems, will not countenance any questioning of the supposedly independent status of his country and his admonitions of Janabari for insubordination affirm this stance (see Mda 1990: 29). It is not until just before their deaths that he finally realises his error and recognises that perhaps he too has rights: 'We have been pushed around and shitted upon too much. That is why I am holding my ground in this park, and I am not moving away from it today or any other day. And I am not paying any more rent for it' (43). Alas, it is too late. Sergeant has exemplified what Hoffer describes as the 'abject poor':

> The poor on the borderline of starvation live purposeful lives. To be engaged in a desperate struggle for food and shelter is to be wholly free from a sense of futility. The goals are concrete and immediate. Every meal is a fulfilment; and every windfall a miracle. What need could they have for 'an inspiring super-individual goal which could give meaning and dignity to their lives'? (1952: 40)

Janabari, on the other hand, has seen the gross unfairness of their lives. He is the one who makes cynical comments and recognises the inequalities of their existence. Although Sergeant's and Janabari's country is, to all intents and purposes, free, Mda questions this freedom and draws attention to the potential betrayal of the revolution. The economy is certainly not under the control of the indigenous population; foreign investment maintained colonialism and it sustains post-independence neo-colonialism. Mr Mafutha, the black businessman, is successful, but only through white acquiescence: 'They say he is worth millions. He is in all the big companies. White companies too' (Mda 1990: 36). The cynical, tacit acceptance of the situation by both black and white people emerges when Banker tells him: 'The only thing you have to do is to listen to our advice' (34).

We Shall Sing for the Fatherland makes it quite clear that neo-colonial attitudes can be just as repressive as those of the erstwhile colonial masters. Real independence means freedom for all people. In 1975, J. Congress Mbata foresaw fundamental change as possible only if there were new and radical arrangements for the redistribution of a country's wealth and resources and if change included 'the formulation of a theory of political development for the African that clearly identifies the link between political power and economic power' (Mbata 1975: 202).

We Shall Sing for the Fatherland is peopled with betrayers and betrayed, and there are several versions of and degrees of betrayal. At its highest level, Sergeant and Janabari play out a game of suspicion. Sergeant insists on total adherence to their survival strategy and will brook no deviations. When Janabari is discovered with money that is unaccounted for, he is accused of 'betrayal and disloyalty to your superior officer' (Mda 1990: 29), but there is no question of Janabari's loyalty to his friend. His extra earnings are always shared but, more potently, his utmost loyalty is demonstrated when he refuses to leave the park for the Old Lady's warm shed at the end of the play. What these altercations amount to is a dignified attempt on Sergeant's part to cling to some form of agency. By pulling rank and controlling Janabari's actions, he still retains, albeit tenuously, a grasp on his own destiny – as a subject, rather than an object. Of course, since he is disabled, he needs Janabari physically, but their combined sense of integrity, exemplified by their refusal to beg, underlines this need for a sense of agency.

Sergeant and Janabari are victims of Ofisiri's petty bureaucracy, as he extracts money from them to stay in the park, but Ofisiri is a victim too. A member of the lower middle class, he has to cling tenaciously to his position, answerable always to his bosses and afraid of losing his job. In the end, because Sergeant and Janabari have died on his beat, he is demoted to guarding the convicts digging their graves. Ofisiri betrays his fellow men by exploiting them shamelessly and arbitrarily and, in turn, he is betrayed by society, which demotes him for something that is really its responsibility.

Sergeant and Janabari are betrayed by the whole of society, including the church. As witnesses to their own funerals at the end of the play, they note the vast difference between Mr Mafutha's funeral and their own and conclude that 'the priests have decided that he was wealthy enough to go to heaven' (Mda 1990: 47). The systematic pattern of betrayal in this play serves to underline the validity of Paulo Freire's contention that if the oppressed 'are drawn into the process as ambiguous beings . . . they will merely *imagine* that they have reached power' (Freire 1972: 98; emphasis added). However, the open-endedness in this play seems to suggest that Mda is issuing a warning, rather than depicting the inevitable.

The Hill, first produced in 1980, narrows and specifies its focus in terms of both location and theme. The action takes place on a particular hill outside Maseru and the play explores the economic dependency of Lesotho on South Africa, the plight of the migrant worker and the consequent breakdown of the family and erosion of traditional values.[2]

The theme of apartheid per se does not appear in *The Hill*, but the system allowed for and, indeed, depended on the exploitation of cheap labour from neighbouring countries. In *The Hill*, Mda shows how the extreme destitution of impoverished rural people makes them extremely vulnerable to exploitation, not only by foreign countries, but also in their own.

The destitution of the protagonists, the Man and the Young Man, is established most graphically in the opening pages in a strongly proprietary argument about the relative quantities of their faeces, both then and on preceding days. That they must resort to handouts and raiding dustbins is bad enough, but what really keeps them going is the sale of their blood to the blood bank – Trans Africa Biologicals – every two weeks.

Poverty, of course, is not theirs alone: both have dependent families in rural villages. Being less tied to the community than other groups, such as the very young, elderly and women, the men of the villages have no choice but to seek an alternative means of subsistence – even if it involves the degradation, hardships and indignities they know they will experience as migrant mineworkers. They can choose either to starve alongside their families or they can try something better. Theirs is the freedom to choose between Scylla and Charybdis:[3] 'Freedom aggravates at least as much as it alleviates frustration. Freedom of choice places the whole blame of failure on the shoulders of the individual. And as freedom encourages a multiplicity of attempts, it unavoidably multiplies failure and frustration. Freedom alleviates frustration by making available the palliatives of action, movement, change and protest' (Hoffer 1952: 44).

In Maseru the men are at the mercy of the well-to-do who are in control: 'The richer they get, the stingier they become' (Mda 1990: 74). The play quite ironically raises the anomaly of the Man being pursued for tax arrears, knowing all the while that 'the safest place in the world when there is a tax and radio licence raid' (84) is the affluent suburb of Maseru West as 'the cops never go there because that's where all the fat ones live' (84). Faced with such glaring inequality, work in the gold mines of South Africa, if they can only get it, is a better option. The mine pay will mean the difference between life and death to their families back home, which is why they are also tempted by a certain cachet to being a 'man of gold' (74), rather than a coal mineworker. Not only is the work in the mines physically demanding and uncomfortable, the life of the worker in the all-male hostels is also degrading, involving the humiliation of communal medical examinations and the pain of injections with unchanged needles (in pre-AIDS days). Worst of all is the shame of life without their women: 'He talks of degradation. What does he know of degradation? We leave our wives at home because the white man doesn't want us to bring them with us to the land of gold. We live in hostels where we fuck each other when the desire comes upon us. And he calls paying a small bribe to secure a good job degradation' (96).

The innocent Young Man and the experienced mineworkers, the Veteran and the Man, embody the patterns of betrayal explored in this play. The Young

Man's father has betrayed his family by his disappearance, thus forcing the Young Man to resort to life in the mines. But the Veteran is a more extreme case. Not only is he betrayed by the prostitutes (who strip him of everything, including his trousers, despite having been paid for their services), he also betrays his family by allowing himself to become a victim of the prostitutes, as he is tempted by 'a little clean fun before going to [his] home village in the mountains' (Mda 1990: 103). As a result of his experiences, the Young Man becomes thoroughly disillusioned. His loss of innocence is expressed in his rejection of cattle in favour of a car, and his abandonment of an entire way of life for a hollow, materialistic and alien value system is potently encapsulated in the sentences: 'I have more important things to live for now. My Valiant and my *gumba-gumba*' (86). His Valiant is simply a car steering wheel and his *gumba-gumba* or record player is a car battery – essential in a rural area without electricity. Both are crucial symbols and represent several aspects of the process: the ease with which the Young Man is deluded by the desire for a car; the fact that his treasures are no more than scrap remnants of a wealthier culture; and the folly of his notion that he can somehow acquire these luxuries piece by piece. By the end of the play, the Young Man has become a cynic. When the Man questions why the prostitutes have helped him, he replies: 'Is it my fault they were not attracted to you?' (112). His conscience is now a poor shadow, as he feels that no matter how he much he transgresses, he has nothing to fear: 'I'll confess, eat the sacrament and ask for forgiveness' (114).

The Young Man has now embraced the maxim of 'every man for himself', as symbolised by the pair of trousers. A man without trousers lacks agency and dignity: at the beginning of the play, the Young Man appears without trousers, as he has just defecated; the Veteran arrives, having been stripped of his trousers by the prostitutes; and in the end, the Veteran steals the Man's trousers. But the Young Man redeems himself by giving the Man his small change and encouraging him to save his blood money for the extra 'green page' for his passport – a bribe for the recruitment officer for the mines.

Mda's next play, *The Road*, first produced in 1982, is a political allegory of apartheid and of the relations between South Africa and Lesotho. The play examines apartheid ideology and the relationship between a black migrant agricultural labourer from Lesotho and a white Afrikaner farmer.[4]

The set of the play is highly suggestive. The road through farmlands suggests the way forward through South Africa, the part of the road on stage being the present, but leading to the horizon and suggesting the future. The tree represents all that is desirable about life in South Africa and the two protagonists represent their respective races – although the Farmer is not just any white man, but a Free State Afrikaner, a racist of the first order.

Through their conversation, we learn that the Farmer is suspicious of the motives of black people and black sympathisers, always suspecting some act of subversion. At the heart of the problem lies 'this beautiful tree God made in our beautiful land' (Mda 1990: 124). The Farmer is not prepared to share the tree on any terms with the Labourer after he discovers his blackness and, later, when he suspects that the Labourer might be plotting to overthrow him, he runs to his tree and hugs it, still holding his gun and saying: 'I am going to defend you. Nobody is going to take you away from me. I'll die fighting for you, my beloved tree' (142). Prior to his discovery of the Labourer's blackness, however, the Farmer is content to share the shade.

The extreme irony and humour of the situation serve to underline the irrationality of prejudice of any kind. Prejudice based on colour is obviously the most visible form, but if one removes visibility, the whole concept becomes ludicrous and, by implication, so do all other forms of prejudice. The casting of a black actor as the white Farmer is essential in order to highlight the incongruousness of colour prejudice. The Farmer's bizarre failure to realise that the Labourer is black until he is told forms the climax of the play – everything else is subsidiary, either as a result of or as a reaction to this discovery.

The Farmer reacts immediately to this news by implementing the policies of apartheid. The Labourer is summarily banished to the other side of the road, to go and 'sit there and develop yourself separately' (Mda 1990: 135) because, as the Farmer tells him, 'This is a white area, you know' (133). But the Farmer can only maintain his position and keep control over the Labourer because he has a gun and constantly threatens violence. He suspects that the Labourer is a terrorist and, when the Labourer intimates that he might take action, the Farmer exclaims: 'Do you mean you are going to use violence on me?' (135). He cannot see the anomaly of their positions or the irony of his greatest fear of becoming a victim of 'anarchy and bloodshed' (135).

Later on, the Farmer steals the Labourer's bundle, telling him that he has no right to it and must work for it if it is to be returned. The contents of the bundle are symbolic of what the Nationalist government has taken from the black population. The food symbolises the Labourer's immediate means of survival, the cooking implements represent his control over his survival in the future and his overalls symbolise his right to work and therefore moral and economic independence. That the Farmer wants the Labourer to work for what is his by right underlines the Farmer's need for the labour and inferior position of the Labourer, which provide the infrastructure of racial superiority.

The untenability of apartheid is alluded to when the Labourer mentions that he is from Lesotho and the Farmer hints at the 'honorary' whiteness that is allowed the Taiwanese and Japanese trading partners. If a country is to survive economically, it must trade. The complications that apartheid imposes become even more bizarre and undermine both the economic and moral fabric of society. Ultimately, the many concessions that apartheid is forced to make erode its foundations, until the whole idea becomes irrelevant.

In *The Road*, Mda explores, together with apartheid, the fundamental issues of prejudice and its more virulent twin, racism. These issues have been comprehensively analysed by Edward Said – metonymically as the Other (Said 1978) and reappraised later as 'not Europe's interlocutor, but its silent other' (Said 1985: 93). Not only is the Farmer anti-black, but he is anti-Jewish, anti-English and anti-communist – in his eyes, a more vehement form of liberal, which he is also against. Unreasoned and unquestioned, his muddled political thinking is only part of his muddled ideology, which is focused on an all-embracing hatred: 'It is my hatred, man. It doesn't concern you . . . I shall hoard my hatred' (Mda 1990: 127). When challenged on religious grounds, he replies: 'I say love your enemy, but shoot him all the same' (127). He is 'anti' everything and anyone who thinks or behaves differently from him. His prejudices are manifested most potently in his racism, which pervades the play from beginning to end.

Abdul R. JanMohamed emphasises the fact that

race is pivotal to the relations in colonial society, in order to provide a phenomenologically accurate description of colonial experience and to avoid two types of distractions. One view misrepresents reality by pretending that racial differences are unimportant in colonial society and thus need not embarrass or concern us; while the other view distorts the world by perceiving everything in terms of class conflict and thus becomes callous to the complexity of lived human experience. (1983: 7–8)

The Farmer feels fully justified in his unchristian behaviour towards his fellow men because he thinks his views on racism are fully justified. This 'Dutch Reformed' version of colonialism is explained by JanMohamed as seeing outside threats from 'Others', in the form of English or African aggression, as a 'divine test and assurance of God's favour' and he argues that for these people, 'in time the uniqueness of their culture acquired a religious significance, and its separation from possibly contaminating agents became a sacred duty: anyone who tried to overcome their separation was considered demonic' (Jan Mohamed 1983: 83).

In *The Road,* the recurring theme of betrayal is couched in sexual terms. The Farmer has betrayed his wife by consorting with prostitutes, first in Swaziland and later in Lesotho. His wife has betrayed him by having an affair with his foreman and he reciprocates by acquiring a regular black mistress. While the Labourer is forced to look for work away from home, his wife becomes the Farmer's mistress. This is the ultimate betrayal for the Labourer. The Farmer has taken from him everything he owns, everything he has by right, first his dog (which the Farmer shot) and now his wife.

Sexual infidelities and betrayal do not stop there. Mda depicts the notion of sexuality in this play as something depraved, unwholesome – thus underlining the depravity of the various betrayals and, ultimately, of apartheid. The language used by both men in connection with sex is usually obscene and all sexual encounters are described in negative terms. The Farmer seeks an outlet for his repressed sexuality occasioned by the strict South African censorship law, as well as the puritanical attitudes of the Dutch Reformed Church. He is a seasoned visitor to the neighbouring states of Swaziland and Lesotho – 'Casinos? Movies! Dirty magazines imported from Scandinavia! Women' (Mda 1990: 150) – especially black women, prohibited to him in South Africa. The Labourer, representing the black peoples of South Africa, reacts to the denigration from his white oppressor and is finally goaded into action and rebels – with disastrous consequences.

And the Girls in Their Sunday Dresses?, first produced in 1988, continues themes first mooted in *We Shall Sing for the Fatherland* and confirmed in *The Hill*. The notions of capitalist exploitation and official corruption in newly democratised post-colonial countries are developed further in this play. But Mda, for the first time, examines gender – specifically femaleness – and the familiar themes of prostitution, poverty and betrayal are viewed from the female point of view.

The thesis postulated in *We Shall Sing for the Fatherland*, of neo-colonialism being an unacceptable alternative to colonialism, is again explored in this play, where ordinary people are no better off than they were before and corruption and exploitation seem to be the preserve of whoever is in power. In *And the Girls in Their Sunday Dresses?* Mda takes a detailed look at the corruption of the petty bureaucracy of the civil service and the misappropriation of what rightfully belongs to the ordinary people.

The focus in this play is on Lesotho and while South Africa is a refuge for the runaway lovers, its relevance is to serve as a commentary on Lesotho and, by inference, the rest of southern Africa. Although the Woman and her lover are at the mercy of the Immorality Act specifically, the apartheid system is used as a symbol of oppression to highlight the inequalities of life in Lesotho. The Lady does not wish to discuss South Africa, dismissing it with: 'They are not our politics. They are politics of another country' (Mda 1993: 26), but the Woman rounds on her and reminds the Lady that 'it is southern African' and is relevant to them all (26).

That the two women represent victims of oppression in Lesotho is made clear. As in *We Shall Sing for the Fatherland*, there has been no real lifting of colonialism. White faces have merely been replaced with black ones. The civil servants whose job it is to distribute the rice donated as food aid are obviously economically better off, as symbolised by their regular, well-paid jobs and attractive clothing – the beautiful Sunday dresses of the title. That they also assume the role of the privileged is made clear in the offhand treatment they mete out to the abject people queuing for the food aid.

But the casual and uninterested manner of the civil servants is mild compared to the bureaucratic corruption described earlier in the play. The rice has been donated by wealthier countries for distribution among the needy, but the capitalist leaders are selling it to 'wholesalers, general dealers and jobbers' (Mda 1993: 14) and there is not enough left for the ordinary people. Not only does the country suffer from this kind of corruption, but Mda also criticises the inefficiency of all public services. The Lady describes post offices, banks or any public government offices as places of waiting, while officials continue their private conversations, or are missing and cannot be found, where files go astray or people are attending interminable meetings. The general populace feels powerless in circumstances like these and, like the Lady, has no recourse but to wait in the 'chair of patience', referring to the chair that the Lady brings with her to sit on while waiting in the queue (37).

Until all the people of a country attain similar rights and quality of life, they cannot be termed liberated. Unless, as Freire says, the people of a country all work together for their communal liberation, they are not free (1972: 103). And one of the reasons for the failure of true liberation would be, in the words of the Woman: 'We say: Well, this is home, we are prepared to accept shoddiness. We are still a young nation so these things are expected to happen. In other words what we are saying is that we don't think we are capable of producing the best results, so we are prepared to tolerate inefficiency and corruption' (Mda 1993: 28). As long as people are prepared to provide excuses for inefficiency and corruption, they are in collusion with their oppressors.

In tackling the theme of poverty, Mda sees clearly the desperation of the poor who can only act according to need, not reason. It makes sense for people to band together and refuse to buy food that was donated and meant to be free; but if you are at the end of the chain of corruption, you join the queue and, as the Lady says: 'Let's face it, you came because you heard it's a bargain . . . you are no different from them' (Mda 1993: 14). But poverty is real, grinding and hopeless. The desperation of people prepared to wait in a queue for four days speaks volumes, but when the Woman complains, 'If it's food aid it must be given to the poor free' (14), she compounds her case by adding: 'And in many cases it helps to keep them where they are – poor' (14).

In this play, prostitution is an issue of poverty. The Lady is at first presented to us in negative terms. She is described in the beginning as attempting to make herself appear '*chic and sexy*' (Mda 1993: 4) but we know what to expect when the Woman criticises her make-up for making her look like a whore. By the end of the play, the defences are down – she is, literally, covered in mud from sitting on the wet ground and she looks dishevelled. By the same token, the front she assumed in the beginning has crumbled and she has to admit her desperation. She reveals that she is destitute – indeed, she has to share her chair with the Woman in exchange for food.

The two women, however, manage to retain some sense of dignity in the face of poverty; the Lady initially keeps up a presentable physical appearance, for instance, while the Woman refuses to 'wallow in degradation' (Mda 1993: 16) for the rice, preferring to give up and go home. In fact, the Woman sees through the Lady's weakness. That she will always be a victim is symbolised by her 'chair of patience'. As long as she has it as a prop to keep her going in the face of all the degradation, she will remain a victim.

The theme of betrayal in this play is an adjunct to the more important theme of gender. The Italian chef betrays both the women by deserting them and leaving them destitute. Indeed, their attitudes to men seem to be coloured by their similar experiences. Apart from denigrating men, the women see them only in terms of salvation or 'insurance' for themselves through marriage, particularly to foreign men, such as the Italian and the Swiss. They are seen not only as a passport to financial security and status, but as providing a way out of their impoverished and corrupt country. But the men, with their predilection for young girls, are fickle and cannot be relied upon.

As far as the women's relationship with each other and with other women is concerned, a certain amount of emphasis is placed on appearance. The Lady's real reason for her obsession with appearance, of course, is the nature of her work. The office girls, initially, are seen as beautiful and, by inference, superior in their summer dresses, and the Woman is also described by the Lady as 'Miss Perfect' (Mda 1993: 23), but in the end there is a mutual recognition of a sisterhood – not only in strengths, but also in weaknesses. Like the Woman, the office girls have been unofficially prostituting themselves to get either their jobs or promotions and therefore are all 'in the same profession' (19) as the Lady. 'Only I do it openly and on my terms, as a free agent. They get laid and still have to sit behind office desks and typewriters before they can get their porridge,' she says.

The two women start off as antagonistic towards each other, but the Lady begins to call the Woman 'sister-woman' and invites her to reciprocate. The explanation and reason for the soubriquet are initially trite – the Lady picked it up from some African-American tourists – but as the play progresses, the two women's lives and philosophies move closer together and the use of the phrase increases. As they hold hands in the final scene, it is evident, apart from the stage direction of '*there is a great warmth between them*' (Mda 1993: 37), that they will face the future together as a unit with a sense of identity and belonging. The men have been well and truly 'Othered' in the final lines: 'Men . . . They are the same. They are like children of one person' (37). Through each other, the two women have forged a sense of self and seized agency. In typical Mda mode, their fate is open-ended: 'I know that never again will I need the food-aid rice, and my chair of patience. Are you coming or not?' (37).

Joys of War, first produced in 1989, is more experimental in form than the earlier plays, marking both a clear departure from and a continuity of Mda's previous work. The play is set on three levels on stage so that events in the play may be presented flexibly in terms of time and place. Simultaneously, scenes may be in the past, present or future or may be taking place in different parts of the country.

With the focus on armed struggle and sabotage, Mda seems to be asserting the relevance of a 1964 ideology to the late 1980s.[5] Armed struggle is not called into question. There is no debate as to its necessity or about alternative means of resistance. Instead, it is shown to be the only effective way forward, especially when compared to the struggles of ordinary people. Metaphorically, this can be seen in the privileged position of the Soldiers on the highest level adopting the positions of statues in a war memorial whenever the focus is not on them. This serves as a powerful icon for eulogising armed insurrection. Yet, the violence of everyday life is constantly foregrounded. Throughout the play we are reminded also of the violence of the burning of people's homes in the squatter camps; the use of tear gas, stones and dogs during protests or riots; the so-called 'suicides' of prisoners in detention; the 'state-of-the-art' torture paraphernalia, and so on. That armed resistance is seen as the only answer in face of such violence is powerfully encapsulated in Soldier One's statement: 'But it looks like all that is left for us to say is "from flowers bullets shall bloom"' (Mda 1990: 100). When Soldier Two asks for 'some little peace' (104), Soldier One responds: 'Oh no, we are not going to have a little peace around here. We are not going to have a little peace anywhere in this country until we win this war' (105).

However, the horrors of war are not overlooked. Both men regret the killing and maiming of civilians during their acts of sabotage, but agree 'this is something we all learn to live with. It cannot be avoided. It is painful, but it cannot be avoided' (Mda 1990: 124). However, despite the civilian casualties, Soldier Two sees the pyrotechnics of war as invigorating and seems to enjoy 'the deafening music of the bombs' (122). Soldier One accuses him of seeing war as a 'festival of fireworks' (122), but he agrees that 'all wars are games. Like pieces of draughts on a board' (123).

The commitment of both soldiers, though different in nature, is constantly alluded to. They are volunteers and both have been specifically chosen for this particular mission. Soldier Two's motives are unclear for most of the play, but Soldier One leaves us in no doubt of the high opinion that Soldier Two is held in by his peers and superiors. Soldier One's motives are clearer and simpler. He is fighting for civil rights and the right of control over his own labour – of necessity and paradoxically, for both altruistic and selfish reasons. By the time Soldier Two's story comes out, we find that he has proved himself committed as a soldier and, personally, to the woman he fell in love with, but the latter is a false commitment as, on being jilted, he is able to transform his commitment into betrayal.

Betrayal, the alter ego of commitment, is thoroughly developed in this play. Initially, Soldier One appears to have betrayed Mama and Nana, who is always convinced of his desertion but, as time passes, we find that he is the least likely to betray anyone, having proved himself loyal to family, comrades and country. The theme of betrayal is manifested mainly in relation to Soldier Two, who betrays his comrade and woman friend by falsely informing on them to the secret police and thereby destroying their lives. His betrayal, though, is doubly insidious: not only does he betray them falsely, he also obtains his revenge in an underhand way by allowing 'the system' to do his dirty work for him. His behaviour is highlighted in marked contrast to Soldier One's integrity in the face of the interrogators.

The basic philosophy that pervades all these early plays is a contemplation of our state of existence as human beings and our relationships to each other. Questions are raised about the importance of individuals, about the need to change our lives and the need to be active in this process. Equally Mda explores the idea of integrity and asks how loyal we are to our fellow humans and our ideals. Betrayal is central to Mda's first play, *Dead End*, and crucial to an understanding of the last play included here, *Joys of War*, which was produced more than a decade later.

Notes

1. The published version of *Dark Voices Ring* was banned and unbanned within five months in 1981. It was singled out initially as 'undesirable' and later, on appeal, it was found that although the play 'contained the language of protest', the setting and references were too vague and the form of the play – a one-act – too brief to have any profound or lasting effect that could 'incite or inflame the feelings of blacks so much as to justify the need for it to be prohibited' (*Report of the Publications Appeal Board*, Case No. 53/81).

2. When *The Hill* was first produced, it was received as 'the emergence of African theatre, spoken in English, which is unique to our place and time' (Fletcher 1980: 14). A revival of the play in 1995 found it to be dated, but this was seen in a positive light 'for, at a time when most cultural creators [were] concerned with reconstruction, development and celebrating how good it [was] to be free . . . it [was] necessary to note that the destruction [was] in full swing' (Khumalo 1995: 35).

3. Scylla and Charybdis refer to a monster and whirlpool in Greek myth – the idea of two dangers or extremes, the avoidance of one increasing the risk from the other; more colloquially, the devil and the deep blue sea.

4. Impoverished Lesotho has had a long and continuing history of migrant labour into South Africa (see Wilson and Thompson 1975: 267–71). In this play, Mda transfers his attention from the mineworker to the farm labourer.

5. It would seem that in this play Mda is reiterating Nelson Mandela's statement at the Rivonia Trial in 1964 that 'our policy to achieve a non-racial state by non-violence,

had achieved nothing . . .' and that eventually 'the time comes . . . when there remain only two choices – submit or fight' (quoted in Benson 1966: 254). The policy of Umkhonto we Sizwe was one of controlled sabotage and, although never explicitly stated, these notions seem to be central to *Joys of War*.

Works cited

Benson, Mary. 1966. *South Africa: The Struggle for a Birthright*. Harmondsworth: Penguin.

Fletcher, Jill. 1980. 'Unique theatre'. *The Cape Times*, 1 March: 14.

Freire, Paulo. 1972. *Pedagogy of the Oppressed*. Translated by Myra Bergman Ramos. Harmondsworth: Penguin.

Hoffer, Eric. 1952. *The True Believer: Thoughts on the Nature of Mass Movements*. London: Secker and Warburg.

Holloway, Myles. 1989. 'Social commentary and artistic mediation in Zakes Mda's early plays'. *The English Academy Review* 6: 28–41.

JanMohamed, Abdul R. 1983. *Manichean Aesthetics: The Politics of Literature in Colonial Africa*. Amherst: University of Massachusetts Press.

Khumalo, Bafana. 1995. 'Positively dated concerns'. *Weekly Mail and Guardian*, 24–30 March: 35.

Mbata, J. Congress. 1975. 'Profile of change: The cumulative significance of changes among Africans'. In: Thompson, Leonard and Jeffrey Butler (eds.). *Change in Contemporary South Africa*. Berkeley: University of California Press.

Mda, Zakes. 1990. *The Plays of Zakes Mda*. Johannesburg: Ravan Press.

———. 1993. *And the Girls in Their Sunday Dresses?: Four Works*. Johannesburg: Wits University Press.

Said, Edward. 1978. *Orientalism: Western Conceptions of the Orient*. London: Routledge.

———. 1985. 'Orientalism reconsidered'. *Cultural Critique* 1 (Fall): 89–107.

Wilson, Monica and Leonard Thompson (eds.). 1975. *The Oxford History of South Africa*. Oxford: Oxford University Press.

3

Mapping Memory, Healing the Land

The Bells of Amersfoort

SHANE GRAHAM

IN ZAKES MDA'S NOVEL, *The Heart of Redness*, the character Bhonco holds on dearly to 'the conflicts of generations ago', because they 'have shaped his present, and the present of the nation' (2000: 4).[1] He bears the marks of these conflicts – the 'scars of history' (12) – on his body: 'Bhonco carries the scars that were inflicted on his great-grandfather, Twin-Twin, by men who flogged him after he had been identified as a wizard by Prophet Mlanjeni, the Man of the River. Every first boy-child in subsequent generations of Twin-Twin's tree is born with the scars' (12). These scars become symbols of traumatic historical memory, which Mda conceives as deeply inscribed on both the body of the individual survivor and in particular places – or perhaps in the relationship between bodies and places. Bhonco's distant cousin Zim, for example, 'talks passionately about [Nongqawuse Valley]. When he began to walk, he walked in this valley. He looked after cattle in this valley. He was circumcised here . . . His whole life is centred in this valley' (50).

Mda pursues related questions of memory and the violent past in his play *The Bells of Amersfoort* (2002), commissioned and co-produced by De Nieuw Amsterdam Theatergroep. In this piece, as in the earlier novel, Mda links memory not only to sensual embodiment, but also to place and to the physical landscape. The main character, Tami, who has fled into exile after being detained and tortured by the security police for her political activism, had pledged with her fiancé, Luthando, who stayed behind in the Eastern Cape, to 'work with the people to mend the scars of the past' (2002: 159). In this play, Mda is clearly aiming to write a piece of 'true theatre of reconciliation', which he claims 'will address the past solely for the purpose of understanding the present . . . It is important that the past is not only addressed. It must be redressed as well' (1995a: 44). Stephanie Marlin-Curiel offers a similar observation about the body of theatre inspired by the Truth and Reconciliation Commission (TRC), which she discusses under the rubric of 'Theatre for Development (TfD)': 'these plays focus on the deep emotional trauma that remains with survivors as the TRC goes about "healing the nation." To varying degrees, they promote the re-humanization and healing of survivors of apartheid, whether they be victims or perpetrators' (2002: 276).

In *The Bells of Amersfoort*, Mda suggests one form that a redress of the past must take before the goals of reconciliation, healing and nation-building can be fulfilled: the people must be restored to the land. In part, presumably, this means a redistribution of land to those dispossessed during colonialism and apartheid; indeed, after the HIV/AIDS epidemic, the inequitable distribution of land is probably the most pressing problem facing South Africa in the twenty-first century. But Mda's diagnosis goes beyond mere ownership of the land; this play calls for whole new modes of producing, negotiating and using space. Luthando, despairing at Tami's refusal to return home even after the ban on anti-apartheid organisations had been lifted and the new dispensation had taken power, reminds her of the resolutions they had made together:

> We promised each other that we would heal the wounded earth. Even though we eat the fruits of freedom, the earth is not healed yet. The damage is too deep to be healed by a stroke of the pen. We need to work with our hands, Tami, as we promised ourselves and our people. We need to heal the land with the warmth of our hands. (2002: 129–30)

Although Luthando later loses sight of this idealism, Tami ultimately embraces the project of healing the 'scars of the past' through working with the earth, which suggests that Mda is calling for the fostering of a holistic relationship between people and the land. His view thus seems to constitute a rejection of both modernist discourses that regard land, nature and space as empty and needing to be traversed, conquered and filled, as well as postmodernist notions that regard places as empty signs to be commodified and marketed on a global scale. Claudia Braude claims that Walter Benjamin calls for a historical memory that is 'citable in all its moments' (1996: 42), which I take to mean a memory that yields to historiographic representation and analysis. I will interrogate and complicate Braude's argument in the course of this chapter; what Mda's play reveals is that if the investment of memory is split between the body and the land, the two must be joined in order to create a historical memory that is citable or representable in *any* of its moments.

The play centres on Tami, who is an anti-apartheid activist from the Eastern Cape living in exile in Amersfoort, in the Netherlands. She fled South Africa years before, after her wedding to Luthando was disrupted by security police who detained her for weeks and tortured her routinely every Sunday morning. Now the sound of church bells evokes a Pavlovian agony every time she hears them. Her principal torturer was a policeman named Johan, who has since reformed his ways, applied for and received amnesty, and is now studying at a seminary in Amersfoort. Tami has meanwhile become an alcoholic and refuses to return home even when Nelson Mandela is released from prison and the other exiles begin their homecoming.

The very structure of *The Bells of Amersfoort* foregrounds issues of space-time through its use of the three 'worlds' or acting areas. The stage directions explain:

> *The stage is divided into three distinct acting areas, located in any manner the director may deem fit . . . One represents TAMI Walaza's present world. The second represents the world she has left behind, which is also the world to which she will return. The third represents the world she will never reach, the world she observes from her window. She vicariously participates in this world as well, although it unfolds across the street. The three worlds, of course, will not necessarily remain static. Sometimes they may collide or even merge and become one world.* (Mda 2002: 114)

For example, in the first scene, Tami and Luthando address each other across the ocean, through letters, telephone, or perhaps telepathy, as Rob Amato suggests (2002: xviii), and then begin to dance in separate spaces, but together as directed: '*Although each of them is dancing in his or her own pool of light, in two different worlds, they are obviously dancing together*' (Mda 2002: 115). Likewise, the stage directions in Scene Two insist: '*It is important that when the two lovers talk they are not looking at each other. They do not address each other directly since they are, in reality, thousands of kilometres apart*' (120).

By thus constructing spatial representations of various temporal stages in Tami's life, Mda attempts to develop new modes of working through the difficulties that traumatic memory poses to narrating the past, thereby achieving reconciliation. Most theorists of trauma who are influenced by psychoanalytical models have focused on the temporal elements of the disorder, attributing trauma, in Cathy Caruth's words, to 'a break in the mind's experience of time' (1996: 61). Dori Laub, for example, says that 'trauma survivors live not with memories of the past, but with an event that could not and did not proceed through to its completion, has no ending, attained no closure, and therefore, as far as its survivors are concerned, continues into the present' (1992: 69). This is dramatised in the play by the flashbacks to Tami's traumatic experiences in South Africa, which are performed in the 'second world' or acting area.

Mda addresses this temporal aspect of trauma and memory in *The Bells of Amersfoort*, most notably through the symbol of the church bells that sound daily in the Dutch town where Tami has set up residence. Every time the bells ring, Tami doubles over in agony; this phenomenon very much resembles the traumatic encounter as Caruth describes it: 'the taking over of the mind, psychically and neurobiologically, by an event that it cannot control' (1996: 58). Ironically, one of the occasions on which the Amersfoort bells sound is in commemoration of a 'day of anti-racism', but to build a monument to anti-racism is necessarily to remember the existence of racism itself, a reminder of the pain symbolised by Tami's agony when she hears the bells.

In the penultimate scene of the play, Tami decides: 'I have to go back. There is unfinished business back home' (Mda 2002: 154). A moment later, the bells toll, but Tami does not feel her accustomed agony. This apparent closure has been brought about, in part, through the artistic process – specifically, Tami-the-trombonist starts a band with her friend Martijn, a drummer from Surinam, and the music they make together seems to perform a therapeutic function. Their mutual friend Katja remarks to Martijn that Tami 'no longer has what she called the "demons" that possessed her. You, the music, or both, have exorcised them' (148). Ina Gräbe's remarks on Mda's novel *Ways of Dying* are relevant here as well: what sets the novel apart 'from the stories told at the TRC hearings is the "solution" to violence, represented as the power of imagination and the escape found in creative outlets, such as singing, drawing and sculpture' (2000: 261).

But Mda's conception of memory goes beyond purely temporal considerations and the closure or healing that Tami seems to find at the play's end is derived from the therapeutic effects of her music and, it seems, from her renewed resolve 'to heal the wounded earth' (Mda 2002: 156). Her own psychic wounds are intimately connected to these scars in the earth and the 'trigger' of the bells not only transports Tami back in time, it also transports her virtually to the prison cell in the Eastern Cape where she was tortured. In one scene, Tami argues with Johan in the 'first world' or acting area, which represents Tami's present in the Netherlands. After she exits the stage, the bells sound and the stage directions declare that Tami '*is flung into the second world*' (146), representing the South African past. The effect of this spatial rendering of memory is to dramatise the psychic agony Tami experiences when she hears the bells – she is not merely reminded of the past, she is transported back to the place where the trauma happened and forced to relive it. For Johan, too, the bells transport him to the same place, but with positive associations: 'Every time they toll, they take me back to my home town in the Eastern Cape . . . The bells of my youth. Their music rings in my ears to this day. It was an idyllic life. The whole rhythm of life was in those bells' (145).

The play thus emphasises the close links between memory and space/place. It also suggests that the body mediates between the two. Tami, for instance, tells Martijn that she has a 'longing for familiar things . . . for ordinary things . . . the smells . . . the rain . . . the thunder' (Mda 2002: 141). In other words, she longs for sensual encounters with the place itself, a longing echoed in a conversation with Johan:

JOHAN: They say [Holland] is my ancestral home, yet I come as a stranger . . . I have even gone to a village that bears my name. It is far removed from

who I am. From what I am. I am of Africa. I do not feel part of this land.
Even the soil smells differently.

TAMI (*emphatically*): The smell of the soil. The peculiar smell of a gravel
path after the rain.

JOHAN: How do you take that with you to Holland? How do you create
that in Holland? (Mda 2002: 145)

This scene bears certain similarities to a scene in John Kani's play *Nothing but
the Truth* (2002), for which Zakes Mda wrote the introduction and which
premiered at the same National Arts Festival in Grahamstown, where *The
Bells of Amersfoort* had its South African debut. Kani's character, Mandisa,
raised in exile in England, visits her uncle and cousin in New Brighton township
for the first time and remarks: 'This is just as my father described . . . even the
smell. Everything . . . The township smell – the dust, coal stoves . . . something
earthy, nothing like England or London especially' (Kani 2002: 17–18). Both
scenes highlight the crucial role that smell seems to play in people's memories
of specific places.

Mda suggests that smell and other forms of bodily memory can transcend
the physical divides that exist between the different 'worlds', as described in
the opening stage directions quoted earlier. As the play progresses, however,
this rigid divide between the first and second worlds begins to erode and Tami
and Luthando address each other more directly, even as their relationship
begins to fall apart. This accelerating breakdown in the play's spatial schemas
is symbolised by the swallow, which shuttles back and forth between Europe
and southern Africa, crossing borders and collapsing space-time – in contrast,
say, to Johan's sense of identity, which is firmly rooted in the African soil.
Wendy Woodward argues that Mda's representation of identities in *The Heart
of Redness* 'suggests that place and identity are mutually imbricated and that
the latter may even be constructed by place. At the same time, identities are
fluid' (2003: 174). Indeed, identities must be fluid, or else invested in something
more stable than the landscape, in the face of rapid and accelerating changes
that are rendering many rural spaces unrecognisable – for example, the
transformation of villages into casino complexes, as the Unbelievers of *The
Heart of Redness* hope to do in Qolorha-by-Sea. The swallow in *The Bells of*

Amersfoort provides a figurative model for such a fluid sense of identity that can transcend place and borders. Tami tells Luthando, long after he has ceased to listen, about seeing the first flock of swallows of the spring:

> *Inkonjane.* The swallow. I knew exactly where they came from. That they have flown from your world. Some of them might even have seen you. Might even have built their mud nests under your eaves. It is April. Your autumn. Our spring. They have flown thousands of kilometres in just one month . . . Dear Luthando, the swallows have come back before time, only to find that it is spring only in name. Snow still covers the ground. (Mda 2002: 121)

Tami, like the swallow, has traversed great distances and displays the sort of confusion over seasons experienced by those who have crossed the equator. Yet the swallow also provides a more direct link between the worlds: in the flashback to the jail cell, after being tortured by an 'unseen force', Tami eventually sits up, stretches out her hand and says: 'Oh, little swallow. You have been my only visitor these past weeks. My only companion . . . Ah, you have built your mud nest under the ledge above the barred window. You have come to stay. Until the seasons change and you fly to other climes' (Mda 2002: 146–47). The swallow thus provides a kind of – perhaps paradoxical – fluid continuity, or connection-through-mobility, which provides a metaphor for Mda's conception of memory.

These changes that take place over the course of the play are due in part to what David Harvey in *The Condition of Postmodernity* (1990) has called time-space compression – the disorientation that results from interrelated phenomena, such as air travel, the Internet and other information technologies, cellular phone networks, just-in-time production methods and the decline of the nation-state. More generally, Harvey diagnoses time-space compression as the symptom of new economic regimes of flexible accumulation and hyper-consumerism:

> We can link the schizophrenic dimension to postmodernity which Jameson identifies . . . with accelerations in turnover times in production, exchange, and consumption that produce, as it were, the

loss of a sense of the future except and insofar as the future can be
discounted into the present. Everything, from novel writing and
philosophizing to the experience of labouring or making a home, has
to face the challenge of accelerating turnover time and the rapid write-
off of traditional and historically acquired values. (1990: 291)

Paraphrasing Karl Marx, Harvey notes that the 'fierce round in that process of
annihilation of space through time that has always lain at the center of
capitalism's dynamic' has intensified in the advanced capitalist countries since
the early 1970s (1990: 293). By designating purposes for every space –
residential, commercial, industrial, agricultural, recreational – and by
constructing built environments according to those designations, capital
effectively 'freezes' space, imposing the stamp of modernity and progress on
the landscape.

In the case of South Africa, this triumph of time over space has been
accelerated since the early 1990s through the ANC's adoption of a neo-liberal
agenda of economic reform and the lifting of economic sanctions and cultural
boycotts. One of the ugliest signs of this new capitalist regime at work in the
political sphere has been the corruption scandals in Parliament, involving an
arms deal and travel vouchers, scandals that have ruined the careers of more
than one Member of Parliament (MP) and even led to the dismissal of the
deputy-president. Mda takes a sarcastic oblique swipe at an MP at the centre of
the arms scandal who received a steep discount on a luxury SUV from an arms
dealer when he has Luthando complain about the colour of a Mercedes four-
wheel-drive he is to receive as a gift (Mda 2002: 159).

Indeed, the most obvious illustration in *The Bells of Amersfoort* of time-
space compression is in the changes that Luthando undergoes over the course
of the play. In the middle years of Tami's exile, he displays a confusion and
disorientation over the changes taking place in his country: 'Dear Tami, years
have passed. The world you knew is no longer the same. It is changing every
day. Even we who live in it can no longer recognise it. Cannot keep up with the
changes' (Mda 2002: 120). Later in the play, he seems to cope with this confusion
by embracing the culture of consumerism and commodification – he drives
only German luxury cars, for example, and develops a fetish for powerful women

in business or Parliament. When Tami finally returns to the mountains of her home in the Eastern Cape, she finds only 'undefinable' figures, 'frozen in agony' (156); their immobility contrasts with Luthando's jet-setting life and emphasises the unevenness of capitalist development in the new South Africa. She asks them where Luthando has gone; one tells her that they elected him to Parliament, but never saw him again. When she goes to look for him in Cape Town, someone else says: 'Luthando? He has left for Johannesburg. The pickings are richer there. Parliamentarians are too poorly paid . . . He was deployed to the corporate world. He is an executive chairman of a black empowerment conglomerate, which recently won a multi-billion-rand tender to supply some defence systems to the army . . . in partnership with a Dutch company' (157). At the end of the play, Tami, dismayed by her fiancé's betrayal of his former ideals and his uncritical embrace of multinational capitalism, laments: 'I am a victim of the twin diseases of the democratic South Africa: instant gratification and conspicuous consumption' (160).

Thus, even as the physical distance between the worlds on the stage seems to shrink due, in part, to time-space compression and even as the distance literally shrinks when Tami finally returns home, the distance between Tami and Luthando's understandings of and goals for the new South Africa has widened into a seemingly unbridgeable chasm. We see this divide in one of their early exchanges across the border between the first and second worlds:

TAMI: I have been walking around the town. I walked for kilometres without going anywhere in particular. Just walked . . .
LUTHANDO: Fortunately my car is air-conditioned. Did I tell you I bought a new car? A BMW Three-Series? I am driving around, thinking warm thoughts about you. (Mda 2002: 134)

This passage reveals that the divide between them is in fact rooted in a radical difference in their interactions with – and use of – space: whereas Luthando seals himself off in climate-controlled luxury, watching the landscape roll past at 120 kilometres per hour, Tami rejects the disorientation of time-space compression and chooses a more direct encounter with the city.

Tami makes her rejection of instant gratification and consumption emphatically clear in the final scene, when she finally meets Luthando in person again. She is riding her bicycle, symbolised on the stage by a wire toy of the type made by township children, which she pushes at the end of a long wire; Luthando, of course, now drives 'a posh Mercedes Benz', which is represented by a 'well-made wire car'. He tells Tami:

> Ah, a bicycle. I hear everybody in Holland rides one. But you know, Tami, here a bicycle is the mode of transportation of the lower classes. The lowest class, in fact. So, you'll have to do away with it. I won't begrudge you if you have one for sporting purposes. I can buy you a very expensive mountain bike. (*Emphatic.*) For sporting purposes. But for the purposes of moving from point A to point B it is a no-no. (Mda 2002: 158)

Tami responds by declaring that the bicycle is 'the only thing I intend to ride for the rest of my life' (Mda 2002: 158) and then condemns Luthando and their former comrades who 'are now involved in self-enrichment activities either as members of the government or of the corporate world' (159). Luthando's attribution of bicycles to 'the lowest class' again underscores the unevenness of development in post-apartheid South Africa and thus the very different relationships with time-space experienced by the rich and by the poor: whereas the working classes and unemployed traverse cities and the countryside by bicycle, on foot, or in minibus taxis that stop and start erratically, the affluent classes zip along in private cars, or fly.

The closing scene of the play underscores Mda's view that true reconciliation requires South Africans to renegotiate their relationship to the land – and, surely, to reconfigure socio-spatial relationships more generally. If it is true, as Tami insists, that there 'can be no reconciliation without justice!' (Mda 2002: 152) and that 'we need to find a new cohesion. The cohesion of free men and women' (160), it appears that justice and this necessary 'new cohesion' are both based in a renewed contact with the wounded earth. It is surely no accident that Tami's degree, which has heretofore gone unused, is in rural development. In the final scene, she offers Johan the opportunity to earn the forgiveness and reconciliation he seeks: 'Help me do what Luthando and I had vowed to do: rebuild the scarred land. Heal the wounds that still ache, that history has imposed on my people' (160).

It is significant that the play's concluding note of hope comes from this alliance between the black former freedom-fighter and the reformed white Afrikaner torturer. Mda, in his note to the publishers, wrote that *The Bells of Amersfoort* 'tries to rehabilitate the Afrikaner in the imagination of South Africa. An Afrikaner man, who was the oppressor and the torturer in the old South Africa, becomes the key element in the development of the country and in rebuilding it in the new South Africa' (quoted in Amato 2002: xviii). Another way to look at this is that the play is attempting to reconcile African and Afrikaner notions of space. Here Neil Smith's discussion of the 'poetic fusion of physical geography with cultural myth' in the conceptualisation of 'poetic nature' in nineteenth-century American literature and culture is useful: 'Where the dominant social symbols of the Old World drew their strength and legitimacy from history, New World symbols were more likely to invest in nature' (1984: 7). Similar symbolic investments can be seen in attitudes towards the land in much Afrikaner cultural mythology – the Great Trek into the interior of an 'empty' land waiting for the mastery of God's chosen people, for example.[2] Yet, as Johan's 'longing for the smell of the gravel roads after the rain' (Mda 2002: 160) reveals, the Afrikaner version of 'poetic nature' is also born out of a genuine love for and connection to the African soil.[3] It is precisely this kind of connectedness to the land that Mda sees as crucial to the construction of a just and reconciled South African future and that he depicts as under threat by a culture of 'immediate gratification and conspicuous consumption' (160).

What solution, then, to the dilemmas of time-space compression does Mda identify in this play? At first glance, it might seem that he is striving for a history that is 'citable in all its moments', as Braude suggests the Benjaminian angel of history represents. Braude notes the existence of many 'incursions into the space of national memory where the past of the apartheid regime is concerned. Attacks on the memory of the activities of the apartheid forces are discernable everywhere we look, threatening the past's complete citability, leaving the lies of the past untouched' (1996: 42). Yet surely what the TRC revealed was the utter impossibility of such a complete citability: even after collecting the testimonies of more than 22 000 victims and more than 6 000 amnesty applicants, the stories that the TRC tells about the past are still full of gaps, blind spots, contradictions and unanswered questions. Dirk Klopper argues that 'the angel of history is described [by Benjamin] in more equivocal terms than allowed for by Braude . . . [T]he angel is impotent in the face of disaster' (2004: 199). Mda's play demonstrates this narrative impotence through, for example, the fragmented presentation of the flashbacks to Tami's torture and the fact that her torturers are never visible on stage while she is actually being tortured.

Klopper further warns of the dangers involved in precisely the kinds of attempts toward totalising closure that Braude's argument implies: '[N]arrative offers a progression from fragmentation to wholeness, from what one might, in the context of the TRC, call disclosure to closure. However, in its pursuit of a telos of closure, the TRC narrative risks foreclosure' (Klopper 2004: 209). Steven Robins sounds a similar warning about the way that narrative closure can be appropriated and mobilised by political forces: '[T]he problem of historiographical representation is further compounded by the tendency of both official and popular accounts of collective suffering to serve (ethnic) nationalist agendas' (1998: 122). Alternatively, as the slogans that Tami mocks Luthando for having learned so well (Mda 2002: 159) reveal, such narratives are equally subject to appropriation by former activists and freedom-fighters to serve as a screen for corruption and self-enrichment. Thus, for Mda, the key to preventing this hijacking of memory is to empower people to determine and retain control over their own (physical and figurative) spaces of memory. This emphasis on autonomy is a recurring theme in Mda's work – as Siphokazi Koyana notes about *The Heart of Redness*, 'Mda emphasizes the importance of having the villagers participate in the transformation of . . . their village' (2003: 54). The shadowy figures in the last scene of *The Bells of Amersfoort* are powerless precisely because they have relied on the likes of Luthando to speak for them and to rebuild their society, rather than taking control over their own lives and spaces. To retain this control, though, Mda suggests that those constructed spaces must be resistant to the kind of 'closure' that is easily appropriated by factions or outside interests.

Two weapons that Tami uses to resist the totalising impulse toward closure or foreclosure are noise and chaos. She tells her friend Katja that her neighbours complain when she plays her trombone: 'I don't know why noise scares them so much. Noise is the essence of life. I can't help it that you Dutch people can't handle chaos. It destabilises you completely' (Mda 2002: 124) and again later: 'I like it so much when Dutch people are destabilised by noise. There is too much order here. We need a little bit of chaos. Noise is normal where I come from. Loudspeakers blaring. Different types of music competing from neighbouring houses! Street noises' (140). There is an irony here: the dissonant noise of Tami's trombone helps her to re-establish her autonomy, while the beautiful music of the bells causes her agony and represents the rigid compartmentalising tendencies of the Dutch/Afrikaner mindset that she identifies in these quotes.

Especially when performed before a South African audience, Tami's jibes at the Dutch sense of order would surely be taken as a comment on the ordering impulses of Dutch-descended Afrikaner nationalists. Indeed, one possible way to understand the history of apartheid social policy is as a series of attempts to contain and subdue the destabilising elements of noise and seeming chaos in the black townships and Bantustans. The fact that Tami remembers the noises of street life so fondly is strong evidence of the failure of these attempts and the persistence of alternative modes of organising and using social space in African cultures.

If Mda refuses totalising narratives of the past, he also rejects a naive faith in the ability of art and narrative to restore people and the land to some harmonious pre-lapsarian wholeness. In one interview, he remarks:

Renaissance involves both 'development' and 'rediscovery'. I would have a problem with 'revival'. It implies 'going back' to the archive to reinvent culture and reclaim a pre-colonial authenticity that is lost. All these, in my view, are conservative and reactionary notions of an African Renaissance. We cannot hope to revive the great civilizations that existed in many parts of Africa. But we can rediscover them – their literature, their philosophy. (Nuttall and Michael 2000: 117)

Mda strives, then, not for recovery of a lost primal unity, but rather for a reinvention of narratives of past times and representations of past spaces in ways that can foster development and transform people's relationship to social and productive space in the present and in the future.

What Mda ultimately advocates is that the communities themselves should define their own memories, places and identities, while leaving these definitions open to revision and renegotiation, rather than allowing them to be imposed from above or appropriated by others. People must not be trapped in the past, he implies, but rather must traverse a dialectic between the past and the present – just as the swallow continually migrates along a Deleuzian trajectory between the 'first world' and 'second world' – in order to imagine and negotiate new possible futures, or the 'third world' that Tami at first sees as attainable only vicariously through voyeurism. By taking part in this mobility herself, but on her own terms and at her own bicycle-slow speed, Tami challenges the codes – what Henri Lefebvre in *The Production of Space* (1991) calls representational spaces – that determine the production and uses of space. Only thus can she, like the characters in Mda's novel *Ways of Dying*, find 'peace with each other and their actual and constructed environment' (Gräbe 2000: 261–62).

The traversals of space-time in ways that both mirror and resist the fragmenting and distorting effects of postmodern time-space compression, as Mda depicts them in *The Bells of Amersfoort*, correlate with what Paul Gready sees as one value of the TRC: it 'facilitated a forward movement in time and an ownership of the full temporal range, a country more at home with its past, present, and future . . . [T]he commission [also] epitomized the newly found capacity to traverse space' (2003: 285) by holding hearings throughout the country, for example. Mda's play is exercising these same new-found freedoms and emphasising the importance for all of South Africa's people do the same, and in the process, forging new modes of constructing and interacting with social space.

Notes

1. I wrote this chapter while working as a Mellon Post-Doctoral Fellow at the University of the Witwatersrand in Johannesburg. My sincere gratitude goes to the Mellon Foundation and the Wits English Department for their generous support. This chapter has been much improved through valuable readings and feedback offered by David Attwell, Christie Fox, Sarah Nuttall and Michael Titlestad. They have my gratitude.

2. Tony Birch's analysis of British settler rhetoric about Australia as '[a] land so inviting and still without inhabitants' (1996: 173) suggests that such tropes of the empty landscape are common to imperialist narratives around the globe.

3. In this regard, the play echoes a passage in *The Heart of Redness* in which Dalton, the white man who has been raised among the amaXhosa, defends Afrikaners from the glib mockery of his white English-speaking friends: the Afrikaner, he insists, 'belongs to the soil. He is of Africa' (2000: 160).

Works cited

Amato, Rob. 2002. 'Introduction'. In: Mda, Zakes. *Fools, Bells and the Habit of Eating: Three Satires*. Johannesburg: Wits University Press, v–xxi.

Birch, Tony. 1996. ' "A land so inviting and still without inhabitants": Erasing Koori culture from (post-)colonial landscapes'. In: Darian-Smith, Kate, Liz Gunner and Sarah Nuttall (eds.). *Text, Theory, Space: Land, Literature and History in South Africa and Australia*. London: Routledge, 173–88.

Braude, Claudia. 1996. 'The archbishop, the private detective and the angel of history: The production of South African public memory and the Truth and Reconciliation Commission'. *Current Writing* 8(2): 39–65.

Caruth, Cathy. 1996. *Unclaimed Experience: Trauma, Narrative, and History*. Baltimore: Johns Hopkins University Press.

Gräbe, Ina. 2000. 'Telling the "truth": Collective memory of South Africa's apartheid heritage'. In: Ibsch, Elrud, Douwe Fokkema and Joachim von der Thüsen (eds.). *The Conscience of Humankind: Literature and Traumatic Experiences*. Amsterdam: Rodopi, 249–63.

Gready, Paul. 2003. *Writing as Resistance: Life Stories of Imprisonment, Exile, and Homecoming from Apartheid South Africa*. Lanham, MD: Lexington Books.

Harvey, David. 1990. *The Condition of Postmodernity*. Cambridge, MA: Blackwell.

Kani, John. 2002. *Nothing but the Truth*. Johannesburg: Wits University Press.

Klopper, Dirk. 2004. 'Narrative time and the space of the image: The truth of the lie in Winnie Madikizela-Mandela's testimony before the Truth and Reconciliation Commission'. In: De Kock, Leon, Louise Bethlehem and Sonja Laden (eds.). *South Africa in the Global Imaginary*. Pretoria: UNISA Press; Leiden: Brill, 195–213.

Koyana, Siphokazi. 2003. 'Qolorha and the dialogism of place in Zakes Mda's *The Heart of Redness*'. *Current Writing* 15(1): 51–62.

Laub, Dori. 1992. 'Bearing witness, or the vicissitudes of listening'. In: Felman, Shoshana and Dori Laub. *Testimony: Crises of Witnessing in Literature, Psychoanalysis, and History*. New York: Routledge, 57–74.

Lefebvre, Henri. 1991. *The Production of Space*. Translated by Donald Nicholson-Smith. Oxford: Blackwell.

Marlin-Curiel, Stephanie. 2002. 'The long road to healing: From the TRC to TfD'. *Theatre Research International* 27(3): 275–88.

Mda, Zakes. 1995a. 'Theater and reconciliation in South Africa'. *Theater* 25(3): 38–45.

———. 1995b. *Ways of Dying*. Cape Town: Oxford University Press.

———. 2000. *The Heart of Redness*. Oxford: Oxford University Press.

———. 2002. *The Bells of Amersfoort*. In: Mda, Zakes. *Fools, Bells and the Habit of Eating: Three Satires*. Johannesburg: Wits University Press.

Nuttall, Sarah and Cheryl-Ann Michael. 2000. 'African Renaissance: Interviews with Sikhumbuzo Mngadi, Tony Parr, Rhoda Kadalie, Zakes Mda, and Darryl Accone'. In: Nuttall, Sarah and Cheryl-Ann Michael (eds.). *Senses of Culture: South African Culture Studies*. Oxford: Oxford University Press: 107–21.

Robins, Steven. 1998. 'Silence in my father's house: Memory, nationalism, and narratives of the body'. In: Nuttall, Sarah and Carli Coetzee (eds.). *Negotiating the Past: The Making of Memory in South Africa*. Cape Town: Oxford University Press, 120–40.

Smith, Neil. 1984. *Uneven Development: Nature, Capital, and the Production of Space*. Oxford: Blackwell.

Woodward, Wendy. 2003. '"Jim comes from Jo'burg": Regionalised identities and social comedy in Zakes Mda's *The Heart of Redness*'. *Current Writing* 15(2): 173–85.

4

Chronicles of Belief and Unbelief

Zakes Mda and the Question of Magical Realism in South African Literature

CHRISTOPHER WARNES

IT HAS BECOME SOMETHING of a critical commonplace to claim that magical realism emerges from contexts characterised by the co-existence of pre- and post-industrial modes of life. As Brenda Cooper puts it: 'magical realism arises out of particular societies – postcolonial, unevenly developed places where old and new, modern and ancient, the scientific and the magical views of the world co-exist' (1998: 216). The Latin American and African examples discussed by Cooper attest to the truth of this statement and show how effective magical realism has been in merging disparate worldviews and in solving certain narrative and aesthetic problems of post-colonial fiction. But it is unlikely that the complicated matter of magical realism can be reduced to straightforward questions of development, or to simplistic distinctions between 'tradition' and 'modernity'. For if socio-economic conditions so easily translate into the aesthetic choices writers make, critics need to explain why magical realism has been so foreign to the South African writing sensibility. After all, South Africa, sadly, continues to outstrip many Latin American countries in terms of income inequality, and stark social, material and phenomenological juxtapositions continue to characterise the country's cultural landscape. Yet, until recently, South African writers have been slow to explore the possibilities of magical realism.

The obvious exception would appear to be Zakes Mda. In the brief biography that prefaces *The Madonna of Excelsior* (2002), we are told that Mda's novels 'have been acclaimed for their introduction of magic realism into South African fiction'. This comment is suggestive of a general consensus – especially among reviewers of his books – that Mda's work represents a new departure in South African writing, one that promises to reconcile some of the cultural polarities of South African reality, while showing the world that South Africans, too, can write magical realism. Detailed critical exploration of the matter has not been forthcoming, however, and it remains unclear what the value of such statements is. The fact that it is the publisher of his novels making claims about Mda's magical realism should provide some cause for concern among critics. Commenting on the Latin American literary context, Jean Franco has observed how ' "[m]agical realism," once taken as the index of Latin American originality, is now little more than a brand name for exoticism' (1999: 204). The very phrase 'magical realism' has proved as marketable as works such as Gabriel García Márquez's *One Hundred Years of Solitude*. The question must therefore be asked whether the enthusiastic use of this term when referring to Mda's novels is simply an exoticist marketing tool, or perhaps a naive expression of a desire for post-apartheid South African writing to be seen as globally relevant. Or does magical realism represent a meaningful way of talking about Mda's work, both in terms of its formal operations and its relations with African and world literature?

Before tackling these questions, it would be wise to spend a few moments outlining what the term 'magical realism' means in literary critical discourse. Condensing the insights of a number of publications, the definition that will be used here is a narrow one in which magical realism signifies a mode of narration that naturalises the supernatural, representing real and non-real in a state of equivalence and refusing either greater claim to truth (Chiampi 1983: 27; Chanady 1985: 3–5; Faris 2004: 7). For a text to be described as magical realist in any meaningful way, there must be clear evidence of the supernatural. As Wendy B. Faris describes it, there must be an 'irreducible element' of magic and this must be represented within a setting that adheres to the usual demands of realism (2004: 7). The text constructs an empirically verifiable object world, but includes within that world events that fall outside the boundaries of rational explanation. I have tried to extend this definition by suggesting that magical realist literature is frequently characterised by either an orientation of faith or one of irreverence. My argument is that writers' deployment of magical realist strategies of narration often corresponds either to the desire to valorise a worldview in which there is no clear distinction between natural and supernatural, or to a quite different drive towards parody, self-conscious critique and epistemological scepticism (Warnes 2005). There are lines of traffic between these orientations, but, as I hope to show with regard to Mda, examining them separately can prove useful in relating texts to their contexts and in supplying a more insightful assessment of the discursive conditions characterising individual deployments of magical realism.

South African writing has, on the whole, been partial to realistic modes of narration. I use the term 'realistic' advisedly here, for realism is a notoriously difficult concept to pin down theoretically and recent research has pointed to levels of experimentation often present in much apparently realistic writing in South Africa. But the fact remains that this experimentation has seldom taken place at the level of form and genre. With the possible exception of the oneiric sequences in J.M. Coetzee's *Waiting for the Barbarians* or the surreality of the last chapter of his novel *Foe*, in the apartheid years virtually nothing was written in English in South Africa remotely resembling fantasy or magical realism. Both Coetzee and Nadine Gordimer in fact explicitly rejected experimentation with non-real modes of narration. The former, in his 1987 Jerusalem Prize acceptance speech laments that he cannot join Cervantes' Don Quixote in entering the 'realm of faery' because 'in South Africa there is now too much truth for art to hold, truth by the bucketful, truth that overwhelms and swamps every act of the imagination' (1992: 99). Gordimer is well known for having declared that the 'essential gesture' of the white writer in South Africa 'can only be fulfilled in the integrity Chekhov demanded: "to describe a situation so truthfully [. . .] that the reader can no longer evade it"' (1988: 250). For different reasons, and in their different ways, these two authors arrive at the same conclusion: writing in South Africa has no place for the creation of other worlds, for fairytales, fantasy and magic.

The most influential commentator on black South African literature of the apartheid years was Njabulo Ndebele. Ndebele's conception of apartheid-era South Africa, drawn from Roland Barthes's analysis of wrestling, is of a society characterised by the 'emptying out of interiority to the benefit of its exterior signs, [the] exhaustion of the content by the form' (1994: 42). Such a society lends itself, in this reading, to representations of the spectacle; indeed, for Ndebele, 'the history of black South African literature has largely been the history of the representation of the spectacle' (41). Protest literature of the spectacular kind yields to the 'pressure of the expository intention': it subordinates choices about aesthetics to political imperatives. Ndebele's antidote to the excesses of spectacular literature is the 'rediscovery of the ordinary'. The ordinary remains an elusive category in Ndebele's writing. As Graham Pechey points out, it 'attract[s] a mainly apophatic definition: we can know what it is *not* rather better than we can know what it *is*.' (1994: 6; emphasis in original) It is not that which can be located in the crude binaries propagated by apartheid, but rather insists on more subtle, intimate and localised ways of seeing, promoting a focus on categories of experience that are overlooked in the literature of the spectacle. 'Ordinary' has a pedigree in critical thought that includes the surrealists' experiments in minute examination, which revealed the extraordinary textures of ordinary objects. We might expect that in breaking the hold apartheid had on protest literature, Ndebele would have had something to say about the place of this kind of experimentation in South African literature. Moreover, given that his project also insists on rescuing African experience from the obliterating effects of urban life under apartheid, might we not conclude that a mode of narration such as magical realism would be well suited to his intentions?

In fact, Ndebele comes very close to setting out a magical realist agenda when referring to Bheki Maseko's 'Mamlambo', a story about a mythical lucky snake. In this story, according to Ndebele:

African folk culture has an independent life of its own right bang in the middle of 'civilisation', of western 'rationality' . . . Bheki Maseko's stories always remind me of Haitian paintings: vibrant with colour, a combination of naturalistic and fantastic elements. Indeed, as [Wole] Soyinka asserts, the rational and non-rational constitute a single sphere of reality in African lore. Bheki Maseko's stories represent this living continuity between the past and the present. (1994: 56)

Interestingly, the blend of 'naturalistic and fantastic elements' that he encountered in Haiti inspired the Cuban, Alejo Carpentier, to write one of the first magical realist novels, *The Kingdom of This World*, in 1949. But, unlike Carpentier, Maseko does not take the representational leap that allows the writer to represent the supernatural on an equal basis with the natural. 'Mamlambo' is a story about characters who believe in the magical efficacy of a certain snake, but it is not a magical realist story because at the level of form, the magical is not afforded equivalent status to the real. Ultimately, the story does not force the reader to confront his or her own assumptions about the nature of reality in the way that most magical realism does. Ndebele's own fictional work operates similarly. His short story 'The Prophetess' dramatises the contest between a residual belief in the supernatural (derived from both African and Christian-derived belief systems) and an emergent rationalist scepticism embodied in the character of a young boy. The story's conclusions about the place of superstition and the supernatural in a modern African society are richly ambiguous, but the story makes available to the reader only the perspective of the doubting boy. It refuses to enter into the worldview of the prophetess or the women who believe they will be cured by her holy water. Ndebele's overall project depends for its authority on the validation of secular, rational models of thought and argumentation. However much space he might be clearing for African modalities of thought and perception, and however much one may sense his striving to, at least momentarily, wish away Western 'rationality' (his scare quotes suggest ambivalence), his case is made not on the authority of otherness, but on the capacity of black South Africans to recognise themselves in terms that are, finally, still familiar to the dominant articulacy.

Ndebele's reference to Soyinka's claim that 'rational and non-rational constitute a single sphere of reality in African lore' is worth highlighting here, as it is one that Mda will echo in interviews and raises suggestively in *The Heart of Redness*. In *Myth, Literature and the African World* Soyinka argues that 'the harmonisation of human functions, external phenomena and supernatural suppositions within individual consciousness merges as a normal self-adjusting process in the African temper of mind' (1976: 122). These 'supernatural suppositions' are most relevant when they concern the relationships between the living and their ancestors, for as Soyinka says with reference to Birago

Diop's poem 'Breathe', relationships between living and dead constitute 'an important, even fundamental, aspect of the world-view of traditional Africa' (133).

Although Ndebele himself does not choose to follow the implications of Soyinka's point into magical realist terrain, others have. Most notable in this regard is Ben Okri, who said of his 1991 Booker-prize-winning novel:

> I'm looking at the world in *The Famished Road* from the inside of the African world view, but without it being codified as such. This is just the way the world is seen: the dead are not really dead, the ancestors are still part of the living community and there are innumerable gradations of reality, and so on. It's quite simple and straightforward. I'm treating it naturally. It's a kind of realism, but a realism with many more dimensions. (quoted in Ross 1993: 337–38)

The Famished Road is a novel composed out of a dense interweaving of natural and supernatural, real and fantastic. Through its spirit-child narrator, the novel is simultaneously capable of representing the cruel banalities of everyday life in a Lagos ghetto and of taking the reader directly into a mythopoetic world of the folkloric grotesque. Okri's comments about his novel suggest that he was trying to demonstrate the extent to which, in his view, African modes of perception differ from their Western counterparts in their partaking of an expanded sense of reality. Only a modified realism – a magical realism – would be capable of adequately representing these ways of seeing. *The Famished Road* thus supplies a useful template for talking about an African magical realism and also embodies what I refer to as a faith-based orientation to both literature and to the problematised notion of the non-real or supernatural. Okri's novel is certainly not the only example of African magical realism, but it is the most useful for the purposes of this chapter because of his stated commitment to describing 'the African world view'.

Magical realism, or the naturalisation of the supernatural, is only one of the more recent ways in which writers have attempted to evoke what Soyinka calls 'the world-view of traditional Africa'. The word 'evoke' here needs qualification, for, as Ato Quayson has argued, it is inadequate to view the relationship between orality and literacy in the African context as simply being one in which the latter reflects or embodies the former. Such assumptions, common in positivistic ethnographic readings of African literature, have had the deleterious effects of homogenising the structure of orality and of eliding the dynamic relationships between orature and literature (1997: 3). By contrast, in the model Quayson develops to understand the place of tradition in Nigerian writing, African writers make 'strategic recourse to indigenous resources' in the service of a 'will-to-identity'. For Quayson, 'the notion of a will-to-identity yields a simultaneous concern with the African nation-state as the implicit horizon, the political unconscious of the literary enterprise as it were, as well as a concern with projecting a viable identity outwards into the global arena' (17). These points, as will be seen, are relevant to the work of Mda. He, like the Nigerian writers studied by Quayson, makes substantial use of an indigenous resource base, which he adapts and modifies for the purposes of elucidating an unfolding post-apartheid consciousness about identities, past and future. His magical realism cannot be understood outside of this context.

It is therefore worth outlining a few of the ways Mda engages with this resource base using techniques common in African literature. One of the most obvious of these is the use of proverbs, also a prominent feature of the work of Chinua Achebe. Here are a few of the proverbs and aphoristic utterances in Mda's novels:

1. A man is never ugly, as long as he has cattle. (1995a: 164)
2. Theirs was the closeness of saliva to the tongue. (1995b: 63; cf. 2000: 13)
3. We are like two hands that wash each other. (1995b: 69)
4. Glowing embers give birth to ashes. (1995b: 106; cf. 2000: 268)
5. The greatest death is laughter. (1995b: 164)
6. We should build a kraal around the word of the deceased, because it is precious like cattle used to be. (1995b: 209)
7. When an owl of the night hoots at daytime, then we must brace ourselves for misfortune. (2000: 174)
8. The ear is a thief. (2002: 119)

As several critics have noted, proverbs in African literature often attempt to inscribe oral paradigms within literary ones, constructing something of an index to the values of the communities that are described. But proverbs should also not be read out of context, as Gareth Griffiths has noted, for in the hands of skilled writers they often signify more or differently than decontextualised assessments might suggest (1979: 69). Such is the case with Mda, whose irony often deflates his use of proverbial wisdom. For example, '[g]lowing embers give birth to ashes' is used in *Ways of Dying* for the purposes of parody, coming as it does from the mouth of the archly satirised 'Archbishop'. In *The Heart of Redness* it emanates from the perspective of the Believers and takes on a far more sombre tone. More important to note is that proverbs such as those in numbers 5 to 8 above are prefixed or suffixed by phrases such as 'in our language there is a proverb'; 'our elders say' and 'they say'. Framed in this way, these proverbs are distanced from the immediate level of the narration. They do not so much index traditional African values as observe the passing of their relevance. The fragments of proverbial wisdom in Mda gesture tentatively towards the various states of flux in which his characters find themselves and need to be viewed in this light, rather than as part of an archaeology of traditional values.

Other strategic deployments of what Quayson calls an 'indigenous resource base' are, among others: the extensive use of non-English words, especially to make reference to items in nature; the direct representation of ceremonial gatherings, whether urban (the funerals in *Ways of Dying*) or rural (the *inkundla* of *The Heart of Redness*); the depiction of traditional practices, such as circumcision rites, the rituals of healing and curse, and *lobola* negotiations; the experimental use of a first-person plural narrative voice in *Ways of Dying* and *The Madonna of Excelsior* (a technique used most memorably by Ayi Kwei Armah in *Two Thousand Seasons*); the use of praise names, and the association of name and destiny. As is the case with Mda's use of proverbs, it is wise not to lift any of these features out of their narrative contexts. For one thing, the protagonists of Mda's novels all treat these topics differently: for Radisene in *She Plays with the Darkness*, tradition is something to exploit to make more money; for Toloki in *Ways of Dying*, it serves as only one ingredient in an eclectic assembly of other identities; for Camagu in *The Heart of Redness*, it is something that must be regained and restored on a personal level; Popi in *The Madonna of Excelsior*, neither black nor white, largely rejects the few pieces of proverbial wisdom offered by her mother. Furthermore, Mda's eye for interesting juxtapositions of past and present, traditional and modern has the effect of problematising all of these categories. His irony is pervasive and his position on matters of custom oscillates between respect, distrust and outright satire – and so it is with his magical realism.

Mda's novels evince a magical realism somewhere between the restraint of Ndebele and the exuberance of Okri. Examples of the supernatural are few in his early novels and non-existent in *The Madonna of Excelsior*. In *She Plays with the Darkness* magical elements cohere around the character of Dikosha. In the Cave of Barwa, adorned with ancient San rock paintings, she feels the warmth of a hearth that was last used centuries ago (1995a: 17). Chastised for trying to paint her mother's *rondavel* (hut) with designs inspired by the San paintings, Dikosha takes refuge in the cave, which becomes a place of healing for her. She wears beads made from ostrich shells (no one in the area has ever seen an ostrich), dances there, eats the honey and herbs of the long-departed San, and is 'healed by medicine men and women who got their power from the land of the dead and extracted all the sickness from her body in the form of arrows' (71). As tourists deface the paintings, the 'men and women with protruding buttocks' are increasingly imprisoned, however, and fewer and fewer are able to dance with her (101). When the dance eventually dies, Dikosha consoles herself with the company and music of Shana, a young boy who is later killed by mist and whose pain Dikosha feels in her body as he dies. Although *She Plays with the Darkness* includes many other references to the beliefs and customs of the people in the village, and although it also memorably evokes the parallel lives of tradition and modernity in the character of Misti, the biochemist training to be a *lethuela* diviner, supernatural elements attach almost exclusively to the character of Dikosha.

What is interesting about Dikosha's experiences in the cave is that she *wills* the paintings of the dancers to life (1995a: 51). The question must be asked, therefore, whether these passages are, in fact, best labelled as magical realism. Traces of a culture that has now entirely disappeared in the region are given life through the imagination of a girl who is herself banished from the life of her community. There is little that is magical – in the sense of supernatural – about the human use of the imagination to transcend the immediacies of suffering. Dikosha does not encounter any essential San presence in the cave, nor are the dancing San present to her in any unmediated way. On the contrary, it is through their art that she is reconciled with their absence. When that art is defaced she can no longer access the imaginative possibilities that it previously offered her. Her dancing – and her playing with the darkness – does not signal the recovery of an essential Africanness in the manner suggested by Okri; it is, rather, towards the invention of tradition that Mda is signalling: towards hybridised, re-enchanting modes of being accessed not through magical means, but through ordinary acts of imagination associated with the redeeming qualities of the aesthetic. Variations on this idea recur throughout Mda's oeuvre.

The passage in *Ways of Dying* that seems most closely to resemble magical realism similarly turns out, on closer inspection, to have little in common with the mode. The poverty-stricken Toloki and Noria, having rebuilt Noria's burnt-down shack, plaster the inside walls with the pages of back issues of *Home and Garden* magazine. They then proceed to stroll through the 'Mediterranean-style mansion', jumping on the soft bed, fighting with continental pillows, baking cakes, listening to music on black leather sofas, watching sit-coms on their wide-screen TV, playing hide-and-seek in the landscaped garden, dining on a lace-covered oak table. As they eat a dinner of cakes (Noria) and Swiss roll and green onions (Toloki), the narrative skilfully returns the reader to the images spread out on the mud floor of Noria's shack, which is 'devoid even of a single stool' (1995b: 114). That this is an imaginative flight of fancy, not a real one, becomes clear at a later stage of the novel when, upset by the lack of empathy shown by the political leaders of the day, Noria and Toloki try to 'walk in the garden' but though they 'stare at the pictures on the wall', they are 'unable to evoke the enchantment' (177). Again, the point seems to concern the empowering qualities of the imagination, fuelled by desire, rather than having anything to do with the supernatural. Juxtaposing stark urban poverty with the markers of bourgeois privilege serves a political purpose and the limits of an approach in which only fancy is required to transcend poverty are also made apparent in the later failure of the imagination. The figurines of Jwara play a less ambiguous role at the end of the novel, reconciling Toloki with

Nefolovhodwe and bringing happiness and laughter to the children of the settlement.

The romantic pattern of relating the aesthetic to liberation and reconciliation through a prose that strives to stir the imagination finds its fullest expression in *The Madonna of Excelsior*. Although it is concerned with enchantment, this prose, like the examples above, has little to do with magical realism, understood in the literary critical sense as the naturalisation of the supernatural. The novel's very dedication – to a bird painted by Father Frans Claerhout – signals the importance that Claerhout's expressionist paintings will have in the narrative. Most of the chapters in the novel begin with intensely lyrical evocations of a scene painted by Claerhout, whom Mda renames 'the trinity' because he is 'man, priest and artist', a combination that has 'tamed the open skies, the vastness and the loneliness of the Free State' (2002: 2). Claerhout is a character in the novel, but more importantly he represents a force that numinously rejoins the religious, the aesthetic and the possibilities of healing the wounds of the past. Thus, it is through a visit to Claerhout that Popi begins the process of recovering a sense of self-worth. Visiting 'the trinity' she is unable to speak, is moved to tears by his work, and leaves feeling that 'she had been healed of a deadly ailment she could not really describe' (238). She is not entirely healed: Popi and Niki achieve financial independence through bee-keeping and the novel concludes with the communal narrative voice informing us that 'the bees had finally completed the healing work that had been begun by the creations of the trinity' (268).

A thread of interconnected ideas about imagination, art and healing can therefore be traced running through *She Plays with the Darkness*, *Ways of Dying* and *The Madonna of Excelsior*. I have suggested that the passages that develop these ideas most clearly – those relating to the Cave of Barwa, Noria's shack and the trinity's paintings – are not magical realist because they do not engage in an unambiguous way with the supernatural. It should be made clear that refusing the label to these passages is not an exercise in critical pedantry, but stems rather from the recognition that Mda's project is not concerned with authenticating an ontology of Africanness, or with valorising particular expanded modes of perception. It is with restoring, on a human level, an affectivity and a dignity denied for generations by the impositions of colonialism and apartheid. In this sense, Mda is a worthy post-apartheid heir to the humanist projects of Gordimer and Ndebele, and the restraint that characterises his use of magical realism corresponds to the normative position on matters of genre taken by these liberal authors.

Of course certain passages in *She Plays with the Darkness* and *Ways of Dying* – though not, interestingly, in *The Madonna of Excelsior* – do display clear evidence of magical realism. Shana's death, Dikosha's telepathic empathy, Noria's voice, her fifteen-month pregnancy and the interpenetration of dream and reality all contain the 'irreducible element' of magic described by Faris. But it is hard to escape a sense in which these deployments of magical realism, while sometimes humorous or moving, are largely gratuitous. The supernatural in these examples is not integrated into the novels' more naturalistic preoccupations and it is hard to find coherent patterns of meaning linking the presence of these textual elements to any extra-textual referents, even unreal ones. The supernatural in these instances does not correspond in any discernible way to religious or traditional belief systems, nor does it further the purposes of satire. By contrast, *The Heart of Redness*, the novel in Mda's oeuvre that makes most use of magical realism, is profoundly connected to historical contexts in which belief and unbelief have affected the lives of millions.

Like Mda's other novels, *The Heart of Redness* uses the aesthetic as a means of accessing reconciliation and healing. But unlike the San paintings, *Home and Garden* gloss, Jwara's figurines, or the trinity's paintings, in *The Heart of Redness* it is the landscape that supplies the material basis for Mda's aesthetics. As Camagu arrives at the Wild Coast, 'he concludes that a generous artist painted the village of Qolorha-by-Sea, using splashes of lush colour. It is a canvas where blue and green predominate' (2000: 61). He is 'fascinated by the yellows, the browns, the greens and the reds that have turned the rocks into works of abstract art' (119). This aestheticised landscape is eroticised by linking it to the character of Qukezwa: she 'sings in such beautiful colours. Soft colours like the ochre of yellow gullies. Reassuring colours of the earth. Red. Hot colours like blazing fire. Deep blue. Deep green. Colours of the valleys and the ocean. Cool colours like the rain of summer sliding down a pair of naked bodies' (223). Though the lyricism of such passages is self-consciously undercut by the rather ludicrous conceit of having Camagu spontaneously ejaculate whenever he hears this singing, in this, as in Mda's other novels, the aesthetic is meant to activate healing through enchantment. Early in the novel, we are told: 'Qolorha-by-Sea is a place rich in wonders' (6). The word 'wonders' is poised ambivalently here between several senses: spectacular natural beauty, marvels that border on the supernatural, or dramatic historical occurrences. All three senses are present in the novel.

The complicating factor in Mda's aestheticisation of landscape is that this particular landscape is thoroughly marked with the traces of history. There are two timeframes operating in the novel, the 1850s and the late 1990s. The period in between – a period of increasing racial repression, culminating in the horrors of apartheid – is dismissively referred to as 'the Middle Generations', the sufferings of which can only be whispered (1). Nongqawuse's pool, the Amathole Mountains, the forests, plains and rivers and, especially, the sea signify locales of false hope in the historical narrative. The potential for the re-emergence of a similar suffering in the post-apartheid era is made clear in the contest over the commemorative value of sites such as the pool. The dangers of reliving the past are rather more obviously signified in the repetition of names in the novel, though there is also an element of irony in Mda's use of this well-worn technique. Chief Xikixa, for example, is notoriously undecided on matters of importance and is referred to as 'the headless chief' – a playful allusion to his namesake, the 'headless ancestor' whose head was boiled by the British so that his skull could be taken home as a souvenir. Although feuds are again a major theme, in *The Heart of Redness* they, like the representation of landscape, carry the signs of history. Thus, the conflict between Believers and Unbelievers threatens to repeat the nightmare of the past in the present. But there is a twist to Mda's presentation of the issue, as we shall see.

The Heart of Redness is concerned less with reconciling Believers and Unbelievers than it is with reconciling Camagu with his roots. In isiXhosa, *camagu*, a common name, signals agreement and can also be used for calling for the blessings of the ancestors. So it is in this sense of agreement and blessing that the protagonist of *The Heart of Redness* is able to contribute to the sustainable development of Qolorha-by-Sea, and in return is reconnected to his language, people and, in a qualified way, traditional belief system. It is not hard to see parallels between Mda and the protagonist of this novel: both spent considerable periods in the United States, both are highly educated, both make a symbolically charged return to the Eastern Cape where they become involved in setting up co-operative, ecofriendly ventures (Kachuba 2004). They even share the same totem, the majola snake (Isaacson 2005). Camagu's reply to Qukezwa's accusation that his head has been 'damaged by white man's education' – 'I believe in the ancestors, dammit!' – (Mda 2000: 119) is therefore revealing for both character and author. This awkward, even forced, affirmation of belief conceals a host of conceptual, historical and cultural complexities. For Camagu, as for Mda, the traces of the disastrous cattle-killing incident are everywhere, and 'belief in the ancestors' must be distinguished from belief in Nongqawuse's prophecies about the ancestors. Mda is a self-confessed romantic who admitted in an interview with Maureen Isaacson that 'moved by the vision of a better world coming, [he] would have embraced this vision in the face of the colonialistic swoop on the lands' (2005). But *The Heart of Redness* suggests a more cautious note: the need to recognise the brutal truth that the cattle killing (and more importantly the refusal to sow) led directly to famine, terror and the capitulation of Xhosa resistance to British imperialism.

The best-informed history of the cattle-killing movement, Jeff Peires's *The Dead Will Arise*, makes apparent the tragic inadequacy of certain mythico-religious worldviews to resist imperialist aggression. Like the Native Americans at Wounded Knee, Xhosa warriors who believed that sacred charms would turn British bullets to water were simply massacred. The prophecies did not come true and thousands perished. Peires's book is sympathetic to the desperate conditions that led to the cattle killing – the lungsickness epidemic, the genocidal impetus of British colonialism – but, in accordance with the norms of academic historiography, he rejects the supernatural as an explanation in itself for what happened in the Eastern Cape in the 1850s. He also makes clear the extent to which the prophecies, and the ways they were received, did not derive exclusively from Xhosa belief in continued existence after death, but were really complex concatenations of historical myth, customary notions of purity and danger, hybridised deities, wishful thinking and even outright deception. Peires also makes clear the ways in which the prophecies generated their own internal causality and logic. The arguments that the dead did not arise because Unbelievers did not kill their cattle, or that the fault lay with the ancestors of the Unbelievers are, after all, irrefutable. Unreason has a reason of its own.

As its dedication makes clear, *The Heart of Redness* draws heavily on Peires's work. There is thus a tension in Mda's novel between the desire to believe expressed by Camagu and Peires's scepticism – between, that is, the desire to affirm the veracity of certain items of belief, but not others. Camagu's shift in affiliation from Xoliswa Ximiya to Qukezwa suggests this movement between the poles of belief and unbelief. It is with the believing Qukezwa that Camagu settles and the position of the Believers with regard to development issues is clearly endorsed in the novel. It is likely that this bias arises because the romantic in Mda wants to align himself with belief, but the realist knows that such a position is untenable with regard to the historical narrative of the cattle-killing movement. Belief in ancestors is, of course, not at all the same thing as belief in Nongqawuse's prophecies. The question that is of relevance here is what impact the movement between these different senses of belief has on the novel's use of magical realism.

'Irreducible elements' of magic in *The Heart of Redness* are distributed equally between Believers and Unbelievers, but carry different valences for each. For those such as Bhonco, who resurrects a 'Cult of Unbelief' for the purposes of recollecting vengeance and suffering, the supernatural is typically negatively charged. The scars inflicted on Twin-Twin as punishment for the alleged witchcraft of his wife, for example, reappear on the first-born male of every subsequent Unbeliever. For the first time in the 1990s, they also appear on the body of a woman, Bhonco's cultivated daughter, Xoliswa Ximiya. She is, needless to say, outraged at the appearance of the scars, not only because they have never before appeared on the body of a woman, but also because she is the most unbelieving – in the many senses in which this word is used in the novel – of all Qolorha-by-Sea residents. The lesson of the scars is clearly that whether one recognises it or not, the pain of the past is always present. But the seriousness of the message is playfully undone by Mda's obvious pleasure at making the prim Xoliswa squirm and by the idea that in the post-apartheid dispensation, even the supernatural has adapted itself to the notion of gender equality. By contrast, magical elements on the Believers' side typically attach to nature. When Zim wants to get revenge on Bhonco, he sends *ing'ang'ane* birds (hadedas) to follow him with their 'rude laughter'. The villagers agree that the war between Believers and Unbelievers 'has advanced beyond human prowess' and speculate about whether Bhonco will send the hammerhead bird to destroy Zim's homestead, but soon realise that 'Bhonco does not know how to talk with birds.' (2000: 227–28). In the case of Qukezwa's immaculate conception, it seems that magic on the Believers' side is so positively charged that it brushes against the sublime.

A useful contrast can be drawn between *The Heart of Redness* and *She Plays with the Darkness* in terms of their uses of magical realism to relate to cultural inheritances from the San. In the earlier novel, as noted, the magical elements are limited and Dikosha imaginatively reconstructs the presence of the dancers in order to effect self-healing. In *The Heart of Redness* the San, or abaThwa, as they are called, appear to Bhonco and his Unbelievers while the latter are in one of the trances they periodically induce in order to recollect pain and sadness by visiting the times of their forefathers (2000: 217). The point of their appearance is to demand the return of the dance that the Unbelievers use in their ceremonies. In true magical realist fashion, Bhonco and his friends show no surprise at the unmediated presence of these 'little men' from beyond the grave. What really perturbs them is that they suspect Zim and the Believers have put the abaThwa up to their demands. But they are afraid of the 'medicine' that might be used against them if they do not comply with the demands and so they resolve to invent their own dance. The episode serves as something of an irreverent spoof on cultural appropriation, suggesting, once again, that traditions are not sacred, but invented and can therefore be added to or subtracted from depending on the needs of those engaging with them. Of more significance is that the San reclaim their dance because the Unbelievers are not using it wisely. By dwelling in the past and indulging their grief, they are spurning the opportunities for healing embraced by Dikosha.

In the light of the ambivalence identified earlier, it is revealing that magical realism is entirely absent from that part of *The Heart of Redness* set in the time of the cattle-killing movement. It appears solely in the sections of the novel set in contemporary South Africa. For all the romantic idealism of Mda's comment to Isaacson that he would have been a Believer had he lived in the time of the prophets, his magical realism tells a different story. Magical realism could, in the manner of Okri, have been used to enter into the mindsets of the historical Believers. It isn't and only in a superficial way can it be said to illuminate the worldviews of the characters in the contemporary narrative. What it does is lend support to certain of the author's positions, allowing him to exercise his romanticism and his sense of hope without condemning him to complicity with a historically destructive set of superstitions. Magical realism assists Mda in generating a gentle mockery, a ludic critique, which leads to the deflation of established truth or seriousness and leads us back to the principal theme of all his works: reconciliation. In this sense, Mda is closer to what I have called irreverent magical realism than he is to the faith-based magical realism of a writer such as Okri.

It is hard to imagine an Okri-style magical realism ever being written in South Africa because the weight of tradition, from Gordimer through Ndebele and including even Coetzee, rests so heavily on the side of realism – at least in so far as realism can be conceived of as the antithesis of the creation of fantastic worlds or ways of seeing. Those South African authors who write in English and who have experimented with magical realism – Mike Nicol, Ivan Vladislavić, Phaswane Mpe – exhibit a tendency to use the mode for playful, self-conscious, critical purposes, showing nothing of Okri's investment in embodying cultural otherness. The settings, characters and themes of Mda's novels all suggest that magical realism might be used to develop Soyinkan ideas about a 'world-view of traditional Africa', in which 'supernatural suppositions' play a central role. But as the earlier analysis of *The Heart of Redness* makes clear, the spectre of Nongqawuse intervenes to remind us of the devastation that some 'supernatural suppositions' have wrought in South African history. What remains is a restrained, gently ironic magical realism that expresses Mda's genius for capturing the reconciliatory spirit of a South Africa striving to heal the wounds of the past.

Works cited

Chanady, Amaryll. 1985. *Magical Realism and the Fantastic: Resolved Versus Unresolved Antinomy*. New York: Garland.

Chiampi, Irelmar. 1983. *El realismo maravilloso: forma e ideología en la novela hispanoamericana.* Translated (from Portuguese) by Agustin Martínez and Márgara Russotto. Caracas: Monte Avila.

Coetzee, J.M. 1980. *Waiting for the Barbarians.* London: Secker and Warburg.

————. 1986. *Foe.* London: Secker and Warburg.

————. 1992. 'The Jerusalem Prize acceptance speech'. In: Attwell, David (ed.). *Doubling the Point: Essays and Interviews.* Cambridge, MA: Harvard University Press, 96–99.

Cooper, Brenda. 1998. *Magical Realism in West African Fiction: Seeing with a Third Eye.* London: Routledge.

Faris, Wendy B. 2004. *Ordinary Enchantments: Magical Realism and the Remystification of Narrative.* Nashville: Vanderbilt University Press.

Franco, Jean. 1999. 'What's left of the intelligentsia'. In: Pratt, Mary Louise and Kathleen Newman (eds.). *Critical Passions: Selected Essays.* Durham: Duke University Press.

Gordimer, Nadine. 1988. 'The essential gesture'. In: Clingman, Stephen (ed.). *The Essential Gesture: Writing, Politics and Places.* Cape Town: David Philip, 240–50.

Griffiths, Gareth. 1979. 'Language and action in the novels of Chinua Achebe'. In: Innes, C. and B. Lindfors (eds.). *Critical Perspectives on Chinua Achebe.* London: Heinemann, 67–85.

Isaacson, Maureen. 2005. 'The Free State madonnas prevail in Mda's new novel'. http://www.theconnection.org/features/zakesarticle.asp, accessed 3 April 2005.

Kachuba, John B. 2004. 'An interview with Zakes Mda'. http://www.tinhouse.com/issues/issue_20/interview.html, accessed 3 April 2005.

Mda, Zakes. 1995a. *She Plays with the Darkness.* Florida Hills: Vivlia.

————. 1995b. *Ways of Dying.* Cape Town: Oxford University Press.

————. 2000. *The Heart of Redness.* Cape Town: Oxford University Press.

————. 2002. *The Madonna of Excelsior.* Cape Town: Oxford University Press.

Ndebele, Njabulo S. 1983. *Fools and Other Stories.* Johannesburg: Ravan Press.

————. 1994. 'The rediscovery of the ordinary: Some new writings in South Africa'. In: Ndebele, Njabulo S. *South African Literature and Culture: Rediscovery of the Ordinary.* Manchester: Manchester University Press, 41–59.

Pechey, Graham. 1994. 'Introduction'. In: Ndebele, Njabulo S. *South African Literature and Culture: Rediscovery of the Ordinary.* Manchester: Manchester University Press, 1–16.

Quayson, Ato. 1997. *Strategic Transformations in Nigerian Writing.* Oxford: James Currey.

Ross, Jean. 1993. '*Contemporary Authors* interview with Ben Okri'. In: Olendorf, Donna (ed.). *Contemporary Authors.* Vol. 138. Detroit: Gale Research, 337–41.

Soyinka, Wole. 1976. *Myth, Literature and the African World.* Cambridge: Cambridge University Press.

Warnes, Christopher. 2005. 'Naturalising the supernatural: Faith, irreverence and magical realism'. *Literature Compass* 2. http://www.literature-compass.com/viewpoint.asp?section=11&ref=459, accessed 3 April 2005.

5

Of Funeral Rites and Community Memory

Ways of Living in Ways of Dying

ROGIER COURAU AND SALLY-ANN MURRAY

I think that one writes also for the dead . . . One writes for a specific dead person, so that perhaps in every text there is a dead man or woman to be sought, the singular figure of death to which a text is destined and which signs. (Derrida 1988: 53)

But these days death was . . . the daughter-in-law of all homesteads. (Mda 2002a: 68; cf. 2002b: 211)

WE BEGIN WITH A JOURNEY, 'Toloki's odyssey to a wondrous world of freedom and riches' (Mda 1995: 51), which moves Zakes Mda's *Ways of Dying* into a powerful imaginative space beyond the limitations of the ordinary novel. The text is marked by a dramatic narrative intensity that provides a suitable vehicle for the larger-than-life action of the novel, with characters whose significance resonates with the histories and stories of black communities in South Africa. In particular, the lamentations of death and the occasion of the funeral become ritual enactments of the memory and loss of relatives, a source of continuity and a form of relation for the larger black urban community. Coupled with this is Mda's attempt to give imaginative weight and historical context to the experience of the migrant labourer and the rite of passage from a poverty-stricken rural life to the even more severe conditions of urban existence.

Toloki describes 'his way to the city to search for love and fortune' (Mda 1995: 60) as a noble quest and his journey's narrative is presented together with that of Noria, his 'homegirl' from the same rural village. He meets up with her again in the city and she becomes his love interest, but she also provides the emotional connection to his rural past, and in this way helps to sustain the energy of Mda's split location of the country and the city. Margaret Mervis suggests that in these two characters we find an allegory of black community life during apartheid and the transition to democracy (1998: 50). Mda attempts, additionally, to convey the resilience of the urban community and its capacity to survive. This is similar to his work in theatre for development, where he 'created plays that have involved the community members in naming their problems from their own perspective, in reflecting on these problems, and in mapping out a definite course of action to solve the problems' (Mda 1994: 106). This suggestion of agency on the part of the urban community is reflected throughout the novel and is vital in relation to the rituals of memory that are the focus of this chapter.

In Mda's narrative, ideas of community and history are expressed and entrenched through the performance of the funeral ritual and the macabre shadows of death and murder that frame it. Whether considered within an explicit political context or in relation to the confusions of socio-political change, these processes of mourning, of finding ways of living by enacting the memory of the dead, carry with them the weight of a turbulent and often distorted history. Unsurprisingly, the city is represented as an ambiguous space, a locus of collective remembrance, as well as a source of spiralling inhumanity, where despair, death and moral decay have intensified. As Mda himself states, the omnipresence of death in the novel 'is congruent with contemporary life in general, not just South African. In most world fiction somebody dies. It has always been like that. Of course in fictions like *Ways of Dying* more people die than is normal in other fictions because this novel is set during the period when death was in abundance in South Africa' (2003).

In *Ways of Dying*, Mda has used as material for his plot recognisable historical events and a socio-political context that draws freely on the typical events of the years between 1990 and 1994, before the democratic elections. However, Mda elects to render the period with a deliberate vagueness, which enables him to reinforce the sense of liminality and uncertainty of the time, thereby disrupting attempts to fix the context specifically and emphasising the nature of the urban milieu that is represented.

In *Ways of Dying* the rituals of death become a performance of the substance of community memory – a source of connection between the worlds of the living and the dead. They are consciously distorted by Mda and merge to become the ambiguous forms that are present in all of his novels but are highly pertinent to his method in *Ways of Dying*, where he demonstrates the co-existence of the worlds of the living and the dead in traditional African societies. In *Ways of Dying* it is Toloki who is able to act as performative mediator. He uses and adapts traditional performance techniques, at once affirming old traditions and reworking them to suit the needs of the new society emerging in South Africa at the time and he becomes the embodiment of the community's dynamic towards survival. In effect, he becomes a contemporary version of the ancient African trickster figure, in that he is able to channel the energies of complex and hybridised patterns of tradition *and* the reality of a new-found Western form of urban living. As Kole Omotoso argues:

> There is a way in which those who are oppressed eke out a living . . . [and] develop mechanisms for their existence. The daily rituals of their lives come to constitute cultures in their own rights, cultures that do not receive much attention from those who concern themselves with the study of the dominant cultures of our societies . . . But the struggle against oppression is not the first thought of those oppressed. Their first concern is to get on with living their lives with the minimum pain – physical, mental and psychological – possible. In order to do this, they evoke a number of deities who have come to be known as the Trickster Deities . . . Trickster Gods and Goddesses of the Black oppressed . . . (2004)

In creating a character such as Toloki, Mda is attempting to give imaginative and experiential weight to the discourses of township culture by filtering them through the traditional knowledges associated with African communal culture. Toloki, a figure of liminal positioning, seeks to mediate between a copious range of cultural forms and expressions, both marginal and mainstream, of modernity and rural past. The act of mourning that he devises is thus a hybridised form of expression, which helps, in Homi Bhabha's formulation, to '[reverse] the effects of the colonialist disavowal, so that other "denied" knowledges enter upon the dominant discourse and estrange the basis of its authority – its rules of recognition' (1994: 112–14), making possible a form of symbolic resistance to apartheid history and knowledge.

In considering the tensions between the forces of colonial and post-colonial history, we might argue that Mda reaches towards postmodernism, rejecting modes that monolithically define human experience in favour of those that acknowledge shifting boundaries and discontinuity. *Ways of Dying* clearly illustrates many of these postmodern aesthetic qualities, as the author challenges official constructions of history and gives a voice to the silenced. Yet the blurring of real and fantastical elements in Mda's text, while evidence of his attempts to decentre received notions of black self and identity, gestures towards the existence of a black self, which, while not coherent, *does* exist and is resourceful in overcoming the cruelties and limitations of the postmodern urban experience by turning postmodern plays of identity towards the discovery of a self, which, for Toloki, is at once ludic and material. Mda thus offers the reader small histories, which displace the primacy of official History, even rendering them visible as a frame of reference.

By engaging fictionally with the city as a postmodern space, it is clear that writers such as Mda are beginning to consider the possibilities of postmodernism in South African writing, even if only in a very preliminary sense. Yet, the postmodern space of the urban is negotiated not only through an erratic magical realism, but also through a distinctive social realism, its distinguishing quality being its representation of an historical condition that is at times undefined and at other times of largely metaphorical value. Sten Pultz Moslund highlights the fact that the representation of history in the novel 'passes a Jamesonian "rigorous judgement" on the present by the future' (2003: 117), allowing for a pastiche of alternate futures, or utopias. The present and future become decentred contestations that place a verdict on one another within the realm of historical possibility.

However, it is also necessary to import the Western constructs of postmodernity into a specifically southern African context with caution. They need to be mediated though a broad range of cultural specificities and to make allowance for the various traditional patterns of thought and cultural practice that are present locally. In *Ways of Dying* the patterns of mourning are themselves part of tradition, yet, as we will show in the next part of this chapter, they take on a new life within the urban context, with its apparently dehistoricised subject, and provide a sense of continuity and potential for the characters and the community as a whole.

Territorialising the city

The nomadic sense of movement with which we began this chapter is meant to affirm the temporal context of *Ways of Dying*, which is that of a nation in formation and society in a state of transition (see Mervis 1998: 39; Van Wyk 1997: 79–80). A sense of uncertainty characterises a society such as this, one that is seeking new ways to define itself, both in relation to the past, with its officially constructed national histories, and the future, which is in some ways part of the intended resolution of the challenging conditions of the present in the novel, as much critical work has shown (see Mervis 1998; Moslund 2003; Van Wyk 1997; Naidoo 1998). In *Ways of Dying*, therefore, we can argue that two states of transition, one temporal and the other spatial, come together in a plot of extreme violence and morbidity, which inflects and directs the course of the narrative, as the central characters find themselves searching for new means of survival and continuity within drastically new geographies and volatile socio-political conditions.

The character as an existential agent within the novel, therefore, constructs relations of location, mediations of identity and means of survival, or 'ways of living', through engagement and wandering within the spaces of the urban. Toloki's interaction with and utilisation of the physical objects at his disposal within the urban landscape is an act of territorialisation, of defining himself in relation to new cultural spaces to which he is becoming accustomed in a context of socio-historical change. An example of this assertive will to become, to define himself, is evidenced in his persistence in procuring the costume that will become the hallmark of his invented trade, that of Professional

Mourner. Toloki sees a beautiful costume in a theatrical 'for hire' store in 'one of the city shopping malls' (Mda 1995: 20) and through his persistent vigil outside the store with his grotesquely mournful demeanour – including exaggerated salivating called 'izincwe, the gob of desire' (22) – the shop-owners finally collect funds in order to purchase the outfit for him so that he will leave them alone. If Mda acerbically represents the expedience of capital in this example, he also attests to the creative persistence of Toloki in acquiring the clothing that becomes the 'venerable costume' of his occupation (22). This claiming of a personal space is reinforced in the name that he gives to the 'quayside shelter and waiting-room where he spends his nights' (10). He refers to it as his 'headquarters', thereby giving personal, professional and emotive context to the public amenities of the cityscape and creating a base of operations for himself and a quaint sense of homeliness that is not often to be found within the urban context. Additionally, he is 'armed with a thick blanket that he keeps in his shopping trolley' (11), suggesting the dually acquisitive and inventive stance that he has taken in the interests of his own survival. As is indicated by Mda's language, these various acts combine an overt peformativity with a military determination, and within them can be found a new means by which Toloki is able to mark out for himself both actual and psychic locations within the urban expanse.

Both of these examples may be theorised in terms of what Gilles Deleuze and Felix Guattari call 'territorialisation' (1987: 315). In their essay, 'Of the Refrain', they use music as a metaphor for the processes involved in marking out one's place in the world. They argue that space is territorialised through the use of periodic, recognisable signs that then establish ownership of 'place'. While the application of this metaphor might imply a deterministic sense of territoriality, given the pitched, ordered and structured quality of music, its rhythm and notation, the performative, interpretive practices associated with music justify its application to Mda's novel, much of which narrates either the use of literal performance as a mode of survival, as in Toloki's securing of his professional clothes and his wailing at funerals, or points to the embedded performative elements of daily life through which individuals make up their ways of living.

In the case of Toloki, this territoriality and its performativity are suggested through the character's innovative use of the objects at his disposal and his ability to live off the conveniences – indeed to reconfigure the inconveniences – that the city provides, be they the public showers at the beachfront, which he uses as a regular bathing facility, the malls, or the docks. The notion of place in *Ways of Dying* is given added meaning if read within the context of Deleuze and Guattari, for 'the territory, and the functions *performed* within it, are products of territorialisation. Territorialisation is an act of rhythm that has become expressive, or of milieu elements that have become qualitative' (1987: 315; emphasis added). Therefore, every subject is formed from a series of milieus, composed of interiors, exteriors and boundaries of these various environments, and space is territorialised through the use of periodic repetitions that signal forms of spatial ownership to others. What Deleuze and Guattari call 'rhythm' entails the traces of encounters between different milieus and the resulting patterns and rhythmic improvisations are the observable changes in the signalling of the ownership of place.

In the city, Toloki gradually develops, through habitual use and familiarisation, movements of behaviour that have the regularity of rhythm, a quotidian repertoire, and he ritualises his conduct in using what is at his disposal on the streets, in roles of existence related to his profession and survival. The musical polyphony of connections that creates different yet intersecting senses of identity and belonging become clearer at this point, for 'just as the spaces of the apartheid city divided, they also generated crossings and intersections' (Robinson 1999: D7). These crossroads of relations, culture and meaning are expressive of a complex set of associations among Mda's characters. The musical metaphor, where performative expressions claim and organise space, is also appropriate in emphasising the vigorous quality of Toloki's spirit; it imbues his otherwise dogged persistence with a creative exuberance that symbolises the energy with which he refashions his urban self and the strange power of cultural continuity with community memory that the act of the funeral entails.

Jennifer Robinson highlights, as examples of Toloki's ambiguously imaginative and utilitarian spirit, the occasion when he brings Noria magazines and catalogues to decorate the walls of her shack and when he filches flowers from the sidewalk gardens (1999: D7). This representation is a recasting of the hostile urban environment, part of Mda's almost allegorical fictional project, in evoking the shifting possibilities of territoriality within the urban context. Toloki's fervent performance as acquisitive nomad is rendered as follows:

> Back in the city, he goes to the furniture stores and gets as many catalogues as he can carry. He tells the salespeople that there are some customers from his village who would like to buy furniture. They would like to see the pictures first before they come to the stores to buy furniture. Of course, the salespeople don't believe him. But they don't see any harm in giving him the catalogues, which are free in any case. Then he goes to a newspaper stall, and negotiates with the owner to buy ten back issues of *Home and Garden* magazine. He buys them at only ten percent of the cover price.
>
> He walks towards the taxi rank, and furtively picks some of the flowers that grow along the sidewalks . . .
>
> He is very pleased that he was able to get roses this time. Their scent fills the whole taxi. Noria will love these. Indeed flowers become her. (Mda 1995: 92)

When Toloki arrives at Noria's shack, together they decorate it with images from the catalogues and magazines, and then imagine that they are walking in a lush garden, a form of escape from the material limitations of urban life. As Robinson suggests: 'The magical realism of the novel does not undo the spaces of poverty – but it refuses to treat experiences of these spaces as one-dimensional' (1999: D7). The suggestion of agency in Toloki's ability to territorialise and negotiate such new, yet still impoverished spaces, is clear. The atmosphere of desolation expressed by Mda is in deliberate relation to the possibility of survival, and the objects of the city become a repertoire for individual use, a 'polyphonic' source, in terms of Deleuze and Guattari's metaphor, of possibility and redemption. The *Home and Garden* episode in *Ways of Dying* with its innovative use of the imagination in mediating the constraints of an oppressive, alienating social reality, a moment of survival, has gained iconic status in South African literature. The suggestion is that Toloki recontextualises cultural practices from their habitual, ephemeral, even banal origins, allowing him to give substance and comfort to his life, to claim the basic human needs for love and homeliness. Through the activity of roving and searching, he finds a sense of resolution and even personal *resolve* and is able to actualise a personal condition in what is otherwise an alienating socio-political context.

In *Ways of Dying*, reality is focalised from an omniscient point of view that presents us with Toloki walking, moving through the city. Yet, the very details that accumulate around Toloki enable us to feel a more multiple nomadic wandering through the streets of the city, as if encountering people, places and events through the subjective perspective of Toloki. Through the act of bargaining and territorialisation, then, we find the signs that connote something of Toloki's peculiar character. The suggestion of beauty and redemption that we sense within the text needs to be considered. We first read this as an instance of magical realism, since the delight expressed in the mundane and ordinary is a mark of this literary style. However, it is a distinctly South African form of fantastical or marvellous expression, for the characters are deeply connected to the indigenous traditions of the country, which they bring to bear on their understanding of the city. Their experience obviously influences their understanding and assignations of meaning for the various elements of the urban milieu, and for them the act of territoriality indicates an awareness of place that is different from that of people from other cultural locations.

But the case of Nefolovhodwe, Toloki's 'homeboy', a man of immense physical girth and a successful businessman who ran 'a flea circus for relaxation' (Mda 1995: 120), recalls Mikhail Bakhtin's notion of 'grotesque realism', as discussed in his study on Rabelais (1993) or, more prosaically, a hint of the burlesque, music-hall character type of Western European tradition. In a similar critical vein, Toloki's wandering is reminiscent of Walter Benjamin's *flâneurs*, those urbane, mid-nineteenth-century, male urban strollers, who revealed the lives of the bourgeois margins through voyeuristic observation, with Benjamin clearly overwhelmed by the city's theatricality, its passion for improvisation and its ironies (Benjamin 1997: 169–71). Yet Toloki, in contrast to these wanderers, is certainly not middle class in economic position, nor does he have the luxury to stroll at will; his roaming is intertwined closely with the need for survival. He is not simply a voyeur of a variously seductive or repellent external world, but is caught and enveloped within it, struggling to find a way through it. Both Toloki and Nefolovhodwe are accordingly the consummate products of intercultural melding, characteristic hybrid points of complexity that further serve to give weight to the claim for *Ways of Dying* as a fictional negotiation between differing cultural worlds in which characters seek individual specificity within the urban expanse. It is as if Mda, in shaping his creative repertoire as a writer, exuberantly and eclectically borrows not only from African tradition, but also from any cultural knowledge that suits his immediate purpose. In this sense, his style is carnivalesque, rather than culturally rigorous.

Ivan Vladislavić distinguishes between the spatial awareness and comprehension of topographical features characteristic of people from the 'countryside' in comparison with the 'busy city person [who must] rely on words and gestures to guide the stranger through a landscape cluttered with irrelevant detail, with dead ends and false turns on every side, some of which might prove disastrous to the unwary' (1999: E11). This intimate knowledge of the urban landscape is relevant to an interpretation of Toloki, for he is able to traverse a multi-stitial network of behaviours and signifying practices within the frenetic and culturally diverse context of the urban. An optimistic sense of familiarity with the urban is suggested in his euphemistic approach to spatial comprehension when, for example, he edits his thoughts in order to replace the negative label 'squatter camp' with 'informal settlement' (Mda 1995: 92). Here, people who might initially be marginalised through a dominant perception as 'squatters' are gradually re-understood by Toloki, as his contact with Noria and the struggles that he sees among 'squatters' to affirm human and humane ways of living coax him towards the emotional recognition that they are people who are settled, who have established domestic routines and who have, out of necessity, attuned a hostile formal economy to their needs. Even in Toloki's use of language, then, we are given an insight into the new ways of living that he has had to seek out within an urban landscape.

Vladislavić's assertion is of use also at the more obvious level of geography, since it emphasises the agency of the city dweller in negotiating physical space. The speaker of Vladislavić's essay (1999: E11) moves between the various streets and points of the South African city of Johannesburg, where the disconnected histories of a multitude of urban subjects and locations are given a purposefully pedestrian exuberance, in which the mundane and everyday contain the incongruous qualities of the monumentally significant. The connection between the urban subject and cityscape is constructed through the territoriality of local histories and knowledges, and for Toloki, this is about the performance of a kind of ritual of survival, while the ways of dying, of death and the funeral orations that celebrate memory and continuity through the ritual, become his ingenious vocation.

Funerals and community memory

The funeral sequence is emblematic of the ability of the black urban community to provide itself with a sense of remembrance and continuity, despite the realities of political violence and the fragile, shifting patterns of association that constitute urban belonging. The funeral is represented by Mda as a powerful enactment of community memory through ritual and a social event that brings people together, both relatives and strangers, and in Toloki's intervention in public mourning, symbolises a community activity that provides opportunities for urban social cohesion and group dynamism. It is challenging, therefore, to discover ways in which community history or community memory is given life and substance in *Ways of Dying*. The rituals of death provide the source of cultural continuity and connection that is needed if memory and history are to survive and Mda reworks some of the traditional roles associated with funeral rites, implying that tradition and community are processes that are evolving in response to the complex demands of survival in the post-apartheid city.

The indigenous forms of performed memory function in relation to the forces of modernity, characterised by the claims for a postmodern condition that typify contemporary South African urban life. On the level of the African urban community, a range of personal histories is narrated and reconstructed during the funeral proceedings, although the funerals themselves became more than just the enactment of an individual's experiential history. The reader's immersion in the action of the funeral, from the first page of the novel, does much to reinforce the poignant atmosphere of human loss that marks the entire text, albeit tempered by brief moments of triumph and evidence of a resilient will to survive:

There are funerals every day, because if the bereaved were to wait until the weekend to bury their dead, then mortuaries would overflow, and cemeteries would be overcrowded with those attending funerals. As a matter of fact, even with funerals taking place daily the mortuaries are bursting at the seams, and the cemeteries are always jam-packed. Often there are up to ten funeral services taking place at the same time, and hymns flow into one another in unplanned but pleasant segues. (Mda 1995: 136)

One could argue, here, that it is in this way that the dead become depersonalised, mere objects in a larger, mechanistic process of production. The funerals certainly become fertile ground for curious, public spectacle and theatrically exaggerated ritual. Similarly, too, at first glance, the use of expressions such as 'jam-packed' and 'bursting at the seams' appears inapt, absurd, in the context of death. Yet, Mda deliberately contradicts the seriousness of the funerals and enriches them with a hilarity that is emphasised by the infectious laughter that spreads around a cemetery where four funerals are taking place simultaneously (1995: 152–53). Paradoxically, then, the final sentence of the excerpt above provides an excellent symbol of death as having a debilitating effect upon the community *and* perversely creating connecting links out of the adversity of urban life. An atmosphere of the carnivalesque is apparent (Van Wyk 1997: 80) and Toloki states: 'In death we laugh as well' (Mda 1995: 152) and that 'in our language there is a proverb which says the greatest death is laughter' (153). Death becomes carnivalised and the progression towards conviviality and irony is a mark of the attempt to find ways of living in the desolate climate of ways of dying.

This strange set of relationships, hilarity and death, living and misery, is characteristic of the shifting conditions and human experiences that are reflected in the novel and Toloki connects himself to these rituals through his innovation of the Professional Mourner, a performative function that enables him to centre himself within the 'ways of dying' of various groups and, by thus embodying the reconciliation of difference, working to create possibilities of communal cohesion or new urban ways of living. Toloki represents the sense of belonging, or even imagined community that is created through sorrow; he carries and conveys the weight of collective grief. The commodification and reification of death allow for the role of Toloki as conduit and performative agent for what many black people have lost: the emotional power associated with oral rhetorical skills that, as in the case of the *imbongi* or praise-singer, for example, work to situate a person within a network of past and present relationships. As he says: 'Death becomes me, it is part of me' (Mda 1995: 106) and he has made the business of death his vocation.

The funeral ritual is marked by a variety of regulated practices that serve as the performed repository of community memory. One of these is of the 'Nurse', although this may have some legitimate connection with traditional practice. The Nurse is a 'designated' (Mda 1995: 1) function at these events, someone who comments on the circumstances surrounding the deceased's demise and is usually the last person to have seen the deceased alive. The title connotes someone in a caring position, who aids in the extension and sustaining of life. This ameliorative role suggests that the Nurse's purpose at the funeral is to act as a moral and emotional support for the community, helping it to react in an appropriate manner to the death of an individual. The Nurse usually provides 'a fountain of fascinating information about ways of dying' (1) and may also serve as the spoken 'voice' of the collective consciousness of the community. This is an established role and into this mix of urban modernity and rural tradition, Toloki attempts to locate a place for himself. At one funeral, the Nurse proceeds to relate in a 'histrionic manner' (146) the death of a certain deceased's elder son. His death is ironically described as 'abnormal' *because* he died of natural causes, although the added importance of the Nurse's speech and its representation lies in the description of the funeral ritual itself and the sense of irony with which he expresses his sentiments. The Nurse, however, is not above the carnivalesque impulses of the funerary moment and when he relates how his compatriot died, he reveals where he hides his money: 'It was fortunate my brothers and sisters, that I had some money in my shoe where I hide it from my grandchildren. Oops, now they know where I hide my money. But don't worry I'll find another place' (149).

This implies that the question of tradition in Mda's representation of the funeral is important, not in terms of cultural essences or assumptions of organic rural connectivity, but because it appears in the novel as a mediating device between different forms of identity. It is clear that for Mda the notion of traditional practice is certainly not essentialised; it is subject to a variety of depictions, explorations and reimaginings as a responsive practice that variously correlates with and resists the tensions of urban modernity. Indeed, Mda is selective in his treatment of inherited practices, appropriating only those that he feels will give energy and cultural detail to the fictional narrative, suggesting that tradition is not fixed, but necessarily subject to change in relation to shifting collective and individual identities. His creation of Toloki relies on a rather eclectic, even haphazard, drawing from various indigenous cultures, though his access to older beliefs and the ways of living is by no means unmediated and is symptomatic of Mda's attempts to negotiate between a confusing array of cultural forms and expressions.

Certainly, it is probable that Mda draws significantly on Xhosa and Zulu funeral practices as a cultural reference in constructing notions of ritual in *Ways of Dying*. Elke Steinmeyer quotes Theo Nyawose (2000: 12; 16–18; 25–29; 31) in setting out the following sequence of practices:

> In the Zulu tradition, the rite takes the following form: 1) the corpse is washed and shaved; 2) the corpse is dressed; 3) the eyes and mouth are closed (there is an additional cleansing element for somebody, who died a violent death); 4) the body is laid out straight inside the hut; 5) vigil during the night before the funeral by family members and friends with continuous chanting; 6) the digging of the grave on the funeral day; 7) preparation of the communal meal by slaughtering an animal; 8) the corpse is taken out of the hut with the feet outwards to the cemetery; 9) testimony by family and friends; mourning; singing or playing music; sermon; walking around the coffin with candles or flowers; 10) praying and throwing soil into the grave; 11) return home; cleansing of hands with specially prepared water. (2003: 164)

As will be shown later in this chapter, Mda draws from and negotiates this representative set of practices within the context of the urban to arrive at the various composite constructions of the ritual that are present in the novel. And it is in this context of cultural hybridity that roles such as the Nurse and

Professional Mourner emerge. Mda is by no means prescriptive or limiting in his use of cultural facts and expands upon them to arrive at the curious cultural dynamics that are observed in *Ways of Dying*.

Consider the role of Toloki at funerals. In keeping with his persistent character, he *claims* his space and a place for community memory through the invented ritualistic rhythms that define his occupation as performer at funerals. Indeed, he focuses and channels these energies into that profession, imbuing the funeral ritual with an organised, potentially respected performative life that gains a place for itself in the urban environment in relation to the needs of community memory and continuity. He takes on the fervour of a religious cleric in the execution of his functions, escaping into an inner world of spirituality. At one particular funeral, he 'sits on the mound and shares his sorrow with the world' (Mda 1995: 17) and with the other mourners. In this way, he finds a medium to channel his own feelings of frustration and helplessness into the public domain of the community. At these funerals, Toloki reinforces his vocal performance with gestures of anguish and pain, with the characteristic sound of 'a goat that is being slaughtered' (144) and strives to convey a grief that is exaggerated and intensified. Toloki's expression of grief becomes an imaginative response to death, while the speech of the person who has the role of Nurse functions as an historical narrative recording the events of death. Indeed, the two work together to heighten the sense of pathos and ill fortune. Toloki struggles to establish a new tradition in which his wailing, weeping and profound expressions of grief come to embody or personify mourning as a visible figure, giving the community an emotive and tangible point of reference towards, and through which, they can channel their grief.

J.U. Jacobs comments: 'This vocal ensemble of Professional Mourner and Nurse may be seen to represent the first stage in the discursive blending that is a feature of Mda's fiction and that increases in complexity in the later novels' (2003: 196). The matter of 'discursive blending' is pertinent, for it is in the expressions of community history, personal information about the deceased and the expressive ramblings of Toloki's hyperbolically performed grief that the funeral ritual is given an emotive quality that could not be achieved through the procedural codes of a conventional memorial service. In Toloki's publicly claiming and affirming the substance of an individual's life, the reader is given access to a form of composite discourse. It is confessional in expressing the feelings of those who are attending the event, be they shared or individually felt, about the deceased, but is also faithful to the memory of the individual who is being memorialised. Toloki's embellishments mediate between the community's sense of self and the memory of the individual being mourned, indicative of a kind of urban subjectivity, present but shifting. The blurring of discourses implies the production of hybrid, syncretic forms of identity: the reader senses the political nature of the public and funerary ritual, while each of the mourners is able to produce a personal construction of the memory of the mourned. This is achieved through the provision of emotional bolstering by the orators, that is, a subjective narrative of the life of the deceased.

Toloki is led to an odd salvation of finding spiritual fulfilment and material reward in ways of dying – he comes to earn his living from the deaths of other people, as a kind of 'assistant to death' (Naidoo 1998: 163). Indeed, Toloki's ability to find a financial-emotional resolution to his problems in such a curious set of practices is yet another example of his innovative disposition and it is from the substance of his own appearance and character that we observe the development of his new vocation:

> But he [Toloki] had the saddest eyes that we have ever seen. His sad eyes were quite famous, even back in the village. We used to sing about Toloki's sorrowful eyes. Slowly he reached the decision that he was going to mourn and that people would pay him for this service. Even the fat Nefolovhodwe had told him, 'Your face is a constant reminder that we are all going to die one day'. He was going to make his face pay. After all, it was the only gift that God had given him. He was going to profit from the perpetual sadness that inhabited his eyes. The concept of a Professional Mourner was born. (Mda 1995: 133)

Death itself has become commercialised and the narrative voice informs us that Toloki at the outset decides to 'profit from death like his homeboy Nefolovhodwe. But after two or three funerals, his whole outlook changed. To mourn for the dead became a spiritual vocation' (Mda 1995: 125). Nefolovhodwe exists in contrast to Toloki, of course, and takes his skill as a maker of coffins to the city where people 'die like flies' (116) and we learn of his coming into wealth through profit from the sorrow of others. Toloki, however, will rely on his physical appearance to profit from death as he 'was going to make his face pay'. This distinctive blending of skills, circumstance and the desire for wealth is characteristic of Mda's approach to the creation of characters who are able to survive deathly social conditions.

The funeral, enactment and source of continuity for community memory, based in rural tradition, thus responds to the forces of modernity in new and curious ways. Some of the consequences are vile to say the least, what with Nefolovhodwe's creation of a 'De Luxe Special' coffin for the wealthy, or the discovery that 'unscrupulous undertakers went to the cemetery and dug the deluxe coffin up . . . and took the coffins to sell again to other bereaved millionaires' (Mda 1995: 126). The rituals of death are exploited by those who are trying to survive – as Venugopaul Naidoo suggests: 'the carnivalesque images that constantly undercut the apocalyptic scenes in the text serve as indicators that death is a process that makes possible another life' (1998: 231–32).

Toloki cleverly displays another form of territorialising activity in fashioning a role for himself, drawn from religious and professional sources. The narrative ventures into a curious range of possibilities, as Toloki finds a sense of grace in the ascetic role that he wishes to assign himself. This role becomes ritualised within the context of the funeral; he becomes the ritual agent of a new, odd profession that intersects with the more traditional role of the Nurse and it is through such intersections that we come to realise the cultural importance of the funeral as a site for the re-enactment and flow of community memory. The ritual processes are usually narrated in sequence and are of great importance in outlining the range of cultural practices that underlies the funeral rite. The first part of the process involves the cutting of the hair of the family members of the deceased in a specific order of hierarchy and seniority (Mda 1995: 146). This is suggestive of a rite of purification, and is also a public way of reinforcing the structures of power within the community, of defining relationships on the basis of patrilineage. This is followed by the oration of the Nurse and of the relatives, at which juncture Toloki finds his clearest moment for serving his purpose, and each mourner, in terms of the hierarchical processional arrangement, shovels soil into the grave (159). Subsequent to this, a communal feast is held (10; 150–54), which allows for some sense of closure after the intense public display of mourning. Toloki mentions the washing of the hands as the concluding act within the ritual (10; 160), which provides a suitable form of symbolic physical and spiritual purification, signifying the return of the communal subjects to the everyday reality of the profane. The washing of hands, then, clearly separates the sacred moment of remembrance from the need to return to the world of the living. It is also clear that Mda is challenging the bases of tradition in the interests of writing a better story: for example, there is little sense in the fact that the old man was killed simply because he does not strictly follow convention (see later in this chapter). Mda creates these circumstances to heighten an atmosphere of moral abandon and depravity, which is the novel's distinct theme: negotiating through the circumstances of transition.

Toloki goes through different developmental phases in the perfection of his mourning technique. He is at first unremarkable in his delivery and does little to convey the anguish and pain appropriate at a funeral. Later, he starts to adopt the characteristics of other members of his community, emulating the 'chants that youths utter during political rallies' (Mda 1995: 108). He modifies them, adding his own gestures and heightened expressions of agony to convey a more profound sense of loss, 'stoking up a frenzy of mourning with his own sighing, heaving and wailing, and is recompensed by the grateful bereaved' (Dowling 1997: 22). His ability to mimic the practices of others is further evidence of his inventive spirit and his process of professionalisation is recognised in his development of the 'modern' form of mourning (Mda 1995: 154). Again, this is a mix of rural traditions and the techniques of urban politics. Toloki channels the feelings for the deceased as part of a community that experiences loss and his theatricality is a form of staged identity that 'enables [the community] to help themselves by employing their traditional performance modes, and to participate in the creation of their own narratives' (Mervis 1998: 40). It is clear that in Toloki's enabling and facilitating group cohesion and interaction through the forces of loss, the community is able to produce its own narratives and meanings, to be an agent in the reconstruction of its own histories. In Toloki, Mda has created a character who is a conduit for the energies of permanence and stability within the community, despite the troubled

times in which these events occur, for he is able to recall atavistic, vestigial practices, recreating them in meaningful ways, connecting himself to the power of
traditional practice with the clear intention of adapting to urban circumstances.

There are obvious tensions between the sense of group belonging (the
supposedly collective beliefs and practices of the funeral ritual) and the authority
of Toloki in relation to the community. These are associated with the difficulties
of his becoming an individual in a modern space, even as he takes on the
responsibility of a collective agency. The collective voice is often not endorsed
by Toloki and is further problematised from within the community by voices
that argue, for instance, for the need to politicise the account of a person's
death in contrast to more traditional funeral orations. Toloki channels the
dual energies of community sentiment and the need for moral reflection and
he is a figure who carries the reader through the narrative and who memorably
hints at the connections between worlds and ways of believing. Toloki's
histrionic positioning is thus more moving than comic, as he is able to imbue
the shattered and violent life of the community with a sense of difficult
humanity.

The clearest example of a funeral sequence as a performative site of
community memory is the one in the eighth chapter of the novel. It indicates,
through the action, the territorialisation of space through qualitative
reassignation of temporal meanings, or the ability of the community to move
beyond grief, finding strength through the enacted memory of the deceased.
The Nurse, here, is 'a toothless old man who has seen many winters' (Mda
1995: 144) and he expresses significant camaraderie with the deceased whose
life he is narrating:

'He was my age mate, this our brother who will not see the new year
. . . We grew up together in a faraway village in the inland provinces.
When we were little boys we looked after calves together, and when
they escaped to suckle from their mothers, our buttocks received the
biting pain of the whip together. When we were older we graduated
from calves to cattle, and we spent months in cattle posts in the snowy
mountains. We went to the mountain school together, where we were
circumcised into manhood. We went to the mines together, and dug

the white man's gold that has made this land rich. Then we came to this city to work in its harbours. When we were too old to make them rich any more, we were thrown out of employment together. I tell you, my brothers and sisters, we travelled a long road with this our brother. Ours was the closeness of saliva to the tongue. And now here he lies, waiting to be laid to rest under the soil. And it is the hands of his own children that have put him in this irreversible state.' (Mda 1995: 144)

The Nurse also feels a profound personal bond between the rural spaces of his youthful experience and the realities of his urban life in adulthood. This is evident in the recitation of individual and communal histories that shape the narrative of the deceased's life. The Nurse is also fulfilling a moral role, not only revealing to the community as is typical of the role of the Nurse, the nature of the man's death, but also emphasising the immorality of his murder by his own sons. The degree of personal relation between himself and the deceased is expressed in an evocative image: 'ours was the closeness of saliva to the tongue', while the descriptions of pastorality and the mountain or circumcision school animate the rural past for living memory. The body's direct association with the surface of the earth indicates an expression of territoriality through the laying of the dead to rest in a location that is removed from the valorised centres of tradition. It is on the most basic and communitarian level a re-enactment of community memory through the Nurse's orature and ability to connect with the latent power of folklore and custom. Again, as with our application of Deleuze and Guattari's theory of territoriality, these functions are suggestive of a nascent performativity and highlight Mda's ability to convey the sway of performance techniques through the innate strength of the community memory's sense of continuity as expressed through the funeral ritual.

The Nurse's kinaesthetic, oratorical abilities are emphasised at this point, as he works himself 'almost into a dance-like frenzy that leaves [the crowd attending the funeral] panting with excitement' (Mda 1995: 144), very similar to Toloki's exaggerated style of mourning. Mda cleverly combines the power of oral delivery and tradition with the passion of the performance and typically we are thrown directly into the moment and have to engage immediately with the fervour and feelings that are being carried to a resounding crescendo of grief and memory. The Nurse's informal obituary additionally expresses a particular sense of togetherness and of community in the presence of the 'irreversible state' (144) of death; the narrative of the deceased's life is an extensive one, encompassing many of the personal histories of migrant labour, village life, urban toils and the climate of death in which the people live. The Nurse later reveals the truth that his friend was murdered by his own sons for failing properly to observe the custom of shaving the heads of his family in a particular hierarchical order and in accordance with funeral rituals. The deceased man 'was a graceful patriarch who loved his family, and was a custodian of his people's customs' (146) and Naidoo emphasises that 'the killing of the acknowledged head of the family is again symptomatic of the entropy experienced by societies caught in the grip of bloodshed during spaces of transition' (1998: 194).

The man's murder by his sons leads to their conviction and possible hanging and Toloki wryly observes that 'funerals acquire a life of their own, and give birth to other funerals' (Mda 1995: 149). The communal voice within the narrative comments on the events in this way: 'We are very angry at the needless death of the patriarch, and we condemn his sons for this abomination' (149). Mda uses this moment to express a range of relations between community, individual and the multiple histories as articulated in memories of village culture and the urban present.

Humorously, we find another example of Toloki's resilient spirit at work, for he uses the funeral events to take advantage of the food that is given out to the entire community as an expression of collective remembrance and he 'usually collects his food, and drifts to some spot where there are no people, and quietly eats from his plate' (Mda 1995: 151); Noria, for her part, only gets to eat meat when at a funeral. Toloki's own act of territoriality is contrasted against that of the burial of the deceased and a claim to a location within the urban topography that is signified through the community's burial of the dead. However, this is not an act removed from the realities of urban existence, for the ways of dying are very much more than the mourning of the dead and are shown to possess qualities that serve to give continuity to community histories and memory, while also providing a site for the collective rituals of enjoyment and the provision of essentials, such as food. These public rituals command much narrative presence in all of Mda's novels, as histories come to locate themselves in the present and in the urban context, such rituals come to possess more mundane qualities, concomitant with the realities of modern life.

The funeral becomes associated with the reconstruction and narration of history by the community. This has been shown to function through the performance of the Nurse and Toloki as Professional Mourner and the sense of memory implies an embedded sense of continuity. The funeral ritual operates in ways that provide at least a provisional certainty for the present, a stability that is much needed during the transitional period in South African history. If anything, these living, vital community histories are given their most tangible presence through the very ways of dying that are the consequence of their arrival. The dynamic is a curious and complex one, as the sense of memory in its ancestral and traditional forms comes to find a place within the uneven modernities – even postmodernities – of the South African city.

Works cited

Bakhtin, Mikhail. 1993 (1941). *Rabelais and His World*. Translated by Hélène Iswolsky. Bloomington: Indiana University Press.

Benjamin, Walter. 1997. *One-Way Street*. London: Verso.

Bhabha, Homi K. 1994. *The Location of Culture*. New York: Routledge.

De Certeau, Michel. 1984. *The Practice of Everyday Life*. Translated by Steven Rendall. Berkeley: University of California Press.

Deleuze, Gilles and Felix Guattari. 1987. *A Thousand Plateaus: Capitalism and Schizophrenia*. Minneapolis: University of Minnesota Press.

Derrida, Jacques. 1988. *The Ear of the Other: Octobiography, Transference, Translation*. Translated by Peggy Kamuf and Avital Ronell; edited by Christie McDonald. Lincoln: University of Nebraska Press.

Dowling, Finuala. 1997. 'Zakes Mda's magical sleight of hand reveals our way of dying as our way of living'. *The Sunday Independent*, 15 June: 22.

Gramsci, Antonio. 1985. *Selections from Cultural Writing*. Edited by David Forgacs and Geoffrey Nowell-Smith. London: Lawrence & Wishart.

Jacobs, J.U. 2003. ' "Singing in a split tone": Hybridising history in the novels of Zakes Mda'. In: Monti, Allesandro and John Douthwaite (eds.). *Migrating the Texts: Hybridity as a Postcolonial Literary Construct*. Turin: L'Harmattan Italia, 191–225.

Mda, Zakes. 1994. 'Another theatre of the absurd'. In: Breitinger, Eckhard (ed.). *Theatre and Performance in Africa: Intercultural Perspectives* (*Bayreuth African Studies* 31: Yearbook of the Association for the Study of the New Literatures in English, band 4). Bayreuth: University of Bayreuth, 105-12.

———. 1995. *Ways of Dying*. Cape Town: Oxford University Press.

———. 2002a (2000). *The Heart of Redness*. Cape Town: Oxford University Press.

———. 2002b. *The Madonna of Excelsior*. Cape Town: Oxford University Press.

———. 2003. Personal correspondence with the author.

Mervis, Margaret. 1998. 'Fiction for development: Zakes Mda's *Ways of Dying*'. *Current Writing* 10(1): 39-56.

Moslund, Sten Pultz. 2003. *Making Use of History in New South African Fiction: An Analysis of the Purposes of Historical Perspectives in Three Post-Apartheid Novels*. Copenhagen: Museum Tusculanum Press.

Naidoo, Venugopaul. 1998. 'Magic realism in Zakes Mda's *Ways of Dying*, 1995 and *She Plays with the Darkness*, 1995'. D.Litt. thesis. Westville: University of Durban-Westville.

Nyawose, Theo. 2000. '"Living in two worlds": Codes and modes of expression at Zulu funerals in KwaZulu-Natal at the turn of the millennium'. Master's thesis. Durban: University of Natal.

Omotoso, Kole. 2004. 'Is White available in Black? The trickster tradition and the gods and goddesses of the cultures of down-pression'. *Rhodes University Centenary Lecture Series*, 5 May. http://www.ru.ac.za/centenary/lectures/omotosolecture.doc, accessed 7 May 2004.

Robinson, Jennifer. 1999. '(Im)mobilizing space – dreaming of change'. In: Judin, Hilton and Ivan Vladislavić (eds.). *Blank: Architecture, Apartheid and After*. Cape Town: David Philip; Rotterdam: NAi Publishers, D7.

Steinmeyer, Elke. 2003. 'Chanting the song of sorrow: Threnody in Homer and Zakes Mda'. *Current Writing* 15(2): 158-74.

Van Wyk, Johan. 1997. 'Catastrophe and beauty: *Ways of Dying*, Zakes Mda's novel of transition'. *Literator* 18(3): 79-90.

Vladislavić, Ivan. 1999. 'Street addresses, Johannesburg'. In: Judin, Hilton and Ivan Vladislaviæ (eds.). *blank___: architecture, apartheid and after*. Cape Town: David Philip; Rotterdam: NAi Publishers, E11.

6

Love and Wayward Women in Ways of Dying

NOKUTHULA MAZIBUKO

> In this society, there is no powerful discourse on love emerging either from politically progressive radicals or from the left. The absence of a sustained focus on love in progressive circles arises from a collective failure to acknowledge the needs of the spirit and an overdetermined emphasis on material concerns. (hooks 1994: 242)

WAYS OF DYING IS a poignant love story that captures the violence, despair and hope of South Africa's democratisation. Zakes Mda takes us through the lives of Noria and Toloki, from their childhoods in a rural village to the squatter settlement where they end up, and fall in love, resolving to teach each other 'how to live' (Mda 1995: 115). Both the nameless village and the squatter camp in a port city where the novel is set can be read as microcosms of the broader South African society. The novel spans apartheid South Africa from the late 1960s to the transition to democracy in the early 1990s and reflects the surge of violence and confusion that happened just before the 1994 elections. In *Ways of Dying* Mda presents the idea of a new dawn in South Africa; however, his renaissance is rooted in the lives of ordinary people, the majority of whom still live in poverty. Mda locates his renaissance within a discourse on love, which not only acknowledges the needs of the spirit, but also privileges a freedom of the spirit rooted in art and creativity that can be accessed by almost anyone.

Central to Mda's discourse on love are wayward women whom he depicts as the custodians of creativity, art and healing. My aim in this chapter is to explore the ways in which Mda presents women as being at the centre of reshaping and rebuilding a post-colonial, post-apartheid South Africa, amidst a nationalist discourse struggling to articulate an African Renaissance. These women are symbols and agents of a spiritual renaissance, operating at the margins of an overly materialist and male-dominated discourse.

Throughout the novel Mda creates tension by exploring opposing ideas and values: the rural and the urban, beauty and ugliness, poverty and wealth, spirituality and the material world, and love and hate. His privileging of spiritual wealth goes beyond the predominant material focus on poverty alleviation strategies as outlined in the current political discourse of African Renaissance. The idea of the African Renaissance has gained currency in post-apartheid South Africa mainly through Thabo Mbeki's efforts to continue the pan-African legacy of the presidents of the first decolonised African states who articulated a vision of a decolonised, prosperous and interdependent Africa: Kwame Nkrumah of Ghana, Gamal Abdel Nasser of Egypt, Julius Nyerere of Tanzania, Patrice Lumumba of Congo, Agostinho Neto of Angola, Eduardo Mondlane of Mozambique and Sir Seretse Khama of Botswana. Their vision led to the formation of the Organisation of African Unity (OAU) in 1963, which became the African Union (AU) in 2002. In South Africa, in his well-known 'I am an African' speech to Parliament in 1996, Mbeki emphasised the need for all South Africans to see themselves as Africans and to work together towards a prosperous future, a future that will be part of an African Renaissance.

In an interview in 2002, Mda emphasised that his African renaissance is not with a capital 'R', as it is a renaissance driven by ordinary people on the margins of centres of power, such as the government and the cities (Mazibuko 2002). He stated also that he sees women as being at the centre of this renaissance in the community work they do and in how they uphold the spiritual and material well-being of their families. Mda's assertions echo those of the South African feminist Nomboniso Gasa who, at the launch of the AU, listened to the African presidents present lauding the 'founding fathers' and wrote about the need to include women in the AU agenda:

Noting the silence on the subject of women, who were part of the earlier African independence movements, those women's names came flooding to mind: Funmilayo Ransome-Kuti and Margaret Ekpo of Nigeria were an obvious entry point. As far back as 1929, women in the southern part of Nigeria combined the struggle for independence with attempts to address gender-specific issues. (2002: 7)

In a paper presented at the University of the Witwatersrand, Shireen Hassim traced the struggle to include gender equity in the national agenda in South Africa. Hassim outlined the competing nationalist and feminist discourses that have led to many debates and conflicts within liberation movements, debates that ultimately led to the inclusion of gender equity in the Constitution:

The 'success story' of the South African women's movement in the transition to democracy is by now a familiar one to feminist scholars and activists. Unlike in many other African countries, the transition to democracy after nationalist struggles did not lead to the marginalisation of women but rather to the insertion of gender equality concerns into the heart of democratic debates. Women's political participation was extended into the realm of representative government and a range of institutions were created to represent and defend women's interests in policy-making. In addition, women's activism ensured that gender equality was protected in the constitution. Unlike the era of national liberation movement politics, during the transition women [organised] as women and [entered] the democratic era with new agendas for women. (2002)

Although, as Hassim states, the Constitution protects women's rights on many levels, in practical terms, high levels of gender violence, as well as continuing poverty, reveal the need to protect and apply these rights. Women still make up the majority in communities at the margins of economic freedom in South Africa.

It is the society at the margins that makes up the world of *Ways of Dying* (see Barnard 2004; Mantjiu 2000; Twalo 2001; Van Wyk 1997). In the squatter camp where Noria and Toloki live, the world of politicians is distant and irrelevant. It is in this world where Noria and the women such as Madimbhaza go about their daily struggle of feeding and clothing the community:

> Toloki notices that the people who are most active in the affairs of the settlement are the women. Not only do they do all the work, but they play leadership roles. At this meeting, they present the most practical ideas to solve the various problems. The few male residents who are present relish making high-flown speeches that display eloquence, but are short on practical solutions. (Mda 1995: 172)

Whether in an urban or rural setting, Mda depicts women as the ones who bear the brunt of the poverty caused by intersecting racial and patriarchal economies. He writes about women who are in constant conflict with patriarchal and economic oppression – colourful, transgressive characters, whose daily dramas are the substance of his African renaissance.

The female protagonist, Noria, her mother, That Mountain Woman, and Toloki's mother are all outspoken and often unkind; as characters they fascinate, as well as antagonise. These three women do not try or pretend to fit into images of calm, 'good' women that a patriarchal value system propagates. They seem to revel in behaviour that contradicts and upsets notions of ideal womanhood. They are the kind of outspoken, boundary-pushing women that Pumla Dineo Gqola refers to in the phrase '*ufanele uqavile*' (2001: 11), an isiXhosa term meant to insult or praise, depending on where the user is coming from ('if addressed to a woman, means, depending on where the accent is placed, either "her (hyper)active mind is to blame" or "your (hyper)active mind is to blame"' (22).

The novel introduces Toloki's mother as not being particularly kind, either about the pampered village child, Noria, or towards her own husband, Jwara: 'The earliest reference to Noria as a stuck-up bitch was first heard some years back when Toloki's mother was shouting at Jwara, her angry eyes green with jealousy, "You spend all your time with that stuck-up bitch, Noria, and you do not care for your family!" '(Mda 1995: 29). Toloki's mother is not happy with her self-absorbed husband, who indulges himself by spending hours creating iron figurines, while there is no food in the house; she not only makes her displeasure known, she shouts it, so that Jwara and anyone else within hearing distance will also know.

Similarly, Mda introduces Noria's mother as someone who does not conform to patriarchal laws that she be humble and obedient in her husband's presence. The first thoughts or words from That Mountain Woman, who is said to have 'razor blades in her tongue' (Mda 1995: 30), are aimed at her husband, whom she chastises for not supporting their daughter's creative talents: '"How dare you, Father of Noria, interfere with the process of creation! Who are you, Father of Noria, to think that a piece of rag like you can have the right to stop my child from doing what she was born to do?"' (30). Mda goes on to explain how That Mountain Woman had got her name because she had come from a village in the mountains and after her marriage to Noria's father, his village gave her the name to bring her down a notch or two, by implying that her background did not equip her with the correct manners for a woman:

> It was not only the razor blades that made people wary of That Mountain Woman. It was also because she was different from us, and her customs were strange, since she was from the faraway mountain villages where most of us had never been. We wondered why Xesibe had to go all the way to the mountains to look for a wife, when our village was famous for its beautiful women. That Mountain Woman had no respect for our ways, and talked with men anyhow she liked. (Mda 1995: 34)

Desiree Lewis's analysis of the reactions to Winnie Madikizela-Mandela as a 'signifier of resistance' (2003: 23) for black womanhood on the margins of a society guarded by intersecting misogynist and racist discourses echoes the villagers' reactions to Mda's wayward women. Lewis says that by constantly being at the centre of controversy Madikizela-Mandela 'offers a symbol of contradiction, of subversion, of disrespect, of impatience, an anarchic symbol, a symbol that appeals to those who have nothing at stake in the available status quo'. That Mountain Woman is seen as 'other' by the villagers and she operates within and outside of village codes as she sees fit. She will not be governed by an illegitimate system that discriminates against women and elevates men, regardless of their worth as individuals. T.G. Twalo's incisive look at subversive gender politics in *Ways of Dying* also makes Lewis's point that in patriarchal society, it is not so much the nature or extent of women's wrongdoing that is questioned, but rather that the woman dares to disregard patriarchal codes. Twalo goes on to argue that Mda challenges these codes 'by privileging female voice' (2001: 40).

In constructing the women in *Ways of Dying*, Mda draws from a range of symbolic figures that circulate within societal constructions of womanhood, as well as within the African literature canon established by Ngugi wa Thiong'o, Chinua Achebe and others. These symbolic figures include the mother (symbolising growth and birth), the healer (healing the nation during and after a period of trauma), as well as the artist/muse (also taking care of the nation's spiritual needs), the virgin, the destructive whore and witch. Mda often uses these symbols in a contradictory manner, where the same character symbolises both growth and destruction (see Moffet 1996).

In portraying That Mountain Woman and Toloki's mother, Mda does not go beyond establishing their symbolic significance. Their birth names remain a mystery since, as Twalo points out, the village renames them according to how it perceives them (2001: 40). Toloki's mother is not given an identity or a history beyond being Toloki's mother and Jwara's wife. Even when she stands up against Jwara's selfishness, she does so in defence of Toloki, whom Jwara ignores while he spends hours with Noria. Although protective of her son, Toloki's mother does not typically represent the nurturing, loving and well-behaved mother. She shows no tenderness towards her son or her husband and her marriage to Jwara seems to be one of economic necessity – before his madness and death, Jwara makes a relatively good living as a smithy. When, after years of Jwara's refusing to eat or leave his workshop, his wife finds him dead and almost skeletal, she does not seem to care. She promptly sells his equipment and goes back to living her life, later becoming the lover of Jwara's friend, Xesibe. Mda seems to suggest that the lovelessness in Toloki's home is what leads to the sadness and hopelessness he feels in his life. As an adult Toloki resolves to free himself by leaving to go to the city in search of 'love and fortune' (Mda 1995: 104). Unlike That Mountain Woman and Noria, Toloki's mother has no special skills or talents. The only other information about her is that after Jwara's death, she is forced to 'get a job doing washing for the manager of the general dealer's store' (110).

That Mountain Woman symbolises both what is good and what is destructive within the village. She is well known and respected for being able 'to make potent medicines for all sorts of ailments' (Mda 1995: 34); however, she is also rumoured to be able to curse people. Like the Prophetess in Njabulo S. Ndebele's short story, 'Fools' (1983), she has special powers; however, That Mountain Woman is a slightly more complex character with her own motives and agendas. That Mountain Woman's work as a healer is not only symbolic of the villagers' capacity and need for healing, but it is also a means for her to support herself. Unlike Toloki's mother, she has some income of her own and is therefore not tied to a man for financial reasons. She is unusual in being a village woman with some access to capital. She has redefined a role for herself as active and one that goes beyond that occupied by many women in rural areas. However, her symbolism, as well as her sense of agency, still remain within the realm of what is possible for a black woman in rural apartheid South Africa. Ironically, That Mountain Woman cannot heal herself and eventually succumbs to cancer of the womb. Here, Mda departs from the trope of the strong woman of Africa. That Mountain Woman is only human after all and cannot walk 'on the rainbow' (34), as she claimed when she first arrived in the village. However, Mda stresses that her fighting spirit prevails till her death; Noria, who is the 'Nurse' at the funeral, describes how her mother 'did not just succumb like a coward but fought bravely against death. She was as much of a fighter in death as she had been in life. Even the specialist from the city had exclaimed in wonderment, as people who suffered from her disease did not last that long' (94). After her death, there is a profound sense of loss that lingers in the village, as it has lost a healer whose power was felt as 'the invisible backbone that supports the community' (Moffet 1996: 15). The respect and awe she commanded during her life is evident from the number of people who come to honour her at the funeral.

Mda's portrayal of That Mountain Woman as a mother does not draw on stereotypical ideas of motherhood. As Florence Stratton states, the mother in the African literature canon is nurturing, protective and often representative of the land that is fertile and must be cared for and, in turn, will care for those who live off it (1994: 39). Unlike the stereotype of the fertile, reproductive mother, That Mountain Woman only has one child whom she spoils. Both That Mountain Woman and Toloki's mother are atypical in this sense; unlike many rural women of their generation, they are not overly burdened by many children. This could be in line with their role of being symbolic of motherhood, yet not fully engaged in the demands of conventional motherhood. Also, motherhood for That Mountain Woman and Toloki's mother does not seem to centre on the patriarchal preference for male heirs. Jwara practically ignores Toloki and his mother's defence of him is against Jwara's bullying and not because of his social currency as a son. That Mountain Woman is also not concerned about bearing sons. She is happy to dote on and support her daughter Noria. Furthermore, she does not seem to share the sentiment that motherhood is a state to be revered – this is shown in how she does not hesitate to have a sexual encounter with the doctor who delivers Noria (Mda 1995: 39). She also often refers to those who anger her as 'botched abortions' (73).

Lewis's examination of depictions of black women as mothers reveals how texts can play into, resist or negotiate prescribed patriarchal myths about the role of women. Her analysis of the way Ellen Kuzwayo's *Call Me Woman* (1985) naturalises the supposedly feminine virtues of 'orderly, obedient, nurturant [*sic*] and domesticated' (1992: 39) motherhood challenges the restrictive stereotyping of women as either good, orderly mothers or deviant (barren women, spinsters, or prostitutes). Mda upsets such binaries by portraying Toloki's mother and That Mountain Woman as taking on motherhood in ways that resist patriarchal prescriptions. However, as they are supporting characters, they are not given textual space that would make them more complex and reveal the processes through which they influence and change their societies.

The character of Noria is more central and thus is given the space and complexity to express a gendered identity in flux. The multiple roles inhabited by Noria embody an identity and subjectivity created at the place where patriarchal discourse, material conditions and her agency intersect. In portraying Noria, Mda has combined the real and imagined in an interesting and contradictory manner. Noria is a combination of the mother, virgin, prostitute, artist and activist.

As a child, Noria is described as beautiful and talented. Her ability to spread joy throughout the village just by laughing is recognised when she is still a baby. This magical quality is constant throughout her life; however, her charms have the equal ability to be abused by the people around her, as when her nursemaids tickle her for the pleasure of hearing her laughter and cause her to cry. The nurses' selfish and exploitative admiration of Noria is typical of how the village appreciates her; their admiration is not generous, as in the same breath they can admire Noria and say just how ugly and unpleasant Toloki is.

Noria develops her gifts of spreading joy when she discovers that she is able to inspire great art through her singing. When she sings, Toloki's father, Jwara, can make weird and wonderful iron figurines. Like the village, Jwara has a voracious and selfish appetite for Noria's gifts, so much so that he once kept Noria singing for a week as he was lost in trance creating his figurines. Although creatively inspired by Noria, Jwara does not share anything substantial with her, except to give her sweets. He also does not share his works of art, but keeps them locked away in his workshop. It is only at the end of the novel, after he dies, that Jwara leaves his figurines to Toloki, perhaps a sign that he recognises the error of his selfishness and lack of support for his son's art. The kind of superficial admiration that Noria gets from the village makes her pompous and unkind, qualities that earn her the title 'that stuck-up bitch Noria'. Like her unconventional mother, she carries this title with pride and disdain.

During her teenage years, Noria leaves school and starts to prostitute herself to bus drivers. She enjoys the financial freedom and other treats and gifts that this lifestyle brings her. She eventually ends up falling in love with Napu, whom she marries after falling pregnant.

As a mother, Noria moves beyond the unconventional into the absurd. She gives birth to the same child, Vutha, twice, and each time the pregnancy is fifteen months long. When she gives birth to Vutha for the second time, it seems to be by immaculate conception and here Mda collapses the two symbols of mother and virgin. Mda's fascination with the trope of the virgin mother is, in part, an ironic comment on the many black women who seem to have conceived immaculately, because there are no men around to help them raise their children. When Noria gives birth to Vutha the first time, she is a teenage drop-out who has no means of supporting herself or her baby. Like her mother, That Mountain Woman, Noria has a taste for risk and finds herself with a baby and no money, not from being born into poverty (as suggested by Twalo 2001: 48), but because of the choice she makes to follow Napu to town. However, once having entered the role of mother and wife Noria is, for some time, not able to extricate herself from the cycle of poverty and Napu's verbal abuse. Even Napu's grandmother, with whom she stays briefly after the birth of Vutha (the first), treats her badly and tries to bewitch her. Napu's grandmother supports the patriarchal system that sees women as objects to be abused (see Twalo 2001: 48). She tries to insist that Noria stay with her, so that she can have access to the monthly allowance that Napu sends.

Napu's relationship with Noria is oppressive and not life-giving. The two are trapped in mutual dependence: Noria depends on Napu's meagre wages and Napu's ego feeds off Noria's financial dependence (he forbids her to work). Noria does not respond submissively to Napu's abuse: 'Noria was hardened by now, and she fought back every time Napu tried to be rude or cruel to her. The bravado that he used to muster when he dealt with That Mountain Woman had fizzled out. On the days when he came home drunk, he would try to assert his manhood. But she would put him in his place' (Mda 1995: 92). The hostility between Napu and Noria eventually ends when Napu kidnaps Vutha and disappears. Napu later leaves Vutha tied to a pole, while he goes on a drinking spree, and Vutha dies, and is eaten by dogs.

Noria's life with Napu resembles Molara Ogundipe-Leslie's description of the multiple systems of oppression that black women have to fight. She describes this multiple oppression as the 'six mountains' carried by black women on their backs: 'One might say that the African woman has six mountains on her back: one is oppression from outside, the second is from traditional structures, feudal, slave-based, communal etc., the third is her backwardness; the fourth is man; the fifth is her color, her race; and the sixth is herself' (1994: 28).

Noria's life is limited by the apartheid context where black women could only exist and work in certain places. This greatly reduces her chances of having access to economic resources. Her chances are further reduced by Napu who forbids her to work. For many years, Noria is trapped by her own decision to stay with Napu.

After leaving Napu, Noria goes to live in a squatter settlement. At the settlement, she conceives Vutha The Second immaculately. When, fifteen months later, he is born, Noria stubbornly ignores the warning of the community and gives her child the same tragic name, Vutha, meaning 'to burn' in Nguni. Noria's prophetic naming is fulfilled when, at the age of five, Vutha The Second is burnt alive ('necklaced') by The Young Tigers. Vutha's necklacing exposes in a grotesque and exaggerated manner one of the saddest casualties of South Africa's race wars – the sacrifice of childhood and innocence. The 1980s mass-based activism swept up children as young as ten. Mda's critique of very young children in the liberation struggle is levelled at both the political movements, as well as the parents of the children. The Young Tigers see nothing wrong in training children as young as five to be fighters in the struggle. Vutha's political experience is described as follows:

> At the age of five, Vutha was already a veteran of many political demonstrations. He was an expert at dancing the freedom dance, and at chanting the names of the leaders who must be revered, and of the sell-outs who must be destroyed. He could recite the Liberation Code and the Declaration of the People's Rights. Of course, he did not understand a single word, since it was all in English. He mispronounced most of the words, too. He also knew all the songs. Even when he was playing with mud in the streets, or with wire cars with the other children, he could be heard singing about freedom, and about the heroic deeds of the armed wing of the people's movement. He, of course, was not displaying any particular precociousness in this regard. All the children of the settlement, even those younger than Vutha, were (and still are) well-versed in these matters. (Mda 1995: 179)

The liberation movement, and especially The Young Tigers, are criticised for using as cannon-fodder children who cannot possibly have any understanding of what the fight for freedom is all about. In Vutha's five-year-old mind, freedom songs about overthrowing the oppressive apartheid regime apply equally to his mother who is determined to curtail his freedom to bully his playmate Danisa, or to go fishing in the marshlands. What is even more tragic is that 'Noria was very proud of her son's political involvement' (Mda 1995: 179). She does not understand her primary role as Vutha's mother is to protect him at all costs and she is satisfied that he is able to join the struggle as an able cadre. The only concern she has is that Vutha should try not to be in front during demonstrations. She shares the community's belief that the children are not too young to be trained as 'the leaders of tomorrow' (185).

This overburdening of Vutha and his peers with war and politics backfires very badly when the followers of the 'tribal chief' who reside in the hostel manage to get Vutha and a friend to betray the details of a planned revenge ambush. The Young Tigers discover the betrayal and murder Vutha and his friend by dousing them with petrol, putting tyres around their necks and making Danisa and another young child set them alight. The Young Tigers are convinced that Vutha and his friend deserved their fate because they are 'sell-outs'. The community shares their view, as they refuse to tell Noria who exactly ordered the death of her child. Furthermore, her shack is set on fire by faceless, nameless people. The community demonstrates its cold and cruel side when it demands that Noria conspire to conceal and forget her son's murder. She is promised by the leaders of 'the political movement' that they will apologise to her in public for the death of her child and acknowledge the pain she must feel as his mother, on condition that Noria quietly accept his death. The political leaders betray their promise, however, and grudgingly apologise in private, while still demanding that she not raise the matter publicly:

> The kind of silence that everyone is demanding from her is that she should not condemn the perpetrators in any public forum, as this would give ammunition to the enemy. Now she sees that what they really want is that she, like the rest of the community, should accept her child's guilt, and take it that he received what he deserved. If she keeps quiet, the whole scandal will quietly die, and no one will point fingers and say, 'You see, they say they are fighting for freedom, yet they are no different from the tribal chief and his followers. They commit atrocities as well.' (Mda 1995: 178)

True to form, Noria is not prepared to let the matter disappear; she 'refuses to be silenced, and tells Toloki that she will fight to the end to see justice is done.

She has kept quiet all these days because she believed that when the national leaders came, they would address the matter openly and with fairness, instead of sweeping it under the carpet' (Mda 1995: 178).

Despite Noria's determination to fight for the truth about her child's death, the novel does not resolve Vutha's murder. It is not clear whether justice is meted out to his killers, or whether they remain anonymous and continue with their lives. Noria tells Toloki that she is determined to continue working for and helping the community, regardless of what The Young Tigers and the political leaders do and say. There is a sense that the underlying tensions and outbursts of violence within the community continue; these are the times and it is not certain how or when the many ways of dying will cease. In the interim, mothers and children such as Noria and Vutha are the casualties. Despite the many anxieties and questions raised by the text, it is nevertheless strangely optimistic. Noria's path is undoubtedly one of redemption and growth through love and art. She reunites with her childhood friend, Toloki, after they have journeyed separately to the city. They fall in love and resolve to teach each other 'how to live' (Mda 1995: 115). It is when they fall in love without reference to material things that Noria and Toloki find happiness and freedom. Through love, they also find the ability to express their art (Noria sings and laughs again, while Toloki paints) and share joy and happiness with others.

Noria's final turn from dispensing sexual favours for money is expressed through her refusal of Bhuti Shaddy's offer of marriage. She stops taking money from men and lives a life of serving humankind. Noria's life of simplicity and service helps her to regain her gift of singing and laughter, which she lost when she left her village. As artist and muse, she symbolises a moral and spiritual power that is to some degree rooted in the village that has produced her. Noria helps Toloki to regain his gift of art; her singing inspires him to draw human faces, which he was unable to do before.

The journeys of women such as Noria, That Mountain Woman and Toloki's mother, who have had to cross boundaries carrying the mountains of racism and patriarchy on their backs, make pertinent bell hooks's insistence that there needs to be a politics of ending the myriad of systems of domination. Like Mda, hooks advocates a politics based on a spirituality that is fair and inclusive:

It has always puzzled me that women and men who spend a lifetime working to resist and oppose one form of domination can be systematically supporting another. I have been puzzled by powerful visionary black male leaders who can speak and act passionately in resistance to racial domination and accept and embrace sexist domination of women, by feminist white women who work daily to eradicate sexism but who have major blind spots when it comes to acknowledging and resisting racism and white supremacist domination of the planet. Critically examining these blind spots, I conclude that many of us are motivated to move against domination solely when we feel our self-interest directly threatened. Often, then, the longing is not for a collective transformation of society, an end to politics of domination, but rather simply for an end to what we feel is hurting us. This is why we desperately need an ethic of love to intervene in our self-centred longing for change. (1994: 244)

In practical terms, hooks emphasises that a love ethic is grounded in service to others. This resonates with Noria and Toloki's service to each other and those around them without necessarily focusing on material gains. This love ethic of service exposes the absurdity of material greed. Mda also counters the absurdity of the oppression and misery that his characters experience by creating his own absurd and magical reality, one that the characters navigate with the grace of art and creativity.

A number of critics have drawn attention to role of the absurd and spirituality through artistic expression in the narration of post-apartheid South Africa in *Ways of Dying*. Rita Barnard describes the novel as 'Janus faced' (2004: 2), looking back at the horror of apartheid, while at the same time hoping for a better future. It is this tension of pulling backward and forward that escalates into the absurd and grotesque, eliciting a liberatory laughter. This is a laughter that takes away the power of the grotesque, but a laughter that can also be cruel (as in the case of Toloki's boss who kills his friend and then laughs) and a laughter that can turn into mourning or sadness (Noria's friend dies laughing). Barnard's point can be expanded to view laughter as a way to gain life and happiness. Noria's laughter uplifts the village and spreads happiness:

> We were not surprised, really, that Noria had all this power to change
> mediocre artisans into artists of genius, and to make the birds and the
> bees pause in their business of living and pay audience to her. In fact,
> one thing that Toloki used to be jealous about even as a small boy, was
> that we all loved the stuck-up bitch, for she had such beautiful laughter.
> We would make up all sorts of funny things in order to make her
> laugh. She loved to laugh at funny faces, and some villagers gained
> great expertise in making them. A particular young man called Rubber
> Face Sehole knew how to pull all sorts of funny faces, and whenever he
> was around we knew that we would all be happily feasting on Noria's
> laughter. (Mda 1995: 31)

Barnard also states: 'Zakes Mda celebrates the generative power of African
popular creativity. The closing pages of *Ways of Dying* represent the people not
as consumers, recyclers, and scavengers, but as fertile and imaginative producers'
(2004: 13). Hence the mental and spiritual high induced by laughter and
creativity can propel individuals to creatively reproduce and change their
environments.

Mpho Mantjiu also explores the spiritual and creative as a way to renaissance;
Ways of Dying, he says, 'is a story of survival and revival, a restoration of human
dignity' (2000: 9). Mantjiu points out that Mda sees love and respect as a way
of living: through love individuals can be pushed to uplift themselves, as well
as their communities. And it is creativity that fuels the love between people:
'The development of individuals sometimes lies in their creativity and both
Toloki and Noria are creators in their own right'. Mantjiu sees *Ways of Dying* as
articulating how ordinary people are achieving the ideals of rebuilding the
nation.

The end of *Ways of Dying* presents a problem that Mda poses to the reader
throughout the novel. The problem is in the form of Nefolovhodwe who arrives
at Noria and Toloki's shack with Toloki's inheritance, a truckload of Jwara's
metal figurines that he has instructed Nefolovhodwe, through dreams, to take
to Toloki. There are so many figurines that they do not fit into the shack and
the lovers cannot decide what to do with them. None of the solutions of what
to do with the figurines that they contemplate is sustainable. They could sell

the figurines and feed the children, but this will last only until there are no more figurines to sell. And finding the space and resources to build a bigger shack for a figurine museum is well-nigh impossible for Noria and Toloki. Mda seems to be suggesting that finding a way to live in the urban spaces is hardly possible and that perhaps they should return to the village.

Throughout Mda's beautifully written novel, jarring and conflicting images are forced together, distancing the reader and forcing a process of constant re-evaluation whether certain ways of living are in fact ways of dying. Will the African Renaissance that places importance on materiality and engaging the global economic agenda be able to provide a way of living? Mda envisions a renaissance that is founded on the principles of love and compassion, a renaissance that puts ordinary people at the centre, led by African women who are the custodians of spirituality as expressed through art and beauty.

Works cited

Barnard, Rita. 2004. 'On laughter, the grotesque, and the South African transition: Zakes Mda's *Ways of Dying*'. *Novel: A Forum on Fiction* (Summer 2004). http://www.looksmarttrends.com/p/articles/mi_qa3643/is_200407/ai_n14680976?pi=dyn, accessed 3 February 2006.

Gasa, Nomboniso. 2002. 'Mothers of the nation and of the continent: Women have a proud history of political activism in Africa'. *The Sunday Independent*, 3 August: 7.

Gqola, Pumla Dineo. 2001. '*Ufanele uqavile*: Black women, feminism and postcoloniality in Africa'. *Agenda* 50: 11.

Hassim, Shireen. 2002. 'Negotiating spaces: Women in South Africa's transition to democracy'. Wits Interdisciplinary Research Seminar. Johannesburg: University of Witwatersrand, 25 March.

hooks, bell. 1994. *Outlaw Culture: Resisting Representations*. New York: Routledge.

Kuzwayo, Ellen. 1985. *Call Me Woman*. Johannesburg: Ravan Press.

Lewis, Desiree. 1992. 'Myths of motherhood and power: The construction of "black women" in literature'. *English in Africa* 19(1): 35-51.

——. 2003. 'No conventional role model'. *Mail & Guardian*, 19 June: 23.

Mantjiu, Mpho. 2000. 'African Renaissance and contemporary South African writing'. http://www.jour.city.ac.uk/international2000/MhoMantjiu/AfricanRenaissance.html, accessed 6 March 2002.

Mazibuko, Nokuthula. 2002. 'Women and social change: An interview with Zakes Mda'. Unpublished interview.

Mbeki, Thabo. 1998. *Africa: The Time Has Come*. Cape Town: Tafelberg Publishers.

Mda, Zakes. 1995. *Ways of Dying*. Cape Town: Oxford University Press.

Moffet, H. 1996. 'Zakes Mda: Ways of living'. *The Cape Librarian* (April): 14–15.

Ndebele, Njabulo S. 1983. *Fools and Other Stories*. Johannesburg: Ravan Press.

Ogundipe-Leslie, Molara. 1994. *Re-Creating Ourselves: African Women and Critical Transformations*. Trenton, NJ: Africa World Press.

Stratton, Florence. 1994. *Contemporary African Literature and the Politics of Gender*. New York: Routledge.

Twalo, T.G. 2001. 'The subversion of nationalist politics in Zakes Mda's *Ways of Dying*'. Master's thesis. Johannesburg: University of Witwatersrand.

Van Wyk, Johan. 1997. 'Catastrophe and beauty: *Ways of Dying*, Zakes Mda's novel of the transition'. *Literator* 18(3): 79–90.

7

Twinship and Humanism in She Plays with the Darkness

T. SPREELIN MACDONALD

TRUE TO THE PARTICULAR aesthetic and humanistic vision that underpins much of his literary project, Zakes Mda's novel *She Plays with the Darkness* (1995) is centrally concerned with undermining social binaries and asserting the role of the marginalised artist in the process of societal transformation.[1] Through the divergent stories of a brother and sister, Radisene and Dikosha, Mda highlights the divisiveness of post-colonial life, asserting the necessity of humanistic values and what one critic has called the power of 'non-instrumental art' in transforming post-colonial cultural identities (Attwell 2005: 194).

Though not of the same father, Radisene and Dikosha become known as 'twins' in their rural mountain village of Ha Samane, Lesotho, due to their being born of the same mother ('Mother of Twins') in the same year. The twins bond intimately as children until Dikosha, a brilliant student, is denied the chance to complete her schooling by local church fathers who see no future for an educated woman in their society. Instead, they sponsor Radisene, himself a mediocre student, to complete his studies in the relatively more urbanised lowlands of the country. This moment marks a split in the lives of the siblings. Radisene embraces the lowland town life of his schooling, disappearing for years at a time from Ha Samane, and eventually becomes an ambulance chaser, defrauding road-accident victims and insurance companies of enormous sums of money. Conversely, in reaction to her disenfranchisement, Dikosha increasingly retreats into a solitary realm of private ritual and art. In rejection of all traditional obligations to and restrictions on her station as a female in her Basotho society she eschews the advances of suitors, does not cook, clean or maintain her appearance, and she refuses to talk to Radisene (or most people, for that matter) for decades.

Mda thus establishes a pattern of tension between a bonded pair of characters that appears fairly frequently in his novels. Through coupled characters, such as Toloki and Noria in *Ways of Dying* (1995), Twin-Twin and Twin, and Bhonco and Zim in *The Heart of Redness* (2000), Popi and Tjaart, and Popi and Viliki in *The Madonna of Excelsior* (2002), the Bored Twins in *The Whale Caller* (2005), and Abednego and Nicodemus in *Cion* (2007) it becomes evident that twinship is invoked in every one of Mda's novels. Of his application of the trope of twinning in *The Heart of Redness*, David Attwell argues: 'Undoubtedly, modernity introduces splitting, a splitting of political allegiances and subjectivities, but against this, Mda asserts the metaphorical and ontological power of twinning . . . This is in keeping with a traditional position that interprets twinship as a *single* identity. In Mda's hands, splitting and twinning comprise a warp and woof, a weaving of pattern and tension that gives definition to South African postcolonial modernity' (2005: 199; emphasis in original).

In a post-colonial climate imbued with divisions, twinship, as a binding '*single* identity', can therefore be seen as that which counteracts the splitting of identities into modernity's common binaries (traditional/modern, male/female, rural/urban, and even self/other). While, as Attwell maintains, this concept may be drawn from 'tradition', it does not necessarily function in Mda's fiction as the traditional antithesis to modernity, in the sense of a traditional/modern dichotomy. Twinship is, rather, a humanistic concept, which undermines the perception of identities as 'split'. It is this concept that Mda pits against the propensity of 'postcolonial modernity' to interpret the world as ultimately divided.

Despite its increasingly clichéd appropriations by politicians, the concept *ubuntu* or *botho*, often defined as 'African humanism', perhaps provides a further philosophical context for Mda's humanistic deployment of twinship. Although it is a broad cultural concept, *ubuntu* is effectively expressed by the proverb common to most South African languages, '*motho ke motho ka batho*' (Sotho), or '*umuntu ngumuntu ngabantu*' (Nguni). Translated as 'a person is a person through other people', this proverb establishes a perception of the world in which the self is not created through self-determination, but primarily through the sacrifices of others (birth, protection, support) and through the interaction of self with others. The self is thus ultimately unable to be split from others.

In this respect, Mda's consistently reapplied trope of twinship throughout his novels seems to strongly endorse this perception of brotherhood and sisterhood as a fundamental and inescapable bond, of continued relevance in a post-colonial age, which is otherwise fractured by identity politics. When applied to divisive issues such as race, class and gender relations, twinship offers Mda a concept capable of surmounting binaries through its ability to both historically establish the validity of humanism in South African society and to map the obligations of twinship over nearly any dominant social, temporal or spatial division.

Notably, twinship in *She Plays with the Darkness*, which preceded *The Heart of Redness* in publication by five years, certainly seems to prefigure the elaborate applications of Mda's later novels. Furthermore, twinship in *She Plays with the Darkness* is significantly more explicit and central than issues of twinship in the earlier *Ways of Dying*. While the coupling of Toloki and Noria in *Ways of Dying* posits some degree of mutual responsibility, their bond carries little of the concreteness that is established between Radisene and Dikosha and between the characters in subsequent novels. Hence, it appears that twinship in *She Plays with the Darkness* is the first instance in which Mda exercises the true potential of this 'warp and woof' of twinship in his fiction.

The splitting of Radisene and Dikosha marks a divide within a single identity, that of their family in the future, as they are their mother's only children. As an ambulance chaser, Radisene becomes fabulously wealthy and thoroughly materialistic in the decades he spends in the capital, Maseru. He lives for his quest to be a self-made, modern man, full of the heartless, independent practicality that allows him to exploit vulnerable road-accident victims in a clear-cut quest for wealth. Dikosha, alternatively, occupies a world of beauty, communing with cave paintings, musicians and dancers, charming and eating snakes, and sustaining herself, un-ageing, for decades through her encounters with figures conjured to life from the walls of the Cave of Barwa, an ancient cave near her village.

In this manner, it appears that Mda establishes a dichotomy between a vulnerable tradition (Dikosha) and the oppressive materialism and rationalism of modernity (Radisene). Yet, any such dichotomous reading of the novel is unfounded as Dikosha's rituals are not truly those of 'tradition', since she rejects nearly all social interaction with the people of Ha Samane. That is, she refuses to be forcibly socialised within and subservient to the traditions of her community. While she produces her beauty largely through communion with an ancient past depicted in cave paintings, the traces left by the absent 'Barwa' population that predated Dikosha's Basotho people in the region, these are not strictly part of a 'tradition' of her people. They are of another, a displaced and erased people who are absent bodily from what is now Lesotho. Therefore, Dikosha's reality, that which she fashions outside of her own Basotho tradition and outside of Radisene's materialistic modernity, is its own brand of modernity. Unlike the 'traditions' of her rural neighbours, or her brother's greedy consumption of the new materials and meanings of the lowland, Dikosha's is a modernity based on the re-creation of life through *another* past, which she selectively combines with various 'new' elements, as well as those of 'traditional' Basotho society.

Attwell describes this trope of summoning up culturally generative processes through art and ritual in Mda's novels as 'the power of non-instrumental art to awaken listeners to their precariousness, to stir up affective capacities, and to remind them that despite the brutalization that is their daily lot, they are still agents of culture' (2005: 194). Dikosha's creativity is 'non-instrumental' in this manner: her prodigious dancing, her communion with these ancient Others through their paintings, her transcendental performances with Shana, the mysterious boy who plays the *sekgankula* instrument, are all rituals of a new generative culture, not technically Basotho 'tradition' and certainly not that of the neo-colonial lowlands. Alone in her private realm of ritual, Dikosha is an agent of her own culture, making beauty through rituals of her own creation.

Above all, Dikosha wishes to become a particular figure painted on the walls of the Cave of Barwa, the 'monster-woman-dancer'. The Cave of Barwa, Mda writes, had red and black paintings of big-buttocked people chasing deer with bows and arrows, or dancing in a trancelike state. Dikosha was spellbound by one painting especially, which showed a dancer with the body of a woman and the head of a beast. It was a fierce looking beast that no one had ever seen before. Dikosha saw herself as the monster-woman-dancer, ready to devour all the dancers of the world, imbuing herself with their strength and stamina, and then dancing for ever and ever, until the end of time. (1995a: 16)

Privately, then, Dikosha seeks to transcend her disempowered position within her society, for it is in privacy that she has agency. In 'devouring' the 'dancers of the world', she is destroying the power that 'the world' has attempted to exercise upon her. As a fierce dancer she aspires to eternal, self-contained power and the beauty of her own new culture. Thus, upon being urged to 'be a lady' by Radisene, she tells him flatly: 'You can be a lady if you want. I want to be a monster-woman-dancer' (1995a: 18).

In her critical engagement with past and present, and in her extreme responses to the structural inequalities of her society, Dikosha seems less to embody 'tradition' or 'the past', in the monolithic sense of the term, than she does an ever-increasing kind of constructive continuity (especially in her later reintegration into Ha Samane). This constructive continuity marks both an awareness of those elements of the past and present, which are surely worth salvaging (the paintings of the Cave of Barwa and her red dress from the lowlands, which she prizes), as well as a stringent critique of those elements that are culturally destructive. In short, Mda is asserting the centrality of *ritual* and individual engagement and choice in relation to both tradition and modernity in post-colonial cultural regeneration.

In its ability to account for the link between ritual processes (cultural generation) and agency, ritual theory is increasingly relevant to the study of peripheral post-colonial communities, such as the rural Lesotho that Mda depicts here. In his study of traditionalist, or 'red', Xhosa performance practices (about which Mda's *The Heart of Redness* is centrally concerned), Patrick McAllister uses Victor Turner's foundational theories of ritual and performance in describing them as ritual activities within post-colonial power dynamics. He summarises Turner's theoretical framework as follows: 'Turner's view of performance, ritual or otherwise, developed from the role of ritual as an aspect of the social process in the "social drama" where it served, in the "redressive" phase of the drama, as a mechanism for the resolution of conflict and social transformation through a realignment of social relations between individuals and groups' (2006: 68). Thus, Dikosha's break from her society is a social realignment, at least for her. Because she perceives her own inability to effect change or gain redress in the shared rituals of her community, Dikosha seeks individual social realignment by claiming private rituals in a private social space. Accordingly, she rejects all imposed human interaction as a means of escaping being ritualised and further subjugated within the traditional power relationships of Ha Samane:

> Dikosha was filled with love for the people of the cave and wished that she could spend all her days with them. She loved the peace that reigned among them. No voice was ever raised in anger, and they did not seem to know any form of violence directed at other human beings. Men did not deem themselves to be more important than women. There seemed to be an equality among them that did not exist in the world of Ha Samane. (Mda 1995a: 52–53)

Catherine Bell argues: 'The deployment of ritualization consciously or unconsciously is the deployment of a particular construction of power relationships, a particular relationship of domination, and resistance' (1992: 206). In ritual, then, power and creativity are inextricable elements. Dikosha's assertion of one of these elements necessarily implies the other. Her quest to create her own cultural identity necessitates that she 'devour' those that impede her progress. She achieves the means to accomplish this only through producing her own private space in which she is able to control both her empowerment and her creativity absolutely.

Dikosha's turn towards this private realm is necessitated by the hopeless corruption she perceives in the paternalistic power dynamics of Ha Samane. Her initial movement towards this realm is made after she is denied further education, but the particular nature of this destructive paternalism is evidenced throughout the novel. The wanton abuse of paternal power by her neighbour, Father-of-the-Daughters, serves as a prime example of both the complete inability of the people of Ha Samane to bring about change through its dominant rituals, as well as the paternalistic power of such rituals to entrench Dikosha's disenfranchisement.

Father-of-the-Daughters' destruction of Dikosha's productive relationship with Shana demonstrates the grounds for her aversion towards Ha Samane's society. Shana, the young wanderer who often accompanies Dikosha's inspired dances with his *sekgankula* instrument, takes up residence at the home of Father-of-the-Daughters. Unlike the other young boys that lodge at this house, Shana refuses to be of much help as a herd boy and is eventually relieved of his duties, being allowed instead to devote himself to playing his *sekgankula*. Eventually, Father-of-the-Daughters loses patience with Shana's indolence and he forces Shana to accompany him into the mountains to retrieve some cattle. Despite Shana's terrified resistance, Father-of-the-Daughters drives him along until Shana is struck down, strangled by the mist that envelopes him.

At the hands of destructive paternalism, Dikosha is robbed of the only individual in her world who shares her commitment to creation. Once again, as when she was denied the opportunity to further her schooling, she has been victimised by the unilateral paternalism of Ha Samane. What makes this loss even more bitter is the way in which the men of the village laud Father-of-the-Daughters at Shana's funeral when he recounts the events leading up to the boy's death: 'Men of the village made speeches in praise of Father-of-the-Daughters. They said his heart was made of gold, and he was a shining example to other wealthy people, for he had taken a poor motherless child and made him his own' (Mda 1995a: 168–69).

This is the suffocating climate of injustice from which Dikosha seeks to escape. Yet, the realm of privacy most closely achieved in the Cave of Barwa is the 'darkness' of the novel's title. In this sense, Mda casts Dikosha's attempted escape in ambiguous terms. Her site of greatest fulfilment, in which she agelessly experiences pure and beautiful relationships, is degenerative on a deeper level. Its greatest benefit is also its greatest fault – it is not *social*. In her quest for the self-contained aesthetic transcendence of her life station, Dikosha risks becoming fully enveloped by the darkness of isolation. Most importantly, this darkness evidences the socially untenable nature of Dikosha's attempted break with her broader community. She cannot possibly create a cultural identity only for herself. Ultimately, she must be part of the broader 'social drama', in Turner's terms, of her society.

The tendency for cultural innovators to seek isolation *and* to be culturally generative is a tendency long-recognised in Western scholarship on Africa. As Turner notes, reflecting on the role of creators in various African societies: 'Prophets and artists tend to be liminal and marginal people, "edgemen", who strive with a passionate sincerity to rid themselves of the clichés associated with status incumbency and role-playing and to enter into vital relations with other men in fact or imagination' (1969: 128).

While Dikosha's character is certainly marked by this desire to transcend her location within Ha Samane society, her darkness springs from her attempt to avoid re-entering this society through 'vital relations . . . in fact or imagination'. Although her imagination is certainly engaged in her private rituals, those painted figures that she attempts to engage with, while certainly very real to her, are ultimately powerless and subservient to 'the world' of people that eventually erase their images in the Cave of Barwa and cut off Dikosha's escape from social life. Dikosha's darkness is firmly rooted in her avoidance of socialisation. While motivated by her traumatic experiences of patriarchal oppression, this attempted escape is ultimately not a tenable solution to her grievances with her society.

Ultimately, Dikosha's ability to create such an entirely private realm of power and ritual is eroded. While she is soaking in the darkness of her cave, the paintings she communes with are deemed a national treasure and increasingly become a site of tourism. Yet, this tourism, rather than inspiring cultural advancement through communion with history and the beautiful, becomes a disaster for Dikosha as tourists increasingly take up the old colonial explorers' practice of scribbling their names on the walls of the cave, effacing the paintings and ultimately erasing Dikosha's ability to access their life-sustaining beauty: 'It finally happened. The people of the cave were totally imprisoned by the scribblings and graffiti on the sacred walls. Dikosha was powerless against the most powerful people in the land, and against the tourists from across the seas, who took their cue from the high and mighty and desecrated the cave with their vain names' (Mda 1995a: 128).

In this manner, the writing on the wall of the cave is truly the 'writing on the wall' in the idiomatic sense, forewarning the erasure of Dikosha's portal into a happier, more peaceful and, most importantly, aesthetically grounded productivity. Furthermore, Dikosha's private realm of ritual has proven to be ultimately transient. Society has encroached upon her rituals and revealed her activities to be, in fact, part of the broader changes or developments of her society.

As much as Dikosha unsuccessfully seeks to be autonomously self-sustaining, so is Radisene ultimately unsuccessful in his quest for purely personal wealth. He builds a fortune through heartless schemes, coercing widows and mortally wounded road-accident victims to sign away much of the sums they are due as third-party claimants on insurance policies. Yet, Mda's primary concern with the role of the artist (Dikosha) is evident in his portrayal of Radisene. Radisene, the businessman, serves more as a device through which to demonstrate the ultimate fruitlessness of an uncritical embrace of the individualistic materialism of modern life. His fortune is eventually lost when he is out-scammed by Nigerian fraud artists and he has virtually nothing further to share with Ha Samane. Even as his interaction with Ha Samane increasingly intensifies towards the end of the novel when he falls in love with Tampololo, one of the daughters of Father-of-the-Daughters, and comes home often in an attempt to enter into better relations with her father, his presence in Ha Samane serves as more of a sideshow than offering any redemptive social engagement. He attempts to engage in the local political frameworks, sitting with other men as they adjudicate civil cases, but with the ultimate effect of alienating himself further from Father-of-the-Daughters and Ha Samane as a whole.

While Dikosha is ultimately able to reintegrate herself back into her community with more success than Radisene, their mutual need for reintegration as citizens and as siblings is equal. Neither can ultimately escape this need. Unlike Dikosha, however, Radisene is unable to carry over anything of worth in his return to Ha Samane's social sphere. The constructive continuity so foundational to Dikosha's life through every phase of her development is ultimately rejected by Radisene. While he is certainly actively engaged in refashioning himself according to the material values of the lowlands, he lacks any historical continuity. Radisene does not have the courage to engage with history and thus exists in avoidance of it.

This is most evident in Radisene's long-time love of herding cattle. His most cherished activity when in Ha Samane is driving cattle along the hills with the sounds of his *lesiba* instrument. At the height of his wealth, Radisene rents cattle from locals in order to satisfy this almost insatiable desire to connect with the fulfilment he experienced herding cattle as a boy. This memory is where he, like Dikosha in her creative activities, tastes fulfilment. Although as a shrewd businessman he could certainly profit in the cattle business, Radisene ultimately denies herding cattle as a viable activity for a modern man such as himself. His aversion to his 'history' is simply too strong.

Here, Radisene and Dikosha's twinship arises as a crucial factor. In their respective quests to be 'self-made', they both refuse to be fully engaged in the rituals of their community. While, as will be discussed later, for Dikosha, this refusal is later supplanted by a more measured engagement with Ha Samane, Radisene's refusal to embrace his history and community is his lasting statement. In the end, each of these two characters is measured in terms of their ability to interact with the community of Ha Samane.

This leads to a more textured understanding of Mda's use of twinship, for it is evident that the twinship of Radisene and Dikosha is not only maintained between them, but also constituted in their respective twinships with Ha Samane. In this sense, they are both twinned twice – to each other and to their community. As they are not able to re-engage effectively with each other, remaining essentially split even when in each other's presence at the end of the novel, their twinships with Ha Samane prove to be the only basis on which the development of their respective characters, vis-à-vis Mda's humanistic vision, can be measured.

She Plays with the Darkness provides another character who seems to bridge the divide between individual and community, past and present, better than Radisene and Dikosha. This is the character of Misti, an age mate of theirs from the neighbouring village of Ha Sache. Misti is fortunate in that her family educates her, even sending her to complete her university studies. Through her intelligence and hard work, she is awarded a bursary to attain her B.Sc. in medical laboratory technology in Ireland. Misti returns and begins a successful career at a hospital in Maseru. Yet, she is eventually forced to confront the dualities of her identity when she is called by the ancestors to become a traditional *lethuela* diviner. Radisene, who has long loved her (before falling in love with Tampololo), is horrified, thinking that she is descending into murky mysticism and throwing away all the sacrifices made for her to become educated and prosperous. Misti's mother is equally distraught:

> Misti's father tried to comfort her: 'There is really nothing we can do about it, Mother of Misti. When the ancestors call, they call. You know that her grandmother, who died long before she was born, was a diviner too. She must be the one who is calling her to follow in her footsteps. We must be proud that she has chosen our child among all her numerous grandchildren.' (Mda 1995a: 120)

Misti's calling reveals a common element of twinship found in many of Mda's novels, the twinship between the past and the present. Mda maps this twinship most richly in *The Heart of Redness*, creating dual plots between ancestral and descendant pairs of brothers, continually reasserting the power of the past in the present. Although this notion of past-present twinship is invested here in a relatively more minor character, Misti's circumstances apparently rehearse it. Her grandmother has summoned her across time and brought her into the fold as her own twin – and it is vital that Mda does not ultimately constitute Misti's duality as irreconcilable. She exists fruitfully, impassioned and actively engaged in both aspects of her total identity, a prospect Mda maintains is possible given his assertion that Misti's character is directly based on a close personal acquaintance of his in Lesotho (MacDonald 2007).

It is tempting to read Misti as a corrective to both Radisene and Dikosha's tendencies towards isolation. As someone who is able to reconcile her status as a 'modern', educated individual with her place within her rural home village, she appears to resolve many of Radisene's conflicts. Misti is a model for the use of relative privilege in embracing twinship and bridging the divide between the claims of traditional and modern culture. But when compared with Dikosha, a severely underprivileged character, Misti serves less compellingly as an alternative model of action. First, without a family wealthy enough to initially sponsor her education, Dikosha could not have similarly gained a foothold in middle-class Lesotho. Dikosha's lack of agency seems to leave little room for gotiate her identity upon similar lines to Misti and she is thus compelled to reject her disenfranchisement by initially isolating herself. Secondly, and most importantly, Misti need not serve as a model for Dikosha's character because, unlike Radisene, Dikosha *does* eventually find some level of integration (though not complete) into Ha Samane. As an artist, Dikosha finds lasting value in her society, despite her disenfranchisement and her initial move towards isolation.

This level of integration and social as well as subjective fulfilment speaks of the need to actively create cultural identity in the post-colony. Stuart Hall has argued for such a process of re-creation that, while seeking the ever-deepening understanding of historical processes fundamental to post-colonial identity, is nonetheless also a process of continual creative regeneration. 'Cultural identity,' Hall states,

> is a matter of 'becoming' as well as of 'being'. It belongs to the future as much as to the past. It is not something that already exists, transcending place, time, history and culture. Cultural identities come from somewhere, have histories. But, like everything which is historical, they undergo constant transformation . . . Far from being grounded in mere 'recovery' of the past, which is waiting to be found, and which when found, will secure our sense of ourselves into eternity, identities are the names we give to the different ways we are positioned by, and position ourselves within, the narratives of the past. (1994: 394)

In this sense, Attwell's identification of Mda's affinity for the protagonist who is a maker of meaning is certainly applicable. Dikosha's role is not to fully *return*, but to build creatively on past traditions (both Barwa and Basotho) as well as the present through a process of selective elaboration. After all, not only does she commune with cave paintings and reclaim the house-painting techniques of Basotho traditions, she also loves her red dress from the lowlands. In Hall's terms, the 'narratives of the past' with which Dikosha is engaged are strands of both her own Basotho traditions and those of the absent creators of paintings of the Cave of Barwa. Dikosha seeks her identity through them in a 'non-instrumental' manner, but with ambiguous results until she is driven outward into Ha Samane by the loss of her paintings.

The ambiguity in which Mda casts Dikosha's position as an 'edgeman' raises an important point of difference between Hall's and Attwell's respective conceptions of a generative post-colonial modernity: for Hall, as much as this process is forward-looking and under 'constant transformation', it is always 1) communal, and 2) unavoidably also 'within' narratives of the past (1994: 394). As a communal experience, Hall describes post-colonial modernity as a process of broader 'cultural identity' formation, which takes precedence over any discussion of subjective experiences of post-colonial modernity. Furthermore, while subjects are able to 'position [them]selves within' the past, they are also 'positioned by' this past. There appears to be little room in such a theory for the activities of Attwell's individual modern creator. Attwell's conception is based on the vitality of individuals who are able to benefit broader society precisely by removing themselves from it. It is only from this distance that the creator can then produce meaning of strategic importance, unsullied by the subservience of the creator to the ritualising powers of the broader society.

In a sense, both positions hold sway. They respectively highlight different dynamics of Turner's conception of the culturally vital 'edgeman', the liminal and marginal figure who strives to free him-/herself of conventional social roles and rather 'to enter into vital relations with other men in fact or imagination' (1969: 128). While Attwell's notion of subjective creativity strongly supports Turner's insistence that such figures necessarily seek some sort of separation from the dominating structures of their society, Hall's interpretation further highlights the reintegration of such figures into society as they actively seek to influence its culture. In doing so, the 'edgemen' must necessarily engage in the structures (which are also structuring) of their society in order to take part in its transformation. There is no pure break available for the 'edgemen', for, at the very least, they must return into the fold of social relations to have relevance beyond their own darkness.

At the moment in which Dikosha realises the inevitability of her return into the fold of her society, she weighs the gravity of this shift: 'It was not only the death of the dance, but the death of a lifestyle as well. Her world and her life with the people of the cave had been destroyed for ever. She would have to find a new way of expressing herself and a new life in the world that was far away from this place' (Mda 1995a: 128). As terrifying as this prospect may be,

Dikosha re-enters Ha Samane society as a much more powerful force than she was when she attempted to extract herself from it. She creates a cabbage patch to feed herself now that she is no longer indefinitely sustained by her interactions with the cave paintings. While everyone in the village covets cabbages, none have ventured to grow their own before. This cabbage patch goes on to inspire a women's self-help movement: 'Women of the village had taken their cue from Dikosha's cabbage patch, and were cultivating cabbages, carrots and spinach in a communal garden. And they were doing this on their own, without anyone's assistance, unlike the lowland communal gardens which were supported by the Germans and the Americans and all sorts of white people who came from across the seas' (166–67).

In this manner, Dikosha certainly uses the unique perspective she has developed in her separation from the community to re-enter it with vitality. Dikosha has further cultural relevance as her contact with Ha Samane society grows. She resumes her youthful practice of attending dances throughout the area, once again establishing herself as the most prominent artist among all her cohort. She further takes on the practice of hearing the confessions of village men: 'In the darkness of her room they began to speak about their beautiful and ugly deeds, and to confess their dark secrets. She merely listened and said nothing. But when the men left they felt relieved' (Mda 1995a: 178).

Dikosha has become one of the key figures in the ritual activities of Ha Samane. McAllister states: 'Ritual involves an "interpretive re-enactment" of experience (Turner 1969: 82, 104) placing experience within the context of basic values and beliefs, allowing people to reaffirm these and adjust to changed circumstances' (2006: 68). What is Dikosha's role in hearing confessions but to enact this very process or ritual, in which subjective experiences are expressed and reflected upon by members of society? Although she does not verbally respond to these expressions, her availability, like ritual performance, functions as *the* site in which individuals seek to situate their experiences within the structures of their society. As Bruce Kapferer maintains, ritual is 'the universalising of the particular and the particularising of the universal' (quoted in McAllister 2006: 69) and the effect of the ritual is that Dikosha's confessors leave her room relieved at the new-found resolution of the 'indeterminacies of their social lives' (McAllister 2006: 69).

Dikosha's most powerful assertion of herself comes, though, after Shana's death, on the day of his funeral. As it comes to a close, Dikosha makes her statement on the matter through dance:

> Suddenly she jumped up and danced. The proceedings of the funeral stopped, as everyone watched her. She danced like a woman possessed . . . like the whirlwind of August. She raised helical dust to the skies, which could be seen for miles around. It was visible even in distant villages.
>
> She danced her last tribute to Shana. Then she walked away to her rondavel. People of the village applauded in spite of themselves. (Mda 1995a: 168)

Dikosha's dancing, which she honed as a girl and then alone in her darkness in the Cave of Barwa, is finally exercised in full force within a ritual context in Ha Samane. She has inspired recognition and possibly movement within the values of her community. As McAllister argues, despite the normative aspects of ritual, those which initially drove Dikosha into darkness, '[a]t times the development and outcome of the social drama involves revolution and reformation, developing and implementing new ways of acting and feeling, restructuring the old order if it is successful. Ritual performances are sometimes agents of change' (2006: 68).

She Plays with the Darkness thus seeks to provide a vision of the role of the marginal creator in bridging the dichotomies of post-colonial existence. Asserting the vitality of the creator of 'non-instrumental' art, Mda's Dikosha is the figure of the post-colonial cultural innovator: isolated yet vital, she necessarily attempts to disengage from the structures of her community in order to find a space of creative generation that will ultimately be of fundamental benefit to the process of transformation in her society in accordance with more humanistic values. Yet, as successful as Dikosha's ultimate reassertion of herself into Ha Samane proves to be, and as botched as Radisene's is, Dikosha and Radisene's lasting estrangement tempers the celebratory statements that the novel may be seen to make, pointing, rather, to a necessary reconciliation that has yet to be completed between these two characters. Mda ultimately asserts Dikosha's twinship with Radisene as an unavoidable aspect of their mutual identity that has been neglected to their mutual detriment. Thus, in the final pages of the novel they are symbolised by two odd doves feeding among a flock of chickens. 'Edgemen' in their respective contexts, Radisene and Dikosha are both necessarily split and twinned with each other and their other twin, their community. Yet, since these two 'doves' must ultimately feed together, as well as within their community, *She Plays with the Darkness* asserts the power of twinship and its humanistic implications, over the divisive forces of post-colonial modernity.

Note

1. An earlier version of this chapter was presented at the 2007 African Literature Association Annual Conference in Morgantown, West Virginia in the United States.

Works cited

Attwell, David. 2005. *Rewriting Modernity: Studies in Black South African Literary History*. Athens, OH: Ohio University Press.

Bell, Catherine. 1992. *Ritual Theory, Ritual Practice*. New York: Oxford University Press.

Hall, Stuart. 1994. 'Cultural identity and diaspora'. In: Williams, Patrick and Laura Chrisman (eds.). *Colonial Discourse and Post-Colonial Theory: A Reader*. New York: Columbia University Press, 392–403.

MacDonald, T. Spreelin. 2007. 'Unpublished interview with Zakes Mda'. 8 April.

McAllister, Patrick A. 2006. *Xhosa Beer Drinking Rituals: Power, Practice and Performance in the South African Rural Periphery*. Durham, NC: Carolina Academic Press.

Mda, Zakes. 1995a. *She Plays with the Darkness*. New York: Picador.

———. 1995b. *Ways of Dying*. New York: Picador.

———. 2000. *The Heart of Redness*. New York: Farrar, Straus & Giroux.

———. 2002. *The Madonna of Excelsior*. New York: Farrar, Straus & Giroux.

———. 2005. *The Whale Caller*. New York: Penguin.

———. 2007. *Cion*. Johannesburg: Penguin.

Turner, Victor. 1969. *The Ritual Process: Structure and Anti-Structure*. Chicago: Aldine.

8

Invidious Interpreters

The Post-Colonial Intellectual in The Heart of Redness

MIKE KISSACK AND MICHAEL TITLESTAD

IN HIS BOOK, *Africa in Modern History* (1978), Basil Davidson offers the useful distinction between a political and a social revolution in order to understand the main dynamics and challenges of the anti-colonial movement that emerged in Africa in the aftermath of the Second World War. Colonial powers, such as Britain, had defined their war aims in their conflict with Germany and Japan in terms of an historic confrontation between, on the one hand, the goals of democracy and individual liberty and, on the other hand, those of totalitarian collectivism and the erasure of individual freedom. In the wake of this momentous and historic struggle to preserve and extend the principle of self-determination for all, countries such as Britain had to confront the ideological inconsistency of preserving their imperial dominions, while simultaneously calculating the financial cost of sustaining their empires. In the latter part of the 1940s and into the 1950s, official sentiment in successive British governments concluded that the relinquishment of empire was the most expedient and commendable strategy to pursue. They had been influenced in their decision by the condemnation of colonialism emanating from the newly constituted United Nations, by the exigencies of post-war economic recovery and by the strident demands for independence emerging from the nationalist leadership in Britain's subordinate territories. By following a policy of relinquishing their empire, British governments thereby rendered their commitment to 'freedom for all' in the post-war world more credible and reduced the crippling burden of the financial costs of imperial administration.

Beginning with the Gold Coast (subsequently Ghana) in 1957, Britain transferred the control of its African possessions to nationalist governments, completing the process by the end of the 1960s, with the exception of Southern Rhodesia, where the transfer of control to a black majority government came as late as 1980, when Robert Mugabe was elected to power as the head of an independent Zimbabwe.

This kind of transfer of power to African nationalist parties constituted *a political revolution*, in that these new African governments and their people could now consider themselves to be the beneficiaries of what Isaiah Berlin calls 'negative liberty' (1969: 122). The term denotes the removal of the control and restraint of the colonial power from the affairs and future of the formerly colonised people (see also Taylor 1985). However, the corollary of this 'negative liberty', of this political revolution, is 'positive liberty', which is a much more challenging and sustained process, for it implies a *social revolution*, which is an engagement with the social reconstruction of the former colony in terms of the African nationalists' professed commitments to the principles of equity and justice, particularly if these are considered in terms of the fair distribution of wealth and the elimination of the oppressive and exploitative practices that characterised the colonial era. The attainment of political power must be complemented by its exercise for the social good of the people if the anti-colonial struggle is to have any substance, credibility and durability. If 'negative liberty' implies the removal of a colonial power's control and restraint, the opportunities that this removal provides for the new nationalist government have to be pursued in a responsible and accountable form of self-determination, thereby constituting a 'positive' exercise of power and liberty.

The politics of social reform, countering the legacy of colonial domination and pursuing a policy of social justice, are effectively the substance of what has been classified as 'post-colonialism'. Robert Young (2003) shows how the post-colonial era has been defined by the struggle of the people to realise the social ambitions articulated by their nationalist leaders in the years preceding the conferment of independence upon the colonies. Different groups have emerged to demand the reforms that would transform the quality of the social lives of ordinary people, focusing on questions such as land distribution and women's rights. These movements and causes must contend with the realities of civil war, the indifference and resistance of some of the new governing elites, many of whom have become complicit in the continuing exploitation of their countries' resources by international business interests, and with the tenacious opposition of cultural practices that have survived the years of colonialism and that refuse to abandon traditional social relationships after the termination of colonial rule.

Throughout most of Africa, the conclusion of the anti-colonial struggle witnessed the physical withdrawal of a colonial power from its former possession. South Africa constitutes one of Africa's conspicuous exceptions, both in the evolution of its colonial experience and in the resolution of its anti-colonial struggle. Interestingly, the formation of the Union of South Africa in 1910, comprising the four British colonies of the Cape, Natal, the Transvaal and the Orange River Colony, marked one of the earliest instances of qualified decolonisation in Africa. The Union signified the attainment of independence for the white members of a former British colonial possession, but it simultaneously impelled this white minority into a protracted struggle with the black majority who became its subjects in the new political dispensation. From the inception of the Union, the 'native question' became a paramount political concern, as black leaders (through the South African National Native Congress, formed in 1912, which subsequently became the African National Congress (ANC)) continually posed the question about when and how South Africa's black subjects would become South African citizens. This issue persisted throughout the decades of exclusive white political control, with its own complex permutations as the age of segregation (1910–48) evolved into the age of apartheid (1948–94), until the dynamics of the anti-apartheid struggle produced the first democratic election in South Africa in April 1994. This event marked the final resolution of the 'native question', as South Africa's black subjects were finally converted into citizens, implying the termination of subservience and the attainment of self-determination, epitomised by the acquisition of the franchise. The April 1994 election denoted the final and belated phase of South Africa's *political revolution*, as the representatives of South Africa's black majority assumed power from the last possessors of exclusive colonial control, the white minority.

Having assumed power through an unexpectedly peaceful process of political transition, the new ANC government, like other post-colonial administrations, faced the formidable task of implementing a *social revolution*, conducting the reforms necessary to counter the legacy of apartheid, consistent with its commitments to the general principles of democracy, justice and redress. Like all governments, the ANC is confronted by the task of converting its general principles and commitments into particular practices in specific situations and it is in such contexts that it confronts the reality of inherited beliefs, preferences and expectations, the very substance of regional and local politics. Such social configurations and alliances can constitute an enduring challenge to the implementation of social reforms and they frequently evince the tenacity of conservative inclinations. It is these inclinations that ensure that change is a protracted, conflictual and often painful process, guaranteeing that the transition from general policies to particular practices will be a gruelling one. Official aspirations to reform expose the limitations of conventional ways of understanding the situation, and make arduous demands on traditionalists for the revision of these perspectives.

The social revolution in *The Heart of Redness*

In post-apartheid South Africa, the focus and progress of the *social revolution* is not only the concern of political analysts, economists, philosophers and, of course, the expectant beneficiaries of the process, the people themselves, but also of literary figures, whose fictional portrayals explore the personal and immediate dimensions of this dynamic to reveal the fraught and paradoxical social complexities of the translation of policies of reform into practices of transformation. One such literary figure is Zakes Mda, whose novel, *The Heart of Redness* (2000), is one that presents a historically sensitive narrative about the experiences of the people of the Eastern Cape village of Qolorha-by-Sea as they face the prospects of change and transformation in the post-apartheid era. Mda establishes an engaging dialectic between retrospective evaluations and prospective visions as he reconstructs the momentous event of the Xhosa cattle killing of 1856–57, tracing the legacy of this event for the Xhosa inhabitants of Qolorha-by-Sea and portraying the constraints and limitations that this historical memory, with its attendant values and expectations, imposes

⟩

upon the present. In Mda's imaginative synthesis of historical reality and fictional construction, he presents us with a scenario of post-apartheid transformation, which is deeply cognisant of the constraining presence of the past on people's anticipations of a better future.

The Xhosa cattle killing of 1856–57 was an anomaly in the history of the subjugation of South Africa's independent black kingdoms, for it marked the self-destruction of the Xhosa polity, in contrast to the conquest of other powerful African kingdoms, such as the Pedi and the Zulu people, who were defeated in armed conflict with British forces in the late 1870s. This controversial and catastrophic event can be interpreted as a desperate attempt by the Xhosa people to secure deliverance for themselves from the cumulative pressure of frontier wars with white settlers on the Cape's Eastern Frontier, which deprived them of much of their traditional land and compressed them into the diminishing territory between the encroaching eastern border of the Cape Colony and the Pondo people to the east of the Xhosa. Diminishing resources and the prospect of final subjugation by the Cape's white colonists supported by regular regiments of the British army, combined with the affliction of lungsickness that decimated the Xhosa cattle herds, generated a chiliastic expectation that the Xhosa ancestors would intervene to expel the invaders from traditional Xhosa territory. This intervention was contingent upon the fulfilment of the ancestors' demand, communicated through the young prophetess, Nongqawuse, that the herds of cattle and stores of grain should be destroyed. The basic rationale behind this demand was that the fundamentals of social life and survival, the twin resources of cattle and grain, had been contaminated by defiled hands, particularly of those involved in practices of witchcraft, which is inherently divisive and destructive. Deliverance could only be effected once these contaminated assets had been purged, thereby meeting the conditions for ancestral intervention and the inauguration of a new, pure and liberated life for the Xhosa people. Compliance by believers in the prophecy resulted in a devastating famine and the Xhosa people were reduced to starving refugees who sought sanctuary in the Cape, thereby terminating their independence and reducing them to the status of subjects and servants in the white colony (see Peires 1989; 1990).

Not all the Xhosa people believed in the inspiration and credibility of Nongqawuse. Mda's novel presents a basic dichotomy between those who were

Believers in the words of the prophetess and those who were Unbelievers, narrating the story of how this cardinal event in the history of the Xhosa people, which culminated in their destruction as an independent people, endures in the memory of the survivors' descendants and defines their relationships of animosity in the post-apartheid village of Qolorha-by-Sea. Zim is a descendant of the Believers, who yearn for the days of Xhosa independence and Bhonco is a descendant of the Unbelievers, who deplore the folly of the Believers that resulted in the destruction of the Xhosa people. This definitive event continues to provide these contemporaries with their identity and with their interpretive perspectives on their situation and their prospects, all of which are crystallised through their incessant recriminations and expressions of regret for what the other failed to do. For the Believers, the ancestors refused to intervene to deliver the Xhosa people from their tormentors and oppressors because of the scepticism and recalcitrance of the Unbelievers, while for the Unbelievers, the gullibility and delusion of the Believers precipitated the total and gratuitous destruction of the Xhosa kingdom, a submission to the Cape under circumstances in which the Xhosa people had no bargaining power at all.

Camagu as secular intellectual
In *The Heart of Redness*, the figure of Camagu arrives in Qolorha-by-Sea, a poor Eastern Cape village, whose occupants are beginning to hope for a better future in post-apartheid South Africa, but who continue to see their situation in terms of the acrimonious legacy of the cattle-killing episode. Their preoccupation with an ossified interpretation of the past imposes limitations on their vision, perpetuating their rivalries and animosities, and curtailing their prospects for a better future. In creating the protagonist Camagu, Mda offers a portrait of an individual through whom the complexities of the post-apartheid *social revolution* can be explored and mediated. Camagu's disposition and contribution may be construed in terms of the notion of a 'secular intellectual', a concept derived from the work of Edward Said and a concise account of whose significance emerges in his Reith lectures, published as *Representations of the Intellectual* (1994), in which he offers a systematic exploration of the role of the contemporary intellectual in society. The brief title conveys a dual meaning, namely the way in which the intellectual is

represented to society by both his/her champions and detractors, and the way in which the intellectual represents social and political issues to the constituent members of society.

For Said, the notion of a 'secular intellectual' acknowledges that any intellectual endeavour occurs in a situated context. The practice of intellectual examination is inextricably located within a particular language, culture and society. To assimilate and deploy a language is a replication of its perspectives and cultural values, which are, in effect, both the enabling and limiting conditions of the activity of critique. It is this immediacy or immanence that constitutes the interminable challenge for the secular intellectual, for he/she has acquired his/her language's cognitive structures and evaluative preferences before he/she tries to effect some critical distance from his/her inheritance. The notion of a 'secular intellectual' implies the experience of immersion in a tradition, whose substance and influence are defined by its linguistic complexity, but the tradition does not offer the prospect of transcendence. As a situated individual, confined and constrained by a linguistic, cultural and historical inheritance, the intellectual strives to secure some critical distance from his/her own society's norms and conventions, while acknowledging the impossibility of complete detachment. For Said, this commits the intellectual to a life of 'exile', in which he/she conducts him/herself in an 'ironic, sceptical and playful manner' (1994: 45), resisting the temptations of cynicism. In doing this, the intellectual is situated between 'loneliness and alignment' (15), assiduously striving to formulate an unconventional or alternative interpretation of his/her collective circumstances and resisting the allure of conformity, which is not only easier but also often more profitable and less invidious. The exilic condition is invidious because it is agitational. It is a condition of 'being unsettled oneself, and of unsettling others' (39) and this process of intentional disruption is effected through the presentation of deliberate challenges to inherited forms of understanding, through a refusal to accept convention as justifiable normality or to accept traditional dichotomies as immutable verities.

Said contests the conventional notion that intellectual objectivity implies a detachment from any particular situation and the adoption of a neutral attitude towards controversial political issues. Citing the example of the famous French intellectual, Julian Benda, who denounced the 'treason of the intellectuals' ('la trahison des clercs'; see Said 1994: 4) in French society before the Second World War, Said exposes the spurious nature of any simple distinction between commitment and detachment. For Said, the situated, secular intellectual is under an obligation to intervene in his/her situation to effect social amelioration consistent with a concept of social justice for all. It is the breadth of one's vision and the inclusivity of one's ambitions that define the labours and interventions of the intellectual, not a resolute detachment and a refusal to participate in the political specificities of one's situation.

Although Said refers neither to the term, nor the context out of which it emerged, his discussion of the role of the contemporary intellectual in society is redolent of the ancient Greek concern with *phronesis*, a concept that evolved into Christian deliberations on the virtue of prudence. André Comte-Sponville (2003) explores the ethical significance of this term by reminding us that prudence complemented the cardinal Greek virtues of courage, temperance and justice. Its significance as a complementary virtue resides in its ability to translate a concern with general principles and prescriptions into concrete and specific actions, one of the most difficult challenges faced by those that adhere to any set of ethical precepts. Comte-Sponville writes: 'Prudence is the disposition that makes it possible to deliberate correctly on what is good or bad for man (not in itself but in the world as it is, and not in general but in specific situations) and through such deliberation to act appropriately' (2003: 32). This is, in effect, a concern with the indispensable features of practical wisdom that enable individuals to implement their moral convictions in particular circumstances, a translation of convictions into practices, which is a key consideration for any situated intellectual who tries to pursue his/her convictions in a socially specific environment. Prudence is a virtue of deliberation that delivers courage from irresponsible impulse and converts cowardly hesitation into informed and rational courage. Such a wise disposition is extremely difficult to attain, for it requires tenacity, resilience and experience, given that it is not a virtue that can be induced by the pursuit of ethical formulas that guarantee particular results. Prudence is developed and practised in situations of uncertainty and risk, always contending with the contingencies of the future, impressing upon any ethical aspirant, such as Said's 'secular intellectual', that one is continually subjected to the ironies and reversals of circumstances, which may confound one's intentions. Within such recurrent situations, one seeks a course between diffidence and arrogance, promoting a responsibly interpretive capability and eschewing any hubristically legislative role.

In *The Heart of Redness*, Camagu evolves into such an exilic and prudentially interpretive figure. Having been in literal exile in the United States for 30 years, where he graduated with a degree in communications and economic development, he returns to South Africa, but finds himself in a state of suspension after the elections of 1994. Although he is a returning exile, with a university qualification and the prospects of employment and promotion through the inception of a post-apartheid system of affirmative action, he does not seek to exploit such opportunities through processes of networking, but professes instead the value of opportunity open to talent and insists on obtaining positions through his own merit. Such a concern with more conventional liberal tenets estranges him from potential colleagues and benefactors, whose patronage he eschews because it would entail unacceptable subservience. Having returned to a liberated country, he finds himself disappointed with the realities of post-apartheid South Africa and is preparing to return to the United States when he is entranced by the voice of a singer, performing at a wake on the rooftop of a nightclub in Hillbrow. He discovers that her name is NomaRussia, and instead of returning to the United States, he follows her to the Eastern Cape village of Qolorha-by-Sea.

Camagu's arrival in the village inserts him into a situation in which his status as an outsider enables him to assess the traditional conflicts of the region with a certain detachment, but he is simultaneously incorporated into the skein of intrigue, suspicion and recrimination that defines the local politics of the area and he struggles continuously with the constraints and pressures imposed upon him by the ossified rivalries of the Believers and the Unbelievers. His arrival coincides with the prospect of imminent change in the area, as a business initiative seeks to establish a casino adjacent to the village. For some, such an initiative is emblematic of modernisation and progress, a qualitative development effecting a commendable change in the lives of a traditional community in the wake of the momentous *political revolution* of 1994. The prospect of this social transformation is, however, controversial, but the particular challenge resides in the terms in which its potential is debated. The disputes over the merits of this development are conducted in terms of the categories defining the rift between the Believers and the Unbelievers and Camagu, a reluctant party to the controversy, is impelled into a situation into which he attempts to inject some rational critique, but finds himself continually confronted by the obduracy of traditional perspectives.

To an increasingly complex extent, he becomes the embodiment of a 'secular intellectual' as he assesses the possibilities and constraints of his situation and contends with the consequences of his dissent. Thus, through his repudiation of the local inhabitants' categories of analysis, he incurs the antagonism of many of the leaders of local opinion in Qolorha-by-Sea. His refusal to align himself unequivocally with any one party to the controversy induces a sense of loneliness and frequent distress, as he enacts the condition of 'being unsettled, and unsettling others' through his individual reformulations of the implications of the debate about development and through his articulation of the moral and economic import of the different proposals for the region. As an outsider, thrust into a completely unexpected situation, which is the consequence of a more limited and personal pursuit of a romantic interest, Camagu finds himself occupying the role of an invidious interpreter. Partisans in the conflict seek his alliance, believing that his status as an educated man will enhance their cause and credibility.

However, his association with these partisans and his participation in their disputes stimulate Camagu's critical response and he confronts the recurrent experience of denunciation from those who think initially that he is a natural ally, but who come to construe his qualifications and criticisms as a betrayal of their cause. This isolation occurs because Camagu is a combination of diffidence and integrity. As an outsider, he does not presume to have a complete understanding of the situation and is, in fact, quite reticent and deferential in his relationships with the village's inhabitants after his arrival, before their demands for his assessment of the situation elicit a response from him. His integrity results in his producing a set of proposals for the economic and social development of the area that are consistent with his beliefs, but his subtle qualifications and individual interpretations become inadvertently antagonistic contributions to the debate.

In what kind of interpretive activities do these themes of diffidence and integrity emerge? Camagu is alerted to the historical rivalry between the Believers and the Unbelievers shortly after his arrival in Qolorha-by-Sea, but he quickly becomes aware that there is a new and equally divisive dichotomy emerging in the village, one that confusingly inverts the traditional nomenclature. He discovers that the contemporary ganglion in the village is the issue of economic development, focusing on the prospect of a new casino being constructed in the area. The historical Believers in the prophecies of Nongqawuse express themselves as Unbelievers in the promise of progress and change, while the historical Unbelievers in the prophecy become the Believers in modernisation. The respective adherents to the historical divide maintain their allegiances, but now the issue has changed, as has the designation of their factions in terms of the notions of 'belief' and 'unbelief'. As Camagu familiarises himself with both the historical and contemporary conflict, he must grapple with the categories of evaluation and recommendation in the specificities of his inherited situation, while simultaneously doubting and qualifying the terms of analysis and their implications for future action in Qolorha-by-Sea.

One of the most ardent proponents of development and modernisation is Xoliswa Ximiya, daughter of the leader of the historical Unbelievers in the village, Bhonco. As a Believer in the establishment of the casino at Qolorha, Xoliswa, a school principal, is the embodiment of a confident, rational and intransigent modernity. Her convictions are strident and unwavering, and she denounces her opponents as irrational apologists for the 'heart of redness', which is synonymous with adherence to tradition, superstition and obscurantism. In economic terms, she sees the establishment of the casino as an employment opportunity for the local population; in cultural terms, she sees the casino project as the advent of civilisation in what she disdains as a 'God forsaken place' (Mda 2000: 69) and she is dismissive of ecological objections to the impact of the construction on the natural environment, claiming: 'We cannot stop civilization just because some sentimental old fools want to preserve birds and trees and an outmoded way of life' (75). Camagu is initially intimidated by her virulence, finding it difficult to respond: 'even Camagu, with all his learning, cannot make up his mind' (104), although he experiences some intuitive reservations about her indomitable confidence.

Camagu's learning makes him neither confident nor arrogant, but his sense of diffidence is gradually dissipated as he is exposed to the multiplicity of perspectives on and interests in the situation in which he finds himself.

Qukezwa, daughter of the leader of the historical Believers, Zim, is the antithesis of Xoliswa and the embodiment of what Xoliswa would consider the 'heart of redness'. Without formal education and occupying a menial position in the village store, Qukezwa nevertheless articulates some challenging views on the prospects of the casino development and Camagu is influenced by her opinions. She denies that the project will provide employment opportunities for the local inhabitants, arguing that the developers will bring in their own labour and she claims that the project will deprive the local population of access to their traditional resources, forbidding them to swim at liberty in the sea and denying them access to the natural resources of the sea, such as the mussels and the oysters.

Camagu struggles to assess and reconcile these divergent perspectives on the situation, effectively deploying his understanding in a straddling and interpretive role that refuses to legislate and prescribe for others. Each of the antagonists, Xoliswa and Qukezwa, considers the other's views as typical of her background in historical Unbelief and Belief, but Camagu resists the constraints of these categories and judgements, seeking a different understanding of the situation. Interestingly, his interpretation of the situation is not confined to an abstract and conventionally intellectual critique, but is expressed through a series of actions that commit him, in a limited manner, to the economic transformation of the area and to a modified understanding of the politics of regional development. In this sense, he evinces some of the characteristics of a 'secular intellectual', who not only wishes to understand his situation, but also to influence and change it. His understandings are translated into action, but these evolve into invidious interpretations, as he incurs the disapproval of both the Believers and the Unbelievers. Xoliswa's father, Bhonco, comes to see him as a perversely retrogressive influence in the village because he does not offer his unqualified support to the party of progress, a disposition that Bhonco finds incredible in an educated man such as Camagu. Qukezwa's father, Zim, begins to see Camagu's proposals as those of an irreverent Unbeliever, who does not have any respect for the historical values and inheritance of his people. This dual opposition initially induces a resistance and resentment from Camagu, as he declares to Zim: 'I am not an Unbeliever. I am not a Believer either. I don't want to be dragged into your quarrels' (Mda 2000: 135), but he quickly realises that even if he can resist the pernicious system of historical classification, he cannot resist involvement and he will have to endure and contend with the consequences of their respective obloquy. He will interact with both to forge a new future and he becomes increasingly resolute as he declares to Bhonco and Zim: 'Neither of you must expect me not to be friends with the other' (165). Occupying the role and location of an intermediary, Camagu begins to experience the travails of a 'secular intellectual' who strives to understand his situation in a novel way and embarks on a course of action that will give effective expression to his hard-won reinterpretation.

As Camagu strives to understand the terms of the situation, in which he is initially an involuntary participant and with which he begins to contend by straddling the dichotomies of the historical divide, he not only grapples with an intellectual appreciation of his circumstances, but he also formulates a course of action that he considers to be a potentially beneficial one for many of the people of Qolorha-by-Sea.

He forms a tentative alliance with the owner of a trading store, Dalton, a descendant of a settler who established his commercial interests in the area after the cattle killing. Dalton is associated with the historical Unbelievers like Bhonco, but, with the emergence of the controversy about the establishment of the casino, Dalton declares himself to be resolutely opposed to its erection. Dalton's vision for the economic development of the area, and Camagu's engagement with him on this issue, further illuminate the complexities of the reconfiguration of the debate between the historical and contemporary Believers and Unbelievers, and help Camagu to crystallise his understanding of the situation and to pursue his proposals with confidence.

Although both Camagu and Dalton oppose the construction of the casino, it becomes apparent that their alliance is based on very divergent and potentially conflicting proposals, reflecting a completely different set of understandings about the culture, customs and identity of the region. It transpires that Dalton's vision is a retrospective one, while Camagu's engages with the difficulties of a perspective that continues to challenge the legacy of inherited categories and understandings. Dalton and Camagu continue to oppose the pressures of the developers and eventually succeed in warding them off by having the area declared a heritage site, but this victory consolidates a rift between them that is very important for the transformation and prospects of the area.

Dalton's preference is for the establishment of a form of cultural tourism that will capitalise on the historical experiences of the Xhosa people and on visitors' fascination with the tragedy of the cattle killing. He proposes the development of a 'cultural village' that will include dancers, stick fighting, original huts and traditional dress. Since Dalton has an association with the historical Unbelievers, his proposal antagonises the contemporary Believers in progress and modernisation, such as Xoliswa, who is appalled by his pursuits, which, she feels, simply perpetuate the historical shame of the Xhosa people and which impede the area's development into a modern society. Xoliswa's criticisms reflect the conventional wisdom of a modern Believer, but Camagu's response to Dalton, while also opposing his suggestions, is more nuanced and perspicacious than Xoliswa's.

Camagu's preference is for a form of ecological tourism, which would involve the promotion of ecological awareness, implying both the restoration and preservation of the flora of the area. Within this context, Camagu seeks the establishment of backpackers' venues, with trips around the heritage sites of Xhosa history. At first sight, there seems to be little to distinguish Camagu's proposals from Dalton's, with the exception that Camagu's seem to reflect a more contemporary concern with the issues of ecology. On closer consideration, however, there is a very significant difference, which reflects the two men's very different attitudes towards history, memory and culture, with implications for the identity, dignity and prospects of the people of Qolorha-by-Sea.

Dalton's concept of cultural tourism and a cultural village presents a focus on the past that panders to commercial interests, fosters stereotypes and impedes a critical engagement with the passage of time, subjecting a particular moment in the Xhosa people's history to an ossifying scrutiny and preservation that deprive them of any meaningful sense of historical evolution and transformational identity. It can be argued that the epithet 'cultural' in Dalton's reference to his concept of tourism and the traditional village is in fact a misnomer, for what he is invoking is the rather two-dimensional notion of 'custom', with its connotations of how a particular people used to live, dress and conduct their recreational activities and referring to vestiges of a way of life that has long since been eclipsed because the social, political and economic context and realities that gave them value and substance have been completely superseded by the dynamics of history.

Camagu's resistance to Dalton's proposals implies this kind of critique, for his focus is more on a veritable notion of culture, which respects the way in which the descendants of groups of people contend with the realities of their contemporary situation, taking cognisance of the inexorability and irrevocability of change, forging a system of values based on their current aspirations and seeking to develop a sense of identity, dignity and hope for the future. For Camagu, the relatively modest notion of ecological tourism offers this, for it acknowledges the momentous changes that have enveloped and overwhelmed the Xhosa people, assimilates the significance of this and seeks to proceed into an uncertain future – it is prospective, imaginative and anticipatory in its encounter with the contingencies of the future. It is an authentic engagement with cultural issues, in that it repudiates nostalgia and any sentimental attempt to preserve the vestiges of a superseded era; it proclaims the futility of trying to protect and perpetuate an allegedly immutable cultural essence, for it affirms the reality of irresistible change, claiming that culture orientates people towards the challenges of the present, addresses the problems of transmuted values and fosters the emergence of dignity in confronting an open future. For Camagu, and the project of ecological tourism, the past is to be remembered, not ossified and revered, while the present must be redefined and reinvented to provide people with the dignity of self-determination, forged within the confines and prospects of their present situation. The vision of ecological tourism can provide this, as it offers the people of Qolorha-by-Sea respectful and conservatory control over their own environment, enables them and others to reflect on the passage of history, with all of its turmoil, conflict and tragedy, through which the region and its inhabitants have passed, and permits them some independence in the construction of a new identity in a time of social transformation.

Camagu's perspective on the changes in Qolorha-by-Sea and its immediate environment is reflected in another conflict that he has with Dalton over the transformation of the village infrastructure. Dalton has been responsible for the provision of better water supplies, but he experiences some conflict with other advocates of modernisation, such as Bhonco, who applauds the provision of services, but does not feel obliged to pay for them. Although sympathetic to Dalton's frustrations, Camagu feels that part of the problem is that Dalton has conducted himself in the manner of a traditional benefactor, doing things *for* the people, but not *with* them. This is consistent with Camagu's view that a people's future, and with it their sense of self-determination and dignity, must be controlled by them – they cannot foster a new sense of cultural pride and confidence if they are simply the recipients of the benefits of another's expertise.

One can, in fact, construe some of the differences between Dalton and Camagu in terms of an illuminating distinction, articulated by some contemporary economists, between growth and development (for example, see Sen 1999). Growth refers to a preoccupation with the increase of material goods, with quantitative indices such as gross domestic product (GDP), while development incorporates this notion into a concept that respects the impact of these material concerns on the more intangible dimensions of culture, identity and dignity. Dalton's focus seems to be confined to the imperatives of growth, whereas Camagu's demonstrates a sensitivity to the complexities of development.

Camagu's provocative interpretations of his situation, which involve a reassessment of the area's legacy and a bold set of proposals for its future, extend beyond his recommendations for the project of ecological tourism. He also forms a co-operative with two women in Qolorha-by-Sea, who sell their catches of mussels and oysters to hotels in East London. Again, Camagu finds that his actions and their justifications are invidious, for Bhonco, leader of the historical Unbelievers, accuses him of embracing the legacy of historical Belief, initiating projects that appear to be inherently traditional and antipathetic to the cause of progress and modernisation. For Camagu, however, this kind of co-operative provides the individuals of the village with the opportunity to benefit from their immediate environment and to establish a commercial relationship with a more influential economic zone. Although simple, this kind of activity confers some dignity and financial independence on the women involved, as they pursue a semblance of self-sufficiency within an ineluctably changing situation. For Camagu, the categories of historical Belief and Unbelief fail to illuminate the situation and guide people into a salutary future, but rather obscure the options and deprive people of their opportunities to pursue a more self-fulfilling life.

He also extends his assistance to the two figures of NoGiant and MamCirha, helping them to establish a clothing co-operative, in which they provide traditional clothing for shops in Johannesburg. Xoliswa is predictably dismissive, telling her father, Bhonco, that Camagu is 'taking the village back to the last century' (Mda 2000: 261), thereby expressing a myopically complacent sentiment that fails to appreciate the subtlety of Camagu's interpretation and initiative. Consistent with the views expressed by Camagu in his criticism of Dalton's water project, Camagu is not doing anything for others, but helping others to do something for themselves, which again provides these two women with a dignifying sense of self-determination and self-sufficiency. The traditional clothes that they make are not an attempt to preserve a mythically static Xhosa identity in the way that Dalton's cultural tourism would, but rather a response to a commercial opportunity in the modern world, producing sartorial items that display artistic merits of their own.

Camagu straddles the traditional and the modern, incurring the wrath of the self-styled representatives of each perspective. Xoliswa's scorn emanates from her modern sentiments, while NoGiant's traditional husband expresses his disapproval for the co-operative project by setting their house on fire, destroying her cloth and equipment because he resents the financial independence that her participation in the project confers upon her. For NoGiant's husband, the project is not a traditional regression, as it is for Xoliswa, but an unacceptable disruption of a traditional power relationship in which he has always enjoyed supremacy. Camagu finds himself excoriated by the contemporary Believers and Unbelievers because his interpretation of the needs of the people in his situation antagonises the inherited understandings of both groups, but he is not prepared to try to comply with the tenets of either in order to obviate or placate their hostility. He is unsettled and he unsettles others, but for Camagu these are the imperatives of his situation as a secular intellectual; he is one who rigorously and courageously evaluates and modifies the inherited categories of understanding and who translates his understanding into actions that affect and transform his environment.

In the figure of Camagu, Mda provides a vivid portrayal of the constitutive features of a post-colonial intellectual confronting the dilemmas and challenges of a secular and protean world. Such intellectuals appreciate the constraints of their cultural, linguistic and historical inheritance, acknowledge the necessity for considered intervention, while simultaneously recognising that they can never occupy a position of scrutiny and influence that will secure complete consensus and evade the invidious consequences of their pronouncements, recommendations and actions. At best, they can strive to emulate the virtue of prudence, which attempts to translate the general precepts of a just and fair proposal into a concrete application in particular circumstances, knowing and anticipating that these will be provocative, antagonistic and transgressive. Such thought and action can never culminate in any final reconciliation or resolution, but must contend with the prospects of indefinite conflict, negotiation and reformulation, immersed in a process of continually reconfigured alliances and compromises as the task of social reform is conceived and implemented. Such a nexus is poignantly delineated in the concluding pages of the novel, in which Camagu visits Dalton, who has been assaulted by an aggrieved and resentful Bhonco, in hospital, where he discusses with him the prospects of the relationship between his system of ecological tourism and Dalton's network of cultural villages. The issue is raised, but Mda offers no account or promise of a consensual conclusion to their exchange, which remains implicitly fraught – Camagu, like the post-colonial intellectuals he represents, continues with the task of invidious interpretation.

Works cited

Berlin, Isaiah. 1969. *Four Essays on Liberty*. Oxford: Oxford University Press.
Comte-Sponville, André. 2003. *A Short Treatise on the Great Virtues*. London: Vintage.
Davidson, B. 1978. *Africa in Modern History: The Search for a New Society*. London: Allen Lane.
Mda, Zakes. 2000. *The Heart of Redness*. Cape Town: Oxford University Press.
Peires, J.B. 1989. *The Dead Will Arise: Nongqawuse and the Great Xhosa Cattle-Killing Movement of 1856–7*. Johannesburg: Ravan Press.
———. 1990. 'Suicide or genocide? Xhosa perceptions of the Nongqawuse catastrophe'. *Radical History Review* 46/47: 47–57.

Said, Edward. 1994. *Representations of the Intellectual*. London: Vintage.

Sen, Amartya. 1999. *Development as Freedom*. Oxford: Oxford University Press; New York: Knopf.

Taylor, Charles. 1985. 'What's wrong with negative liberty?' In: *Philosophy and the Human Sciences*, Philosophical Papers Vol. 2. Cambridge: Cambridge University Press, 211–22.

Young, Robert J.C. 2003. *Postcolonialism: A Very Short Introduction*. Oxford: Oxford University Press.

9

Culture and Nature in The Heart of Redness

HILARY P. DANNENBERG

'I am just saying I have a problem with your plans. It is an attempt to
preserve folk ways . . . to reinvent culture. When you excavate a buried
precolonial identity of these people . . . a precolonial authenticity that
is lost . . . are you suggesting that they currently have no culture . . .
that they live in a cultural vacuum?'

'Now you sound like Xoliswa Ximiya!'

'Xoliswa Ximiya is not capable of saying what I have just said. She
talks of civilization, by which she means what she imagines to be western
civilization. I am interested in the culture of the amaXhosa as they live
it today, not yesterday. The amaXhosa people are not a museum piece.
Like all cultures, their culture is dynamic.' (Mda 2003: 248)

THIS EXCERPT FROM a lively discussion on the culture of the Xhosa people
between Camagu and John Dalton in Zakes Mda's *The Heart of Redness* touches
upon many of the issues of culture at the heart of the novel: culture is both
dynamic and complex, and local cultures are irrevocably changed when they
come into contact with other cultures, notably when the other culture, be it
colonialism or the forces of economic globalisation, seeks a hegemonic position.
Nevertheless, as the extract from the novel above indicates, cultures are dynamic
and need not fear a loss of authenticity through the hybridisation that comes
with intercultural contact. Their dynamism makes them continually valid as

cultures, notwithstanding a loss of purity. Moreover, Camagu's words point to the fallacy of the neo-colonial mindset in which cultures are placed in a hierarchy around a Western-driven concept of a 'universal civilization' (Achebe 2001: 85), which orders and influences geographical territories and their cultures according to selective criteria, particularly technological or economic advancement.

In proposing a complex definition of the different levels contained within the concept of culture, Edward Said highlights one particularly hierarchical and selective way of understanding culture:

> Second, and almost imperceptibly, culture is a concept that includes a refining and elevating element, each society's reservoir of the best that has been known and thought, as Matthew Arnold put it in the 1860s . . . In time, culture comes to be associated, often aggressively, with the nation or the state; this differentiates 'us' from 'them', almost always with some degree of xenophobia. Culture in this sense is a source of identity, and a rather combative one at that . . . (Said 1994: xiii)

Mda's novel strongly counters such a culturally imperialistic and exclusive notion of culture in two different ways: first, *The Heart of Redness* provides counter-cultural narratives to those powering the colonial and neo-colonial cultural forces portrayed in the novel; second, it traces a complex network of intercultural dynamics, which in some ways subverts the idea of 'us' and 'them' by showing how both individual human beings and cultural narratives are affected by intercultural contact. In Mda's novel, the cultures of the Xhosa and Khoikhoi peoples, and the life stories of key characters within these cultures, are represented as particularly colourful and dynamic. The novel's emphasis on both colour and a knowledge and wisdom concerning the local natural environment are calculated precisely to counter the colonial idea of African culture as one of 'darkness' and as 'the antithesis of Europe and therefore of civilization' (Achebe 1990: 3), as is portrayed by Conrad's novella, *Heart of Darkness*, a text to which the title of Mda's novel refers.

The overall timeframe of *The Heart of Redness* makes it a significant *post-colonial*, as well as *post-apartheid*, South African novel. The central geographical location of the novel's two time levels is the village of Qolorha-by-Sea in the

Eastern Cape. The earlier time level, set in the mid-nineteenth century, depicts the invasion of the lands of the Xhosa people by the British. On the contemporary time level at the end of the 1990s, the people of Qolorha-by-Sea are also facing an invasion, but one in which they have a little more choice: they are debating whether to allow a new holiday and gambling complex to be built in their village and thus whether to allow their local culture and environment to be transformed in the hope of creating new jobs and technological progress. The apartheid period is only referred to obliquely as 'the sufferings of the Middle Generations' (Mda 2003: 3) and is not the focus of the text. Just as, in the excerpt that begins this chapter, Camagu advocates an orientation to contemporary Xhosa culture, so the novel itself focuses on issues facing contemporary South Africa and Africa as a whole within the wider historical and cultural context of colonialism, as opposed to the specific history of apartheid. The colonial time level often presents a deeply ironic study of the forces and effects of British colonialism in South Africa; the depiction of the cultural processes taking place in this earlier time level play an important role in the overall discussion of cultural interaction that the novel addresses. One of the key functions of the colonial time level is to underline the present-day dangers of embracing the neo-colonial forces of globalisation from the West; the novel does this by presenting the two historically separate invasions as analogically dangerous processes: 'Mda's intertwining of the two narratives, through both structure and characterization, highlights the key issues and demonstrates the intervention of the past in the present' (Bell 2003: 68).

In this chapter, I try to show how Mda's narrative succeeds in living up to its fictional hero's claim that culture is *dynamic* by tracing the many ways in which the novel depicts the forces and forms of culture and cultural interaction. Underlying the novel's complex and multi-levelled narrative, the local natural environment of the village of Qolorha-by-Sea itself provides a unifying and positive force and constitutes the novel's most powerful statement about the necessity of protecting local environments from the invasion of Western economic forces: 'There is dialogue between Qolorha (place and physical landscape) and the varied meanings and interpretations of the events that occurred there in the past . . . and the present reality' (Koyana 2003: 52).

As J.U. Jacobs observes in his analysis of the novel's structure, *The Heart of Redness* presents

... the dialectic between, on the one hand, *ubuqaba* (backwardness and heathenism) and, on the other, *ubugqobokha* (enlightenment and civilisation). Backwardness and enlightenment, and traditional belief and skepticism, are contrasted and relativised in both main narrative periods of the novel ... Both the 1856 and 1998 narratives are coded in terms of ambivalence and cultural heterogeneity that resonates back and forth between the past and the present. (Jacobs 2002: 230)

Mda's novel reflects the recognition that issues of cultural interaction and choice regarding cultural development are highly complex by representing both division and hybridity (see Feldbruegge 2004). The novel's intricate discursive and representational strategies embrace and reflect two different forms of cultural dynamic: contrast and confrontation, and the intermingling of cultures and cross-cultural influence. The argument that follows explores aspects of this complex structure, showing how, ultimately, the local colour and very specific natural environment of Qolorha-by-Sea emerge as a positive cultural and natural force, which provides a firm ground against which the shifting cultural dynamics of the text are enacted.

Cultural and rhetorical polarisations

On the novel's broadest historical scale, cultural interaction is represented as a tendential, hostile confrontation of different traditions. On both time levels, external cultures enter South African space and pose a threat to it. On the nineteenth-century time level, the novel sardonically and satirically presents the cultural imperialism and hegemonic ambitions of the British colonisers:

Sir George Grey ... had arrived with great enthusiasm with a mission to civilize the natives. Those amaXhosa who had become amaGqobhoka – the Christian converts, that is – believed in Grey ... He had been a governor in Australia and New Zealand, they said, where his civilizing mission did many wonderful things for the natives of those countries. Of course he had to take their land in return for civilization. Civilization is not cheap ... Grey believed that all men were equal – well, almost equal – as long as they adopted a civilized mode of dress and decent habits. (Mda 2003: 84–85)

Moreover, when Nongqawuse makes the prophecy that if the Xhosa kill all their cattle they will be saved by a new race of people who will come from the sea, the colonial intrusion is shown to have the effect of polarising the Xhosa people into the opposing camps of those who believe and those who do not believe in her prophecy: 'Believing brothers fought against unbelieving brothers. Unbelieving spouses turned against believing spouses. Unbelieving fathers kicked believing sons out of their homesteads. Unbelieving sons plotted the demise of believing fathers. Unbelieving fathers attempted to kill believing sons. Siblings stared at each other with eyes full of blood' (Mda 2003: 86).

The cultural processes taking place on the contemporary time level are depicted as being subject to the same dynamics of polarisation: the novel's parallel time levels therefore rhetorically enforce the equation of British colonialism with contemporary Western-driven globalisation, which is also represented as an external threat to local culture. By paralleling a nineteenth-century colonial invasion with a contemporary economic assault, Mda suggests that Western economic progress and the forces of globalisation should not be automatically embraced as bringing benefits but should, like colonialism, be treated with extreme caution and suspicion because they pose as much of a potential threat as they appear to offer benefits to local culture – precisely because of the power of such an invasion to permanently transform local cultures in the way that colonialism did. As Siphokazi Koyana observes: 'The casino project is without a doubt the strongest symbol in the village of Western capitalism as it is appropriated by blacks' (2003: 55). In the novel, the Unbeliever, Bhonco, is a fictional embodiment of what Chinua Achebe refers to as 'those who believe that Europe and North America have already invented a universal civilization and all the rest of us have to do is hurry up and enrol' (2001: 104). '"The Unbelievers stand for progress," asserts Bhonco, to the assenting murmurs of his followers . . . We want to get rid of this bush which is a sign of our uncivilized state. We want developers to come and build the gambling city that will bring money to this community. That will bring modernity to our lives, and will rid us of our redness"' (Mda 2003: 92).

Thus, as on the colonial time level, Mda represents the serious divisions at a local level, which are created by external cultural forces; as in the nineteenth century, the Believers and Unbelievers are polarised around the issue of how to deal with an invasion. Whilst the satirical subtext of Bhonco's words quoted above emphasises the negative aspects of blindly embracing 'progress', the novel does not present the issue in such clearly polarised terms. A greater initial ambivalence is achieved, above all, through the presentation of Camagu's own developmental story as a newly arrived stranger in Qolorha-by-Sea. Like many locals, he is initially perplexed about whether the Believers or the Unbelievers embrace the more sound position; the issue is thus represented as a serious dilemma and by no means as a foregone conclusion:

> It is difficult for many people to know which side to take. Even Camagu, with all his learning, cannot make up his mind . . . He has tried to observe the patterns of believing and unbelieving at this village, to try to make sense of them. And they remain beyond comprehension . . . Camagu concludes that these people select positions in such a way that they are never found to be on the same side on any issue. (Mda 2003: 91–92)

Camagu's observations here underlie another thrust of the novel's cultural observation – that cultural divisions and binary polarisations are not simply to be blamed on external forces, although it is sometimes a convenient explicatory strategy to blame external cultural factors, such as colonialism. Polarisation is here represented as being in the nature of human social interaction and politics – right down to the local level in Qolorha-by-Sea.

Camagu's decision-making process regarding the question of believing or not believing in *ubugqobokha* forms the central rhetorical structuring of the novel. This process is also intertwined with the love plot. Mda follows the highly effective strategy of firing the reader's interest via the love plot around Camagu and his quest for the 'right' woman in Qolorha-by-Sea, but combines it with the novel's key thematic and cultural concerns. While Camagu first arrives in the village in search of NomaRussia, whose singing at a Hillbrow wake enchants him, the subsequent narrative is structured around his dual attractions to two other women, Qukezwa and Xoliswa Ximiya, who come from Believer and Unbeliever families respectively. Mda orchestrates the confrontation of Believing and Unbelieving attitudes by creating a contrasting relationship between these two female characters, thereby underlining and reinforcing the ongoing debate about the desirability of embracing the new 'invasion'. The two women are clearly foil characters. However, whilst Xoliswa's values are represented in the same satirical tones as those used for her father Bhonco, Qukezwa's attractions and positive aspects are only gradually discovered by Camagu and revealed to the reader, so that ultimately both Camagu (literally) and the reader (rhetorically) are slowly seduced by Qukezwa and the natural world she represents.

Thus, in the initial description of Xoliswa, the values of Americanised or stereotypical Western culture are presented satirically and negatively. Her beauty is 'cold and distant'; she is attractive in *Western* terms: she is highly intelligent and ambitious, but cool in personality and angular in body: 'She . . . is quite tall and well proportioned – which is good if you want to be a model in Johannesburg, but works against you in a village where men prefer their women plump and juicy . . . people never stop wondering how she is able to walk among the rocks and gorges of Qolorha-by-sea in those high heels' (Mda 2003: 11). And later on:

> Camagu's eyes are glued on Xoliswa Ximiya. He does not remember seeing anyone quite so beautiful before. Her beauty exceeds that of the hungry women who are referred to as supermodels in fashion magazines. It is the kind of beauty that is cold and distant, though. Not the kind that makes your whole body hot and charges it with electric currents . . . If she could only bring herself to smile a bit. (Mda 2003: 64)

Even more than her father, Xoliswa's enthusiasm for Western culture, especially her deep admiration for US cultural icons, is represented in satirical fashion:

> Xoliswa Ximiya is more fascinated by the fact that the stranger [Camagu] was on his way to the United States of America. She informs him that he will be happy in that wonderful country. She herself has lived there, empowering herself with the skill of teaching English as a second language. It is a fairy-tale country, with beautiful people. People like Dolly Parton and Eddie Murphy. It is a vast country that is highly technological. (Mda 2003: 64)

In terms of the question of the new development project, Xoliswa argues wholeheartedly for the advantages that will come with modernisation, and disregards potential dangers to the local environment: 'You have seen how backward this place is. We cannot stop civilization just because some sentimental old fools want to preserve birds and trees and an outmoded way of life' (Mda 2003: 67).

Qukezwa, by contrast, is the antithesis of Xoliswa in every conceivable way; she does not embody contemporary Western norms of female attractiveness; she is not cool, but playful, physical, and earthy: 'Qukezwa smiles at him and impishly says, "I am not married." Camagu takes a close look at her, his eyes betraying his shock. She is short and plump. She wears a skimpy blue-and-yellow floral dress. Although she is not particularly beautiful, she is quite attractive' (Mda 2003: 56). Whilst Camagu is not immediately impressed by Qukezwa's appearance, by the end of the novel he has been seduced by her rebelliously free, colourful and creative spirit, and convinced by her arguments against the ideas of the Unbelievers and their conception of progress; in touch with the local environment, she introduces him to the natural world of Qolorha-by-Sea.

Camagu's responses to the two women thus plot his own cultural development in the novel. He establishes a cerebral connection with Xoliswa due to their shared knowledge of and influence by Western culture, but ultimately he becomes a captive of his fascination for Qukezwa. The struggle for these two cultural systems within his consciousness is represented as so complex that at one point he wishes, in vain, that he could find 'respite' 'in Xoliswa Ximiya's icy beauty' (Mda 2003: 152). This can be interpreted as Camagu's desire to cling to the value systems that he has imbibed during his long period of exile in the United States. In his first confrontation with Xoliswa's pro-Western thinking, the narrative makes it clear that Camagu by no means shares Xoliswa's enthusiasm for the United States: 'There is nothing wonderful about America. Unless you think racial prejudice and bully-boy tactics towards other countries are wonderful' (66). Nevertheless, the struggle to fully distance himself from Western cultural norms is represented as a difficult process: both his decision to side with the Believers and his developing feelings for Qukezwa are structured as a gradual, dialectical process and not as a conceptual and romantic fait accompli.

The Heart of Redness represents the choice between Western and local culture as one connected with one of the most fundamental aspects of human culture – clothing. The novel's emphasis on the cultural implications of clothing goes straight to the heart of its title. Xoliswa's high heels are a key part of her rejection of traditional Xhosa culture – above all the redness of traditional clothing – as being symptomatic of *ubuqaba* or 'backwardness', as represented by her mother:

> NoPetticoat is one of the *amahomba* – those who look beautiful and pride themselves in fashion. She is wearing her red-ochred *isikhakha* dress . . . To the *amahomba*, clothes are an art form. They talk. They say something about the wearer. But to highly civilized people like Xoliswa Ximiya, isiXhosa costume is an embarrassment. She hates to see her mother looking so beautiful, because she thinks that it is high time her parents changed from *ubuqaba* – backwardness and heathenism. They must become *amagqobhoka* – enlightened ones – like her. She has bought her parents dresses and suits in the latest European styles. (Mda 2003: 43–44)

In the novel as a whole, clothes do a lot of the talking – providing statements about characters' cultural positions and forming a central strand in the depiction of cultural confrontation. Thus, when, shortly after the passage above, the novel switches to the nineteenth-century time level, the same terms are repeated in the colonial context. Mhlakaza, or Wilhelm Goliath, as he calls himself in his temporary period of conversion to Christianity, preaches to his own people a combined and comically ridiculous message of Christianity and clothes culture:

> '. . . Do away with *ububomvu* or ubuqaba, your heathen practices, your superstitions, and become amaGqohoka . . . civilized ones . . . those who have converted to the path that was laid for us by Christ. Throw away your red ochre blankets! Wear trousers! Throw away your red isikhakha skirts! Wear dresses! For our Lord Christ died for us on the cross, to save us from eternal damnation.' (Mda 2003: 49)

Likewise, later in the novel, as the narrative of cultural choice and positioning plays itself out on the contemporary time level, the Ximiya family becomes divided by this very issue. Xoliswa's attitude to clothing initially marks her out as more radical than her Unbeliever parents; gradually, however, the positions of her parents polarise and this is again articulated through the culture of clothes:

> The Unbelievers stand for civilization. To prove this point Bhonco has now turned away from beads and has decided to take out the suits that his daughter bought him . . . From now on he will be seen only in suits. He is in the process of persuading his wife also to do away with the red ochre that women smear on their bodies and with which they also dye their isikhakha skirts . . . NoPetticoat must do away with this prided isiXhosa costume. But she is a stubborn woman. (Mda 2003: 71)

NoPetticoat's continuing choice of traditional clothing is symptomatic of her ultimately differing position within the cultural divide and foreshadows her later rebellion when she changes to the side of the Believers.

Cultural hybridisation and Mda's representation of cultural dynamics

In terms of its depiction of the interplay of overall cultural forces, the novel is thus structured around oppositional patterns, which are implied to be the combined results of the inherent polarising urge of human culture, the polarising effect of the invasion of local culture from outside, and the novel's overall rhetorical position, which inclines towards the position of the Believers on the contemporary time level. However, the novel's finer details and dynamics, notably the representation of many of its characters, reflect complex and ambivalent processes of cultural choice in individual life stories. Apart from certain key characters who fully take up one or the other position, notably Zim, Qukezwa and Xoliswa, the novel is full of characters who are bound up in a process of making cultural choices and are part of a larger process of cultural intermingling and hybridisation, the inevitable result of contact between different cultures. Mda's concept of cultural dynamics, which was expressed in the excerpt at the beginning of this chapter, is very much the result of an awareness of the fluidity of cultures arising out of colonialism, migration and the diaspora. It thus echoes post-colonial theories of hybridity born of a sense of the shifting constellations of cultural difference, as for example discussed by Hall (1993), Bhabha (1994), and Young (1995).[1]

Camagu's cultural position and his extended decision-making process constitute the novel's central exploration of culturally hybridised identity, but many other characters are bound up in analogous processes. As already indicated in the discussion of cultural polarisation through clothing, NoPetticoat (on the contemporary time level), and Mhlakaza/Wilhelm Goliath (on the colonial time level) are two characters who are caught up in the dynamics of cultural choice to the extent that they switch from one side to the other. On the colonial level, the life stories of the brothers Twin and Twin-Twin explore different aspects of cultural interaction. Twin decides to marry Quxu, a Khoikhoi woman (who is called Qukezwa by the amaXhosa (Mda 2003: 22) and henceforth retains this name), and in doing so alienates his brother Twin-Twin. This particular episode comes to a head when Twin becomes influenced by Qukezwa's Khoikhoi beliefs: ' "Now my brother dreams of foreign prophets that have nothing to do with the amaXhosa people . . . We have had our prophets. The prophets of the amaXhosa, not of the Khoikhoi or the abaThwa. We had Ntsikana and we had Nxele. What more do you want?" asked Twin-Twin' (75–76).

On the colonial time level, the novel thus represents the hybridisation and mutual influence of cultures as a complex process, with a character like Mhlakaza succumbing to the proselytising British Christians, and others like Twin crossing indigenous cultural borders. The intrinsic complexity of the colonial time level's multi-directional cultural interchange is embodied in the figure of Qukezwa. Not only is she criticised by Twin-Twin for bringing her Khoikhoi culture into that of the Xhosa people, but she is also lambasted by Twin-Twin because she is one of the 'Khoikhoi women [who] sold their bodies to the British soldiers in order to smuggle canisters of gunpowder to their fighting men' (Mda 2003: 21). The Khoikhoi woman Qukezwa is thus at the centre of an intercultural triangle in which she undertakes either voluntary or strategically necessary cultural mergings with both the Xhosa people and the British.

Despite his criticism of his brother's Khoikhoi wife, Twin-Twin is no less a victim of a complex cross-cultural dilemma. Twin-Twin takes up a firm position as an Unbeliever and rejects Nongqawuse's predictions. As a result, he ends up having to throw in his lot with Xhosa Christian converts. Like his brother's wife, in fact, he is forced to strategically have reluctant relations with the British:

> 'And these are your friends, my brother? These people who believe in the rule of the white man and in his god?' [Twin] asked mockingly.
>
> This made Twin-Twin very uncomfortable. His unbelief in the false prophets . . . had forced him to form a strange alliance with people who had deserted their own god for the god of the white man. People like Ned and Mjuza, who were descendants of amaXhosa heroes but were now followers of white ways. (Mda 2003: 85)

On the contemporary time level, John Dalton, a descendant of the Briton John Dalton who came to Africa as a coloniser in the nineteenth century, faces a different cultural predicament. Dalton is a white man with 'an umXhosa heart' (Mda 2003: 8) and he identifies with the Xhosa people of Qolorha-by-Sea much more than with his Anglo-Saxon counterparts. Thus, when, in the new post-apartheid climate of white nervousness, his ethnic compatriots are following the tribal and economic instinct to migrate to predominantly white former British colonies, such as Australia, Dalton continues to experience a sense of belonging to Qolorha-by-Sea:

> 'You are the only one who will remain in this mess, John . . . everyone is leaving.'
>
> 'Not everyone,' says Dalton, not bothering to hide his irritation. 'The Afrikaners are not leaving.'
>
> 'Do you fancy yourself as an Afrikaner, just because you married one?'
>
> 'I am staying here,' says Dalton. 'I am not joining your chicken run. This is my land. I belong here. It is the land of my forefathers.' . . .
>
> They can leave for all he cares. Yes, let them go. He does not need them. He has his community of Qolorha-by-Sea. And his wife's people. (Mda 2003: 139–41)

As on the colonial time level, contemporary Qolorha-by-Sea is represented as being the product of a dynamic mingling of different peoples. This is also made clear in the description of the different features that surface in individual faces through the mixing of genes:

> Zim, the leading light of the Believers, owes his existence and his belief to his great-grandfather, Twin, and Twin's yellow-coloured wife, Qukezwa . . . Zim himself is a yellow-coloured stocky man with the high cheekbones of the Khoikhoi. He has taken more from his great-grandmother's people. So have his children. Their Khoikhoi features were enhanced by their mother, NoEngland, who was from the amaGqunukhwebe, the clan that came into existence from the inter-marriages of the amaXhosa and the Khoikhoi people even before the days of Nongqawuse. (Mda 2003: 37)

Thus, as Jacobs notes, on the 1856 time level, 'Heitsi Eibib, son of Tsiqwa . . . is the bearer of the ancient traditions of both the Xhosa and the Khoi-khoi' (2002: 230). Moreover, on the contemporary time level, Qukezwa's son Heitsi – magically fathered by Camagu – will thus be a new blend of the already hybridised Xhosa and Khoikhoi, further mixed with Camagu's amaMpondomise blood and his transnational acculturations: 'The hybrid figure par excellence in the novel is only born at the end . . . paradoxically born to the sounds of the Believer-Unbelievers-division, the ululating and heckling' (Feldbruegge 2004: 82). The network of intercultural relations that the novel depicts is therefore intricate in terms of its overall structure and presents a highly complex dynamic of identity for many of the individuals concerned.

While, therefore, in overall global terms, the novel traces the confrontation of cultures, it also traces the complex and finer realities of this cultural interaction – above all in Twin, Camagu and John Dalton of the contemporary time level, who are all caught between the polarised fronts in some way and must make a decision. All these individual stories attest to the mixing of peoples and cultures that is the consequence of the confrontation of cultures that the novel also depicts. *The Heart of Redness* depicts both hybridisation and polarisation as a fact of life, offsetting the polarising aspects with the individual stories and choices that are made within the dynamics of cultural contact.

The Heart of Redness also explores the hybridisation of cultures as manifested by specific cultural narratives and belief systems.[2] Here Mda shows, sometimes ironically, the meeting of cultures as a mingling and sometimes bizarre misunderstanding and reassembling of narrative elements from other cultures and belief systems. The biblical narratives of the Christian religion are, for example, defamiliarised and undermined as part of Mda's critique of the British colonisation of Africa. However, Mda also traces the blending and interaction of different narratives of belief beyond the colonial context. On the colonial time level, for example, Twin is drawn towards the specific narratives of his Khoikhoi wife's culture:

> [Qukezwa] explained, 'To place a stone on this grave of Heitsi Eibib is to be one with the source of your soul.'
>
> 'How can one man have so many graves?' Twin asked.
>
> 'Because he was a prophet and a savior,' she said. 'He was the son of Tsiqwa. He lived and died for all the Khoikhoi, irrespective of clan.'
>
> Twin was sad that no one had ever died for the amaXhosa people in the same way that Heitsi Eibib had died for the Khoikhoi.
>
> At night she taught him about the stars . . . 'They are the seven daughters of Tsiqwa, the Creator. The Seven Sisters are the star mothers from which all the human race has descended,' she explained. (Mda 2003: 23)

The foregrounding of the Khoikhoi narrative of belief with its parallels to the Christian narrative of the crucifixion has the additional effect of displacing the narratives of the Christian missionaries, which also feature on the nineteenth-century time level. A complex dialogue of belief systems also occurs in a later conversation between the brothers. Speaking from a staunchly Xhosa perspective, Twin-Twin tells Twin: 'We have our own god. And he has no son either. Unlike the god of the white man or of your wife's people' (Mda 2003: 76). Here Twin associates the Christian and Khoikhoi belief systems with each other for his own rhetorical purposes. This association is immediately undone, however, by Twin, who 'replie[s] defensively, "Unlike the white people, the Khoikhoi did not kill the son of their god"' (76). This last point, that only the Christian religion is founded on the murder of the son of a god, is made repeatedly in the novel and underlines the intrinsically destructive elements upon which the Christian narrative is founded.[3]

Mda, however, not only defamiliarises and subverts the authority of the Christian narrative, but also traces the developmental dynamics of different strands of cultural narrative among the Xhosa people. Thus, because the news arrives that a nation called the Russians have dealt the British a decisive blow in the Crimea, the Xhosa of the nineteenth-century time level associate 'Russians' with the prophecies of Nongqawuse and believe that the Russians are a black people who will come to save them: 'Although the British insisted that they were white people like themselves, the amaXhosa knew that it was all a lie. The Russians were a black nation. They were the spirits of amaXhosa soldiers who had died in the various wars against the British colonists' (Mda 2003: 82). In this example, Mda shows how cultural narratives grow dynamically out of incongruous and chance elements; he underlines the basic human need to construct vital narratives of belief, even if these belief systems are objectively untrue: the narrative of salvation by a race of black Russians is a very powerful and real one for the Xhosa people, seen in the context of their hopes of salvation from the British.

A further key element of the dynamic blending of cultural narratives and belief systems in the novel concerns the question of the *origins* of narratives. This touches the question of the origins and originality of specific local cultural narratives and thus of each belief system's authenticity, authority and originality. Again Mda adopts various strategies that reflect a dual tendency to undermine colonial authority, but also show the interactive dynamics of human culture. For example, the narrative authority of the Christian religion is explicitly undermined by the novel's narration of a key episode in the history of the Khoikhoi people, in which the originality and authenticity of a Khoikhoi narrative in relation to the Christian one is underlined:

Heitsi. The one who parted the waters of the Great River so that his people could cross when the enemy was chasing them . . . the Great River closed upon the enemy. And the enemy all died . . . Camagu smiles to himself when he remembers how he learned all this from Qukezwa when she was teaching him about the sacred cairns. He also learned that the Khoikhoi people were singing the story of Heitsi Eibib long before the white missionaries came to these shores with their similar story of Moses and the crossing of the Red Sea. (Mda 2003: 249–50)

The question of the origin of Nongqawuse's prophetic narrative is subject to a more complex treatment on the nineteenth-century time level. Here Mda traces the different narratives and rumours created by the young girl's prophecy that the cattle killing would lead to a 'resurrection' (Mda 2003: 208) of the ancestors. While the use of the word 'resurrection' implies possible influence from Christian narratives, the text also presents various other interpretations of the origins and causes of Nongqawuse's prophecy. Thus, while Twin and the Believers see Nongqawuse's prophecy as central to Xhosa culture in terms both of belief and survival, Twin-Twin reads it as originating from quite a different source – British colonial policy. Twin-Twin holds the 'view that The Man Who Named Ten Rivers [Sir George Grey] had planned the whole cattle-killing movement. And that he had cleverly invented these prophecies and used Nongqawuse, Mhlakaza, and Nombanda to propagate them among the amaXhosa people. He wanted the amaXhosa to destroy themselves with their own hands . . .' (157). By contrast, commenting on Nongqawuse on the contemporary time level, Dalton reads the prophetess as 'a little girl who craved attention' and who 'decided to concoct her own theology', using the model of the Christian narrative of the resurrection (245–46). Camagu provides a less negative but at heart an equally relativistic interpretation: ' "She was a young girl, yes, and young girls are prone to seeing visions . . . Who's always seeing visions of the Virgin Mary? Young girls . . ." ' (246).

Nature in *The Heart of Redness*
Camagu's development from outsider to integrated member of the village of Qolorha-by-Sea forms the central narrative of the many narratives contained in *The Heart of Redness*. As stated above, Camagu is one of many characters who find themselves forced into a decision-making process within the overall phenomenon of cultural polarisation that the novel depicts. Camagu's story is one of multiple interactions of cultures. Ultimately, however, it is the forces of nature, the locality, sensuality and colour of place – personified by the attractions of the Qukezwa of the contemporary time level and reinforced by rhetorical elements in the discourse concerning the cultural forces and the

value of knowledge and education – which structure his decision-making process and power the novel's central statement about how to respond to the contemporary invasion by the forces of Western culture.

When Camagu takes a detour to Qolorha-by-Sea in search of NomaRussia at the beginning of the novel, he is about to leave South Africa and return to the United States because he cannot find a role to play in the political and economic circles of contemporary urban South Africa. While he is not a worshipper of the United States like Xoliswa, he is nevertheless a product of Western culture in so far as he has completed a doctorate during his years of exile and 'acquired so much knowledge in the fields of communication and economic development' (Mda 2003: 29). For this reason, he is by no means initially convinced of the Believers' case: 'Camagu wonders why the Believers are so bent on opposing developments that seem to be of benefit to everyone in the village' (71). It is only as a result of his deepening contact with Qukezwa that his attitude changes. As Qukezwa initially tells him, he is one of those, like Xoliswa, 'whose heads have been damaged by white man's education' (104). From this point, Qukezwa commences his cultural re-education in the realities of the local natural environment.

A key aspect of the figure of Qukezwa on both time levels is an affinity with and deep knowledge of the local environment, which are represented as the most positive forces in the novel because they provide a concrete framework for forms of action and orientation that stay true to the spirit – and needs – of the local community. Early in the novel, the Khoikhoi woman Qukezwa of the colonial time level is represented in terms of natural wisdom and knowledge which fascinates Twin when he first meets her:

'Tsiqwa is the one who tells his stories in heaven. He created the Khoikhoi and all the world. Even the rocks that lie under water on the riverbed. And all the springs with their snakes that live in them. That is why we never kill the snake of the spring. If we did, the spring would dry out.'

Twin was captivated by her wisdom. He did not let on that her words were beyond him . . . (Mda 2003: 22)

On the contemporary level, Qukezwa's knowledge and authority concerning the natural environment is also established. Early in the text, in an argument with Zim, Bhonco contrasts his daughter Xoliswa's advanced social status and education with that of Qukezwa in very negative terms: 'Those whose daughters are not secondary-school principals but sweep the floors of white people should stop talking nonsense' (Mda 2003: 45). However, by the end of the text, Xoliswa and Qukezwa's relative values to their communities and the role of formal education in this process have been radically reconstituted and Xoliswa has departed from Qolorha-by-Sea for good, leaving it to 'wallow in redness' (261).[4]

A key factor in Qukezwa's rise to a superior position in the novel's character constellation concerns the role of different species of flora in the local natural environment. In the novel as a whole, trees play a key role in Mda's textual evocation of the natural environment of Qolorha-by-Sea. There are frequent references to different types of trees in a variety of contexts. Twin and his wife survive by eating the bark of the 'mimosa tree, or the *umga*' (Mda 2003: 212) during the starvation period caused by the cattle killing; Zim is described as often sitting 'under his wild fig tree', which 'knows all his secrets' (38); an *umsintsi* tree is a site where the 'elders of the Unbelievers' hold a meeting (72); Qukezwa and Zim walk 'past *usundu* palms among the wild irises', while having a discussion (46). The *usundu* palm also plays a role in a description of the beauty of the natural environment of Qolorha-by-Sea as one of 'lush colour' (55), as narrated from Camagu's perspective, and Dalton is dismayed when 'a rare fig tree' is 'chopped down' (149). Moreover, the destruction of trees becomes part of the overall neo-colonial confrontation taking place on the contemporary time level. The Unbelievers talk about planting 'civilized trees . . . from across the seas . . . that have no thorns' (146) and the representatives of the development project (which calls for a large-scale cutting down of local trees), contemplate the possibility of building 'a retirement village for millionaires' in Qolorha-by-Sea, which they would call 'Willowbrook Grove': ' "We'll plant other trees imported from England. We'll uproot a lot of these native shrubs and wild bushes and plant a beautiful English garden" ' (202–03).

The tree motif culminates in the court case, or *inkundla*, which establishes Qukezwa's superior knowledge about the specific role of trees in her local environment. In a much earlier meeting with Camagu, she is depicted, from Camagu's perspective, as 'destroying . . . beautiful plants that have such nice purple flowers' (Mda 2003: 90). Camagu's response here, that Qukezwa's behaviour is wild and irrationally destructive, reflects his own state of underdeveloped knowledge with regard both to Qukezwa and the local environment. Qukezwa must enlighten him: 'This is the inkberry. It comes from across the Kei River. It kills other plants . . . And this plant is poisonous to animals too' (90). In the later court case Qukezwa gives an explanation to the village elders for her further apparent acts of vandalism:

'The trees in Nogqoloza don't harm anybody, as long as they stay there,' explains Qukezwa patiently. 'They are bluegum trees. The trees that I destroyed are as harmful as the inkberry. They are the lantana and wattle trees. They come from other countries . . . from Central America, from Australia . . . to suffocate our trees. They are dangerous trees that need to be destroyed.' (Mda 2003: 216)

Qukezwa is thus depicted as applying specific knowledge and observation of the local environment as part of a contemporary ecological form of post-colonial restoration of the Eastern Cape. While a character like John Dalton, the progeny of the former colonial invader, is depicted as being culturally integrated into the local community and no longer a threat, the battle is still being waged against the botanical descendants of the colonists.

The village accepts Qukezwa's argument and the court case against her collapses. The establishment of Qukezwa's practical knowledge of the environment goes hand in hand with Camagu's discovery of her personal attractions and those of the natural world of Qolorha-by-Sea, where he gradually puts down his own roots. On the level of the love plot, Camagu experiences Qukezwa as a colourful, natural, and erotic force:

Qukezwa sings in such beautiful colors. Soft colors like the ochre of yellow gullies.

Reassuring colors of the earth. Red. Hot colors like blazing fire. Deep blue. Deep green.

Colors of the valleys and the ocean. Cool colors like the rain of summer sliding down a pair of naked bodies . . .

'I love you, Qukezwa! I love you!' he shouts breathlessly.

'You know nothing about love, learned man!' she shouts back. 'Go
back to school and learn more about it!' (Mda 2003: 193–94)

In the dynamics of the love plot and the question of local versus Western
values, this passage is decisive. Camagu's sensual response to Qukezwa's singing
depicts her literally as the personification of local colour – not only of the
traditional redness of ochre, but of the variety of colours that the novel uses to
characterise the beauty of the local environment. It also shows Qukezwa
assuming a position of power over Camagu and demanding that he abandon
the kind of 'knowledge' that a Western education has given him because it is
less relevant for the local context. Here she actually taunts him for being formally
educated, stating that although he is much older than her, he still has a different
and more important kind of education to complete. Following this, the other
key component of Camagu's new education along local, natural lines concerns
his discovery of the sea and the wealth of its seafood through his visits there
with Qukezwa. This in turn leads to his initiative to found the seafood co-
operative with two local women. The sensual discovery, but also the practical
utilisation of the natural world of the sea, provides the final means for Camagu
to become established in the community.[5]

Qukezwa's influence on Camagu is thus that of the 'pedlar of dreams'
(Mda 2003: 36), which he feels he needs at an early point in the novel when he
is still disoriented and alienated in Johannesburg. By the end of the novel,
however, Camagu himself has been refashioned into the 'pedlar of dreams'
that he 'used to see himself as' (36) in that his initiative empowers the seafood
co-operative and other local impulses. Restored to a sense of local identity, he
is also given the role of articulating one of the novel's concluding statements
on the question of belief and the role of human 'dreams' in the context of
Nongqawuse's prophecies in another debate with John Dalton:

'Believers are sincere in their belief. In this whole matter of Nongqawuse
I see the sincerity of belief, John. It is the same sincerity of belief that
has been seen throughout history and continues to be seen today where
those who believe actually see miracles . . . What I am saying is that it
is wrong to dismiss those who believed in Nongqawuse as foolish,' says

Camagu. 'Her prophecies arose out of the spiritual and material anguish of the amaXhosa nation.' (Mda 2003: 245)

This statement recontextualises the question of belief as one that is directly linked to the material conditions under which people live.

Against the novel's vast and complex cultural-historical backdrop it is, therefore, the specific local and natural world that plays the decisive role in powering its argument. In the representation of the globalising Western forces of 'progress' and 'civilisation' versus local culture, the representation, appreciation and understanding of nature plays a key role. On the late twentieth-century time level, Qukezwa is the symbol of the awakening forces of the local world and the kind of advanced local cultural knowledge about the natural world that is most useful to local needs and is opposed to the infiltrating widespread norms of Western civilisation.

While it depicts the forces of cultural hybridisation and change as part of the relentless dynamics of human culture, the novel nevertheless states that when it comes to practical life and socio-political realities, there should be no Western-dominated cultural hybridising, since this will result in a process of assimilation into US-driven globalisation and the loss of both cultural identity and the specific local character of the natural world – embodied by the invading alien species of tree such as the wattle. *The Heart of Redness* therefore depicts the preservation of regional cultural identities as a necessity if local cultures are to protect themselves from larger globalising cultural forces and suggests that a clear sense of local cultural allegiance should override the kind of amorphous hybridity that is represented by the expanding and economically monopolising forces of Western culture.

Notes

1. 'The diaspora experience as I intend it here is defined, not by essence or purity, but by the recognition of a necessary heterogeneity and diversity; by a conception of "identity" which lives with and through, not despite, difference; by *hybridity*.' (Hall 1993: 401–02; emphasis in original)

2. Feldbruegge (2004: 73–80) explores forms of religious syncretism in *The Heart of Redness*.
3. See also Mda (2003: 259): ' "He [the god of the white man] is not powerful at all," said Twin-Twin dismissively. "Is he not the one who sat idle while the white people killed his son?" '
4. The relationship between Xoliswa and Zim's dead son Twin (Qukezwa's brother), which forms one of the novel's several background love stories, is also a story of estrangement through contrasting educational values: 'As time went on, Xoliswa Ximiya outgrew Twin as she became more educated' (Mda 2003: 43).
5. Camagu 'teams up with [the two women] in such a way that they use their knowledge of the sea to harvest the mussels and oysters, while he uses his knowledge of the city and markets to distribute the produce' (Koyana 2003: 54). Koyana also highlights the fact that 'one of the most remarkable aspects of successfully overriding the casino project is that the villagers challenge the practice of keeping Africans away from the beautiful beaches, as has been the case in South Africa for many years.' (55)

Works cited

Achebe, Chinua. 1990 (1988). 'An image of Africa: Racism in Conrad's *Heart of Darkness*'. In: Achebe, Chinua. *Hopes and Impediments*. New York: Anchor, 1–20.

———. 2001 (2000). 'Today, the balance of stories'. In: Achebe, Chinua. *Home and Exile*. New York: Anchor, 73–105.

Bell, David. 2003. 'The persistent presence of the past in contemporary writing in South Africa'. *Current Writing* 15(1): 63–73.

Bhabha, Homi K. 1994. *The Location of Culture*. London: Routledge.

Feldbruegge, Astrid. 2004. 'The representation of hybridity in Zakes Mda's *The Heart of Redness*'. Master's thesis. Leipzig: Institute of English Studies, University of Leipzig.

Hall, Stuart. 1993 (1990). 'Cultural identity and diaspora'. In: Williams, Patrick and Laura Chrisman (eds.). *Colonial Discourse & Postcolonial Theory: A Reader*. Hemel Hempstead: Harvester Wheatsheaf, 392–403.

Jacobs, J.U. 2002. 'Zakes Mda's *The Heart of Redness*: The novel as *umngqokolo*'. *Kunapipi: South Africa Post-Apartheid* 24 (1 & 2): 224–36.

Koyana, Siphokazi. 2003. 'Qolorha and the dialogism of place in Zakes Mda's *The Heart of Redness*'. *Current Writing* 15(1): 51–62.

Mda, Zakes. 2003 (2000). *The Heart of Redness*. New York: Picador.

Said, Edward W. 1994 (1993). *Culture and Imperialism*. London: Vintage.

Young, Robert J.C. 1995. *Colonial Desire: Hybridity in Theory, Culture and Race*. London: Routledge.

10

Community and Agency in
The Heart of Redness *and*
Joseph Conrad's Heart of Darkness

GAIL FINCHAM

ZAKES MDA'S WORK HAS elicited strong critical responses over the past decade. Rogier Courau, discussing 'literary and political historiography in the postcolony', draws attention to Mda's fusion of 'official history and community stories in the postcolonial context' (2004: 7) through his use of 'the speaking voice of a communal consciousness' (8), his ability to draw on the past to invigorate the present and his engagement in 'artistic and cultural translation' (12). Johan van Wyk speaks of what he takes to be a literature of transition marked by a 'resurgence of the repressed, loss of the reality principle, dream and mysticism' (1997: 80), while Margaret Mervis sees Mda as using a combination of 'Brechtian didacticism and indigenous African participatory story-telling' (1998: 55) that incorporates oratory and magic realism to move beyond anger arising from apartheid towards the reconstruction of individuals and their communities. David Lloyd discusses the 'polyphony of voices that allows Mda to present a richly complex and ironized debate about the issues facing contemporary South African society and its historical colonial antecedents' (2001: 35), while J.U. Jacobs, writing of the new Constitution's refusal to define Africanness by race, colour, gender or historical origins, points out that unlike the stereotyped figures of liberationist writers, Mda's characters are 'allowed . . . complex and (extra)ordinary individuality' (2000: 68). He also

191

draws on African music to show how 'Mda turns to traditional performance to mediate a culture in the process of transition and renewal' (2002: 227), arguing that *The Heart of Redness* is a 'split-tone narrative', employing a 'palimpsest structure'. Wendy Woodward shows how Mda as a post-colonial writer deconstructs Western dualisms in order to rehabilitate a traditional Xhosa worldview grounded in the 'contemporary issues of post-1994 South Africa' (2003: 173). She demonstrates the imbrication of place with identity in Mda's fiction and discusses his use of the Bakhtinian carnivalesque.

These writers insist on the importance for Mda of community,[1] history and memory in constituting post-colonial agency. Underlying their thinking is the concept, important from late 1996 onwards, of an 'African Renaissance', set out in visionary language and incorporating five crucial principles: 'the encouragement of cultural exchange; the emancipation of African women from patriarchy; the mobilization of youth: the broadening, deepening and sustenance of democracy, and the initiation of sustainable economic development' (Vale and Maseko 1998: 274).[2] Equally important in the aesthetics of liberation post-1994 is the work of the black South African writer Njabulo S. Ndebele. In *Rediscovery of the Ordinary* Ndebele critiques the writing of politically engaged South African writers of the 1970s and 1980s as a literature of spectacle:[3] 'I came to the realisation . . . that our literature ought to seek to move away from an early preoccupation with demonstrating the obvious existence of oppression. It exists. The task is to explore how and why people can survive under such harsh conditions. The mechanisms of survival and resistance are . . . far from simple' (1991: 158).

In this chapter I propose to juxtapose Mda's text of survival and resistance, *The Heart of Redness* (2000), described by David Attwell as 'the most ambitious work of fiction by a black South African writer in well over a decade' (2001), with Joseph Conrad's *Heart of Darkness*, written more than a century ago (1898). My purpose is twofold: to demonstrate Mda's post-colonial deconstruction of the tropes of empire and his redeployment of history to create a transformed African reality and to demonstrate Conrad's insight into the processes of colonial domination, which his protagonist Marlow simultaneously exposes and colludes with. I want to draw attention to salient similarities between Mda's and Conrad's texts: their rich intertextuality, their foregrounding of the importance of the reader's role in creating the meaning of the text, their interrogation of the binary thinking underlying Western thought and their exposure of colonial strategies of appropriation in mapping and naming. It is also worth exploring the contrasts between the texts' depictions of landscape (Conrad's chiaroscuro settings versus Mda's vibrant, colourful Africa), the divergent cultural significance of song and dance in both texts, and considering the dream-world, examining Conrad's departures from realism into surrealism and Mda's departures from realism into magic realism.

In the Dedication at the beginning of *The Heart of Redness*, Mda acknowledges J.B. Peires's book, *The Dead Will Arise* (1989), as the main historical source for the story of the prophetess Nongqawuse and the Xhosa cattle killing of 1856–57. His indebtedness to *Heart of Darkness* is equally obvious. Kurtz's postscript – 'exterminate the brutes' – is transferred to the beheading of Xikixa, ancestor of the Believers and Unbelievers of Mda's novel, under British colonial rule. Marlow's appalled vision of heads on stakes as he approaches the Inner Station in the Congo is echoed by Mda's chief protagonist, Camagu, who recoils in horror when he sees five dried-out heads of Bushmen in London's Natural History Museum and is equally shocked to discover that 'in Paris, the private parts of a Khoikhoi woman called Saartjie Baartman are kept in a bottle' (Mda 2000: 194). In these extracts, both Mda and Conrad interrogate the relationship between 'barbarism' and 'civilisation'. Other intertexts suggested for *The Heart of Redness* include Zoë Wicomb's *David's Story* (also written in 2000), with its protagonist's Griqua ancestry reverberating with Mda's fusion of Xhosa and Khoikhoi genealogies and Gabriel García Márquez's *One Hundred Years of Solitude*, with its magic realist narrative techniques (Jacobs 2002: 228). Intertexts for *Heart of Darkness* include works by Virgil, Dante, Goethe and Plato (Lothe 2001 and Fincham 2003). What the density of these intertextual connections foregrounds is a richness of figurative language, a juxtaposition of textual and cultural referents, and a deployment of irony and ambiguity that complicates the reader's response to both texts.[4]

Shared terrain
Both Mda and Conrad challenge conventional Eurocentric ways of reading. The narrative structure of *Heart of Darkness* undermines teleological readings

of history, for Marlow's journey, a travesty of the quest, is circular, ending where it began and recording a black hole at the centre of the story where – geographically and psychologically – Kurtz is situated. Where the frame narrator presents a version of history that is 'heroic, progressive, incontrovertible' (Fothergill 1989: 15), Marlow's narrative is fissured by hesitations and contradictions as his story poses moral and epistemological challenges to the conventional binaries familiar to Western thought: 'lightness/darkness . . . illumination/blindness, idea/idol, civilized/savage, conqueror/conquest, vital/ dead, and dream/nightmare' (22). Mda's narrative transposes this binary structure into the specifically African world, undermining 'dualistic . . . thinking about differences between the human and the nonhuman, as well as between the living and the dead, and the spirit world' (Woodward 2003: 183).

Neither text allows the reader to reach a centre; in both ironies proliferate. J. Hillis Miller has remarked that 'Marlow promises to pass . . . illumination on to his hearers . . . the fulfilment of this promise to reveal . . . remains always future, something yet to come, eschatological or messianic rather than teleological' (2002: 32–33). *Heart of Darkness* ends inconclusively, with Marlow unable to profit from his quest or to pass on comforting redemptive truths to the frame auditors or the reader. In fact, by the end of his story, the frame narrator, whose earlier pronouncements were so full of jingoistic confidence, has taken on Marlow's bleak focalisation, seeing the Thames as continuous with the Congo River: 'the tranquil waterway leading to the uttermost ends of the earth flowed sombre under an overcast sky – seemed to lead into the heart of an immense darkness' (Conrad 1946: 162). And what of Mda's central protagonist, Camagu? He has become, by the end of the novel, one of a 'little trinity' (Lloyd 2001: 38). United with Qukezwa, the modern reincarnation of the prophetess Nongqawuse, and father to a baby named Heitsi in honour of his Khoikhoi ancestor, Camagu appears to bring together Western know-how with African wisdom, 'the modernization of redness' (38). But this triumphant resolution is undercut by the novel's closing pages where the omniscient narrator records Camagu's pleasure at his integration into Qolorha-by-Sea, but issues a warning about the future:

[Camagu] feels fortunate that he lives in Qolorha. Those who want to preserve indigenous plants and birds have won the day there. At least for now. But for how long? The whole country is ruled by greed. Everyone wants to have his or her snout in the trough. Sooner or later the powers that be may decide, in the name of the people, that it is good for the people to have a gambling complex at Qolorha-by-Sea. And the gambling complex shall come into being. (Mda 2000: 319)

For Mda, as for Conrad, the self-identification achieved by his protagonist is individual and provisional; it does not guarantee closure.

Both texts are striking in the dramatisation of the strategies of mapping and naming by which the coloniser controls the colonised. Early in his story Marlow recounts how

when I was a little chap I had a passion for maps. I could look at South America, or Africa, or Australia, and lose myself in all the glories of exploration. At that time there were many blank spaces on the earth, and when I saw one that looked particularly inviting on a map . . . I would put my finger on it and say, when I grow up I will go there. (Conrad 1946: 52)

But by the time Marlow is old enough to become an explorer himself, the enticing blank space of his childhood dream 'was not a blank space any more. It had got filled since my boyhood with rivers and lakes and names. It had ceased to be a blank space of delightful mystery – a white patch for a boy to dream gloriously over. It had become a place of darkness' (Conrad 1946: 52). As David Spurr notes, 'the name of the principal blank space is repressed in Conrad's narrative, the name of Africa being everywhere displaced by the ambiguous and portentous phrase which serves as the title of the text. By means of this displacement of the referent, Africa is no longer bound in time and space, but becomes the *figure* of darkness and "nothingness"' (1993: 94; emphasis in original). Marlow does not recognise this suppression of the referent in the 'blank space' of Africa because as adventurer, he wants to insert himself there. He does, however, register the corruption of colonial appropriation, which turns the 'blank space' into 'a place of darkness'. But this recognition is short-lived, for in Brussels, visiting the Company offices prior to his departure for the Belgian Congo, he is once again stirred to excitement as he looks at the Company map and those places claimed by Britain in the scramble for Africa: 'there was a vast amount of red – good to see at any time, because one knows that some real work is done in there, a deuce of a lot of blue, a little green, smears of orange and, on the East Coast, a purple patch, to show where the jolly pioneers of progress drink the jolly lager-beer' (Conrad 1946: 55).

Of the map-as-logo in imperial cartography, Benedict Anderson writes illuminatingly:

> Its origins were reasonably innocent – the practice of the imperial states of coloring their colonies on maps an imperial dye. In London's imperial maps, British colonies were usually pink-red, French purple-blue, Dutch yellow-brown, and so on. As this 'jigsaw' effect became normal, each 'piece' could be wholly detached from its geographic context. In its final form all explanatory glosses could be summarily removed lines of longitude and latitude, place names, signs for rivers, seas, and mountains, neighbours. Pure sign, no longer compass to the world. In this shape, the map entered an infinitely reproducible series, available for transfer to posters, official seals, letterheads, magazine and textbook covers, tablecloths, and hotel walls. Instantly recognizable, everywhere visible, the logo-map penetrated deep into the popular imagination. (1983: 175)

Colonial cartography, then, not only imposed an alien identity on indigenous territory; its purpose was equally to sever that territory from everything that constituted its social and geographical identity. Colonial cartography replaced indigenous names with names of its own devising: in *Heart of Darkness* Marlow's first sighting of the African coast is of places 'with names like Gran'Bassam, Little Popo, names that seemed to belong to some sordid farce acted in front of a sinister back-cloth' (Conrad 1946: 61). Elsewhere I have argued for the intertextual significance of this portentous description, suggesting that Conrad intends us to recognise in it Plato's Cave and to understand his novella as a reverse parable, in which the coloniser is doomed to see only shadows on the wall while the colonised may escape from entrapment and delusion (see Fincham 2003).

In Mda's novel, the nineteenth-century chronotope is dominated by the governor Sir George Grey, 'The Man Who Named Ten Rivers'. This nickname is derisively given to him by the amaXhosa, who are well aware that 'he is a thief' (Mda 2000: 96). The omniscient narrator sarcastically remarks: 'Of course he had to take their land in return for civilisation. Civilisation is not cheap' and 'it did not matter that the forebears of those natives had named those rivers and mountains from time immemorial' (95). Grey's role in suppressing indigenous resistance becomes increasingly clear. Initially the trader Dalton had interpreted for Grey, claiming that he only wanted to spread British civilisation and bring peace to the area; but as the narrative progresses, The Man Who Named Ten Rivers is revealed as a systematic destroyer of Xhosa laws and customs, as he institutes a judicial system that suppresses them. Bringing to the area his experience in Australia and New Zealand, Grey offers the indigenous people not extermination, but assimilation. But after the cattle killing when thousands are dying of starvation, many are forced to work as slaves in white settlements, 'being paid only in food rations' (296). Grey's plan to turn the amaXhosa into 'useful servants, consumers of our goods, contributors to our revenue' (291) appears to have triumphantly succeeded.

Mda gets his own back on Grey, however: his novel is studded with Xhosa names for people and places that a European reader would not understand. Where *Heart of Darkness* dramatises cultural and linguistic imperialism in the names that the 'Pilgrims' give the indigenous population ('enemies', 'rebels', 'criminals'), Mda challenges his reader's historical understanding by using many of the same names in his novel's colonial and contemporary chronotopes. Where The Man Who Named Ten Rivers is revealed as a dangerous ideologue, Mda creates a powerful counter-voice in the prophet known by his people as 'The Man of the River'. Furthermore, Mda reappropriates the African landscape by giving his chief protagonist, Camagu, mystical, erotic dreams about rivers. These play a crucial role in his achievement of identity and his eventual incorporation into the Qolorha-by-Sea community. Mda's novel, then, is acutely aware of names as carriers of identity. Conrad's novella is no less so. Its only named protagonists are Marlow and Kurtz; the rest of the characters are defined by their roles. In the frame narrative, we have the Lawyer, the Accountant and the Director of Companies; in the Congo narrative, we have the Pilgrims, the

Chief Accountant, the Manager of the Central Station, the Harlequin, Kurtz's Mistress and the Intended. What these nominations centrally foreground is loss of agency: *Heart of Darkness* is peopled by characters whose identity is conveyed entirely through their (public and instrumentalising) function rather than through their individual voices.

Salient contrasts

There are several salient contrasts between Mda's and Conrad's texts, starting with their depiction of the African landscape. Mda's text is saturated with colour. There are the rocks around the sea at Qolorha-by-Sea where the women harvest oysters and mussels: 'Camagu is fascinated by the yellows, the brown, the greens and the red that have turned the rocks into works of abstract art' (Mda 2000: 118); there is Zim's tree, in which red and green and yellow birds live (41) and there is the village itself, which seems to Camagu on first arrival to have been painted by a 'generous artist . . . using splashes of lush colour. It is a canvas where blue and green dominate. It is the blue of the skies and the distant hills, of the ocean and the rivers that flow into it. The green is of the meadows and the valleys, the tall grass and the usundu palms' (61). In a striking synaesthesia, Qukezwa 'sings in glaring colours. In vibrant colours. Dreamy colours. Colours that paint nightmares on barren landscapes. She haunts yesterday's reefs and ridges with redness' (312). *Heart of Darkness*, from its opening paragraph, generates only black, white and grey. The instances of this evoked chiaroscuro are too numerous to discuss. Suffice to say that the same tension between darkness and light recurs on almost every page – in the frame narrative, in the central narrative, in Britain, Brussels and the Congo. Critics have made much of the systematic inversion of black/white stereotypes on which the story turns, but its lack of colour seems to me equally interesting. There are only two places where the text erupts into colour and both instances are suspect: the multi-coloured map in Brussels, as already discussed, and the gaily patched Harlequin with his bright red and blue pockets whom Marlow encounters as he approaches Kurtz's Inner Station. Neither of these epiphanies has any real connection with the African landscape. The map imposes falsely constructed identities on Africa; the Harlequin takes on an identity of shreds and patches that parallels his cultural and psychic emptiness, his spirit of adventure that connects to no principles or value systems other than that of fervent discipleship.

However, it is when we move to the cultural arena of song and dance and the unconscious arena of dreams that the differences between Mda's and Conrad's texts are most striking. Marlow, surrounded by what he experiences as primeval savagery, steels himself to resist 'going ashore for a howl and a dance' in the alien surroundings of 'an empty stream, a great silence, an impenetrable forest' (Conrad 1946: 93). When he catches sight of black people on the shore, his vision of them is both fragmented and paranoid:

> . . . there would be a glimpse of rush walls, of peaked grass-roofs, a burst of yells, a whirl of black limbs, a mass of hands clapping, of feet stamping, of bodies swaying, of eyes rolling, under the droop of heavy and motionless foliage. The steamer toiled along slowly on the edge of a black and incomprehensible frenzy. The prehistoric man was cursing us, praying to us, welcoming us – who could tell? We were cut off from the comprehension of our surroundings . . . They howled and leaped, and spun, and made horrid faces; but what thrilled you was just the thought of their humanity – like yours – the thought of your remote kinship with this wild and passionate uproar. (Conrad 1946: 96)

For Marlow, the antidote to regression to savagery is immersion in the conscious world of work – rivets, fixing the tinpot steamer, navigating among countless snags. He fears the unconscious world of dreams, fears libidinous atavistic excess once he succumbs to sleep. The dream is not a release. It partakes of the frightening isolation and solipsism that is the human condition: 'We live, as we dream, alone' (Conrad 1946: 82).

In *The Heart of Redness*, by contrast, dance and dreams play a central role. Camagu returns to Africa after 30 years' absence in the United States and was out of the country when the *toyi-toyi* dance became fashionable at freedom rallies. Consequently, he suffers from discrimination at job interviews, when potential employers enquire: 'Who is he? We didn't see him when we were dancing the freedom dance' (Mda 2000: 31).[5] If the *toyi-toyi* or 'freedom dance' has become the exclusive property of the 'Aristocrats of the Revolution' (36), dancing among the amaXhosa at Qolorha-by-Sea fulfils an antithetical function, uniting the community in a commemorative celebration of the ancestors. Here Mda achieves a remarkable cross-over between the Believers – the traditionalists – and the Unbelievers – those who want technological development. Both clans need to enact their connection to the past. Zim, patriarch of the Believers, sits under his wild fig tree, listening to the song of the birds. His tree is visited by the ancestors: 'there are four different kinds of ancestors: the ancestors of the sea, the ancestors of the forest, the ancestors of the veld, and the ancestors of the homestead. They are all regular visitors to the tree' (41). Similarly, Bhonco, patriarch of the Unbelievers, treasures the dance that has been taught to his followers by the original people of the area, the Bushmen or abaThwa, whose knowledge of local plants and animals is unequalled. The dance takes his people back to the land of the ancestors by inducing a trance, in which they experience a sadness that makes future happiness possible: 'Under the umsintsi tree the elders present a wonderful spectacle of suffering. They are invoking grief by engaging in a memory ritual' (83).

When, towards the end of the novel, the abaThwa threaten to take back the dance because the Unbelievers have become alienated from their traditions, Bhonco asks despairingly: 'How will the Cult of the Unbelievers survive without the dance?' (Mda 2000: 259). The novel insists on the cathartic function of grief and the centrality of memory in creating a community's future. Memory and grief are embodied in dance, for (as David Coplan points out) dance, like orature, makes meaning visible (see Jacobs 2000: 72). And as Mda points out: 'Among the marginalised and disadvantaged in the rural areas and in urban slums . . . art is still part of the common festival. We all sing and dance' (1994: 145). Equally, the world of dreams constantly intersects with the waking world, linking the present to the past. In the nineteenth-century chronotope, Qukezwa plays the *umrhubhe*, a musical instrument like the voice of mountain spirits, which 'creates a world of dreams' (Mda 2000: 177), particularly the vision of the new people who will arise from the waves and drive the colonists from the land. In the modern chronotope, the latter-day Qukezwa is angry that Camagu 'of late . . . has been featuring in her dreams. And she tells him so. She does not like that. He has no business imposing himself on her dreams' (196). For Camagu – like Marlow – dreams are connected with the sexual drive; Qukezwa has the power to sing him to orgasm. But his connection with her is ultimately healing, for she teaches him to understand himself and his new environment. By the end of the novel they have married and given birth (magically!) to a son.

The importance of the dream-world for the characters in *The Heart of Redness* derives from Mda's indebtedness to an African oral tradition[6] that frequently converges with what has been called, in the South American context, 'magic realism'. In an interview with Venu Naidoo, Mda stresses that his preoccupation with magic realism pre-dates his familiarity with Márquez and is specifically African: 'as Africans we always live with magic' (1997: 250), just as his use of a communal narrator derives from African oral traditions: 'this is how African people tell stories' (254). Insisting that he was writing in a magic realist mode 'long before [he] heard of the Latin Americans', Mda declares:

> In magic realism the supernatural is not presented as problematic, or as contradicting our laws of reason. It does not contradict empirical reality. It is not a matter of conjecture or discussion. It happens and is accepted by other characters and by the reader as an event . . . I wrote in this manner from an early age because I am a product of a magical culture. In my culture the magical is not disconcerting. It is taken for granted. No one tries to find a natural explanation for the unreal. The unreal happens as part of reality. The supernatural is presented without judgement. A lot of my work is set in the rural areas, because they retain that magic, whereas the urban areas have lost it to westernization. (Mda 1997: 281)

It was not until I read Theo L. D'Haen's essay, 'Magical realism and postmodernism: Decentering privileged centers' that I saw connections between Conrad's use of surrealism in the colonial context of *Heart of Darkness*[7] and Mda's use of magic realism in the post-colonial context of *The Heart of Redness*. D'Haen expands on Carlos Fuentes's insight that 'there [are] no privileged centers of culture, race, politics' (1995: 194). He explains: 'It is precisely the notion of the ex-centric, in the sense of speaking from the margin, from a place other than "the" or "a" center, that seems to me an essential feature of that postmodernism we call magic realism' (194). D'Haen sees magic realism as continuing the tradition of its progenitor, surrealism. He maintains that magic realism appropriates the techniques of the central line and then uses these 'to create an alternative world *correcting* so-called existing reality' (195; emphasis in original). What magic realism does, then, is to expose the fact that 'systems of generic classification are complicit with a centralizing impulse in imperial culture' (Slemon 1995: 408). It seeks to achieve 'psychic liberation from Old World domination and its cognitive codes' (413). Or as Brenda Cooper puts it: 'Magical realism at its best opposes fundamentalism and purity; it is at odds with racism, ethnicity and the quest for tap roots, origins and homogeneity; it is fiercely secular and revels in the body, the joker, laughter, liminality and the profane' (1998: 22). What these writers foreground is the literary technique of decentring, which is a key feature of both *Heart of Darkness* and *The Heart of Redness*. Where Conrad abandons realism to create surreal encounters – Marlow meeting the knitting women in Brussels, for example – it is precisely with this purpose of exposing the absurdity of colonial administration as dangerously self-absorbed and morally compromised. Mda uses magic realism to force the reader to suspend disbelief and to allow his characters – principally Camagu and Qukezwa – to transcend their physical limitations and access the visionary plenitude glimpsed in their dreams.

Conclusion

Conrad, a major metropolitan writer who remains always an 'outsider' in the country of his adoption, sees the coloniser in Africa as suffering from diminished agency and a loss of cultural community. Mda, as post-colonial writer, appropriates a profoundly colonial incident, which he recontextualises. He creates agency by reconfiguring history and invoking memory, insisting on the possibility of meaningful community. His project is not unproblematic in that it risks androcentrism and essentialism[8] in the gendered representation of the prophetess Nongqawuse in the nineteenth century and her reincarnation, Qukezwa, in the modern chronotope. Nevertheless, Mda creates a richly layered, vivid narrative that effectively 'writes back' to Conrad's dense, disturbing interrogation of 'barbarism' and 'civilisation'.

Notes

1. Several critics dispute what I see as Mda's evocation of the ideal of community. Grant Farred remarks that in *Ways of Dying*, 'Toloki the artist represents the benign face of postapartheid society's preference for the upwardly mobile black individual rather than the demands of the township masses; he is a character obsessed with creative expression and spiritual self-improvement . . . focused on the exceptionalism and singularity of the individual subject' (2000: 192). For Farred, 'Mda's novel may be said to enunciate the death of radical politics, of the commitment to transforming and materially improving the lives of the black underclass' (196). Konstantin Sofianos sees *The Heart of Redness* as attempting to reconcile not only Believers and Unbelievers, 'but more importantly the contradictions within the discourse of African Renaissance' (2004: 31). Sofianos remarks: 'It is a stark reality that the cumulative trickle-down prosperity prompted by the prophets of neo-liberalism and the free-market has remained as elusive in postapartheid South Africa as the sight of fattened cattle rising from the waves was in 1856–7' (35). He concludes: 'To speak with Benedict Anderson, the white middle-class is . . . invited to join the imagined community of the nation, but the price the text is willing to pay for this accommodation is the betrayal of those "co-operative" values it has invested with such redemptive possibilities' (38).

2. On Mbeki and a 'people-centred society', see also J.U. Jacobs (2000).

3. 'We can now summarise the characteristics of the spectacular in this context. The spectacular documents; it indicts implicitly; it is demonstrative, preferring exteriority to interiority; it keeps the larger issues of society in our minds, obliterating the details; it provides identification through recognition and feeling rather than through observation and analytic thought; it calls for emotion rather than conviction; it establishes a vast sense of presence without offering intimate knowledge; it confirms without necessarily offering a challenge. It is the literature of the powerless identifying the key factor responsible for their powerlessness. Nothing beyond this can be expected of it' (Ndebele 1991: 46).

4. Particularly useful for both texts is John Frow's definition: 'The concept of intertextuality requires that we understand the concept of text not as a self-contained structure but as differential and historical. Texts are shaped not by an immanent time but by the play of divergent temporalities' (Worton and Still 1990: 45).

5. 'Liberation movements have always been attuned to the importance of their cultural expression in the power of manifestos, speeches, slogans, songs and insignia. In South Africa, during the states of emergency in the 1980's, the *toyi-toyi* dance – a combination of traditional African rhythms and military drill – added movement to the spectacle of the political funeral at which the praise poet, in defiance of the police ringing the cemetery, would eulogise the fallen comrade' (Chapman 1998: 3).

6. 'Central themes in the oral traditions of southern Africa – in the tales, histories, heroic poetry and songs – have to do with tradition and freedom, and the implicit dilemma created in the conflict between the two concepts' (Scheub 1996: xxi). *The Heart of Redness* centrally addresses this conflict.

7. Conrad's work, in its swings between realism and romance, anticipates the surrealist movement of the 1920s with its emphasis on dream-like sensations and the expression of the subconscious. In Conrad, such distortions of reality verge on the grotesque and are consistently negative, whereas post-colonial writers employing magic realism do so to create a positive, transfigured reality.

8. On androcentrism, see Helen Bradford (1996); on essentialist depictions of women, see Dorothy Driver (1990; 1992). I see Mda's presentation of Nongqawuse's story as problematic in two areas: she is 'voiced' by a male omniscient narrator and the elements of male sexual transgression contained in her narrative are, as in traditional accounts, simply omitted. In linking Qukezwa in the modern chronotope to the prophetess Nongqawuse in the colonial chronotope, and in attributing to both figures an essentialising identity that links women to nature rather than culture, Mda would seem to repeat uncritically 'the rigid categories passed down to us in different versions of patriarchy' (Driver 1990: 253). Editors' note: see also Meg Samuelson's chapter, 'Nongqawuse, National Time and (Female) Authorship in *The Heart of Redness*', in this volume.

Works cited

Anderson, Benedict. 1983. *Imagined Communities: Reflections on the Origin and Spread of Nationalism*. London: Verso.

Attwell, David. 2001. 'Mda turns to Nongqawuse for inspiration'. *The Sunday Independent*, 28 January.

Bradford, Helen. 1996. 'Women, gender and colonialism: Rethinking the history of the British Cape Colony and its frontier zones'. *Journal of African History* 37: 351-70.

Chapman, Michael. 1998. 'The aesthetics of liberation: Reflections from a southern perspective'. *Current Writing* 10(1): 1-16.

Conrad, Joseph. 1946 (1898). *Heart of Darkness*. London: J.M. Dent and Sons.

Cooper, Brenda. 1998. *Magical Realism in West African Fiction: Seeing with a Third Eye*. London: Routledge.

Courau, Rogier. 2004. 'Re-imagining community histories in the South African fiction of Zakes Mda'. Master's thesis. Durban: University of KwaZulu-Natal.

D'Haen, Theo L. 1995. 'Magical realism and postmodernism: Decentering privileged centers'. In: Zamara, Lois Parkinson and Wendy B. Faris (eds.). *Magic Realism: Theory, History, Community*. Durham: Duke University Press, 191-208.

Driver, Dorothy. 1990. 'Women as mothers, women as writers'. In: Trump, Martin (ed.). *Rendering Things Visible: Essays on South African Literary Culture*. Johannesburg: Ravan Press, 225-55.

————. 1992. 'Women and nature, women as objects of exchange: Towards a feminist analysis of South African literature'. In: Chapman, Michael, Colin Gardner and Es'kia Mphahlele (eds.). *Perspectives on South African English Literature*. Johannesburg: A.D. Donker, 454-74.

Farred, Grant. 2000. 'Mourning the postapartheid state already? The poetics of loss in Zake
    Mda's *Ways of Dying*'. *Modern Fiction Studies* 46(1): 183–206.
Fincham, Gail. 2003. '"Heart of Darkness" and Plato's *Republic*: A reverse parable'. *L'Epoque
    Conradienne* 29: 95–109.
Fincham, Gail (ed.). 2001. *Conrad at the Millennium: Modernism, Postmodernism, Postcolonialism*.
    Boulder: Social Science Monographs; Lublin: Marie Curie-Sklodowska University.
Fothergill, Anthony. 1989. *Heart of Darkness*. Milton Keynes: Open University Press.
Jacobs, J.U. 2000. 'Zakes Mda and the (South) African Renaissance: Reading *She Plays With
    Darkness*'. *English in Africa* 27(1): 55–74.
————. 2002. 'Zakes Mda's *The Heart of Redness*: The novel as *umngqokolo*'. *Kunapipi* 24(1 &
    2): 224–36.
Lloyd, David. 2001. 'The modernization of redness'. *Scrutiny2* 6: 34–40.
Lothe, Jacob. 2001. 'Cumulative intertextuality in "Heart of Darkness": Virgil, Dante, and
    Goethe's *Faust*'. In: Fincham, Gail (ed.). *Conrad at the Millennium: Modernism, Postmodernism,
    Postcolonialism*. Boulder: Social Science Monographs; Lublin: Marie Curie-Sklodowska
    University, 177–97.
Mda, Zakes. 1994. 'Learning from the ancient wisdom of Africa: In the creation and
    distribution of messages'. *Current Writing* 6(2): 139–50.
————. 1997. 'Acceptance speech for the Olive Schreiner Prize (1997)'. *English Academy Review*
    14: 279–81.
————. 2000. *The Heart of Redness*. Oxford: Oxford University Press.
Mervis, Margaret. 1998. 'Fiction for development: Zakes Mda's *Ways of Dying*'. *Current Writing*
    10(1): 39–56.
Miller, J. Hillis. 2002. 'Should we read "Heart of Darkness?"' In: Fincham, Gail (ed.). *Conrad
    at the Millennium: Modernism, Postmodernism, Postcolonialism*. Boulder: Social Science
    Monographs; Lublin: Marie Curie-Sklodowska University, 21–41.
Naidoo, Venu. 1997. 'Interview with Zakes Mda'. *Alternation* 4(1): 247–61.
Ndebele, Njabulo S. 1991. *Rediscovery of the Ordinary: Essays on South African Literature and
    Culture*. Johannesburg: COSAW (Congress of South African Writers).
Peires, J.B. 1989. *The Dead Will Arise: Nongqawuse and the Great Xhosa Cattle-Killing Movement
    of 1856–7*. Johannesburg: Ravan Press; Bloomington: Indiana University Press; London:
    James Currey.
Scheub, Harold. 1996. *The Tongue is Fire: South African Storytellers and Apartheid*. Madison:
    University of Wisconsin Press.
Slemon, Stephen. 1995. 'Magic realism as postcolonial discourse'. In: Zamara, Lois Parkinson
    and Wendy B. Faris (eds.). *Magic Realism: Theory, History, Community*. Durham: Duke
    University Press, 407–26.
Sofianos, Konstantin. 2004. 'Formal politics and informal settlements: The realism of Zakes
    Mda's *The Heart of Redness*'. Unpublished senior research project. Cape Town: University
    of Cape Town.
Spurr, David. 1993. *The Rhetoric of Empire: Colonial Discourse in Journalism, Travel Writing, and
    Imperial Administration*. Durham: Duke University Press.

Vale, Peter and Sipho Maseko. 1998. 'South Africa and the African Renaissance'. *International Affairs* 74(2): 271–87.

Van Wyk, Johan. 1997. 'Catastrophe and beauty: *Ways of Dying*, Zakes Mda's novel of the transition'. *Literator* 18(3): 79–90.

Woodward, Wendy. 2003. '"Jim comes from Jo'burg": Regionalised identities and social comedy in Zakes Mda's *The Heart of Redness*'. *Current Writing* 15(21): 173–85.

Worton, Michael and Judith Still (eds.). 1990. *Intertextuality: Theories and Practices*. Manchester: Manchester University Press.

Zamara, Lois Parkinson and Wendy B. Faris (eds.). 1995. *Magic Realism: Theory, History, Community*. Durham: Duke University Press.

11

The Ecological Imperative in The Heart of Redness

HARRY SEWLALL

And for all this, nature is never spent.
(Gerard Manley Hopkins, 'God's Grandeur')

Ecological awareness, then, will arise only when we combine our rational knowledge with an intuition for the nonlinear nature of our environment. Such intuitive wisdom is characteristic of traditional, nonliterate cultures, especially of American Indian cultures, in which life was organized around a highly refined awareness of the environment. (Capra 1983: 25)

IN THE OPENING paragraphs of *Cry, the Beloved Country*, Alan Paton sententiously proclaims of the land: 'Stand unshod upon it, for the ground is holy, being even as it came from the Creator. Keep it, guard it, care for it, for it keeps men, guards men, cares for men. Destroy it and man is destroyed' (1958: 7). The land, as a primordial symbol in humankind's struggle for survival, finds a deep resonance in the South African literary imagination. It is a potent metaphor of possession and dispossession, colonisation and oppression, and it has been explored in the works of writers as diverse as Paton and Zakes Mda, and J.M. Coetzee and Nadine Gordimer.

Mda's novel, *The Heart of Redness*, is very much about society and its relationship to the land. While the main theme of the novel derives its impetus from the plot involving the prophetess, Nongqawuse, and the tragic episode of the cattle killings in the Eastern Cape in the mid-nineteenth century, its secondary theme is energised by the dialectic between the demands of metropolitan culture on the environment and the ecological injunction to 'guard it [and] care for it' in the quasi-religious sense of Paton. Linked to the earlier plot of the inappropriate thaumaturgical response of the ancestors, with its catastrophic consequences, is the modern-day debate of their descendants about the development of the pristine real estate of Qolorha-by-Sea. Just as the ancestors were locked in a self-destructive, ideological struggle with the British almost 150 years previously – a struggle emanating directly from the political issue of land possession – the post-apartheid generation is implacably split over the future of the seaside paradise.

This chapter, located within an ecocritical matrix, proposes to explore the tensions in Mda's novel occasioned by the historical clash of ecological ideologies, juxtaposed with the exigencies of metropolitan life on the present generation. In presenting a revisionist reading of the historical event described in early school texts as the 'national suicide' of the amaXhosa, Mda also recuperates the nature-culture dialectic to demonstrate how binaristic responses to this debate can be reconciled by the recognition of the need for a symbiotic balance between nature and culture, on the one hand, and modernity and tradition, on the other hand.

In his poem, 'God's Grandeur', composed in the latter part of the nineteenth century, Gerard Manley Hopkins wrote about the depredations of Western society's materialism on the resources of the earth. Lamenting that '[g]enerations have trod, have trod, have trod' upon this earth, to the extent that 'all is seared with trade; bleared, smeared with toil;/And wears man's smudge', Hopkins ends his poem on an optimistic note, affirming his undying faith in 'the Holy Ghost' to regenerate the environment (1994: 26). More than a century after Hopkins's assertion that 'nature is never spent', we cannot be easily solaced by the grand narrative implicit in his reassuring theophany. As one newspaper caption proclaimed recently, we confront the frightening prospect of 'using up the Earth faster than it can regenerate' (Fowler 2004: 2).

According to a report by the World Wildlife Fund: 'We are running up an ecological debt which we won't be able to pay off unless governments restore the balance between consumption of natural resources and the Earth's ability to renew them' (quoted in Fowler 2004: 2).

In the last three decades, the public has become increasingly aware of the impact of the greenhouse effect on our environment and of how the destruction of the ozone layer, and the consequent warming of the atmosphere, is already upsetting the ecology of the Arctic region. The world's governments, prompted by their scientists, have recognised this threat to our existence and have periodically sponsored conferences on this theme. In the face of an ecological crisis that threatens our existence on this planet, the actions of certain governments, such as the United States under President George W. Bush, become incomprehensible. Bush's refusal to sanction the 126-nation Kyoto protocol in 2001 was based on the argument that curbs on greenhouse gas emissions would be too costly for a nation such as the United States. Arguing in support of the United States, which is the world's top polluter, The Competitive Enterprise Institute maintains that while the United States may be wasting a lot of the world's resources, the country is also producing far more of the world's resources (Fowler 2004: 2). Such an argument is not only specious but also points to the need to recognise the impact of developed and developing nations on the ecological landscape of our planet and to find a balance between the demands of metropolitan existence and the imperative to conserve and protect our environment.

What, one might ask, has this preamble on the state of the planet got to do with a reading of Zakes Mda's *The Heart of Redness?* Such a question, rhetorically, goes to the very heart of the ongoing debates about the status and ontology of literature in contemporary society and academe, as well as its hermeneutics. It also intersects with the fraught issues of the role of the environment in literary texts and the legitimacy and viability of ecocriticism as a mode of intervention in literary studies. At a conference of the Association of University English Teachers of Southern Africa held at the University of Zululand in 1992, Ivan Rabinowitz declared:

In order to explore the intersections of literature, nature and the environment, we shall have to theorize a genuinely post-colonial version of cartographic semiosis, the study of the relation between the act of mapping and the negotiation of territory and identity. Our pure and timeless texts will have to be read as cultural signs which point to a narrative of possession, appropriation and epistemic aggression; our maps, including our maps of time and the material body, will have to be reinterpreted as hybrid texts and as forms of cultural inscription. (1993: 23)

This conference, the first of its kind on the subject of ecology in the discipline of English studies in South Africa, was themed 'Literature, Nature and the Land: Ethics and Aesthetics of the Environment'. Considering that in the United States the first Modern Language Association (MLA) session on ecocriticism was only held in 1991 (see Glotfelty and Fromm 1996: xvii–xviii), the South African endeavour must rank as a landmark achievement. Rabinowitz criticised the sterile orthodoxies of the New Critical literary culture, hence his ironic allusion to 'pure and timeless texts'. Whether Mda's *The Heart of Redness* will prove to be a timeless text is for history to decide, but hybrid it certainly is, and it fits the bill as a post-colonial literary document that satirically explores, among other issues, the epistemic aggression of the early colonisation of South Africa, particularly the Eastern Cape region, and the ecological implications of this event for the present generation of protagonists in *The Heart of Redness*.

The history of the cattle killings has been well documented in South African historical texts. In recent times, the story of Nongqawuse has been viewed from alternative standpoints, both historically and fictionally. J.B. Peires has attempted to answer why the amaXhosa in the late nineteenth century were prepared to listen to a prophetess:

The Cattle-Killing cannot be divorced from the colonial situation which was imposed on the Xhosa in 1847 by Sir Harry Smith. Although it has been necessary in this history to examine the personal role of Sir George Grey in detail, it should be remembered that the essential objectives of Grey were identical to those of Smith and of colonial rule generally: to destroy the political and economic independence of the Xhosa . . . to make their land and labour available to the white settlers, and to reshape their religious and cultural institutions on European and Christian models. (1989: 312–13)

Peires further draws attention to the fact that the idea of cattle killing had been widespread before Nongqawuse started to speak. The existent religious belief was a strange mix of Xhosa cosmology, according to which the dead do not die, and the Christian notion of resurrection, a belief popularised by the prophet Nxele before 1820. So, Nongqawuse's ideas were not original. The logical conclusion was therefore that the sick cattle, once destroyed, would be resurrected. In Mda's novel, 'lungsickness' is thought to have originated in Europe: 'It was brought to the land of the amaXhosa nation by Friesland bulls that came in a Dutch ship . . . in 1853. Therefore even the best of the isiXhosa doctors did not know how to cure lungsickness' (2000: 55).

A decade before Peires's historical account of the cattle killing, the narrator-protagonist of one of Mtutuzeli Matshoba's short fictional works presented a dialectical view of the Nongqawuse story in one of his reflections as he journeys to the Transkei, the newly created Bantustan of the apartheid government: 'In order to understand my interpretation of past and present events in relation to each other, I think it is necessary to review the tale I heard from my instructional voices' (1979: 164). Matshoba depicts Nongqawuse as a young, idealistic maiden who dreams of the emancipation of her downtrodden people. In his highly polemical rendering, the land policy of the British government was continued by the Union Government's introduction of the Natives Land Act of 1913. According to Anne McClintock, through the Land Acts of 1913 and 1936, 'a scant 13 percent of the most arid and broken land was allocated to black South Africans, though they comprise 75 percent of the people' (1995: 324). In a similar way to Matshoba, Mda provides a revisionist reading of this tragic event, presenting both sides of the story, so that neither the Believers nor the Unbelievers are essentialised (see Jacobs 2002: 232). In *The Heart of Redness*, this double-voiced perspective is provided by the character of Camagu, 'the hybrid, mimic man' (Sewlall 2003: 342), who has obtained a doctorate in communications in the United States and is neither a Believer nor an Unbeliever: ' "What I am saying is that it is wrong to dismiss those who believed in Nongqawuse as foolish . . . Her prophecies arose out of the spiritual and material anguish of the amaXhosa nation" ' (Mda 2000: 283).

That Mda's text recommends itself as an exigent site for an ecocritical investment is borne out by a recent study by Wendy Woodward. Coupling *The Heart of Redness* with two other southern African texts, Woodward locates her study in the comparatively new field of Animal Studies. While her focus is on the interaction between humans and animals in these literary works, the general tenor of her argument, especially in its exploration of the symbiotic relationship between two generations of Xhosas with their cattle and birds, intersects with some of the main concerns of my project. She goes to the core of the cattle-killing controversy when she draws attention to the belief of the ancestors that 'these slaughtered cattle would be resurrected and new ones come from the spirit world [illustrating] the sacred nature of these animals within the amaXhosa worldview' (2003: 302). In a similar vein, David Lloyd makes the following observation about Zim, the head of the modern generation of Believers (or traditionalists): '[Like] the traditional Xhosa, he perceives sacredness in nature. He is so much a part of the natural world that he can talk with birds' (2001: 36).

To the literary critic, actions such as communing with birds and animals, as instantiated also in Mda's *The Madonna of Excelsior* (2002), where Niki shares an uncanny relationship with her bees, would fall within the realm of magic realism. But in Mda's work, the world of magic interfaces seamlessly with the world of reality, so much so that its presence in his writing does not obtrude as a stylistic mannerism, but is consonant with the worldview of the amaXhosa. In his acceptance speech for the Olive Schreiner Prize in 1997, Mda drew attention to the fact that he was still at high school in Lesotho when he wrote the play *We Shall Sing for the Fatherland* (1990),[1] which presents the interaction between the living and the dead:

> I wrote in this manner from an early age because I am a product of a magical culture. In my culture the magical is not disconcerting. It is taken for granted. No one tries to find a natural explanation for the unreal. The unreal happens as part of reality. The supernatural is presented without judgement. A lot of my work is set in the rural areas, because they retain that magic, whereas the urban areas have lost it to Westernization. (Mda 1997: 281)

'Magic' is used by Mda both as an apparatus for subverting Western religious orthodoxy and as a way of symbiotically reconciling the elements of nature and culture, as this dichotomy is understood in its broadest context. Throughout the text, events and phenomena occur that defy the modern rational intellect, but sit easily within the wider context of the thaumaturgical response of the older generation to the utterances of prophets and prophetesses. Events such as the immaculate conception of Qukezwa's child, the death of Zim who dies with a smile as soon as he hears of his son Twin's death, followed the next day by the death of NomaRussia, who had once slept with the married Zim, and the marks of flagellation inexplicably appearing on the body of the modern woman, Xoliswa, are all reminiscent of Gabriel García Márquez's phantasmagorical flourishes in *One Hundred Years of Solitude*. In *The Heart of Redness* the elements of magic interlace with the narrative fabric of the novel. They serve as a link between the modern, secular world of the present generation and the spiritual world of the ancestors, denoting the mysterious and inexplicable nature of that world in contrast to the palpable, materialistic one of their descendants. When Bhonco of the Middle Generation, who is the link between his Unbelieving ancestors and the new generation of Unbelievers, such as his daughter, Xoliswa Ximiya, is stung by the bees which have inhabited his home, his daughter's insistence that he be taken to a clinic is met by the response:

> Education has made this girl mad, thinks Bhonco. Has she forgotten that, according to the tradition of the amaXhosa, bees are the messengers of the ancestors? When one has been stung, one has to appease the ancestors by slaughtering an ox or a goat and by brewing a lot of sorghum beer.
>
> 'It must be that scoundrel Zim,' moans Bhonco. 'He must have talked our common ancestor [the one beheaded by the British] into sending me these bees. And the headless old man complied! Don't they know? Bees are not for playing games of vengeance!' (Mda 2000: 262)

Even though Bhonco is in favour of the development of Qolorha-by-Sea, he still believes in the malignant forces of the unknown. He is convinced that his enemies, the Believers, have been responsible for sending the large birds, the ibises, to torment him wherever he goes. When he and the villagers meet to discuss the building of the casino and the holiday resort, the narrative voice records: 'There he is, surrounded by his supporters. The hadeda ibises have given him some respite and are no longer mocking him with their laughter' (Mda 2000: 229). Such is the universe occupied by Bhonco, in which tradition and modernity, magic and realism, coexist in credible measure.

Bhonco and his supporters, who regard the ancient prophetess Nongqawuse as false, represent the forward push of modernisation in the village of Qolorha-by-Sea. Although Bhonco is pleased to hear Mr Smith, one of the white entrepreneurs, outline his wonderful vision of a resort with merry-go-rounds, jet-skiing and a roller-coaster over the sea, he is 'suspicious of this matter of riding the waves. The new people that were prophesied by the false prophet, Nongqawuse, were supposed to come riding on the waves too' (Mda 2000: 230). This reminder of the disastrous past when wondrous things were prophesied for the salvation of the Xhosa nation resonates ironically with the promises of an equally wondrous future for Qolorha-by-Sea.

But not everyone is enamoured of the idea of a bustling seaside resort where people will ride waves in the way that 'civilized people do in advanced countries and even here in South Africa, in cities like Durban and Cape Town' (Mda 2000: 231); not least of all, Camagu, who questions the benefit of such 'wonderful things' for the local people. He points out that the children of Qolorha-by-Sea are too poor to enjoy such facilities, which will be monopolised 'only by rich people who will come here and pollute our rivers and our ocean' (231). To these reservations, Zim, a Believer and an inveterate enemy of the descendants of Unbelievers, adds his voice: 'This son of Cesane [Camagu] is right. They will destroy our trees and the plants of our forefathers for nothing' (231). Camagu, who is the mediating voice between the Believers and the Unbelievers, and who, to use a construct of Homi Bhabha, occupies the zone of the 'liminal space, in-between the designations of identity' (1994: 4), is not totally opposed to the idea of developing the potential of Qolorha-by-Sea, but his vision is an ecocritical one – 'promotion of the kind of tourism that will benefit the people, that will not destroy indigenous forests, that will not bring hordes of people who will pollute the rivers and drive away the birds' (232).

Challenged by Bhonco's daughter, Xoliswa Ximiya, who asks how he would 'stop civilization' (233), Camagu shouts: '"How will I stop you? I will tell you how I will stop you! I will have this village declared a national heritage site. Then no one will touch it. The wonders of Nongqawuse that led to the cattle-killing movement of the amaXhosa happened here. On that basis, this can be declared a national heritage site!"' (233).

Xoliswa's intense desire to break away from backwardness, symbolised by the 'redness' in the title of the book, takes her finally to Pretoria where she lands the high-profile job as a deputy-director in the national Department of Education. Once fancied by the villagers as the lover of Camagu, she leaves Qolorha-by-Sea when Camagu turns his attention to the young and voluptuous Qukezwa. David Attwell suggests that in Camagu's quest for his cultural self, 'the choices before him are modelled by Qukezwa and Xoliswa' (2004: 173). With Xoliswa now gone from the village, it is in and through Qukezwa that Camagu finds his new interstitial identity, a condition which, according to Michael Titlestad and Mike Kissack, 'embodies a persuasive postdialectical (post-*anti*-apartheid) mode of secular intellectual politics' (2003: 268). Qukezwa is the descendant of Twin, the Believer, who married a woman also named Qukezwa. When Xoliswa confronts Camagu about his relationship with the 'child' Qukezwa, who is pregnant by Camagu through a miraculous, asexual conception, Camagu's rejoinder is: '"Where you see darkness, witchcraft, heathens and barbarians, she sees song and dance and laughter and beauty"' (Mda 2000: 219). If Xoliswa embodies the attributes of the modern feminist, or as one villager comments, '[she] is a man in a woman's body' (302), Qukezwa represents a feminist of a different mould – the ecofeminist.

An enigmatic figure, who shaves her head in the manner of her father Zim, a Believer, Qukezwa thrusts herself into the gaze of the villagers (and ours) when she appears at the traditional court on the egregious charge of vandalising trees. Camagu, who attends the proceedings, is mystified at her alleged behaviour, since she was also opposed to the destruction of the natural environment of Qolorha-by-Sea in order to make way for the casino resort. What adds to his puzzlement is that she simply cut down the trees and left them there, not even using them as fuel. According to Xhosa tradition, her father ought to have been charged with his young daughter's crime, but Qukezwa insists on answering the charges herself. Dressed in her red blanket, which is perceived by the Unbelievers as the mark of her backwardness and barbarism, Qukezwa humbly, but emphatically proclaims her guilt: ' "I cut the trees, and I shall cut them again" ' (Mda 2000: 247). The court notes that this girl has in the past cut down the inkberry tree because it is poisonous. It is for this very same reason that she has cut down the recent spate of trees, as she testifies in her defence:

> The trees that I destroyed are as harmful as the inkberry. They are the
> lantana and wattle trees. They come from other countries . . . from
> Central America, from Australia . . . to suffocate our trees. They are
> dangerous trees that need to be destroyed . . . Just like the umga, the
> seed of the wattle tree is helped by fire. The seed can lie there for ten
> years, but when fire comes it grows. And it uses all the water. Nothing
> can grow under the wattle tree. It is an enemy since we do not have
> enough water in this country. (Mda 2000: 248–49)

She surprises the elders who nod in agreement, even if they do not condone what she has done. One of them muses on the source of her wisdom for such a young a girl who, at her age, should be focusing on 'red ochre and other matters of good grooming and beauty' (Mda 2000: 249).

What emerges at the village trial of Qukezwa is that the indigenous people of this land have always had their own laws to protect the environment. While Qukezwa's actions are considered criminal because there are no laws proscribing wattle trees, there are traditional laws in place that allow the destruction of noxious weeds and plants, such as the mimosa. We also learn during the court deliberations that only a week earlier some boys had been punished by the same court for killing the red-winged starling, or the *isomi* bird, regarded as being holy:

> It is a sin to kill isomi. Yes, boys love its delicious meat that tastes like
> chicken. But from the time we were young we were taught never to kill
> isomi. We ate these birds only when they died on their own. We watched
> them living together in huge colonies in the forest or flying in big
> flocks of thousands . . . These are sacred birds. If an isomi flies into

your house your family will be blessed. Isomi is a living Christ on earth. If you kill isomi you will be followed by misfortune in every direction you go. When we punish boys for killing red-winged starlings, we are teaching them about life. We are saving them from future misfortune. (Mda 2000: 249–50)

These traditional laws may be rooted in superstition, or even religious belief, but they effectively legislate on matters of conservation. In the extract above, the preponderance of the plural pronoun 'we' encodes a communal proprietorship over the ecology of the land. The purpose of punishing the boys is not to hurt them, but to educate them about their future. What is foregrounded in this extract is the imperative for ecological education, without which the future of any nation, no matter how sophisticated, would be doomed. William Beinart draws attention to the potential of humans to endanger their environment if left to their own devices: 'All human societies, from metropolitan industrial Britain to the Easter Islands, have had the capacity to destroy the natural resources on which they depend' (2002: 223).

If metaphors are carriers of ideology, as C.A. Bowers (1993: 22–23) proposes, the coding of religious and ecological metaphors in the language of the amaXhosa reflects an epistemology that is at variance with established Western belief. The melding of Christian faith, as personified by the figure of Christ and symbolised by the anthropomorphised *isomi* bird, with what may be regarded as superstitious belief in luck and misfortune, suggests a syncretism which accommodates the timeless wisdom of the elders and the abiding faith of the colonisers. Such hybridity of faiths allows the amaXhosa to accept ancestor worship along with the Christian notion of the resurrection of Christ. The prophecy of Nongqawuse is accepted as an outcome of this millenarian doctrine. Opposed to the syncretism of the indigene Xhosa society is the Western dialectical tendency to think in terms of binary categories of us/them, true/false, superiority/inferiority, salvation/perdition, right/wrong and culture/nature. Such categories of thinking, or 'root metaphors', can be 'traced directly back to Enlightenment thinkers' for their 'fundamental legitimation', according to Bowers (1993: 25), whose study, *Critical Essays on Education, Modernity, and the Recovery of the Ecological Imperative*, is echoed in the title of this chapter. In such an anthropocentric universe, where human rationality is the measure of all things, the environment is seen as instrumental to society's needs. The appropriation of the land, its conquest and taming to the needs of humans is the predominant trope of Enlightenment thought, which gives rise to the nature/culture dichotomy that posits culture as civilisation and nature, usually personified as a woman, as unruly and primitive. As a corollary to this, the owners of uncultivated land were viewed as savages, a view thematised in the words of Sir George Grey in *The Heart of Redness*, when he capitalises on the tragic consequences of Nongqawuse's prophecy:

> 'The advance of Christian civilization will sweep away ancient races. Antique laws and customs will moulder into oblivion . . . The strongholds of murder and superstition shall be cleansed . . . as the gospel is preached among ignorant and savage men. The ruder languages shall disappear, and the tongue of England alone shall be heard all around. So you see, my friends, this cattle-killing nonsense augurs the dawn of a new era.' (Mda 2000: 237)

The novel abounds in the kind of irony invested in this extract. Western religious doctrine is constantly juxtaposed with indigenous beliefs to show the supernatural elements of both systems of cosmology. No one system is privileged over the other. Grey's arrogant claim about 'Christian civilization' is satirically undercut by the refrain 'they who have murdered the son of their own god!' (Mda 2000: 268), something the amaXhosa find incredulous. Religion and language have always been strong semiotic markers of the other, hence Grey's policy of proselytising and Anglicising the amaXhosa. In this regard, Leon de Kock postulates that the policy of the colonisers in reducing the language of the amaXhosa to 'a written orthography' was to translate the Bible 'into the semiology of a previous oral culture' (1996: 65).

Ravi Rajan observes that from 1850 to 1950, a vast network of scientific institutions and international conferences was set up in parts of the British Empire to facilitate 'efficient exploitation of the natural resources of the colonial hinterland' (2002: 263). Lance van Sittert, who describes the Eastern Cape frontier of the late nineteenth century as a 'cultural transition zone', populated by hunter-gatherers, pastoralists and farmers and European colonists, writes: 'Scorched earth was an integral part of the military campaigns which levered Africans off their land, and pushed the colonial boundary steadily northwards. In their wake, the land was converted to private property and seeded with European settlers, stock and crops' (2002: 142). In Mda's novel, the governor, Sir George Cathcart, frustrated like his predecessor, Sir Harry Smith, in being unable to quell the Xhosa insurrection, 'order[s] his soldiers to go on a rampage and burn amaXhosa fields and kill amaXhosa cattle wherever they [come] across them' (Mda 2000: 25). His successor, Sir George Grey, whom the indigenes refer to not by name, but by the mocking sobriquet, 'The Man who Named Ten Rivers', completes the task begun by his predecessors. At the end of the novel, he is heard, filtered through the narrative voice, proclaiming his great achievement: "'Finally I have pacified Xhosaland!"'" (312). While he perceives his land policy of penetrating Xhosa land to settle whites as a victory, the ecological and human toll on the region is incalculable: 'Pacified homesteads are in ruins. Pacified men register themselves as pacified labourers in the emerging towns. Pacified men in their emaciated thousands. Pacified women remain to tend the soil and build pacified families. When pacified men return, their homesteads have been moved elsewhere, and crammed into tiny pacified villages. The pacified fields have become rich settler farmlands' (312).

This stylised passage encapsulates, in rhetorical terms, the ambivalent nature of conquest in the name of progress. It would be true to say that such settlements ushered in the kind of progress that makes South Africa a mighty engine of commerce and industry on the continent of Africa today. It would also be true to say that the deleterious impact of such progress on the indigenes is felt even to this day in the Eastern Cape, which is rated the poorest and most underdeveloped province in the country, its social and political woes exacerbated by corrupt governance – a fact acknowledged by Mda in *The Heart of Redness*. The extract above testifies to the destruction of the ecological relationship between the men of the region and their land and to the evils of the migrant labour system as a consequence of it.

Opposed to the anthropocentric root metaphors in which men such as Sir George Grey think, are the anthropomorphic frames of reference imbricated in the worldview of primitive cultures, such as the Xhosa, in which the incommensurables of religious belief, superstition, tradition and secularism are accommodated. The spiritual and the secular become the warp and the weft of the fabric of their existence. Enriching this variegated texture of their lives, are animals, which exist in an interpersonal relationship with humans. The dualistic Western view of the human kingdom versus the animal kingdom is replaced by a prismatic one, in which we see humans interacting symbiotically with animals, as instantiated when lungsickness begins to take its toll on the cattle of Twin-Twin, the Unbeliever and ancestor of Xoliswa: 'Twin-Twin wept as he watched his favourite bull die a horrible and protracted death' (Mda 2000: 55). When Twin, a Believer and an ancestor of Qukezwa of the present generation, loses his favourite horse Gxagxa (later, also the name of Qukezwa's horse) to lungsickness, he agonises over its death, refusing to eat the best dishes prepared by his wife. He continues to keep vigil until his beloved horse's hide 'cover[s] only a pile of bones' (84).

This bond between humans and animals endures over the years into the present generation, when we see weaverbirds and the horse Gxagxa keep vigil over the dying Zim, the father of Qukezwa: 'Amahobohobo weaverbirds fill the homestead with their rolling, swirling song. They miss the man who spent most of the day sitting under their giant wild fig tree. Gxagxa refuses to move from his vigil outside Zim's door' (Mda 2000: 305). The human emotion registered by the word 'miss' transfers seamlessly, and to any animal lover, plausibly, to the birds and Zim's horse. After Zim dies, his spirit transmigrates to Gxagxa who, as Zim's proxy, becomes devoted to Qukezwa:

> Whenever the horse has had its fill of grazing, it comes looking for her everywhere. If she is not at the cottage, it goes to Nongqawuse's Valley. If she is not there still, it goes to the sea, particularly to the lagoon. She is sure to be there. They love each other, Gxagxa and Qukezwa. It was her father's favourite horse. Her father lives in this horse . . . She gives it the same kind of respect she gave her father. (Mda 2000: 316)

It is significant that Zim dies in the environmental ambience of his village, attended not only by his loving daughter Qukezwa, but also the non-human creatures that have been a part of his *lebensraum*. NomaRussia, whom Camagu once saw at a funeral wake in the bustling and sleazy neo-city of Hillbrow, Johannesburg, returns to Qolorha-by-Sea suffering from terminal cervical cancer. She dies the morning after Zim's death, a fact that angers the villagers who feel that this 'unscrupulous woman', Zim's former mistress, 'would not leave Zim alone' (Mda 2000: 309). To Zim, death does not come easily. He lingers between 'the Otherworld – the world of the ancestors that runs parallel to this world' (308) and the world of Qolorha-by-Sea. But when death does come, it comes gently, if suddenly. The night he hears of his son's death, he expires 'smiling' (308).

Twin, of course, had died some time ago in the streets of Hillbrow, 'drunk and frustrated' (Mda 2000: 307). It was at his funeral that NomaRussia had sung so beautifully and captured the heart of Camagu whose quest for her brings him to Qolorha-by-Sea. Like Xoliswa, a professional, who goes away to the city of Pretoria, Twin was an émigré from the village, living in Hillbrow and struggling to make a living by selling carvings of Xhosa people. One of the consequences of landlessness, caused by the economic restructuring of the land, is the deracination of young men such as Twin, as Robert Young has commented: 'Without land to cultivate, the only alternative is to drift to the slums of the big cities. Even the sanctuary of the slum is itself vulnerable, as in apartheid South Africa, or contemporary Mumbai' (2003: 45). The polarisation of the country and the city, with the ecological inequalities implicit in it, results in the tragedy of Twin, who, unlike his father Zim, dies of deprivation in Hillbrow, once the cultural milieu of the avant-garde, now the haven of illegal immigrants, prostitutes and drug addicts:

> Twin had been frustrated for a long time. No one was buying his carvings any more, for he carved people who looked like real people. No one wanted such carvings. Buyers of art were more interested in twisted people. People without proportion. People who grew heads on their stomachs and eyes at the back of their heads. Grotesque people with many arms and twisted lips on their feet. Twin refused to create things that distorted reality . . . He starved and died a pauper. (Mda 2000: 307)

The satirical treatment of intellectualism in the above extract underscores the dichotomy between the sterile, metropolitan world of high art, with its connoisseurs and charlatans, and the plenitudinous world once inhabited by Twin and his ancestors, the promise of which still exists in the worldview of Qukezwa, the sister of Twin, in the village of Qolorha-by-Sea.

Earlier, I posited the notion of Qukezwa as being an ecofeminist. Cheryll Glotfelty and Harold Fromm (1996: xxiv) define ecofeminism as a hybrid label to describe a theoretical discourse whose theme is the link between the oppression of women and the domination of nature. But the term 'ecofeminism' is itself in danger of becoming hierarchical and essentialised if one takes the feminist movement as being rooted in the Western psyche as anti-men and pro-nature. Michael Bell points out some of the problems associated with the term 'ecofeminism'. Apart from perpetuating the 'dichotomy between men and women as well as the negative stereotypes of women as irrational, as controlled by their bodies, and as best suited for the domestic realm' (1998: 170), the term also suggests that Western societies are more patriarchal than Eastern ones, and this is manifestly not true. Eastern societies, and even African ones – Zimbabwe being a good example – have demonstrated their patriarchal dominance over nature. Bell advocates a middle position, avoiding such dualisms and recognising 'the gray areas and the interactiveness and interdependence of our categories' (171).

The sub-continent of India has witnessed the most sustained struggles by women environmental activists who have opposed the male-dominated interests of commerce and trade in their country. Long before Arundhati Roy made environmental issues a cause célèbre, Indian rural women were at the forefront in protecting their natural resources from what Young terms 'men . . . ideologically colonized by the short-term commercial values of the market place' (2003: 102). The earliest example of resistance by peasants to the deforestation of their land goes back to the 1940s, when Mira Behn, a devotee of Gandhi, established an ashram in the foothills of the Himalayas to focus on the problem of deforestation and the planting of non-indigenous cash crops, such as the pine tree. Like the kind of intuitive ecological awareness shown by Qukezwa in Mda's *The Heart of Redness*, the women 'possessed repositories of intimate knowledge both of husbandry and of the medicinal and nutritional value of a wide variety of plants' (Young 2003: 102). A case in which both men and women were involved in protecting their environment, which finds a resonance in Mda's novel, is that of the tree-hugging, or Chipko, movement which began in 1972–73 in northwest India when the local people successfully protested against the sale of 300 ash trees to commerce. According to Young, men and women gave up their lives in the struggle (2003: 102). The Chipko movement opposed the government's forestation plan to plant non-indigenous trees, such as the eucalyptus, which produces no water-conserving humus and destroys the food system.

Alfred Crosby proposes that European expansion was not only facilitated by military superiority, but also by 'a biological, an ecological, component' (1986: 7). Such colonisation of public land by an invading force or by the central government, acts to the detriment of the local people. In Mda's novel, Qukezwa's seemingly reckless act of cutting down 'foreign trees . . . not the trees of our forefathers' (Mda 2000: 248) is a protest against such invasion by what Crosby has termed 'portmanteau biota' (1986: 270), a collective term for the organisms that Europeans took with them to the lands they colonised. Qukezwa's actions, which stem from ancestral wisdom, register a strong message to governments that exploit the planet without regard for the deleterious consequences of their actions. Qukezwa's stance is vindicated by the present-day situation in South Africa where the legacy of 'portmanteau biota' is costing the country millions of rand. According to a recent newspaper report, 'exotic plants and weeds are destroying our grazing and farming lands, forests, nature and game reserves. The government spends half a billion rand a year on fighting this scourge, but it is far from winning the battle' (Makhaye 2005: 17).

The case against Qukezwa for cutting down foreign trees eventually 'fizzles out' because the elders of the village apparently 'have more important things to deal with' (Mda 2000: 280). The battle over the immediate future of Qolorha-by-Sea is won by Camagu, Qukezwa and the Believers. Camagu's plan for a co-operative society that harvests the sea and manufactures Xhosa attire and jewellery finally triumphs when a court order from the Department of Arts, Culture and Heritage puts a stop to the building of the casino and declares Qolorha-by-Sea a 'national heritage' site (311). But for how long? The answer to this question comes unequivocally towards the end of the novel when Camagu drives back to Qolorha-by-Sea after visiting Dalton at a hospital in East London. Dalton is recovering from a vicious attack by the frustrated Unbeliever, Bhonco, who still harbours a grudge against him and his settler forebears for cutting off his ancestor's head during one of the many wars between the settlers and the amaXhosa over natural resources in the Eastern Cape. That greed and the exigencies of survival will eventually impact on the ecology of the area, as it did during the time of Sir Harry Smith and Sir George Grey, appears to inevitable:

> As he drives back home he sees wattle trees along the road. Qukezwa taught him that these are enemy trees. All along the way he cannot see any of the indigenous trees that grow in abundance in Qolorha. Those who want to preserve indigenous plants and birds have won the day there. At least for now. But for how long? The whole country is ruled by greed. Everyone wants to have his or her snout in the trough. Sooner or later the powers that be may decide, in the name of the people, that it is good for the people to have a gambling complex at Qolorha-by-Sea. (Mda 2000: 319)

In an onslaught on the ecocritical approach to literature, Sven Birkerts has written: 'I will speak as a literary purist and assert that literature cannot and should not be used as a pretext for examining man and nature, certainly not more than it is a pretext for examining any other thing or relation' (1996). Birkerts's contention, arising from his review of Glotfelty and Fromm's *The Ecocriticism Reader* (1996), is that literature should explore human nature, its avariciousness, rapacity and the will to power (1996). Birkerts's broadside on ecocriticism serves as a timely critique on the trivialisation of literature in the interests of any agenda, not only ecocriticism. But if, as he suggests, literature's focus should be on the human condition in its multifarious facets, an ecocritical perspective serves literature all the better, for, as Glotfelty defines 'ecocriticism', it is a study of the relationship between literature and the physical environment, taking an earth-centred approach to literary studies (1996: xviii). As a perspective, or approach, it problematises the literary encounter, whose main purpose, echoed by Birkerts, is the exploration of humans' relationship with the universe. Mda's novel, in highlighting the present-day struggle over the future of Qolorha-by-Sea, articulates a post-colonial nexus that critiques the British occupation of indigenous Xhosa land and its ecological impact on the Eastern Cape today.

In 2004, Wangari Maathai, who started the Greenbelt Movement in Kenya in 1977 (Young 2003: 107), was awarded the Nobel Peace Prize. This was the first time in the history of the Nobel that this ultimate accolade for peace was awarded to an African woman, and to an environmental campaigner. When she was asked by Stephan Faris of *Time* magazine, 'What's the planet's biggest challenge?' her response was: 'The environment. We are sharing our resources in a very inequitable way. We have parts of the world that are deprived and parts of the world that are very rich. And that is partly the reason why we have conflict' (Faris 2004: 4). On the subject of colonial expropriation of the land and its effect on indigenous people, Edward Said argues that for the geographical identity of the land to be restored, due to the presence of the coloniser, 'the land is recoverable at first only through the imagination' (1994: 271). The ecological imperative in Mda's novel for an identity with the ancestral land answers to that imaginative recovery of a historical past when indigenous communities were displaced by violence of epistemic proportions.

Note
1. In his introduction to *The Plays of Zakes Mda* Andrew Horn states that the play was written in 1973. In a footnote he further explains that it was first performed in February 1979 (see Mda 1990: xii; note 22).

Works cited
Attwell, David. 2004. 'The experimental turn in black South African fiction'. In: de Kock, Leon, Louise Bethlehem and Sonja Laden (eds.). *South Africa in the Global Imaginary*. Pretoria: UNISA Press, 154-79.

Beinart, William. 2002. 'South African environmental history in the African context'. In: Dovers, Stephen, Ruth Edgecombe and Bill Guest (eds.). *South African Environmental History: Cases & Comparisons*. Cape Town: David Philip, 215-26.

Bell, Michael M. 1998. *An Invitation to Environmental Sociology.* Thousand Oaks, CA: Pine Forge Press.

Bell, Nigel and Meg Cowper-Lewis (eds.). 1993. *Literature, Nature and the Land: Ethics and Aesthetics of the Environment.* Collected AUETSA Papers 1992. Ngoye, Zululand: University of Zululand.

Bhabha, Homi K. 1994. *The Location of Culture.* London: Routledge.

Birkerts, Sven. 1996. 'Only God can make a tree: The joys and sorrows of ecocriticism'. *The Boston Book Review* 3(1) Nov/Dec. http://www.asle.umn.edu/archive/intro/birkerts.html, accessed 22 October 2004.

Bowers, C.A. 1993. *Critical Essays on Education, Modernity, and the Recovery of the Ecological Imperative.* New York: Teachers College Press.

Capra, Fritjof. 1983 (1982). *The Turning Point: Science, Society, and the Rising Culture.* London: Flamingo.

Crosby, Alfred W. 1986. *Ecological Imperialism: The Biological Expansion of Europe, 900–1900.* Cambridge: Cambridge University Press.

De Kock, Leon. 1996. *Civilizing Barbarians: Missionary Narrative and African Textual Response in Nineteenth-Century South Africa.* Johannesburg: Wits University Press.

De Kock, Leon, Louise Bethlehem and Sonja Laden (eds.). 2004. *South Africa in the Global Imaginary.* Pretoria: UNISA Press.

Dovers, Stephen, Ruth Edgecombe and Bill Guest (eds.). 2002. *South African Environmental History: Cases & Comparisons.* Cape Town: David Philip.

Doyle, Alister. 2004. 'No more polar bears by 2100'. *The Star,* 9 November: 2.

Faris, Stephan. 2004. '10 questions for Wangari Maathai'. *Time,* 18 October: 4.

Fowler, Jonathan. 2004. 'We are using up Earth faster than it can regenerate'. *The Sunday Independent,* 24 October: 2.

Glotfelty, Cheryll and Harold Fromm (eds.). 1996. *The Ecocriticism Reader: Landmarks in Literary Ecology.* Athens, GA: University of Georgia Press.

Hopkins, Gerard Manley. 1994 (1918). *The Works of Gerard Manley Hopkins.* Edited by Robert Bridges. The Wordsworth Poetry Library. Ware, Hertsfordshire: Wordsworth Editions.

Jacobs, J.U. 2002. 'Zakes Mda's *The Heart of Redness*: The novel as *umngqokolo*'. *Kunapipi* 24 (1 & 2): 224–36.

Lloyd, David. 2001. 'The modernization of redness'. *Scrutiny2* 6(2): 34–39.

Makhaye, Chris. 2005. 'Alien plants are sapping our land'. *Sunday Tribune,* 16 January: 17.

Márquez, Gabriel García. 1970. *One Hundred Years of Solitude.* London: Jonathan Cape.

Matshoba, Mtutuzeli. 1979. *Call Me Not a Man.* Johannesburg: Ravan Press.

McClintock, Anne. 1995. *Imperial Leather: Race, Gender and Sexuality in the Colonial Context.* London: Routledge.

Mda, Zakes. 1990. 'We shall sing for the fatherland'. In: Mda, Zakes. *The Plays of Zakes Mda.* Introduction by Andrew Horn. Johannesburg: Ravan Press, 23–48.

———. 1997. 'Acceptance speech for the Olive Schreiner Prize (1997)'. *The English Academy Review* 14 (December): 279–81.

———. 2000. *The Heart of Redness.* Oxford: Oxford University Press.

————. 2002. *The Madonna of Excelsior*. Cape Town: Oxford University Press.

Paton, Alan. 1958 (1944). *Cry, The Beloved Country: A Story of Comfort in Desolation*. Harmondsworth: Penguin.

Peires, J.B. 1989. *The Dead Will Arise: Nongqawuse and the Great Xhosa Cattle-Killing Movement of 1856-7*. Johannesburg: Ravan Press.

Rabinowitz, Ivan. 1993. 'Under western words: The post-colonial landslide'. In: Bell, Nigel and Meg Cowper-Lewis (eds.). *Literature, Nature and the Land: Ethics and Aesthetics of the Environment*. Collected AUETSA Papers 1992. Ngoye, Zululand: University of Zululand, 18-23.

Rajan, Ravi. 2002. 'The colonial eco-drama: Resonant themes in the environmental history of southern Africa and South Asia'. In: Dovers, Stephen, Ruth Edgecombe and Bill Guest (eds.). *South African Environmental History: Cases & Comparisons*. Cape Town: David Philip, 259-67.

Said, Edward W. 1994 (1993). *Culture and Imperialism*. London: Vintage.

Sewlall, Harry. 2003. 'Deconstructing empire in Joseph Conrad and Zakes Mda'. *Journal of Literary Studies* 19(3/4), December: 331-44.

Titlestad, Michael and Mike Kissack. 2003. ' "The foot does not sniff": Imagining the post-*anti*-apartheid intellectual'. *Journal of Literary Studies* 19(3/4), December: 255-70.

Van Sittert, Lance. 2002. ' "Our irrepressible fellow colonist": The biological invasion of Prickly Pear (*Opuntia ficus-indica*) in the Eastern Cape, *c.* 1890-*c.* 1910'. In: Dovers, Stephen, Ruth Edgecombe and Bill Guest (eds.). *South African Environmental History: Cases & Comparisons*. Cape Town: David Philip, 139-59.

Woodward, Wendy. 2003. 'Postcolonial ecologies and the gaze of animals: Reading some contemporary southern African narratives'. *Journal of Literary Studies* 19(3/4), December: 290-315.

Young, Robert J.C. 2003. *Postcolonialism: A Very Short Introduction*. Oxford: Oxford University Press.

12

Nongqawuse, National Time and (Female) Authorship in The Heart of Redness

MEG SAMUELSON

THE HEART OF REDNESS is set in two interconnected time zones, the time of Nongqawuse's prophecy and the post-apartheid present and it provides an exemplary case study through which to analyse contemporary cultural attempts to grapple with the legacy of Nongqawuse. A survey of recent reinscriptions of Nongqawuse's story reveals three central trends: the trope of virgin birth, a framework of sacrifice and redemption that intersects with the national narrative crafted within the Truth and Reconciliation Commission (TRC) (see Wilson 2001: 114–19), and a continued interest in questions of heritage, modernity and development, central also in earlier writing on Nongqawuse.[1]

The recent revival of interest in Nongqawuse can, in part, be attributed to the publication in 1989 of J.B. Peires's authoritative study, *The Dead Will Arise: Nongqawuse and the Great Cattle-Killing Movement of 1856–7*, which created fertile ground for new cultural interpretations that draw their symbolism from Christian resurrection theology. Mda cites Peires as the primary source for his fictionalised account of the historical event. Indeed, so closely does he tie his fictional version to Peires's account that there is little room for interpretative work on the historical narrative in *The Heart of Redness*. Hence, I initiate my reading of the novel with a discussion of Peires and point to alternative versions of the event forsaken in Mda's account, which faithfully follows its historical source text. The novel's present-day narrative provides an arena in which we can grapple with Mda's exegesis of the historical narrative. Before doing so, I discuss the novel's achievements in countering a linear model of history and challenging ideologies of development. As its conceptions of time are embodied in female characters, however, its recourse to female fertility as privileged metaphor compels the settling of narrative time into national formations. Moreover, the use of the female form as index of national time and container of textual meaning depends on a gendered conception of authorship that presents women as either leaky or empty vessels.

The character Qukezwa is rendered as one such empty vessel for Mda's vision when she bears a son while still a virgin. Qukezwa is a manifestation of what Florence Stratton calls the 'Mother Africa Trope'. This trope, according to Stratton, 'legitimates the critical practice of excluding women from the creation of culture, of writing them out of the literary tradition' (1994: 52). Figuring Qukezwa as Mother Africa, the novel shifts the site of authorship from the female prophet to the male writer. The author function claims the status of the Author-as-God; it claims, in other words, what Roland Barthes terms the 'theological' principle in the text (1977: 146). Such disembodied authorial transcendence is achieved through the identification of women with the physical body and the embodiment of textual meaning in women's flesh. Equated with the body, women are excluded from cultural production and the contested and unruly meanings of Nongqawuse's words are managed and contained when transposed into the 'message' that women convey through their wombs.

Historical controversies: Gender, cattle and women's words
The story of Nongqawuse, in brief, is that claiming to speak on behalf of the ancestors, she instructed the amaXhosa to kill all their cattle and cease cultivation. Adherence to this injunction, she foretold, would result in the ancestors, along with new cattle, rising from the dead, new grain being available in abundance, and the world returning to its original, pristine state (see Gqoba in Jordan 1973: 70-75 and Peires 1989: 79, 126, 98). If controversy surrounds the events of 1856-57,[2] historians agree unanimously on their consequences. Following the failure of the prophecies, approximately 40 000 amaXhosa died of starvation, another 40 000 had no option but to seek waged labour in the British colony. Independent Xhosaland had been decimated and the last vestiges

of Xhosa political sovereignty soundly quashed, as the British used the events of 1856–57 as an excuse to confiscate massive tracts of land and to round up chiefs, exiling them to Robben Island. From this point onwards, little stood between the amaXhosa and their incorporation into the colonial order.

Nongqawuse was approximately fifteen years of age when she began to prophesy in 1856. She lived in Independent Xhosaland under the guardianship of her uncle, Mhlakaza. At this time, the amaXhosa had already suffered severe losses in the face of imperial aggression. Their social and political organisation had been placed under intolerable strain by a near century of colonial incursion and conflict, and their final substantial military challenge to colonial encroachment, the War of Mlanjeni of 1850–53, had failed. The situation was exacerbated by a lungsickness epizootic, spreading rampantly through British Kaffraria and Independent Xhosaland in the mid-1850s. Peires's great contribution to scholarship on the events of 1856–57 was to draw attention to the impact of the lungsickness epizootic in an argument claiming that the 'cattle-killing' was a rational and logical response to colonial pressures and unprecedented livestock mortality. However, while he has enriched our understanding of the events of 1856–57 through his attention to lungsickness, his failure to draw gendered conclusions about cattle dearth and cattle killing has left a palpable blind spot in his narrative. This lacuna then finds its way into Mda's novel.

Cattle were the glue of Xhosa society and the primary markers of status and wealth. Their central function was that of *lobola*, or bride-wealth, used to appropriate the reproductive potential of women. Through the payment of *lobola*, future offspring were incorporated into the patrilineal line of the husband's clan. Human capital was central to the social organisation of the agrarian amaXhosa, and cattle, as the means to the reproduction of human capital, were pivotal (see Guy 1990: 39–41). Xhosa social organisation underwent a period of startling disruption in the 1850s. To adopt the evocative phrase with which Judith Butler titles her book, it was a time of 'gender trouble' (1990), as cattle, the means through which gender was produced and performed, were in increasingly short supply. Young men were unable to raise sufficient cattle for *lobola*; patriarchs were unable to sue men who engaged in extramarital sexual relations with their female kin; chiefs lost power along with their herds.

The cattle dearth was 'wreaking havoc with older ways of regulating sexuality' and thus with the regulation of reproduction and legitimacy (Bradford 1996: 362).

Helen Bradford points out that the prophecies – with their injunctions against cultivation and their order for cattle to be killed – freed women from the onerous task of cultivation that fell to them within the gendered division of labour, while demanding that men destroy the very currency through which 'male power over women' was symbolised and practised (1996: 366). It is remarkable that Nongqawuse, a young unmarried woman, should have claimed authority on the subject of cattle. That her prophecies were addressed to the resource through which female fertility and labour was controlled seems most suggestive.

Peires records claims that the prophecies and their staunch female following had a gendered agenda, but then hastily dismisses them, along with what he calls the 'dubious cliché' that 'women's oppression in male dominated societies such as that of the Xhosa predisposes [them] to participate in ecstatic religious movements' (1989: 172). Extrapolating from a mere three examples of women who did not support the prophetic movement (including one Mfengu and one royal woman, women inhabiting either marginal or exceptional positions in amaXhosa society), he concludes categorically: 'Clearly, the believer/unbeliever divide followed no set pattern of kinship, age or even gender' (174). Jeff Guy, in contrast, proposes that the prophecies and their broad female support base constituted 'an attack by women on existing male structures and power bases weakened by cattle losses' (1991: 231).

At one point in the *The Heart of Redness*, Mda appears willing to admit what Peires denies: 'Women became the staunchest supporters of the prophets. Many of them left their husbands and went to live with their parents. Women were the leaders of the cattle-killing movement' (2000: 126). Context is everything, however, and this bold statement is undercut by its positioning in the novel. The reference to women's support of the movement is inserted to highlight the surprise of one character, Twin, when his wife shows doubts about the wisdom of following it too faithfully, rather than to emphasise the gendered characteristics of the movement. For the first time in their marriage, Twin goes 'against the wishes of his wife' (125). The statement that women were the leaders and supporters of the movement is undermined by juxtaposition. What the novel shows, rather than tells, is men supporting the prophetic movement in opposition to their wives. Thus does Mda remain true to Peires's version and inattentive to the gendered implications of the events of 1856–57. This surface denial is, however, belied by strong undercurrents of gendered anxiety that later become the focus of my analysis.

Another of Peires's depictions taken up by Mda is the attempt to construct a richer biographical narrative for Nongqawuse. Forging 'historical links' out of no more than 'hints in the sources' (Guy 1991: 227), Peires argues that Nongqawuse's guardian, Mhlakaza, was the disenchanted gospel-man, Wilhelm Goliath, who had toured the Eastern Cape with the Anglican archdeacon, Nathaniel Merriman, previous to Nongqawuse's prophecies. By way of this claim, Peires concludes that the prophecies were strongly influenced by the Christian resurrection theology with which Wilhelm Goliath was conversant. The unspoken implication is the attribution of the prophecies' authorship to Mhlakaza, rather than Nongqawuse. As Bradford observes: 'Peires places a black man who, on his own confession, mouthed the words of a woman, centre-stage'; he 'has awarded [Nongqawuse's] words and historical significance to a man' (1996: 366).

A recurrent theme in Nongqawuse's legacy is that of her as an empty vessel for the words of others. Most historical and cultural interpretations of Nongqawuse's prophecy, including Mda's, join Peires in going to considerable lengths to work around the female authorship of the prophecies. Convoluted plots are constructed, by way of which Nongqawuse's authorship – both her message and its authority – is ascribed to a range of male historical actors: Sir George Grey, the chiefs, Mhlakaza or Xhosa paramount, Sarhili. Another androcentric strategy at work in both Peires and Mda's accounts is the portrayal of Nongqawuse as one offering little more than a pastiche of previous prophecies by Nxele and Ntsikana.[3] At issue is not the originality of Nongqawuse's prophecy, but its authority: Nongqawuse's speech acts achieved widespread adherence where previous prophecies had failed to do so.

While denying the authority of female authorship, Peires's Mhlakaza narrative – which treats the prophecies as a syncretic bricolage of Xhosa ancestral beliefs and Christian resurrection theology – is also slanted towards the kind of redemptive story prevalent during the South African transition. This narrative, replete as it obviously is with hope and desire, exerts a powerful influence over cultural work produced during the transition. *The Heart of Redness*, which refuses a linear narrative structure, purportedly challenges a redemptive scripting of history. But the symbolic baggage weighing down on women's bodies proves overwhelming. Ultimately, the novel's representation of the female reproductive body draws it in line with the dominant national narrative.

Entangled time: Non-linear histories

The presence of the past is palpable in the twentieth-century narrative of the novel, most notably in the social division between Believers and Unbelievers (inherited from the time of Nongqawuse and from which stems the division between 'red people' and 'school people').[4] Enmity between Believers and Unbelievers is reinvigorated in Mda's present-day narrative as Qolorha-by-Sea, the site of the prophecies, faces a new crisis in the late twentieth century. Believers and Unbelievers quarrel over the merits of 'progress' in the form of a proposed tourist development. The Unbelievers campaign in favour of the development, arguing that it 'will bring modernity to our lives, and will rid us of our redness' (Mda 2000: 105). The Believers resist it because it will destroy the local ecology, in the interests of national and global capital, and alienate them from their natural surroundings. Insisting also on the contemporaneity of their non-modern cultural practices, they reject the attempt to package this culture for tourist consumption.

The proposed development, vaunted as being of 'national importance' (Mda 2000: 230), promises to modernise the village, while retaining vestiges of 'redness' in the fixed format of the tourist spectacle. As such, it reiterates the colonial imposition of the nineteenth century, which aimed to consign a lived present to the static past of the museum exhibit, while transforming the amaXhosa into a waged-labour underclass, servicing colonial capital. Both colonial and national projects aim to produce 'modern' subjects in the interests of economic 'progress' by fixing in the 'past' any identified 'non-modern' attributes (see Lloyd 2000: 219); the complicity between them is revealed through the novel's interpenetrating time zones and reiterated crises.

Resistant to the time of origin and telos, to the linear movement through past, present and future, Mda responds to such colonial and national projects by giving literary voice to the preoccupations of theorists such as Partha Chatterjee, Achille Mbembe and Dipesh Chakrabarty. Chatterjee and Mbembe argue for an understanding of time in the post-colony as 'heterogenous, unevenly dense' (Chatterjee 1999: 131) and 'fundamentally fractured' (Mbembe 2002: 272), in short, as an 'entanglement . . . of multiple dureés made up of discontinuities, reversals, inertias, and swings that overlay one another, interpenetrate one another, and envelop one another' (Mbembe 2001: 14). These conceptions of time in the post-colony are antithetical to what Benedict Anderson terms the 'homogenous, empty time' of nationalism (1983: 31). 'Homogenous, empty time', notes Chatterjee, is not only the time of nationalism, it is also 'the utopian time of capital', with its attendant discourses of linear progress and development (1999: 131).

Mda's return to Nongqawuse thus differs from Thabo Mbeki's in his 'I am an African' speech.[5] Mbeki states: 'I am the child of Nongqause [sic]. I am *he* who made it possible to trade in world markets in diamonds, in gold, in the same food for which my stomach yearns' (1996; emphasis added). Evoking Nongqawuse in order to speak a narrative of progressive modernisation, Mbeki lays an overtly teleological claim on the historical story. The meaning that Nongqawuse holds for Mda is, at first glance, quite different and appears to have more in common with what Chakrabarty terms 'subaltern pasts' (1998: 18) than with nationalist historiography.

The blending of time periods and the exploration of disjunctures in the present that we find in *The Heart of Redness* apparently undoes the imposed binary of 'traditional' and 'modern' (or, in this context, 'red' and 'school') through the assertion of what Chakrabarty terms 'a shared "now"' or 'a relation of contemporaneity between the non modern and the modern' (1998: 28). The entanglement of past and present and the insistence on the contemporaneity of 'redness' found in the novel is radically antithetical to colonial culture's 'denial of co-evalness', to use Johannes Fabian's expression (1983: 55). In his exploration of 'how anthropology makes its object', to quote his subtitle, Fabian finds that colonial culture constructs its spatial and cultural others as temporal others, as those who inhabit a temporally prior position on the evolutionary ladder. This 'denial of co-evalness' is exemplified in the novella to which Mda's title alludes, in which Joseph Conrad's Marlow likens his spatial movement up the Congo to 'travelling back to the earliest beginnings of the world' (1973: 48). Mda's inscription of time is equally antithetical to the progressive, modernising temporalities espoused by new nationalist discourses, such as that spoken by Mbeki.

On a thematic level, Mda equally fends off the threat posed by 'development' to his fictionalised village by attempting to take the 'subaltern past' seriously, allowing it to disrupt the present rather than fixing it in the past (see Chakrabarty 1998: 24). The Believers triumph when the valley – the place of Nongqawuse's visions – is declared a heritage site. The prophecies, which promised to restore the world to its original state, are fulfilled as Nongqawuse finally saves the village from the impingement of 'modernity', whether as part of the colonial or nationalist project.

However, the symbolic weight placed on women's bodies during the nation-building transition exerts a new set of pressures on the text. We are confronted with contradictory textual desires and a fissured textual politics. The novel's embodiment of time in women and its reliance on a set of gendered tropes spawned in both colonial and nationalist discourses hamper its ability to escape the poetic logic of nationalist and colonial temporality. While Conrad uses female figures to exemplify his 'heart of darkness', Mda equally depends on the female form to house his 'heart of redness' and shares with Mbeki a gendering of the child of the future as male.[6]

The question then arises of whether it is possible to destabilise colonial and nationalist edifices while leaving intact the gendered representations that prop them up. I suggest not. In the following section, I attend to the use of women as temporal figures. This focus renders visible the operations within the text of what Svetlana Boym terms 'restorative nostalgia', which expresses a nation-orientated memory that 'tends to make a teleological plot' by suturing the 'gaps and discontinuities' of memory with 'a coherent and inspiring tale of recovered identity' (2001: 53). Structured according to this nation-oriented memory, time settles into a Janus-faced structure, its heterogeneity divided into two homogenous parts: 'modern' progressive movement and 'non-modern' repasts.

Embodied time: Women as temporal figures

The Heart of Redness grapples with Nongqawuse's contradictory and contested legacy in the present-day drama by twice splitting it between three female characters: Qukezwa, Xoliswa Ximiya and NomaRussia. All three women enter the plot as love interests of Camagu, the character most closely associated with the author.[7] Like Mda, Camagu returns to South Africa after the democratic elections following an extended period in exile. Camagu is quickly disabused of any idealised notions of the South African 'miracle' and becomes the spokesman for Mda's strongly worded critique of the 'new' South Africa. However, the articulation of this critique through the lens of male desire sees it founder on an essentialised gender politics.

Disillusioned by his experience in Johannesburg, Camagu prepares to return to the United States. On the eve of his departure, he encounters NomaRussia, from the rural Eastern Cape village of Qolorha-by-Sea, singing at a Hillbrow wake. Captivated by her 'hearthly beauty' and her song, which conjures images of 'a folktale dreamland' (Mda 2000: 27), Camagu delays his departure in order to make a spontaneous trip to the village in search of her. This will be where Mda sets his 'African renaissance' and, as this renaissance is figured through a literal rebirth, female bodies become implicated in a nostalgic restoration of an 'African identity'.

Following Camagu's arrival in Qolorha-by-Sea, NomaRussia, the object of his quest, eludes him, and he finds himself oscillating instead between the favours of Xoliswa Ximiya and Qukezwa. This is the text's first attempt at splitting Nongqawuse's ambiguous legacy. Xoliswa Ximiya and Qukezwa are, respectively, the only living descendants of the Unbelieving and Believing branches of the family on whom the novel centres and are emblematic of the social division of the amaXhosa into 'red' and 'school' people (or 'non-modern' and 'modern'). The dichotomy drawn between the two female characters reveals the extent to which the novel defines women – and that which they represent – according to their fertility. Elsewhere it commendably smudges the boundary between 'red' and 'school'. However, this boundary becomes rigid in representations of the female reproductive body: the Unbelieving Xoliswa Ximiya is childless; the womb of the Believing Qukezwa is the site of miraculous fertility. Each woman provides an emblem, respectively, of the 'modern' and 'non-modern'.

Xoliswa Ximiya represents the 'school people'. She is the principal of Qolorha-by-Sea Secondary School and is an embarrassingly effusive supporter of US-style 'civilisation'. She epitomises the legacy of Nongqawuse celebrated by Mbeki, one that ushered the time of nation and capital into the pre-capitalist world of the amaXhosa. Through its association with Xoliswa Ximiya, whose first mention in the novel refers to her childless state, this discourse is rendered barren.

In contrast to Xoliswa Ximiya, Qukezwa gives birth to a son in extraordinary circumstances. The only surviving child of the Believing line, Qukezwa is closely associated with heritage. She provides the novel's most persistent gateway to the world of the past as she speaks, sings and dreams herself into the body of her ancestral namesake, Qukezwa the first, who lived in the time of Nongqawuse.

Having failed to find a 'home' in Johannesburg and unsuccessful in his efforts to locate the 'hearthly beauty', NomaRussia, in Qolorha-by-Sea, Camagu regretfully plans his return 'to Xoliswa Ximiya's U.S. of A.' (Mda 2000: 111). He is interrupted by the screams of a hotel cleaner, who has discovered in his blankets a brown mole snake, the Majola clan totem. Camagu is returned to a cultural tradition when he is visited by, and in turn acknowledges, his totem. Up to this point, Camagu has been courting Xoliswa Ximiya. Following the visitation by Majola, she is summarily dismissed from his attentions and replaced by Qukezwa, who is finally able to convince Camagu that the proposed development will have a negative impact on the village. As Qukezwa begins to dominate the plot, the sharp fragments of heterogenous time begin to melt under the soft glow of nostalgia.

Mda admits to being a romantic, drawn to Nongqawuse's beautiful dream of a better world (see Isaacson 2003). The authorial voice is openly sympathetic to her when it states: 'In reality . . . all [she] wanted was to save the amaXhosa nation' (Mda 2000: 182). At the same time, it is keenly aware of the devastation that followed in the prophecies' wake, of the unspeakable sufferings of the 'Middle Generations', in the novel's genealogy. The 'dis-ease' introduced into the text by this awareness of immeasurable loss is enhanced by a latent disquiet concerning the gendered power struggle that historians such as Bradford have found in the prophecies. Such contestation is anxiously denied in the above quote, with its insistence on amaXhosa unity and the altruistic, nation-centred motives of Nongqawuse.

Torn between the romantic dream of a better world and the horrifying consequences of this act of female authorship, the text manages its ambivalence by again splitting aspects of Nongqawuse's legacy. This second split is embodied in NomaRussia and Qukezwa. The duality established between them is a duality between the maimed and the miraculous reproductive body.

The name 'NomaRussia' ('Mother of the Russians') alludes to the redemptive promises of the prophecies and locates its bearer within this legacy as maternal figure. After disappearing for much of the novel, NomaRussia reappears near the end, once marriage negotiations for Camagu and Qukezwa's union have concluded. She is dying of cervical cancer and a stream of blood gushes from her reproductive organs. Temporal juxtaposition is used to powerful effect when the narrative cuts back to the past and the devastating effects of the prophetic movement are revealed in all their horror: 'People were dying. Thousands of them. At first it was mostly old people and children. Then men and women in their prime. Dying everywhere. Corpses and skeletons were a common sight. In the dongas. On the veld. Even around the homesteads. No one had the strength to bury them' (Mda 2000: 292). This aspect of Nongqawuse – a terrifying harbinger of death – is embodied in NomaRussia. Her diseased reproductive organs provide the vehicle through which the horrors of the failed prophetic movement are exposed.

If NomaRussia's body figures authorial anxieties, Qukezwa's figures authorial desires in at least two respects: claims of autochthony and dreams of redemption. Her ancestral namesake (Qukezwa the first) was a Khoikhoi woman and the two Qukezwas carry much of the novel's symbolic weight. The emphasis placed on them reveals a deep investment in the politics of origins. As Twin asserts, Qukezwa the first is 'the original owner of this land' (Mda 2000: 124). Qukezwa the second inherits from her predecessor both her Khoisan features – her 'yellow thighs', for instance (64) – and her entitlement to the land, which she in turn passes on to her son. Such claims are established through women's – mother's – bodies and conferred to men.

The novel's deployment of autochthony is troubling both in terms of its dependence on the figuration of women as mothers and in the extent to which it untangles the text's temporality. According to Mbembe, celebrations of autochthony belong to an impoverished African nationalist tradition that 'has come to conceive politics either along the lines of a recovery of an essential but lost nature – the liberation of an essence – or as a sacrificial process' (2002: 272). Autochthony and sacrificial redemption, origin and telos, meet in the body of Qukezwa the second. In contrast to NomaRussia's oozing, diseased body, it expresses the integrity of parthenogenesis, or virgin birth, and alludes to Christian redemption myths.

When Qukezwa is found to be pregnant, the grandmothers attest that she is still a virgin, 'that she has not known a man – in the biblical sense' (Mda 2000: 250). The reader might assume, as Camagu does, that Qukezwa was impregnated during their mystical midnight horse-ride. Camagu, seated behind Qukezwa, with his thighs wrapped around her, is enraptured by her singing. Afterwards he discovers that his pants are wet. Impregnation without penetration is the 'rational' explanation for Qukezwa's conception. Yet little weight is attached to this explanation. Instead, the novel positions the conception as a 'miraculous' event. Qukezwa and Camagu pass Nongqawuse's Pool and narrative splicing between past and present suggests that Qukezwa's conception is a fulfilment of the redemptive longings of her Believing ancestors, Qukezwa the first and Twin. A comparison with Sindiwe Magona's *Mother to Mother* is illuminating: virgin birth, in *Mother to Mother*, carries no 'magical' implications, but comments instead on the social positioning of women within and between South African patriarchies (see Samuelson 2004: 133, 137).

In *The Heart of Redness*, Xhosa, Christian and Khoikhoi cosmologies are drawn together in Qukezwa's virgin birth, with Khoikhoi beliefs taking ascendancy as syncreticism gives way to autochthony. The child born from these unusual circumstances is called Heitsi – after the Khoikhoi prophet-god in whose honour Qukezwa the first named her own son. Heitsi Eibib, as both Qukezwas relate, is the son of the storytelling creator, Tsiqwa, 'who tells his stories in heaven. He created the Khoikhoi and all the world' (Mda 2000: 23). Heitsi Eibib is both 'the earliest prophet of the Khoikhoi' and saviour: 'He lived and died for all the Khoikhoi' (24).

While readings of the prophecies as syncretic cultural products tend to foreground Mhlakaza at the expense of Nongqawuse, the turn here to the autochthonous sees the female prophet-woman displaced in favour of the male prophet-god. 'Miraculously' conceived and named after Heitsi Eibib, Heitsi the second (the son of Qukezwa the second) is encoded as a messianic figure and the text's romantic dream of a better world is deflected from Nongqawuse onto him.

Historians argue that the redemptive symbols of the Christian resurrection narrative were introduced to the amaXhosa by the Khoikhoi (who had earlier imbibed them from missionaries).[8] Mda, in contrast, keeps Khoikhoi beliefs inviolable. Camagu comes to learn that 'the Khoikhoi people were singing the story of Heitsi Eibib long before the white missionaries came to these shores with their similar story of Moses and the crossing of the Red Sea' (Mda 2000: 288). Thus, the Khoikhoi women – Qukezwa the first and second – are the bearers of a 'pure' and 'uncontaminated' African cultural tradition invested in the son, Heitsi.

The sublimated sexuality of Qukezwa's virgin birth is equally telling. Qukezwa the first, as a guerrilla during the War of Mlanjeni, is among the 'Khoikhoi women [who] sold their bodies to the British soldiers in order to smuggle canisters of gunpowder to their fighting men . . . prostituting themselves' to save 'the amaXhosa nation from utter defeat' (Mda 2000: 22–23). Stratton claims that the prostitute provides a metaphor of national degradation under colonial conquest, which finds its post-colonial counterpart in the figure of Mother Africa, symbol of national recovery (1994: 48–50). Qukezwa the second is cleansed and reclaimed as a Mother Africa figure, her body uncontaminated and whole. The shift from prostitute to virgin-mother that we find in *The Heart of Redness* is one from the nation penetrated by foreign incursion to the nation redeemed through its recovery of an authentic cultural tradition. This trajectory is followed also in Mda's previous novel, *Ways of Dying*, where redemption is signalled by the movement of the central female character, Noria, from prostitute to ascetic. The story told through these women's bodies follows a linear structure, untangling narrative temporality and rearranging it into a teleological formation that stretches from colonial loss to post-colonial recovery.

Given the textual value laid on Qukezwa's body, it comes as no surprise that of the three women, she is the one that Camagu chooses for his wife. The closing paragraph of the novel retains an emphasis on Qukezwa as the figure of heritage. Here, the binary of 'modern' and 'non-modern' settles into the twin poles of Janus-faced national time, conventionally expressed through a troubling gendered configuration. Marked as conserving figures, women protect the spiritual and cultural identity sloughed off by their menfolk, who follow colonial and nationalist narratives of progress outside the sanctuary of the home, or, in our context, the cultural tradition to which Camagu is returned in a symbolic act of homecoming.

Throughout the novel, shoreline and sea are associated with Qukezwa's Khoikhoi heritage and the Xhosa ancestors awaited in the time of Nongqawuse. When Heitsi refuses to swim in the sea, Qukezwa is stunned: 'How will he survive without the sea? How will he carry out the business of saving his people? . . . Heitsi screams even louder, pulling away from her grip, "No, mama! No! This boy does not belong in the sea! This boy belongs in the man village!" '(Mda 2000: 320).

In the closing words of the novel, Heitsi rejects both his autochthonous heritage and (apparently) his messianic destiny. But the gendered split is indicative. As Anne McClintock has shown, nationalism's 'temporal anomaly' – with its one face gazing back into a primordial past, its other into an infinite future – is managed by having women embody 'nationalism's conservative principle of continuity', while the national sons act out its 'progressive, or revolutionary principle of discontinuity' (1995: 358–59). As national son-citizen, Heitsi assumes for himself the principle of temporal discontinuity, while also laying a specific claim on the village space as male (the 'man village'). Unlike Xoliswa Ximiya, Heitsi is not subject to textual censure for taking this stance and is, moreover, given the last words in a novel that has expelled Xoliswa Ximiya. Qukezwa, who is embraced by the narrative, continues to play her female role as the conserving and conservative temporal aspect of nationalism, as the 'repository of the national archaic' (McClintock 1995: 359).

The Heart of Redness contradicts its own attempts to write time as entangled by shifting into a teleological historical narrative of autochthony, sacrifice and redemption. This not only undercuts its more radical inscription of time, but also offers a limited script for women to inhabit. Women embody heritage and carry redemption in their wombs. The packaging of the novel is instructive here: the first South African edition depicts a Xhosa woman, cloaked in the 'traditional' red blanket, with a baby on her back. The 'red' woman, with baby in tow, signifies on the pregnant promises of a recovered cultural identity and, with the Madonna as interchangeable signifier, its redemptive quality.

The alacrity with which the novel – itself located in literate culture – dismisses Xoliswa Ximiya, the only highly literate woman in the story, is revealing. Women bear men's messages through their bodies and are firmly discouraged from seizing the tools of writing themselves. The 'heart of redness' beats within the breast, or womb, or a woman; the future and the pen are the preserve of men. Thus does the novel participate in an androcentric appropriation and displacement of women's authorship, even as it ostensibly focuses on a woman whose words fundamentally altered the political landscape of South Africa.

Leaky vessels, empty vessels: Gender and authorship

Leaky vessels, observes Marina Warner, provide an image of female (mis)rule, of women's lack of control and of a lack of control over women: 'the ideal female body, fitting container of high and virtuous meanings, should be an impossible object, like a sieve which does not leak' (1985b: 266; see also 248–49). Through the leaky vessel of NomaRussia's body, the novel offers anxious commentary on female assumptions to authorial power and women's entry into the public sphere. Her condition alludes to what Bradford, in an earlier version of her paper, has called the 'reproductive imagery' of Nongqawuse's prophecies – their references to blood-red suns and moons, to milksacks and bukka roots, fed to young women to prevent miscarriages.[9] These elements of the prophecies mark them as explicitly female – to some, intrinsically female – and have been read, moreover, as pointing to a female, even a 'proto-feminist', agenda (Bradford 1996: 366). The failure of the romantic dream of the prophecies is thus ascribed in part, by the novel, to their gendered nature: to their female authorship and reproductive imagery.

NomaRussia's story is also used to deflect what Bradford identifies as Nongqawuse's most 'original contribution' in an era of prophecy (1996: 363). A substantial portion of Nongqawuse's prophecy concerns the sexual indiscretions of promiscuous men. This aspect of her prophecy, along with the authority her utterances achieved, distinguishes Nongqawuse from a legion of prophets. Yet, it has been largely ignored in historiography and is displaced in the novel. *The Heart of Redness* shifts the emphasis from containing promiscuous men to punishing promiscuous women. The cause of NomaRussia's cancer, she insists, is retaliatory witchcraft, bitter recompense for an adulterous affair.

NomaRussia's travails are traced back to women's sexual incontinence, which is in turn symbolically linked to the devastation following the prophecies that stem from women's verbal incontinence. Her leaky body thus suggests a conception of female authorship as disruptive, its meaning unstable as it spills out uncontrollably, and its effects disastrous. In Renaissance English drama, Gail Kern Paster finds that 'the female body's moisture, secretions, and productions' are marked as 'shameful tokens of uncontrol' (1993: 52). Menstrual blood, in particular, serves as a sign 'of woman's inability to control the workings of her own body' (83). In the African Renaissance represented in Mda's novel, a similar symbolic field holds sway: NomaRussia's inability to stop bleeding provides a visible reminder of women's lack of restraint and casts a shadow back upon the historical figure of Nongqawuse.

Mda responds to Nongqawuse's verbal incontinence by asserting what Sandra M. Gilbert and Susan Gubar describe as 'the patriarchal notion that the writer "fathers" his text just as God fathered the world' (2000: 4). Speaking from outside the text, Mda describes writing as a process of being 'in control' (quoted in Robertson 2001). When asked about his use of fictional devices associated with magical realism, Mda replies: 'The world that I was writing about was the world that I created . . . I am the God of that world, so I can make things happen the way I want them to happen' (Naidoo 1997: 250). Rather than enabling the 'subaltern past' to disrupt meaning, magical realist devices allow this author to claim the function of creator and controller of meaning, and to exclude women from authorship. This gendered conception of authorship is first suggested in *Ways of Dying*.

In *Ways of Dying*, Noria's mother, That Mountain Woman, who offers a fundamental challenge to patriarchy, is killed off with cancer of the womb. Mda strikes at the centre of her matriarchal power and, thus disabling her, turns his attentions to the reproductive body of her daughter.[10] Noria bears what the Yoruba call an *abiku* child. Like Qukezwa's womb, Noria's is also the site of a miraculous conception. Discussing *abiku* children in West African fiction, Brenda Cooper finds that they represent the plight of a nation that refuses to be born and that spirals through bloody cycles of violence. This is an image of birth that emphasises 'circularity' and 'repetition', rather than change (Cooper 1998: 88). Thus, Noria's reproductive body becomes a vessel for the author's message about the nation: it is made to speak both the terrible cycle of violence gripping the transitional state and messianic hopes for a redemptive future. Revealingly, the young Noria plays the part of muse to Toloki's father.[11] Her later shift from prostitution (suggesting incontinence) to asceticism – the 'sealed fountain' (Warner 1985a: 73) – sees her resuming the role of muse, now to Toloki himself, whose artistic products inspired by Noria are declared 'the work of a genius' (Mda 1995: 187). And genius, as Christine Battersby shows in *Gender and Genius*, is a conventionally male condition (1989).

The troubling, leaky secretions of the reproductive body – symbolic of an uncontrolled and uncontrollable act of female authorship – are displaced onto the unfortunate NomaRussia and That Mountain Woman, both of whom are emblems of dis-ease. Qukezwa's virgin body, in contrast, avails itself to authorial penetration. The virgin female body, argues Susan Gubar, is a 'blank page' on which male authors inscribe their messages: '[the] model of the pen-penis writing on the virgin page participates in a long tradition identifying the author as a male who is primary and the female as his passive creation' (1986: 295). Mda tellingly describes his acts of authorship as being 'in the God business', when he talks of the importance of commanding control over the texts he writes (Naidoo 1997: 250; quoted in Robertson 2001). He thus casts himself in the mould of the storytelling Khoikhoi God, Tsiqwa (father of Heitsi Eibib) and we are left to ponder the implications of Qukezwa's miraculous conception of the child Heitsi. Stratton claims that in the male African literary tradition, women bear the author's interpretation of history like a baby in the womb. When Qukezwa bears Heitsi (named after Tsiqwa's mythical son), she bears Mda's message, transforming his words into flesh and bringing the text's desires to life. Stratton's comments about an earlier generation of male African writers are applicable to Mda: 'He is the subject-artist, she is the aesthetic object, the repository of his meaning . . . her function is to embody his vision' (1994: 52).

The Author-as-God fixes the meaning of an undecidable text. We are returned again to an androcentric historiography that attempts to manage the unruly words of a female prophet. Nongqawuse has been pathologised in oral and written historical traditions as sexually frustrated. Mda represents this position in his Unbelieving Twin-Twin, a largely unsympathetic character, who says: 'Bring that foolish girl Nongqawuse to me so that I may sleep [with] her. I will give it to her so hard that she will stop spreading lies! She is telling all these lies, dreaming all these dreams, seeing all these imaginary visions, because she is starved of men!' (Mda 2000: 99).

While explicitly critical of the position voiced by Twin-Twin, the novel, riven as it is contradictory desires, finds itself reiterating this stance on another level: the Author-as-God silences Nongqawuse, or harnesses her voice to his purposes, by transposing her verbal acts onto the reproductive ones of Qukezwa. Bradford exposes the historical tradition – both oral and written – as one characterised by men responding to Nongqawuse through 'exercising sexual power', as Twin-Twin does in the above quote (Bradford 1996: 367 n.100). Mda metaphorically wields such power when he impregnates Qukezwa with his redemptive message.

As a young woman of marriageable age in a time of cattle dearth that threatened to deprive her of the authorising subject position of legitimate motherhood, Nongqawuse may have laid claim to the voice of the ancestors as a means to enter the public sphere to which she, as an unmarried woman, had no access. Qukezwa's relation to cattle, in contrast, is that of bride rather than prophet, she is spoken for rather than speaker. Qukezwa welcomes the customary exchange of cattle that transfers her miraculous fertility from her father to Camagu. We are reminded of the significance of the cattle killed in the prophetic movement: cattle are the currency through which women's reproductive potential is appropriated by the clan. Magona's *Mother to Mother* again provides a useful intertext as the female writer, who draws on a similar symbolic and historical field to Mda, offers a very different response to the institution of customary marriage. Unlike Qukezwa, Magona's Mandisa deeply resents the exchange of cattle that bequeaths her fertility to the head patriarch and his ancestral line.

Bradford points also to Nongqawuse's injunctions against incest and extramarital sexual relations as intimations that she may have claimed the voice of male ancestors in order to counter her female vulnerability and voice her female rage (1996: 363–64). Her insistence on the female signature of the prophecies offers a useful counterweight to Peires and Mda's gender-blind readings, as, indeed, the comparison with Magona reveals. I, however, wish to chart a route between the two positions. If Mda marshals the 'subaltern past' to express his meaning, so too does Bradford, who appropriates Nongqawuse as 'proto-feminist'. I am reluctant to rely on woman's signature as transparent sign that renders invisible differences within the category 'woman' and equally keen to unseat the authorial authority Mda asserts over the text of the novel and over Nongqawuse herself. It may be more productive to situate Nongqawuse's utterances at the juncture of feminist and postmodernist practices. While forgoing the full presence of female speech, an anti-phallocentric postmodernism may productively displace the authority and legitimacy of male authorship.

In a fascinating reading of Nongqawuse that pre-dates Mda's novel, Lewis Nkosi points to her assumption of ancestral voices as an instance in which postmodernism, far from being disabling, can have 'subversive and discomposing effects not only on the hegemonic discourse of the imperial centre but also those created by traditions to underpin hierarchical structures of age and patriarchy' (1998: 89). He reads Nongqawuse's authorship as decentred *through* men, rather than inhering *in* men and points to her

> 'narcissism,' her spectacular self-identification when she peers into a pool of water and thinks she can hear voices of the ancestral spirits speaking to her. Was claiming to have seen visions and to have heard voices of the ancestral spirits not perhaps Nongqawuse's attempt – not fully conscious to be sure – to clear space for herself in which as a woman, traditionally forbidden to participate in political discourse, she could then speak with some authority and be listened to? (Nkosi 1998: 88)

The scene of Nongqawuse's 'spectacular self-identification' is of particular pertinence. Evocative of the Lacanian 'mirror stage', it suggests the imaginary process of identification by which the fragmented, or leaky, body is projected as unified subject (see Lacan 2001: 1–8). The imaginary unity of the 'I' – in this case the speaking subject – is achieved through an act of mis-recognition, a projection of the (lacking or leaky) 'I' onto the ancestors. As Nkosi concludes: 'What passes for the "subject of discourse" is speaking from many places at once' (1998: 88).

While *The Heart of Redness* retains Nongqawuse's Pool as heritage site, the scenes in which she 'hears voices' are transferred to misty fields and choppy seas. Her 'spectacular self-identification' is erased from the novel. Furthermore, by depicting Nongqawuse as little more than a mouthpiece for the ancestors or Mhlakaza, Mda avoids taking up Nkosi's challenge to consider the implications of Nongqawuse's 'voice throwing' regarding questions of authorship. Instead, he persistently shows her availing herself as a receptacle for other voices. The spectre of woman as leaky vessel – and of authorship as dispersed and decentred – is dispelled. Nongqawuse is posited, instead, as empty vessel: an uncontaminated container for the words of men.

Splitting off all anxiety with regard to the troubling legacies of the prophecies' female authorship and unrecuperable losses, the novel centres its desire on Qukezwa's virginal and maternal body. She reveals the 'ideal' Nongqawuse of masculinist and nationalist fantasy: one who was no more than a mouthpiece for the patrilineal ancestors, one who wished for no more than to save the Xhosa nation. Cast out is an image of Nongqawuse as a woman who entered the public sphere with her own gendered agenda. While the Nongqawuse of male nationalist fantasies transmits the male-authored message through her mouth, Qukezwa, her representative figure in Mda's present-day narrative, transmits it through her body. Qukezwa, then, is proposed as a domesticated, culturally 'pure' Nongqawuse, her obedient womb replacing Nongqawuse's unruly, slippery voice.

Qukezwa's parthenogenesis thus sees Mda reasserting the author function that Nongqawuse both claimed and destabilised. The novel shows no interest in reading Nongqawuse as one engaged in 'postmodern' acts of decentring that grant authority to the female self through a cunning act of displacement and, in the process, destabilise the boundaries between *intombi* and male ancestors, and between medium and author. Moreover, rather than grappling with the implications of Nongqawuse's assumption of the ancestral voice –

the most authoritative in the patriarchal and patrilineal hierarchy – Mda, curiously, reduces it to a weak analogy. Faced with the disturbing claim that Nongqawuse was 'a little girl who craved attention' and 'concoct[ed] her own theology', Camagu accounts for the prophecies as follows: 'Young girls are prone to seeing visions . . . Who's always seeing visions of the Virgin Mary? Young girls. Our Lady of Fatima . . . our lady of this and that . . . all places where young virgins saw visions of the Virgin!' (Mda 2000: 283). Compared to a virgin seeing visions of the Virgin, Nongqawuse's authority is multiply mediated and can be achieved only through woman's relation to the blessed son.

In her discussion of the male historiographic tradition, Bradford suggests that 'gender imperialism' of this nature is a compensatory response to the 'strength of Nongqawuse's challenge to patriarchal power' (1996: 366). Her observation applies equally to *The Heart of Redness*, in which the author-function reasserts an androcentric power that Nongqawuse appealed to only to challenge in her decentred acts of (female) authorship.

Notes

This chapter has also been published in an expanded form as 'Chapter 2: Nongqawuse: National time and (female) authorship' in Samuelson (2007: 51–83).

1. Allusions to the Virgin Mary alongside accounts of Nongqawuse's prophecy appear in Mda's *The Heart of Redness* (2000), Sindiwe Magona's *Mother to Mother* (1998), Mike Nicol's *This Day and Age* (1992) and Brett Bailey's *The Prophet* (2003). The use of the TRC as an explanatory context for Nongqawuse's story is evident in *The Heart of Redness*, *Mother to Mother*, *The Prophet*, *The Day of the Two Suns: The Trial of Nongqawuse* (1999) and *Nongqawuse: The Truth Commission* (2003). Nongqawuse's prophecy is drawn on to provide commentary on 'development' (particularly capitalist development) in *The Heart of Redness*, Jeremy Cronin's poem 'The Time of Prophets' (1997) and Kelwyn Sole's poem 'Miss Nongqawuse 1997' (1998).

2. A note on terminology: the events of 1856–57 have conventionally been dubbed 'the Xhosa National Suicide' or the 'Cattle-Killing movement'. Due to significant problems with both these formulations – outlined below – I refer to them as 'the events of 1856–57'. The phrase 'National Suicide' is a discredited one that today appears only in tourist brochures, luring visitors to Nongqawuse's Pool or grave. Far from attempting mass suicide,

believers in the prophecies, as recent historical literature persuasively argues, sought to save themselves and their lifestyle, from colonial encroachment. On the other hand, 'Cattle Killing', as Jeff Guy points out, 'is more than a misnomer. It conflates, distorts and oversimplifies the events to which it refers, thereby excluding a number of the most important elements'. Focusing on the male-associated realm of cattle at the expense of female agricultural labour, it conceals the significance of the latter: 'As damaging as the killing of cattle and the resultant deprivation was, it was the destruction of crops and the suspension of cultivation which turned deprivation into catastrophe' (Guy 1991: 229).

3. In this regard, see also *Nongqawuse: The Truth Commission* (2003). Bailey's *The Prophet*, which represents women as the main supporters driving the movement, evokes a more terrifying Nongqawuse than any other transition text and reaches its resolution in a ritual exorcism of the spirits possessing Nongqawuse.

4. The reference to 'redness' in the novel's title is specific to the Eastern Cape, where 'red' denotes the ochre used as ornamentation by 'traditional' amaXhosa and the terms 'school people' and 'red people' are used to differentiate between those who have embraced 'modernity' and those who have not.

5. Presented on the occasion of the adoption by the Constitutional Assembly of *The Republic of South Africa Constitution Bill* in 1996, when he was deputy-president, this has become Mbeki's signature speech and was performed by John Kani at the 'We are Finally Free' concert, celebrating Mbeki's inauguration for a second presidential term on 27 April 2004.

6. Editors' note: see Chapter 10 for a discussion of Mda and Conrad.

7. As Maureen Isaacson relates: 'Mda says he identifies with Camagu' (2003). Camagu and Mda both return from exile to a democratic South Africa, having received advanced degrees in communication and, significantly, both share the clan totem of the Majola. In his interview with Isaacson, Mda tells of his two encounters with Majola, and Isaacson quotes him instructing her: 'You must say I have seen it' (2003). I will soon discuss Camagu's encounter with Majola.

8. Elizabeth Elbourne claims that 'it is striking how much faster mission Christianity was adopted by the battered remnants of Khoikhoi communities of the eastern and western Cape in the late eighteenth and early nineteenth centuries than it was by less politically and economically damaged African societies outside the colony' (1995: 65). She finds that their 'interaction with Christianity was shaped by existing Khoisan beliefs', with often syncretic results (72). Thus, far from inviolable, Elbourne points to the 'permeability of Khoisan religiosity' at this time, along with its 'readiness to turn outside influences to "national" ends' (74).

9. This phrase was used in the version of Bradford's paper presented in the Africa Seminar Series, Centre for African Studies, University of Cape Town in 1995 (38 n.139).

10. My reading of That Mountain Woman's unfortunate fate developed out of a dialogue with Nokuthula Mazibuko at the 'Postcolonialism: South/Africa' conference (Durban, 5–7 July 2004), at which we presented papers on gender in *Ways of Dying* and *The Heart of Redness* respectively.

11. By inscribing woman as muse and bearer of his message, Mda misses an opportunity to allude to the renowned Venda artist Noria Mabasa, who is more reminiscent of That (indomitable) Mountain Woman than of the character who bears her name in the novel. Mabasa's significance in South African culture is signalled, among other things, by the naming of a street in her honour in Johannesburg's new inner city precinct.

Works cited

Anderson, Benedict. 1983. *Imagined Communities: Reflections on the Origin and Spread of Nationalism*. London: Verso.

Bailey, Brett. 2003. *The Prophet*. Performed by Third World Bunfight at the Standard Bank National Arts Festival, Grahamstown, 1999. In: Bailey, Brett. *The Plays of Miracle and Wonder: Bewitching Visions and Primal High-Jinx from the South African Stage*. Cape Town: Double Storey, 167–93.

Barthes, Roland. 1977. 'The death of the author'. In: Barthes, Roland. *Image-Music-Text*. Edited and translated by Stephen Heath. Glasgow: Collins, 142–48.

Battersby, Christine. 1989. *Gender and Genius: Towards a Feminist Aesthetics*. Bloomington: Indiana University Press.

Boym, Svetlana. 2001. *The Future of Nostalgia*. New York: Basic.

Bradford, Helen. 1996. 'Women, gender and colonialism: Rethinking the history of the British Cape Colony and its frontier zones, c.1806–70'. *Journal of African History* 37: 351–70.

Butler, Judith. 1990. *Gender Trouble: Feminism and the Subversion of Identity*. New York: Routledge.

Chakrabarty, Dipesh. 1998. 'Minority histories, subaltern pasts'. *Postcolonial Studies* 1(1): 15–29.

Chatterjee, Partha. 1999. 'Anderson's utopia'. *Diacritics* 29(4): 128–34.

Conrad, Joseph. 1973 (1899). *Heart of Darkness*. Harmondsworth: Penguin.

Cooper, Brenda. 1998. *Magical Realism in West African Fiction: Seeing with a Third Eye*. London: Routledge.

Cronin, Jeremy. 1997. 'The time of prophets'. In: Cronin, Jeremy. *Even the Dead: Poems, Parables and a Jeremiad*. Cape Town: David Philip, 36–38.

The Day of the Two Suns: The Trial of Nongqawuse. 1999. Screenplay by Zakes Mda. Directed by John Matshikiza. Produced by Mark Newman. *Saints, Sinners and Settlers* Series. SABC 2.

Elbourne, Elizabeth. 1995. 'Early Khoisan uses of mission Christianity'. In: Bredekamp, Henry and Robert Ross (eds.). *Missions and Christianity in South African History*. Johannesburg: Wits University Press, 65–95.

Fabian, Johannes. 1983. *Time and the Other: How Anthropology Makes its Object*. New York: Columbia University Press.

Gilbert, Sandra M. and Susan Gubar. 2000. *The Madwoman in the Attic: The Woman Writer and the Nineteenth-Century Literary Imagination*. 2nd ed. New Haven: Yale University Press.

Gubar, Susan. 1986. ' "The blank page" and the issues of female creativity'. In: Showalter, Elaine (ed.). *The New Feminist Criticism*. London: Virago, 292–313.

Guy, Jeff. 1990. 'Gender oppression in southern Africa's precapitalist societies'. In: Walker, Cherryl (ed.). *Women and Gender in Southern Africa to 1945*. Cape Town: David Philip; London: James Currey, 33–47, 348–49.

———. 1991. 'A landmark, not a breakthrough. Review of *The Dead Will Arise: Nongqawuse and the Great Xhosa Cattle-Killing Movement of 1856–7* by J.B. Peires'. *South African Historical Journal* 25: 227–31.

Isaacson, Maureen. 2003. 'Free Sate madonnas prevail in Mda's new novel. Review of *The Heart of Redness* and *The Madonna of Excelsior* by Zakes Mda'. *The Connection*. 3 October. http://www.theconnection.org/features/zakesarticle.asp, accessed 3 October 2003.

Jordan, A.C. 1973. *Towards an African Literature: The Emergence of Literary Form in Xhosa*. Berkeley: University of California Press.

Lacan, Jacques. 2001 (1977). 'The mirror stage as formative of the function of the I.' In: Lacan, Jacques. *Écrits: A Selection*. Translated by Alan Sheridan. London: Routledge, 1–8.

Lloyd, David. 2000. 'Colonial trauma/postcolonial recovery'. *Interventions* 2(2): 212–28.

Magona, Sindiwe. 1998. *Mother to Mother*. Cape Town: David Philip.

Mbeki, Thabo. 1996. 'I am an African'. Statement of Deputy-President T.M. Mbeki, on the occasion of the adoption by the Constitutional Assembly of The Republic of South Africa Constitution Bill. 8 May. http://www.anc.org.za/ancdocs/history/mbeki/1996/sp960508.html, accessed 15 January 2005.

Mbembe, Achille. 2001. *On the Postcolony*. Translated by A.M. Berrett, Janet Roitman, Murray Last and Steven Rendall. Berkeley: University of California Press.

———. 2002. 'African modes of self-writing'. Translated by Steven Rendall. *Public Culture* 14(1): 239–73.

McClintock, Anne. 1995. *Imperial Leather: Race, Gender and Sexuality in the Colonial Contest*. New York: Routledge.

Mda, Zakes. 1995. *Ways of Dying*. Cape Town: Oxford University Press.

———. 2000. *The Heart of Redness*. Cape Town: Oxford University Press.

Naidoo, Venu. 1997. 'Interview with Zakes Mda'. *Alternation* 4(1): 247–61.

Nicol, Mike. 1992. *This Day and Age: A Novel*. New York: Vintage.

Nkosi, Lewis. 1998. 'Postmodernism and black writing in South Africa'. In: Attridge, Derek and Rosemary Jolly (eds.). *Writing South Africa: Literature, Apartheid, and Democracy, 1970–1995*. Cambridge: Cambridge University Press, 75–90.

Nongqawuse: The Truth Commission. 2003. Performed by Community Arts Project. Cape Town: Cape Town Festival.

Paster, Gail Kern. 1993. *The Body Embarrassed: Drama and the Disciplines of Shame in Early Modern England*. Ithaca: Cornell University Press.

Peires, J.B. 1989. *The Dead Will Arise: Nongqawuse and the Great Xhosa Cattle-Killing Movement of 1856–7*. Johannesburg: Ravan Press.

Robertson, Heather. 2001. 'You can take your hat off'. *Sunday Times*, 25 March. http://www.suntimes.co.za/2001/03/25/lifestyle/life02.htm, accessed 2 October 2003.

Samuelson, Meg. 2004. 'The mother as witness: Reading *Mother to Mother* alongside South Africa's Truth and Reconciliation Commission'. In: Koyana, Siphokazi (ed.). *Sindiwe Magona: The First Decade*. Pietermaritzburg: University of KwaZulu-Natal Press, 127–44.

———. 2007. *Remembering the Nation, Dismembering Women? Stories of the South African Transition*. Pietermaritzburg: University of KwaZulu-Natal Press.

Sole, Kelwyn. 1998. 'Miss Nongqawuse 1997'. In: Sole, Kelwyn. *Love That Is Night*. Durban: Gecko, 99.

Stratton, Florence. 1994. *Contemporary African Literature and the Politics of Gender*. London: Routledge.

Warner, Marina. 1985a (1976). *Alone of All Her Sex: The Myth and Cult of the Virgin Mary*. London: Picador.

———. 1985b. *Monuments and Maidens: The Allegory of the Female Form*. London: Weidenfeld.

Wilson, Richard A. 2001. *The Politics of Truth and Reconciliation in South Africa: Legitimizing the Post-Apartheid State*. Cambridge: Cambridge University Press.

13

A Politics of Doubt

GRANT FARRED

. . . for there is no Covenant with God, but by mediation of some body
that representeth Gods Person; which none doth but Gods Lieutenant,
who hath the Soveraignty under God. (Hobbes, *Leviathan* 1996: 122)

Introduction

One of the most deplorable aspects of the postmodern era and its so-
called 'thought' is the return of the religious dimension in all its different
guises: from Christian and other fundamentalisms, through the
multitude of New Age spiritualisms, up to the emerging religious
sensitivity within deconstruction itself (so-called 'post-secular' thought).
(Žižek 2000: 1)

THE THEOCRATIC IS, almost invariably, the space of the politically dissensual
precisely because it attempts, vigorously, to suppress dissent. It is a public site
that, despite its desire for conformity, opens up – sometimes only in the most
inconspicuous ways, sometimes as full-blown opposition – into disagreement,
contestation, conflict and possibly even violence. Because of its declared
adherence to the multitudinous, observant One as the apex of the hierarchy,
the theocratic cannot function as anything but the space of inequality. It is
here where transcendentally derived or socially authored hierarchies order
existence, where those hierarchies are most strictly enforced, where the

relationship between God and humans, priests (holy men, prophetesses, shamans) and followers, the faithful and atheists or agnostics, men and women, or some combination of these and other inequalities, structure daily political life. The theocratic determines public morality and culture, and it scripts the community's history.

The crucial paradox about the theocratic *res publica* is that it marks the space where fundamentalism, in Slavoj Žižek's terms, is not most assured but, on the contrary, most concerned about its articulation, about how it is practised as a faith and about whether its orthodoxy holds. The theocratic is the repository of anxiety because of its aporetic nature, because of how it operates in the crucial gap between the impure condition of the now (the condition of living in imperfection) and the anticipation of an immanent transcendence (the perfect eternity that is promised to the faithful). It constitutes the space of politics, the pregnant, contradictory historical moment in which the 'here' both obstructs the fulfilment of the eternal future and functions, through temporal force, as its only possible condition for fulfilment. The 'here' is always the site of the ultimate theocratic stakes because it marks the moment in which the potential for failure is inconceivably high, where things can go fatally wrong, where the hereafter can be lost, ceded to other forces. The promise of the theocratic also, because of the potential political costs of damnation, functions as a threat to the polis. Transformed into a threat, the terms of the promise provide the theocratic with the legal mechanisms, the technocratic language and the moral and spiritual justification necessary to enforce the promise; the promise, in other words, cannot be delivered; it cannot perform its utopian possibility, without a coercive underside.

The fundament of every religion, of course, is its promise of transcendence, the possibility – guarantee, we might say – of exceeding its immediate, restrictive temporality and spatiality, which will be succeeded by eternity and establishing itself as the final, unending epoch. In his essay, 'Technologies of the self', Michel Foucault argues that religions, especially Christianity, are 'supposed to lead the individual from one reality to another, from death to life, from time to eternity' (2000a: 242). In order to achieve its 'post-temporal' status, its fulfilment, every religion requires an event, normally one of cataclysmic, paradigm-shifting dimensions, which illustrates its truth, illuminates and elucidates its singularity, makes visible, physically manifest, the terms of its holy text and sets it apart from its rivals. The 'event' of the religion, such as the crucifixion and resurrection in Christianity, is such that it reveals those other faiths to be untrue, establishing a hierarchy, offering salvation to and glorifying those who adhere/d, damning those who doubt/ed. It is the basic tenet of fundamentalism: it divides the world along the simplest, yet decisive, fracturing: the saved and the lost, those who have been redeemed and those who have been punished into perpetuity; or, more ideally, those who have never doubted and those whose doubt now. The truth of the event apparent (or, 'the Truth Event', in Alain Badiou's phrasing (2001: 41–42; 67–71)), will exact the ultimate cost: the life, both in the here and in the afterlife, of those who did not, who refused, to believe.

While the desire for the primal, inaugural event is inscribed everywhere in Zakes Mda's *The Heart of Redness*, in the words of the Xhosa prophetess Nongqawuse, in the longings for liberation that stretch across the centuries from mid-nineteenth-century British colonialism to the unfulfilling history of the post-apartheid South African present, there is in the novel only the insistent presence of the Fall. There are only thwarted attempts at salvation, at the resurrection of the amaXhosa. For the ironically named 'Believers', the *Heart of Redness* protagonists who reject modernity and Christianity, Mda's work offers little in return for their faith. Believers such as the 'historical figures' of the nineteenth century, the Xhosa Twin and his Khoikhoi wife, Qukezwa, and their contemporary heirs Zim and his daughter, Qukezwa, receive nothing for their faith except what the novel terms a series of 'Disappointments' (Mda 2000: 131); there is no 'good news of the resurrection' (133). While the 'Believers' are felicitous in their 'faith' (which can sometimes be reduced to the historic culture of their community), they are no less dependent on the notion of sacrifice than their counterparts, the 'Unbelievers', of whom only some are Christian, but all of whom are on the side of modernity. It is significant, however, that among the chief Unbelievers in *The Heart of Redness*, Twin-Twin (twin brother of Twin) and his latter-day progeny, Bhonco and his daughter, Xoliswa Ximiya, none are Christian. However, *The Heart of Redness* is suffused with, if not the ethos, then certainly with the discourse of Christianity.

In his work on the 'technologies of the self',[1] Foucault, in his critique of modernist teleology, holds that the early Christian church borrowed many of its practices and rituals from surrounding pagan religions, including a dialogic engagement on notions of the 'self' with the Stoics. Foucault's is, of course, a reversal of the modernist logos that situates Christianity as the genesis of 'Reason' and traditional practices. In *The Heart of Redness*, however, Foucault's reversal is itself reversed, in no small measure because of the familiar elision in his work of the politics of colonialism and post-colonialism. This post-apartheid novel reveals how, often unwittingly, the 'pagan' Believers took many of their prophetic cues from Christian religious practices, practices borrowed, absorbed, and rearticulated from the colonialist Christians who ruled them and the colonised converts with whom they shared, almost always antagonistically, a socio-political space.

The clearest expression of the Believers' 'cultural' debt to Christianity can be identified in the discourse of the prophetess Nongqawuse, the movement's leading figure, whose predictions to the amaXhosa constitute the basis of the novel's main narrative. In a pivotal moment, Nongqawuse issues instructions, via one of her spokespersons, to her followers in a language laden with the portent and promise of the resurrection, blending the Mosaic foreboding of the Old Testament with the proselytising prospect of the New Testament's St Paul:

> 'The new people who will arise from the dead will come with new cattle, horses, goats, sheep, dogs, fowl and other animals that the people may want. But the new animals of the new people cannot mix with your polluted ones. Destroy everything. Destroy the corn in your fields and in your granaries. Nongqawuse has told us that when the new people come here there will be a new world of contentment and no one will lead a troubled life again.' (Mda 2000: 155)

In order to achieve the 'new' world, the old has to be completely and utterly destroyed; neither crops nor livestock of the old can be spared. The new can only be born, can only become, once, Old Testament plague-like, all the material vestiges, the property, of the old have been eliminated. Nongqawuse's promise of purity is reminiscent of, but not analogous to, the New Testament Jesus clearing the money lenders out of his Father's house, the act of making the physical site of the sacred holy again, cleansing that contaminated by commerce. The relationship of the various 'faithful' to the material is, as this chapter will show, problematic. Both the Believers and the Unbelievers embrace the ownership of property, the private and the public, and do not require its full and permanent renunciation as a precondition for their faith, as in Nongqawuse's case where it demands, at most, a temporary sacrifice after which full restitution is promised.

The 'new people' will replenish the cattle and refill the granaries, but only after all the amaXhosa have sacrificed their possessions (the prophecy refuses the distinction that has emerged between the Believers and the Unbelievers). In addition to replacing what has been sacrificed with that which is uncontaminated, there is a further, anti-colonially crucial, guarantee: 'the spirits would arise from the dead and drive the white people into the sea. Who would not want to see the world as it was before the white conquerors?' (Mda 2000: 77). However, not even a return to the pre-lapsarian, pre-colonial condition is something every Believer, to say nothing of the Unbelievers, is willing to risk his/her property for and because of this intra-political 'disobedience' and dissent, the promised land cannot, perforce, be achieved. The unfaithful Believers found themselves exposed to the felicitous wrath of the zealous Twin: 'But chiefs who were Believers continued to cultivate their land. Their territories became targets of Twin's marauding destroyers' (112). This double splitting of the amaXhosa, into Believers and Unbelievers and observant and unobservant Believers, makes evident a certain theocratic hollowness in Nongqawuse's prophetic conditionality: 'As long as the amaGogotya – the Unbelievers – continue to unbelieve, the prophecies shall not be fulfilled' (107). Twin's raids show that it is not only the amaGogotya's recalcitrance, their construction of unbelieving as a faith, that produces a tension between the two camps that endures over the centuries. It also suggests that the Unbelievers alone cannot be interminably condemned, except in fundamentalist terms, as the 'enemies of the nation' (107). Moreover, the Believers' infelicitousness, the 'doubting' chiefs who hedge their material bets, suggests that the prophetic is unachievable, unarticulable, even, without the precondition of universal obligation. Fealty to the prophetic is not specific to the Believers. It applies, as a precondition for transubstantiation, absolutely, indiscriminately, to the entire Xhosa nation. It is this absolutist politics that explains why the prophetic is historically unfulfillable: the prophetic requires complete transformation before change is possible or, can be promised. The prophetic demands absolute reconstitution before absolute transubstantiation can take place.

Because of the double dissensus that marks life in Qolorha-by-Sea, the promise of Nongqawuse is historically unfulfillable because it could only have been achieved by submission at the precise conjuncture, by following absolutely the dictates of the prophetess. The amaXhosa could, as it were, only have been liberated from colonial rule and born again, like Christ, if they had all forsaken all their material goods. However, unlike Christ, they were not required to sacrifice their lives, only that which they owned and that which they, had they been true to and in their faith, would have regained in the moment after their rebirth as a people, a people no longer contaminated, a people no longer polluted by their past. Unlike the Old Testament's Abraham, who was, even though it was with grave reservation, 'willing' to sacrifice his son Isaac in order to follow God's commands, the amaXhosa are not required to do violence to their children, or other loved ones. Unlike contemporary anti-colonialists, such as the San Domingan sans-culottes, fighting under the direction of Toussaint L'Ouverture, they were not required to risk their lives in battle against the (French) colonialists, and unlike the San Domingan slaves, they did not achieve freedom and independence, although had they done so, it would have been without human bloodshed. Nongqawuse's cattle killing, as the event is commonly known in South African history, which *The Heart of Redness* dates to 16 February 1857, required nothing but obedience, the first tenet of faith, and sacrifice, another crucial tenet of faith.

This chapter is a critique of the inability of *The Heart of Redness* to comprehend fully the complexity of Christian discourse, especially Christianity's dialogic relationship to the prophetic tradition articulated by Nongqawuse. Central to this argument is the role that the politics of doubt plays in the advocacy and sustenance of a faith. Despite Mda's underdevelopment of Christianity's theocratic status in *The Heart of Redness*, his sometimes prosaic rendering of it as the faith of the colonialists, as a secondary, out-of-place structure of belief, this faith of some Unbelievers is saliently and generatively present in *The Heart of Redness*. However, the discursive force of Christianity is only available if the village of Qolorha-by-Sea, the post-apartheid community where Nongqawuse once lived and the place from which she as a pubescent girl issued her directives about the cattle-killing movement to the amaXhosa, is read as the site of theocratic dissensus. It is the place that pits one new system of belief against another, that comprehends more critically the modernity of both the Believers and the Unbelievers that emerges in direct response to the cattle-killing event, a hermeneutic that interrogates the political complications of positing Xhosa culture as the basis for a faith. Qolorha-by-Sea is the political space where the Believers and the Unbelievers, after the suspension of struggle that was the 'Middle Generations' (colonialism and the apartheid era), renew their battle. This time, however, Nongqawuse, now 'reborn', or, 'returned', in the person of Qukezwa, is engaged in a different struggle with the Unbelievers: the environmental future of the region where she once, however briefly, 'reigned'. The struggle is now between late-capitalist modernity and 'tradition', between venture capitalists, a group of investors whom contemporary Unbelievers, such as Bhonco and his daughter Xoliswa Ximiya, support and who want to build a casino complex in Nongqawuse's old territory, and Believers who want to preserve their physical surroundings and their history. Most importantly, however, this chapter demonstrates how a dissensual politics requires its own scepticism because it can, and does in *The Heart of Redness*, produce a politics fraught with the potential for exploitation (of the historically disenfranchised) and co-optation (with global capital) as any politics of consensus that it is opposing.

Not equal to sacrifice
> Excess is the essence of the promise. (Ranciére 1995: 5)

The discourse of the sacrificial is fundamental to Christianity, as much as it is to any other faith. Sacrifice is part of an equitable system of exchange. In return for the crucifixion, there is the resurrection, the harbinger of eternal life for all, not simply for God's own son, Jesus Christ; in exchange for faith, there is the promise of everlasting life. The concept of the sacrifice is what the Believers, who, given their name, should understand not only perfectly well but without any struggle, fail to grasp. The Believers' resounding critique of their counterparts, especially the Christians in the ranks of the Unbelievers, is the crucifixion: 'What else could one expect from people who were a product of different creation from that of the amaXhosa, people who were so unscrupulous that they killed the son of their own god?' (Mda 2000: 133). This inconceivability on the part of the Believers is a constant, but singularly unconvincing, refrain throughout the novel. It is, to say the least, a disingenuous position. After all, how could a community of believers willing to put their all, their faith, their future and their material well-being in the hands, or words, more precisely, of a pubescent girl, not comprehend the possibility of a miraculous death and rebirth? Especially when they are willing to stake themselves on the mystical arrival of those variously named the 'spirits', the 'Strangers' and even the 'Russians' by ship on an appointed, or, anointed, day?

In a paradoxical turnabout, Zim, chief latter-day Believer, puts it in a fashion that exposes the Believers' fallacy that the mystical, miraculous content of Christianity is inaccessible to them: ' "If your Christ can walk on the sea and turn water into wine, so can Nongqawuse's cattle rise from the sea," declares Zim' (Mda 2000: 245). The vernacularisation of Christ's miracles – the act of walking on water, to test the faith of his disciples, especially Peter who, like at the Garden of Gethsemane, fails the test, and the first miracle of turning water into wine during the wedding at Canaan – reflects the depth of the dialogic between the Believers and the Unbelievers. These discourses have become so integrated into each other that one cannot function metaphorically without the other. However, more salient is the first miracle Zim invokes. Taken from the Book of Matthew (14:22–33) and occurring just after Jesus has fed the multitude with five loaves and two fishes, it is a telling choice because it is all about faith, or, more specifically, about the lack thereof. Jesus urges his disciples to walk towards him on water (after he had walked to them in a choppy sea) and, following his directive, they do so. However, when the sea again shows signs of turbulence, their trust in him wavers and they begin to sink. Jesus rescues them, but he adds a memorably gentle rebuke to Peter: 'O thou of little faith, wherefore didst thou doubt?' (Matthew 14:31).

While in the Old Testament God presented Abraham with a test of faith, Jesus' sacrifice, the crucifixion, in the New Testament is so much more central to Christianity. The Christians could countenance, *ex post facto*, the killing of 'god's own (and only) son' because it represents the constitutive event of their faith, what Žižek has named the 'perverse core of Christianity':[2] without Christ's death (the crucifixion) there would be no resurrection and without Christ's arising from the dead, there would be no Christian religion. Similarly, without the failed prophetic, the amaXhosa could not have constructed a faith able to withstand its own non-fulfilment and the particular demands of its own historic suspension, the Middle Generation. It is through Nongqawuse's predictions, her scripting of a 'new people', that the nation of the amaXhosa can be born. Just as Christ's death produces eternal life for Christians, so the near-death of the amaXhosa, when thousands starved, literally, to death because of the cattle-killing movement, produces a 'national' life out of prophetic failure. Nongqawuse's prophecies represent the death of those whose adherence to her utterances proved fatal, but mythically generative in the capacity of the prophetic to sustain her followers a century and a half later, a Xhosa life-in-death (the death of the promise of deliverance and resurrection) that is also, like Christianity, a life-because-of-death.

The singular aspect of Nongqawuse's prophecy – what distinguishes it from Christianity – is that its notion of the sacrificial does not call for 'self-renunciation' (Foucault 2000a: 249). It is premised, instead, on the temporary and communal renunciation of the self, and the self's property, in order to gain a reborn, purified self now in possession of uncontaminated and presumably bountiful property. The prophetic does not so much require self-renunciation as self-preservation, the preservation of the self through a temporary social death that will soon be reversed by a more glorious rebirth. What is clear is that both the prophetic and the unbelieving have an intimate, non-renunciatory relationship to property; both faiths have as a central tenet either the preservation of property (Unbelievers) or the reclamation of new, sanctified property (Believers). *The Heart of Redness* constitutes the theocratic meeting point of Žižek and Foucault: the novel advocates practising faiths based on what one might term the 'perverse, non-sacrificial care of the self'. These are faiths that do not require the permanent sacrifice of the self's (or the community's) property.

It is thus through the 'failed' prophetic that the Xhosa nation enters modernity dialectically. It is, of course, out of and because of the impurity and material deprivation of colonial modernity that the prophetic can be articulated. The crisis of colonial modernity provides the condition for the germination of the prophetic. This variegated historic dialectic makes what is theocratically at stake so apparent: how do two articulations of a critical faith, derived from the struggle to define a people in their encounter with colonialist modernity, occupy the same political space, a site surrounded on all sides by, in the novel's two historical moments, either the repressive practices of colonialism or the urgent demands of capital expansion?

At the most facile level, *The Heart of Redness* posits a struggle between those who have faith and those who do not, the Believers and the Unbelievers, between two modes of black anti-colonial life, those who seek a reflective return to Nongqawuse's 'redness', which is, for the Unbelievers, the sign of the 'uncivilised', and those who stand on the side of post-apartheid 'progress'. However, while the Believers consistently represent themselves as the historic incarnation of those who came before, not simply as ancestors but as direct descendants of their theocratic legacy, the bloodlines of *The Heart of Redness* will not sanction such a claim because all the inhabitants of Qolorha-by-Sea trace their roots back to the same progenitor, Xikixa, father of the twins, the Xhosa chief decapitated by the colonists: 'Everyone is always at pains to stress that Twin's and Twin-Twin's lines are distinct, even though they are joined at the top by the headless ancestor' (Mda 2000: 62). Furthermore, the Believers and the Unbelievers are both movements founded and regenerated in response to historical crisis. They originate because of the increasing encroachment upon black life by the British colonists. Governors such as Harry Smith, George Cathcart and George Grey want to bring the indigenous peoples more firmly under their control, giving the colonists direct access to their resources and their labour and quelling the regular rebellions on the frontiers of the colony. Similarly, a century and a half later, after the end of apartheid, the Believers and the Unbelievers are reborn because of the dangers to their community that derive from the new state's accommodation with capital. According to Bhonco, the Unbelievers are in favour of building a casino resort and accruing to the community a new source of wealth: ' "The Unbelievers stand for progress

. . . We want to get rid of this bush which is a sign of our uncivilized state. We want developers to come and build the gambling city that will bring money to this community. That will bring modernity to our lives, and will rid us of our redness"' (92). The turn to modernity also marks the moment of decision. Modernity trumps 'tradition' for the Unbelievers because they choose, not always with deliberateness, civilisation and development, rather than adherence to excessive promises offered by the legacy of Nongqawuse.

However, what binds the contemporary Unbelievers to the Believers, besides history and physical proximity, is a glaring lack of political acumen. Both groups suffer from an ideological blindness to the causes of black material deprivation in a post-apartheid society and a refusal to recognise that the vulnerability of Qolorha-by-Sea emanates only in part from outside (venture capital) because there is no internal economic structure that can sustain the community. However, Bhonco's endorsement of 'progress' and 'modernity' cannot be figured as simply the hollow gesture of the politician. Much as Bhonco speaks from a position that too readily enunciates support for the casino complex, his speaking is girded by a deeply grounded, dialectical historical truth. The Unbelievers represent the struggle, which animated and sustained the anti-colonial project for centuries, against the misrepresentation of the 'native' as uncivilised, or 'red', in the iconography of Mda's novel, and therefore less than human. However, by reiterating so vehemently their support for 'civilisation', by trying to escape the 'heart of redness', the Unbelievers inadvertently give credence to the colonialists' representation of them. They add substance to the pronouncements of one of the colonial governors in *The Heart of Redness*, Sir George Grey: '"They will give up their barbaric culture and heathen habits, and when they take over their chiefdoms they will be good chiefs. I want the chiefs to undertake to send their sons to school"' (Mda 2000: 127).

Implicitly, by insisting upon themselves as 'civilised', the Unbelievers acknowledge that dreaded, unspeakable a priori era of their own history: their moment of 'barbarism'; implicitly, by virtue of their opposition to the colonialists and to the Unbelievers, the Believers establish themselves as the protectors, full inhabitants, of the Xhosa tradition, as those who reject modernity because of their principled opposition to colonialism's project of

Othering, denigrating, exploiting and enslaving indigenous communities. However, because of their pragmatism, their refusal of the sacrificial element of the prophetic, their belief in a rationalist materiality of self- and 'national' preservation, the Unbelievers cannot be simplistically figured as agents of complicity. They are not the Judases of betrayal, that scion of the nation who sold the amaXhosa for 30 head of cattle, even though some of the Christians in their ranks accept the ideological terms of colonialism. There are Unbelievers willing to trade resources for the elimination of their own 'redness'. Speaking of Grey's policy of the appropriation of indigenous land, an Unbeliever defends the governor's actions: 'Of course he had to take their land in return for civilization. Civilization is not cheap' (Mda 2000: 84). However, it could be argued, as Bhonco does in a conversation with Camagu, that Nongqawuse's was the real betrayal and that her standing has not been affected by her 'wrongdoing' because of the mythic status afforded her by history: '"It is you learned ones who have turned her into a goddess who must be worshipped. Yet she killed the nation of the amaXhosa"' (61).

This complex interplay between betrayal and pragmatism, between loyalty and disavowal (of the prophetic) lends Bhonco and the Unbelievers' support for modernity, (post-) industrialisation, employment and the production of ethnicity and pleasure for xenotropic consumption a hermeneutic indeterminacy. If nothing else, it allows for their anti-environmental politics as a considered economic choice, as a historically conscious, contextually produced pragmatism. Without jobs of one kind or another, Qolorha-by-Sea will become a ghost town, remembered only nostalgically as the place that houses Nongqawuse's Pool. The Unbelievers are struggling against a new post-apartheid history that, as it were, has officially given them back their history of Nongqawuse without redressing the devastation suffered by the Middle Generation – a legacy which all of Qolorha-by-Sea confronts daily, from Bhonco, who cannot obtain his pension from the state, to his daughter, who finds her school's prospects and her own chances of promotion thwarted by bureaucracy and the distance of the village from the provincial and the national capital. Bhonco and Zim's village could easily become, as it already largely is, one run by the 'white amaXhosa', John Dalton, the resident trader, local storekeeper and entrepreneur who organises a small-scale ecotourist agency that takes mainly white and often

European visitors to see Nongqawuse's Pool. Within this entangled historical paradigm, the Unbelievers cannot be dismissed as merely representing the politics of the unfaithful. When the Unbelieving elder proclaims, ' "They want us to remain in our wildness! . . . To remain red all our lives! To stay in the darkness of redness!" ', he is simultaneously raging against the Believers (who oppose 'progress'), unreflectively pronouncing on the failure of that self-same modernity and venting the entire community's frustration and helplessness about their post-apartheid material lack (Mda 2000: 71).

In this way, Bhonco and Zim, Unbeliever and Believer, speak, together and discordantly, from the place that Jacques Ranciére names 'democracy'. In their rhetorical skirmishes, Bhonco and Zim inadvertently rescue the term 'democracy' from post-apartheid inanity and misuse and restore to it a philosophical veracity. Between the Believers and the Unbelievers, they redeem democracy from its overdetermined political invocation, a modality of the political that promised so much but delivered, to Qolorha-by-Sea and other places like it, so little. In Ranciére's terms, democracy is 'neither compromise between interests nor the formation of a common will. Its kind of dialogue is that of a divided community' (1995: 103). The Believers and the Unbelievers are in this difficult, potentially unresolvable dialogue: they animate the Ranciérean definition; the point is not to produce political consensus, but rather to reject compromise and any construction of a common will, a shared political outlook. Democracy in Qolorha-by-Sea signifies a historic agreement born out of enforced détente (the Middle Generation) and decades of sustained strife: the institution of animus as the political modus operandi of the place, the insistence upon a dissensus as the only political practice worthy of the name of democracy. This is not, as Camagu, the interloper from Johannesburg, would prefer it, a place where the political combatants want rapprochement, let alone an enduring truce; this is a space that neither desires consensus nor makes it possible.

Qolorha-by-Sea is not the site where the ethos and ideology of the 'new South Africa', with its insatiable appetite for public reconciliation obtains. *The Heart of Redness* village is, in the philosophically demanding terms of Ranciére, the only democratic locale of substance. Its standing as a democratic space is borne out by a telling exchange between Bhonco and Camagu. At a village meeting to discuss the building of the proposed gambling resort, the disagreement between these two proves revealing. Not only do they represent different generations of black South Africa, but also different modalities, the barely literate, untravelled Unbeliever and the educated, cosmopolitan, Believer-fellow traveller, although Camagu never fully adopts Zim's position. They stand for divergent ideologies, the former for unreflective capitalism and the latter for a problematic, environmentally grounded liberalism.[3] In a critical encounter, the 'history teacher from the secondary school' (Mda 2000: 95) (whose position is commensurate with Camagu's), reveals himself as a proponent of liberal-democratic process. The history teacher argues: ' "That is what democracy is all about. Citizens must first debate these matters. There must be consensus before a decision is taken." "Such are the ills of democracy!" remarks Bhonco.' Bhonco's response is, in part, a laconic, off-handed comment. Mainly, however, it stands in sharp contrast to the history teacher and Camagu's argument for 'consensus', for the bridging of difference, for the reconciliation of the newly reopened split between the Believers and the Unbelievers. The history teacher's/Camagu's is, in salient ways, the voice of post-apartheid South Africa's representative, accountable democracy: the privileging of unity over dissent; this position advocates a politics that creates very little possibility for dissent of the Ranciérean variety, any politics that remains trenchantly dissensual, that regards democracy as the practice of holding unyieldingly to its own oppositionality. Political consensus, that mode of ideological engagement favoured by parliamentary democracy, can be described as a politics without a genesis, without democratic substance because it works on the premise of a preordained terminus: it already knows where it wants to arrive, it presupposes its final articulation; consensus is simply a matter of following a prescriptive – and prescribed – political trajectory. Unlike a Ranciérean (and Bhonco-nean) democracy, where the struggle does not envisage its endpoint, where there is not the always anticipated meeting in the middle, consensus concedes every potentiality of the radical. It is for this reason that it is not, as *The Heart of Redness* fails to recognise, Camagu but Bhonco who represents the democratic. He refuses Camagu's tendency to reduce democracy to the inevitable production of consensus.

For Bhonco, consensus represents, as an instance of the political, an ill because it cannot conceive of either the practice, in the post-apartheid dispensation, or the continuation, from the strife-riven days of the twins, of historic animosity. Bhonco speaks for the retention and the sharpening of the divide, as problematic as his anti-environmental position is; his is an urging for the repeated reinscription of the ideological gap, the long-standing antipathy that separates the Believers from the Unbelievers. It is a form of the political totally inconceivable to Camagu, not only an adrift, returning exile, but also a figure who has neither, in the colloquial, a grasp of the political stakes, which Bhonco is so ardently arguing for, nor a complex understanding of how democracy might be conceived as anything other than a series of compromises.

Bhonco, and not Camagu, comprehends that this is a place, Qolorha-by-Sea, the village meeting, possibly even the post-apartheid state, where the history of long-ago choices continues to hold with a rare absolutism, even an obstinacy. In Qolorha-by-Sea democracy means the capacity to sustain divisions, to bring Twin and Twin-Twin, and the differences they incarnate(d), back to political life every day. Zim and Bhonco play out in post-apartheid society what happened centuries ago when families were torn apart: 'Believers fought against unbelieving brothers. Unbelieving spouses turned against believing spouses. Unbelieving fathers kicked believing sons out of their homesteads. Unbelieving sons plotted the demise of believing fathers' (Mda 2000: 86). Qolorha-by-Sea's is the legacy of tumult, strife and the most intense internal splitting so that, as *The Heart of Redness* makes clear, in this tiny corner of post-apartheid society, the universal franchise is new, but the history of division is old; it is, in fact, much, much older. This ancient conflict contains within it, according to Ranciére, the essence of democracy. For him, 'democracy is closely linked to tragedy – to unsettled grievance' (1995: 102). *The Heart of Redness* is nothing, for both the Believers and the Unbelievers, if not the narrative of repeated historical 'tragedy'. On the appointed day, 16 February 1857, when the Russians are supposed to rise from the sea but do not, the 'Unbelievers went about their usual work. But for the Believers it was the day of the Great Disappointment' (Mda 2000: 211).

On the other hand, for Xoliswa, it is Nongqawuse who 'killed the nation of the amaXhosa' with that precise injunction of the prophetic. It was the young prophetess who initiated the (un)called for sacrifice, of not only crops and livestock, but also an entire way of life; it was she who inaugurated the division by marking, with a lasting historical emphasis, that moment before division from the moment that came after. It is because of Nongqawuse that the moment of Xikixa, whose time is symbolically and politically 'sacrificed' by Nonqaqwuse's pronouncements after he is himself 'sacrificed' by the British, now doubles as the moment before the political. The 'Great Disappointment' was the prophetess's definitive and most consequential act because it divided the amaXhosa forever by setting families against each other, which tore the amaXhosa's temporality into two. Such was Nongqawuse's effect that she reinforced the doubling of the two, irreversibly making a 'Twin' and a 'Twin-Twin' out of Xikixa's twins (Mda 2000: 61).

However, Bhonco's anti-environmental position, even as it inscribes itself as 'democratic', reveals a crucial paradox. A democratic politics does not guarantee a radical politics. As instructive and philosophical as his dissensual politics is, Bhonco's is explicitly an argument for capitalist expansion. Not only will the environment be destroyed, but Bhonco's lament: 'The village itself lost a glittering gambling paradise that would have changed life for everyone. Instead it got a rustic holiday camp that lacks the glamour of the gambling city' (Mda 2000: 273), is a short-sighted critique of the Believers' putative triumph. The 'glittering gambling paradise' would have yielded very few, if any, decent-paying, non-dead-end jobs. Without understanding how globalisation operates, democracy can easily find itself performing as a functionary for global capital. The democratic, in *The Heart of Redness* instance, may ironically be more dangerous to the economically vulnerable than a liberal environmentalist politics. *The Heart of Redness*, however, resists such a political palliative. At the very end of the novel, Camagu understands that the Believers' political 'victory' and that of 'consensus' represents nothing but a political stay of execution: 'Those who want to preserve indigenous plants and birds have won the day. At least for now. But for how long?' (277). The casino, it appears, is an inevitable construction in Qolorha-by-Sea. And, with it, not an inauguration of the Rancièrean democratic, but its liquidation; accompanying it will be the destruction of the environment and the elimination of Nongqawuse, as well as the history of prophetic political she dialectically embodied.

It could be argued that the temporary liberal environmental triumph over capital reveals the conservative core of the prophetic. Nongqawuse's pronouncements, the Believers' struggle, are primarily about preservation, not rebellion, the ousting of the British colonialists notwithstanding. The cattle-killing movement turned on the exchange of property, old for new, not its renunciation or its redistribution. The Unbelievers, too, were focused on preservation. In the face of prophetic demands to destroy their property, they sought to save and protect, to refuse the promise of exchange because of their faith in their historic possession.

The politics of doubt
> Every man's work shall be made manifest: for the day shall declare it, because it shall be revealed by fire; and the fire shall try every man's work of what sort it is. (Corinthians 3:13)

The cattle-killing movement instantiated not only a social and material death, but also, conceptually, speculatively, a rare historical moment: the equality of the amaXhosa. That is what is most important about that moment between the death of the nation's resources and the replenishing thereof by the 'Strangers', the substitution of the new for the old, which is tantamount to an act of grace, of plenitude, of '*agape*',[4] 'love as charity'. In the time of the decision all the amaXhosa would have been equally bereft, equally vulnerable and, potentially, equally felicitous, all equally true in their belief that Nongqawuse's promises could and would be fulfilled. In the act of social death, before the 'entire amaXhosa nation' tasted the 'sweet fruits of the resurrection' (Mda 2000: 86), there was the potentiality for a brief equality of life. At the heart of the faith of and in redness there was, just for that brief instant, that prospect that Camagu desires and Bhonco, in his Ranciérean fashion, dreads – the elliptical possibility for consensus: the capacity of the amaXhosa to act as One because they are, if only for that pre-16-February-1857 moment, united in their relationship to the promise, dependent upon it for their deliverance. Contained prophylactically in that instant is the amaXhosa's liberation from colonialism, from ethical contamination, from the past that saw them reduced to servitude, and from the future that would induct democracy as a tragic separation of the One from its Self.

It is in the Nongqawuse-inspired movement, which produces the Unbelievers in the splitting of the Xikixa-One into the Two, the doubling of 'Twin' into 'Twin-Twin', that the 'unsettled grievance' is conceived. Of course, Nongqawuse's prophecies give rise to not one but two grievances. For the Believers it inaugurates their animosity toward the Unbelievers for their refusal to adopt the faith advocated by Nongqawuse and a couple of other lesser prophetesses; for the Unbelievers, those Nongqawuse agnostics and atheists, it marks the origins of their dislike for the 'redness', the 'uncivilised' propensities that are given full articulation by the *thanatos* instincts, the death drives, of the Believers, what Twin-Twin understands as the unthinking tendency toward obedience that will bring about the physical death of the amaXhosa. In the terms of this grievance, and contrary to the position of the Believers, it is not believing that will save the nation, but its exact opposite: unbelieving, the refusal of the prophetic as the basis for a faith, is what saves the amaXhosa by physically preserving the life of Xhosa subjects from self-elimination. It is through the act of doubt, the activist rebuttal of the prophetic by organising unbelieving as a viable, countervailing, life-sustaining faith, that the nation's life, if not its prophetic salvation, is achieved. In the struggle between believing and unbelieving, a doubly productive dialectic emerges out of the Unbelievers' doubt. According to Žižek's reading of the crucifixion-resurrection narrative, it is only through doubt, for which Jesus ironically chided Peter, that God, as Jesus Christ, can redeem humanity: 'But in that terrific tale of the Passion there is a distinct emotional suggestion that the author of all things (in some unthinkable way) went not only through agony, but through doubt' (2003: 15).

On the one hand, it is because of Twin-Twin and the Unbelievers' doubting Nongqawuse's prophecies that the 'Cult of the Unbelievers' can harden into a faith in rationality, as an interrogative device for questioning the prophetic, of putting it to the materialist test and then rejecting it (Mda 2000: 5). On the other hand, it is because of the threat posed by the Unbelievers' doubt that the Believers can affirm their faith. As Zim says, ' "It is an honor to pine on behalf of those who waited in vain" ', conjoining in that moment the discourses of the absolute and the sacrificial (177).

Zim's felicity, however, is Sisyphean and without the equivocation that would make his faith a more critical political tool. He has never questioned why Twin 'waited in vain'. He is, furthermore, performing the 'martyrdom' of the non-penitent believer/Believer. The Believer's is not, as Foucault would have it, the 'affect of change, of rupture with self, past and world' (2000a: 245), a break with the past, but rather its opposite: a reconnection, an affective resurrection, the suturing of the post-apartheid moment to its prophetic origins, the current act of mourning that elides the violent rupturing that was the Middle Generation. Zim's is the theatricality of faith that makes visible the affective costs of the prophetic, even if all that is patent is the futility of having 'waited in vain', of having endured 'Great Disappointment' after 'Great Disappointment'. This is precisely why doubt is at once the great impermissible for a faith and its most valuable facilitator, provided it is engaged and transcended. The overcoming of doubt, like conversion, which is what Twin euphorically undergoes, is a powerful experience, what the Apostle Paul in his letters to the Corinthians names a 'fire', an acid test, because it signals the triumph over temporary unbelief, which produces a surer, more critical, re-embracing of the faith; now, most likely, as an absolute faith. The reformed, or re-convinced, doubter, like the biblical Thomas, symbolically eviscerates unbelief and steps fully, reflectively, infinitely, into the faith.

The most critical of the Unbelievers, among whom Twin-Twin numbers foremost, are not attracted by Christianity, but by the rationality of modernity. It is he who had 'elevated unbelieving to the heights of a religion' because he rejected the blind faith Twin assumed and which consumed the believing brother (Mda 2000: 5). Twin-Twin, already sceptical of the discourse of the sacrificial, is firmly opposed to the irrationality of Nongqawuse's preachings; he is not willing to exchange his crops or his cattle for new ones. For Twin-Twin, it is rationalism, the ability to operate critically in the world, to resist the seductions of the spirit, that constitutes the core of 'unbelieving'. He will not trade in the unknown; he will not put his faith in 'Strangers' or mysterious 'Russians' or 'spirits'. Twin-Twin is, unlike his brother, a man of profound logic; he is, unlike his heir Bhonco, a consistently assiduous thinker, a historically conscious agent.

It is precisely Twin-Twin's strict rationalism, the deliberateness with which he acts, that makes him ill suited for a radical politics. He is too much, epigrammatically phrased, the 'capitalist' to engage in a politics of risk. His proclivity for materialist calculation proves a double-edged sword: the refusal to endure property loss is precisely what makes him such a keen opponent and interlocutor of the prophetic, but this tendency to tabulate gains and losses is also what would make him recoil from the uncertainties, the lack of materialist guarantees that are integral to a radical politics. A radical politics requires a critical dispensation that extends beyond the interrogative; it requires, as it were, an approach that is willing to engage in the act of potentially, more than temporarily, renouncing the self in order to transform, not simply maintain, the polis. The radical demands creativity and imagination, not only the dissensual demos. It is appropriate, then, that Bhonco should be Twin-Twin's heir. Twin-Twin may lord over a larger domain and possess greater material resources, but they are both protagonists limited by and satisfied with minimum material gains. Twin-Twin is intent on maintaining the Xhosa status quo; unlike the Believers he will not engage in a politics of risk. Bhonco, operating under infinitely greater material strictures, is willing to trade his history and culture for the promise of a few jobs at a 'glittering gambling casino'. The price of pragmatism is the impossibility of a radical politics. It is not so much that both Twin-Twin and Bhonco are or would be willing to pay this price, but that the alternative never occurs to either of them as a political possibility.

However, politically cyclopean as he is, Twin-Twin continues to represent, if not an entirely viable politics, then certainly a protagonist who emerges in *The Heart of Redness* as a figure of political challenge. Twin-Twin, as a historical actor who has witnessed the effects of colonialism, Christianity and the division of the amaXhosa, performs, ironically, a prophetic role in relation to the post-apartheid Qolorha-by-Sea. His grounded critiques suggest that the village, its history and its dialectic relationship to the prophetic, will not endure unless it confronts the consequences of the moment of decision, especially because it is living with the consequences of both historical moments. Nongqawuse's old haunt will, unless it can fashion a political practice that combines the dissensual and the radically creative, succumb to the twin inefficacies of a non-radical democracy and a politically impotent liberalism.

It is out of this difficult, dually inscribed temporal conjuncture between modernity and the 'faith' of Nongqawuse that the post-apartheid theocratic is born. It is out of the conflict among modernity, the prophetic and the agnostically inflected pragmatic, that *The Heart of Redness* reveals itself to be a deeply eschatological text. It is, as Camagu finally reflects, a novel of grave endings, of impending biblical catastrophe – an eschatology, crucially, that democracy as the practice of sustained division cannot avert. If the theocratic contains within its articulation nothing so much as its own incipient critique, the *Heart of Redness* opens up into a democracy of doubt, a dissensual critique of democracy that begins to understand the politics of division and prophetic politics that is open to opposition from within.

Notes

1. See Foucault's essay 'Technologies of the self' and the interview, 'The ethics of the concern of the self as a practice of freedom' in this regard.
2. This phrase is the subtitle of Žižek's *The Puppet and the Dwarf: The Perverse Core of Christianity* (2003).
3. The construction of resorts is an economic strategy with a less than venerable history in South Africa. Pleasure resorts, such as the infamous Sun City, were constructed in the then nominally independent black homelands (Bophuthatswana, in this case) to lure white South Africans with gambling, prohibited in the nation proper, and X-rated shows, similarly prohibited by the Calvinist apartheid regime.
4. This term is borrowed from Žižek (2000: 113–14).

Works cited

Badiou, Alain. 2001. *Ethics: An Essay on the Understanding of Evil*. Translated by Peter Hallward. London: Verso.

Foucault, Michel. 2000a. 'Technologies of the self'. In: Foucault, Michel. *Ethics: Subjectivity and Truth*. Translated by Robert Hurley et al.; edited by Paul Rabinow. *Essential Works of Foucault: 1954–1984*, Vol.1. London: Penguin, 223–51.

———. 2000b. 'The ethics of the concern of the self as a practice of freedom'. In: Foucault, Michel, *Ethics: Subjectivity and Truth*. Translated by Robert Hurley et al.; edited by Paul Rabinow. *Essential Works of Foucault: 1954–1984*, Vol.1. London: Penguin, 281–301.

Hobbes, Thomas. 1996 (1651). *Leviathan*. Edited by Richard Tuck. Cambridge Texts in the History of Political Thought. Cambridge: Cambridge University Press.

Mda, Zakes. 2000. *The Heart of Redness*. New York: Farrar, Strauss and Giroux.

Ranciére, Jacques. 1995. *On the Shores of Politics*. Translated by Liz Heron. London: Verso.

Žižek, Slavoj. 2000. *The Fragile Absolute*. London: Verso.

———. 2003. *The Puppet and the Dwarf: The Perverse Core of Christianity*. Cambridge, MA: MIT Press.

14

Towards a South African Expressionism

The Madonna of Excelsior

J.U. JACOBS

ZAKES MDA HAS SPOKEN of the way in which the end of apartheid has freed the imagination of the artist in South Africa. He has argued that during apartheid there was a strict social prescription for writers to address the political situation, but now they may 'create with all the freedom in the world and define for themselves what their role is as an individual artist' (Temkin 2002: 3).

Mda has identified two thrusts to his own writing. The first is his emphasis on *place*: he always begins with an actual place, he says, never with a story and, as he builds his characters, the story emerges in their interactions with that place (Anstey 2001: 12). When a book is historical, moreover, he bases his narrative heavily on research because he sets great store by accuracy. This realistic or historiographic strain in Mda's writing sits paradoxically alongside a second, highly imaginative one, however, that has frequently earned his fiction the description of 'magic realism'. This label has prompted the author's repeated denials that he has been influenced in any way by the Latin American magic realists. He writes magical novels, he says, because he is himself 'a product of a magical culture' (Mda 1997: 281); in his African culture, 'the magical is not disconcerting. It is taken for granted. No one trie[s] to find a natural explanation for the unreal. The unreal happens as part of reality. The supernatural is presented without judgement.' Mda reconciles these two contradictory fictional modes, the realistic and the magical, in his view of his own role as a writer in

South Africa as a dual one. 'My stories have that historical backdrop,' he says, 'but first and foremost I write them to entertain. I'm a storyteller, but also a social critic and a teacher.' (Temkin 2002: 3; see also Mervis 1998).

Mda's dual commitment, on the one hand, to place and its history and, on the other hand, to an African epistemology and storytelling tradition, has shaped all his works of fiction to date. In each of his novels the narrative has arisen out of a particular southern African region and all are characterised by a hybridised fictional discourse, combining historiography with a narrative mode that transcends conventional realism and is informed by African performance traditions. This fictional syncretism is metonymically represented in his novels in the figures of paired or twinned protagonists, usually siblings, who form part of the deep narrative structure. In his first novel, *Ways of Dying* (1995), the events take place mainly in a squatter settlement in a harbour city and the transitional period in South Africa between 1990 and 1994 forms the historical context for the lives of the two main characters, who are not actual siblings, but are conjoined by their special bond of being a 'homeboy' and 'homegirl' from the same village: Toloki is a talented artist and a 'Professional Mourner' and Noria, an inspirational singer.

The narrative of the second novel, *She Plays with the Darkness* (1995), traces the modern history of coups and military governments in Lesotho from 1970 to 1994, with reference to the lives of the fraudster Radisene and his sister Dikosha, who is not literally his twin but was conceived only four weeks after the birth of her brother, thereby earning their mother the nickname, 'Mother-of-Twins'. Dikosha personifies the song and dance culture of the Basotho; not only does she perform their traditional, rural songs and dances, she also participates in the contemporary music culture that has evolved in the townships, which symbolises in various ways the Basotho mediation of the modern world (see Jacobs 2000).

The third novel, *The Heart of Redness* (2000), takes this fictional doubling still further. The historical narrative is presented in terms of two Eastern Cape chronotopes in palimpsest: the hypotext dealing with the story of the prophetess Nongqawuse, the Xhosa cattle killings and the subsequent starvation in Xhosaland in 1856-57 and inscribed over this, the contemporary hypertext set in 1998, dealing with the issues of democracy, reconstruction and development in the new South African state. The nineteenth-century plot is driven by the conflict between the Xhosa twin brothers, Twin-Twin, who is one of the Unbelievers, and Twin, one of the Believers, while the twentieth-century plot takes its impetus from the conflict between Twin-Twin's Unbelieving descendant, Bhonco, and the latter-day Believer, Zim, who is the great-grandson of Twin, for whom Zim named his own son, Twin. Other names are also duplicated across the two chronotopes, the most significant being that of Zim's traditionalist daughter, Qukezwa, who is named after her Khoikhoi great-great-grandmother, Qukezwa, wife of the ancestral Twin. The split/doubled narrative strands are metonymically represented in *The Heart of Redness* by traditional Xhosa songs and dances, especially the ancient Xhosa tradition of *umngqokolo* or overtone/split-tone singing (see Jacobs 2002, 2003).

A significant feature of each of these hybridised and performative fictional texts is that they foreground metadiscursive episodes by means of which Mda consciously draws his reader's attention to the role of artistic performance in the narrative construct. In *Ways of Dying* the fictional merging of the everyday and the surreal is symbolised in the narrative by means of Toloki's artistic talent, his fantastical decoration of Noria's shack and her inspirational singing. In *She Plays with the Darkness* Mda presents his fictional negotiation of ancient values and modern politics in the detailed accounts of Dikosha dancing to the rhythms of the sacred drawings in the Cave of Barwa until they are covered in graffiti and no longer accessible, and also in the descriptions of her participating in a whole range of traditional rural and modern urban dances. And in *The Heart of Redness* the traditional Xhosa *umngqokolo* singing is described in performance by both the ancestral Qukezwa and her great-great-granddaughter Qukezwa, in prose that attempts to evoke the colours of its unique blend of overtones and undertones as a way of understanding the narrative blending of past and present, history and fiction, and the mundane and the fantastic.

The Madonna of Excelsior: The historical narratives

Mda's fourth novel, *The Madonna of Excelsior* (2002), similarly focuses on two historical periods in a particular region: 1970–71, which saw the notorious arrests and charges under the Immorality Act of apartheid South Africa in the eastern Free State town of Excelsior, and present-day, democratic South Africa.

The 1970–71 narrative provides a thinly fictionalised account of the various transgressions of the Immorality Act by local, respected white men and poor, young Sotho women, the conspicuous increase in the number of illegitimate, 'Coloured' children in the community and the subsequent arrests and charges, which caused the attention of the world press to focus on Excelsior. This peculiarly South African drama unfolds in the novel against a backdrop of the puritanical sexual morality of the late 1960s, as officially championed by the two most powerful Afrikaners in the country at the time: Prime Minister John Vorster, whose government formulated and implemented the Afrikaner Nationalist segregationist ideology that was at least professed, if not practised, locally in Excelsior, and his brother, Dr J.D. ('Koot') Vorster, who was elected moderator of the general synod of the Nederduitse Gereformeerde Kerk in October 1970 and whose church provided apartheid with its imagined scriptural authority.

The Bloemfontein newspaper, *The Friend*, reported the arrests and convictions under the Immorality Act in the region as assiduously as did all the other newspapers in the country. Mda drew on these reports in *The Friend* in different ways for his fictional recreation of the events in Excelsior. First, there were the regularly reported Immorality Act transgressions that obviously provided the general context for Mda to realise his narrative obligation to the place and its history. The Free State was the place and 'immorality', with variations, was its dominant story at the beginning of the 1970s, as the following two of the many cases reported in *The Friend* between October and December 1970 illustrate:

TWO ON CHARGE OF IMMORALITY
A 31-year-old immigrant, Dieter Lausch, of Kellner Street, Bloemfontein, and a 19-year-old African woman, Norah Khoban, appeared before Mr J A Hamman in the Bloemfontein Magistrate's Court yesterday on a charge of immorality.

No evidence was led and bail of R40 was granted to Lausch. Khoban was remanded in custody.

The hearing was adjourned until November 23.

Mr D Nel is prosecuting and Laubsch and Khoban are acting in their own defence. (*The Friend*, 27 October 1970, 2)

Figure 1: *To Market.*

Figure 2: Untitled (village houses).

Figure 3: *Please God!*

Figure 4: Untitled (man with donkey).

Figure 5: *Winter.*

Figure 6: Untitled (mother and child).

Figure 7: Untitled (mother and child).

Figure 8: Untitled (mother and child).

Figure 9: Untitled (mother and child).

Figure 10: Untitled (mother and child).

Figure 11: *Catcher of the Sun.*

Figure 12: *The Sick Child*.

Figure 13: Untitled (nativity).

Figure 14: *The Committee.*

MAN FOUND HANGING IN CELL

Vereeniging

A fifty-year-old married man was found hanging in the Vereeniging police cells shortly after he and an African woman had been detained on allegations of contravening the Immorality Act.

The man, a German immigrant and resident of Vanderbijlpark, and the African woman were arrested late on Wednesday. At 10.20 p.m. an officer visited his cell and all was in order.

Forty minutes later the man was found hanging behind his cell door from a rope made from his shirt. (*The Friend*, 6 November 1970, 6)[1]

Secondly, to recreate this history, Mda reproduces, very slightly edited, a number of the actual reports from *The Friend*, with accounts of the humiliating arrests under the Immorality Act, the fear, the unequal treatment of white and black transgressors, their separate trials, the discriminatory sentences, the public disgrace, the suicides – in short, the whole sordid and sorry human drama around the perversion of morality by apartheid. In the chapter, 'An outbreak of miscegenation', Mda includes verbatim, with the omission of a few sentences or occasional paragraphs, four actual cases that were reported in *The Friend*. An article on 7 January 1971 records the trial of Anna Tsomela, a 36-year-old African mother of a light-skinned, fair-haired baby of three months and a white man from Bloemfontein, Petrus François Smit, who was the father of her child and who had tried to provide for Tsomela and their baby (see Mda 2002: 89–91). In his melodramatic testimony, a Constable Griesel of the South African Police told how he had followed the couple along farm roads at night and surprised them in sexual embrace in the front seat of Smit's delivery van. Mda contrasts this report about a consensual relationship, albeit an illegal one, across the colour bar with another one which involved sexual assault, but which was also dealt with under the same Immorality Act, miscegenation being the greater offence. The case of the 33-year-old former traffic inspector, Barend Jacobus Nolan, who, pretending to be a policeman, had made indecent physical advances to a 19-year-old African school teacher, Cecilia Mapeta, then offered her money for sex, and finally assaulted her when she refused, was first mentioned briefly in *The Friend* on 12 November 1970, under the heading 'Immorality: Two in court' and then more fully reported on 23 January 1971. Mda, again citing virtually the entire newspaper report (but without its headline) incorporates into his fictional construct the account of Nolan's wife and three children being present in court to hear Mapeta's story of how Nolan had abducted her in his car and the account by Constable Nel of the South African Police of how he had found them parked in a grove of bluegum trees off the main road outside Rouxville and of how he had arrested Nolan after Mapeta had made her escape (2002: 92–93).

It is in this general climate that five Afrikaner men and thirteen African women were charged with attempting to contravene the Immorality Act in Excelsior in November 1970 – the culmination of a period about which Mda's communal narrative voice in *The Madonna of Excelsior* remarks sardonically: 'It was the Golden Age of Immorality in the Free State. Immorality was a pastime' (Mda 2002: 93). Thirdly, then, it was from the national scandal of the Excelsior case that Mda drew the main body of material for his novel. The case was first reported in *The Friend* on 2 November 1970 under the headline, 'Immorality Act: 13 charged' and then again on 4 November 1970 under the headline, 'Four farmers on bail; ten African women held for immorality', where the full details were provided. Ten African women (the number was later increased to fourteen), each the mother of a 'Coloured child', were being held in custody in Winburg jail and four well-known farmers of the Excelsior district were out on bail of R150 to R200, 'following a large-scale police swoop'. They had been arrested under the Immorality Act for offences allegedly committed over a period of five years, since 1965. Originally five men had been held, but the fifth, 51-year-old J.M. Calitz, 'the only butcher of the town', had been found dead, with a shotgun lying next to his body, after his appearance in court. The four other men who appeared before the magistrate of Excelsior, Mr J.H. Visser, were: Johan Christian Bornman (48) of the farm Vergelegen, 'charged with having relations or attempting to have relations with two African women, Ellen (32) of the African township, and Anna (23), of the farm George'; Tjaart Nicolaas van der Walt (38) of the farm Blougomboom, 'charged with immoral relations with three African women: Julia (32) of his own farm, Eliza (18) of the farm Dwaalspruit, and Alice (20), of the farm Elim'; Stephanus Esias de

Vries (28), of the farm Mooivlei, 'charged with immoral relations with Elizabeth (21) of the farm Mooimeisieshoek and Eliza (30) of Mooivlei'; and Adam Johannes Bezuidenhout (42), of the farm Tweespruit, 'charged under the Immorality Act together with Sanna (40), a domestic servant of the African location'. Although the women, too, had been granted bail of R50 each, they could not pay and were therefore detained. In addition to the names of the white farmers and their farms in the report signifying a particular Afrikaner cultural heritage and the use of only the 'European' first names of the African women reflecting the depersonalising racial discourse of the time, the report in *The Friend* of 4 November 1970 goes on to elaborate on the standing of some of these men in their community. Calitz had served on the Excelsior town council, Bezuidenhout had served on various committees, and both of them were well known in Free State angling circles. When the public prosecutor in Excelsior opposed bail for Bezuidenhout on the basis of his having had a previous conviction for violence (an African woman had been killed), his lawyer pleaded a total personality change, a heart condition, an elderly father who could not manage to farm 7 000 morgen of land on his own and, finally, a wife and four children.[2]

Mda's fictionalisation of the Excelsior events is minimal. Names are changed, or else transferred to other characters: J.M. Calitz, the butcher who committed suicide, in the novel becomes the butcher Stephanus Cronje, his first name borrowed from Stephanus Esias de Vries; Tjaart Nicolaas van der Walt gives his first name to Cronje's son, Tjaart; the surname of the farmer Johan Christian Bornman is transferred to the Dutch Reformed minister, Reverend François Bornman; and Adam Johannes Bezuidenhout's middle name is given to the predatory Johannes Smit. None of the African women's names is reproduced in the novel. The fictional plot follows the events fairly faithfully: the arrests, charges and the eventual withdrawal of the charges.

Whereas the 1970 Excelsior history is documented in the novel from archival sources, the contemporary one relies on readers' familiarity with this context. It includes the liberation of Nelson Mandela, Walter Sisulu and Govan Mbeki from imprisonment; Afrikaner and African nationalist political developments and conflicts post-1990; political in-fighting at local government level; equity and affirmative action undermined by nepotism and corruption in the new administration; *broedertwis* (literally, 'conflict between brothers'; family conflict) among Afrikaners; the rewriting of their roles in apartheid history by opportunistic whites in the new dispensation; the delivery and non-delivery of housing under the Reconstruction and Development Programme; the problem of squatters, demolitions and forced removals even under the new government; the culture of non-payment for services and a growing dependence on pensions and disability grants; a new black racism; family killings among whites; the HIV/AIDS pandemic; the plight of the former soldiers of the apartheid state, now abandoned by their bosses; greed and corruption in Zimbabwe, etc. Mda's even-handedness in his representation of the new South Africa is remarkable.

As in Mda's previous novels, in *The Madonna of Excelsior* these past and present histories are also narrated with reference to twinned protagonists – only here in a tripled configuration: the 'Coloured' Popi is paired, as a result of her mother Niki's participation in all the miscegenation in Excelsior, on the one hand with her black, Mosotho half-brother, Viliki and, on the other hand, with her white, Afrikaner half-brother, Tjaart Cronje. The narrative tells the story of Niki and her daughter Popi, who is doubly discriminated against and rejected: as a so-called 'Coloured' by the whites and also by the black community who revile her as a 'Boesman'.

Frans Claerhout, Flemish expressionism and Mda's ecphrasis

In his fictional project to recover a language of colour from the black-and-white script of apartheid, Mda's text once again foregrounds its metadiscourse: the novel opens with Popi's recollections of the Eastern Free State painter-priest, Father Frans Claerhout, working in his studio on his canvases 'of distorted people and skewed houses and donkeys and sunflowers' (Mda 2002: 3). The actual Frans Claerhout, who is referred to in Mda's novel as the 'trinity: man, priest and artist' (5), was born in Pittem, West Flanders, in 1919 and came to South Africa in 1946 to work as a Catholic missionary, eventually settling at Thaba Nchu in the eastern Free State (see Jonckheere 1975; Van Wilderode 1986: 7). In *The Madonna of Excelsior*, Mda's narrative is not directly informed by indigenous African artistic/cultural performance, as in the earlier novels, but rather by a Western European one, as indigenised by a European-born artist working in Africa. In the second chapter, the narrative voice reports: 'Popi tells us that it all began when the trinity was nourished by Flemish expressionists' (5). (Popi first learns about Flemish expressionism from an art book in Claerhout's studio, and later furthers her knowledge of art and artists through books from the local library.)

According to Leon Strydom (1983), from whose authoritative and illuminating analysis of the Flemish-South African artist's *Catcher of the Sun* series I have derived the theoretical basis for my reading of Mda's novel in this chapter, Claerhout first began painting in the style and also in the spirit of the Flemish primitives and expressionists – Brueghel and Constant Permeke in particular – and then adopted mainly early twentieth-century expressionist and late nineteenth-century symbolist styles, both of European origin. Claerhout's work, Strydom argues, 'developed from plastic expressionism – inspired by the material – in the style of Constant Permeke (1886–1952) and Gustaaf de Smet (1887–1943), to symbolist expressionism – inspired by the mystical – in the manner of Albert Servaes (1883–1966) and Gustaaf van der Woestijne (1881–1947)' (1983: 9). Flemish expressionism, like German expressionism, was a protest art, but Strydom says that for Claerhout, it was the mystical element that drew him to Flemish expressionism. His work may also be compared in certain respects to that of Vincent van Gogh, Paul Gauguin, James Ensor, Edvard Munch, Marc Chagall and Georges Rouault – all artists whose work is both expressionist *and* symbolist.

As a painter, Claerhout needs also to be seen in terms of two local contexts. Regionally, he was a member of the so-called Bloemfontein Circle, a small group of artists in Bloemfontein, including painters such as Alexander and Marianne Podlashuc and Stefan and Iris Ampenberger, who, together with Eben van der Merwe, Mike Edwards, Walter Westbrook, Renée le Roux and Rose-Marie Budler, launched an indigenous artistic movement in 1958. Nationally, as Arie Kuijers points out, Claerhout should also be situated within the overall development of South African expressionism (1999: 16). The first wave, based on German expressionism, is represented by Irma Stern and Maggie Laubscher; the second wave is represented by Flemish immigrants, such as Maurice van Essche, Herman van Nazaret and Claerhout himself; the third wave includes a whole range of black artists of the 1960s, such as Gerard Sekoto,

Sydney Kumalo, Julian Motau, Tshidiso Motjuoadi, Louis Maqhubela, Lucky Sibiya, Cyprian Shilakoe and Dan Rakgoathe; and later waves include artists such as André van Vuuren, Phillip Badenhorst and Marnus Havenga.

Strydom suggests that Claerhout followed the Flemish tradition of depicting aspects of folk life, taking as his subject matter the immediate surroundings of the mission – the daily lives of the black people amongst whom he works. 'The office of his priesthood . . . has become the constant source of his inspiration as an artist. He regards nothing he encounters as being outside the range of human experience or unworthy of the art of painting' (1983: 8–9) (see *Figure 1*). Claerhout portrays daily life from a variety of perspectives, identifying with his subjects and also distancing himself from them and, as Strydom puts it, 'painting with compassion and with humour, religiously and philosophically, through the eyes of Africa and from a Western point of view, enervated and serene' (9). Or (to set up a dialogue between the art critic and the fictional aesthetic discourse in *The Madonna of Excelsior*), as the narrative voice in Mda's novel says of the 'trinity': 'His subjects are ordinary folk doing ordinary things. Yet God radiates from them' (Mda 2002: 131) (see *Figure 2*). For Claerhout, what is important is not life-like portrayal, but rather, interpretations of the human situation; for him to paint, according to Strydom, 'is to concentrate and capture the essence of being human' (1983: 9) (see *Figure 3*). Claerhout attempts 'to work out in terms of art a philosophy of life that will reconcile the physical and the spiritual, the social and the mystical, and one in which the visual and the visionary, the ethical and the aesthetic complement one another' (9). A similar metaphysic, it may be argued, informs Mda's fictional project in *The Madonna of Excelsior*.

In his analysis of Claerhout's painting technique, Strydom explains the economy with which the Flemish-South African painter conveys a wealth of meaning (see *Figure 4*):

[Claerhout] invariably works out a composition in its entirety by drawing in oil directly on the panel. These construction lines fade or vanish under the colours he then applies, but he generally draws them in again so that the sharply defined contours bind the colour areas and lend the desired rhythm to the image. He applies his paint thickly, with powerful sweeps of the brush; he seems almost to model in paint. The effects he achieves are indeed partly the result of the large quantities of paint he applies, layer upon layer, so that the colouring is worked through in a unique way . . . Typical of his work is the minimum of distinguishing colours, of which the contrast and intuitive cohesion finally dictate the form of the entire painting. The colours . . . are telling because of their coherence, and not because they happen to correspond to reality outside. (1983: 8; see also Edwards 1982: xii; Kuijers 1999: 14; Rock 1975: 31; Scott 1975: 107; Schwager 1994: 27, 43)

Arie Kuijers says that Claerhout's cloisonné technique was introduced in the nineteenth century by Emile Bernard and also employed by other artists such as Rouault. Or (to continue the dialogue between the art critic and the novel), as Mda, through Popi, describes the effect of the 'trinity's' impasto technique in *The Madonna of Excelsior*: 'His work had a robustness that had escaped the Flemish expressionists. Perhaps it was the broad strokes, some of which were created with palette knives instead of the usual broad brushes. And the multiple glazes that seemed to suck her into the canvases, making her walk the same soil that the trinity's subjects walked' (Mda 2002: 236).

The expressionist style – to return to Strydom's analysis of Claerhout's work – might at first appear to be crude and uncontrolled, but its characteristics of contrast, dynamic movement and distortion are used 'to convince the viewer in a direct and emphatic way of the artist's (emotional or intuitive) interpretation of reality' (1983: 10) (see *Figure 5*). An expressionist painting invites the viewer to become involved, rather than remain detached in experiencing the work and to approach it not in judgement, but with a sense of wonder and compassion, even humour; the expressionist painting offers 'a view of reality rather than a mere representation of reality, one which is felt rather than [only] seen'. Whether in the form of a statement of belief or a social narrative, the viewer is confronted with reality, rather than allowed to evade it. In expressionist art, conventional beauty is sacrificed for purposes of expression and meaning emanates from the form, rather than from the object or model depicted. As Strydom formulates it:

The expressionist painting therefore represents the beginning of the abstract in art and heralds the 20th century approach in which the two-dimensional canvas or panel is no longer the background against which a three-dimensional reality is projected, but a plane on which the artist, using colour and line, creates shapes that are subject to the laws of that plane and not to those that apply in the world of time and space. The shift of focus is from the representation to the viewer's consciousness, from the content of form to the function of form, and the result is that the barrier between subject and object is lifted, and the viewer becomes creatively involved in the image, whether it be purely colour and form, or whether it harks back to observable reality. (1983: 10)

Or (to continue the aesthetic dialogue between the art critic and the novel), as the narrative presents Popi's response to the 'trinity's' paintings:

The same questions were in Popi's eyes as she moved from one canvas to another. *What did it all mean? Did it matter that she did not understand what it all meant? Was it not enough just to enjoy the haunting quality of the work and to rejoice in the emotions that it awakened without quibbling about what it all meant? Why should it mean anything at all? Is it not enough that it evokes? Should it now also* mean? . . . The works exuded an energy that enveloped her . . . (Mda 2002: 236, 238; italics in original)

As Claerhout's art developed, Strydom points out, his palette became brighter, more subtle and more richly nuanced than his Flemish models', direct observation deepened into mood in his paintings, and an increasing interiorisation resulted in a pictorial world that evinces the features of both expressionism and symbolism, that is both direct and suggestive, mundane as well as mystical, and socially committed as well as religious and mysterious.

To appreciate fully how in *The Madonna of Excelsior* Mda narratively further indigenises a Western European art form that has already been indigenised by Claerhout, one needs to understand his fictional discourse in this novel in terms of ecphrasis, 'the literary description of a work of art' (Hollander 1998: 86). More precisely, Mda's fictional discourse needs to be distinguished from the merely *iconic*, for, as John Hollander explains, quoting Jean H. Hagstrum

(1958), ecphrastic literary works are those 'that purport to give "voice and language to the otherwise mute art object."' And even more precisely, *The Madonna of Excelsior* is, as has been seen, an example of *actual* ecphrasis, where a literary work incorporates actual, particular works of art that pre-exist it, as opposed to *notional* ecphrasis where a literary text incorporates descriptions of purely fictive works of art.

The Madonna of Excelsior is one of the most self-reflexively ecphrastic novels in South African writing. First, in terms of genre, Mda owes something of the structure of his fictional narrative to the major series or cycles of paintings that Claerhout produced, such as *Christ in Tweespruit*, *Reconciliation by Women*, *The Dance of the Farm Labourer*, and especially the series of 29 canvases, *Catcher of the Sun*. To return to Strydom for a critical language to adapt and apply to Mda's work: paintings can be organised into a coherent group in two ways, namely as a cycle, or as a series. The difference is that 'the cycle is the development of a theme in a time-space continuum, and thus entails a horizontal or linear arrangement. This group depicts a history, and the paintings illustrate the consecutive episodes or phases of that narrative or process' (1983: 16). The series, on the other hand, 'is a repetition of a theme discontinuous in time and space, and thus necessitates a vertical arrangement. The paintings in the group are all variations on a sustained theme, each painting accentuating a different aspect of the chosen theme, or presenting a different perspective to illustrate the theme by means of other objects'. Each of these theoretical possibilities has its limitations, however. The paintings in a series are interchangeable and the theme can be varied endlessly, without affecting the overall meaning and without reaching any conclusion. Simple, boring thematic repetition can, however, be turned into ever-deepening variations on a theme by bringing into a series the development or continuity principle of the cycle. And, conversely, by bringing into the cycle the repetition principle of the series, simple, chronological narrative progression can be enriched with variously repeated colours, lines or images. Claerhout's *Catcher of the Sun* group of paintings, Strydom argues, derives its impact and meaning from the dialectic between cycle and series (see 1983: 16–18).

Mda's fictional text in *The Madonna of Excelsior*, I would argue, similarly engages the reader through a narrative dialectic between the cyclical principle of development and the serial principle of repetition. The best example of serial repetition in the novel is perhaps the range of variations on the theme of musical performance in the novel: the traditional, mocking wedding songs sung to Niki and Pule on their wedding day; the hymns sung in the mission church that Niki attends; Pule's drunken singing on his way home from the shebeen; the Afrikaans songs that the children sing at the Cherry Festival in Ficksburg, followed by the singing of the Cape Coons and the music of the Bloemfontein Caledonian Pipe Band; the victory song and dance of the women outside the courtroom when the immorality charges are withdrawn by the Attorney General; the Methodist hymns that Popi joins in singing when she becomes a member of the Young Women's Union of the Methodist Church; the liberation *chimurenga* songs from Zimbabwe that Popi learns from her brother Viliki; her heartrending solo at Pule's funeral; Viliki's ghetto-blaster that introduces South African freedom songs into their lives; the celebration song when Viliki is elected mayor of Excelsior; Popi's regular singing at the funerals of AIDS victims; the new liberation songs of the squatters on the land earmarked for housing under the Reconstruction and Development Plan; the singing of itinerant musicians and Christmas carollers, the nostalgic singing of old struggle songs from Zimbabwe and Mozambique – and finally the penny-whistle playing of the Seller of Songs, a Coloured busker who celebrates her mixed identity and teaches Viliki to play the accordion and fills his house with songs. All these variations are deepened by the development of the cyclical narrative about all the miscegenation in Excelsior and the subsequent personal and public lives of Niki, Popi and Viliki to the conclusion where Popi comes to accept and celebrate her own colour. In this connection, it may be argued that the serial principle of repetition also has close affinities with the oral storytelling tradition, whereas the linearity of the cycle tends more to be a characteristic of Western narrative.

The second, more obvious and perhaps most important ecphrastic aspect of the narrative, that makes the novel a true iconotext, is to be found in Mda's conscious attempt to create a prose equivalent of Claerhout's plastic (inspired by the material) and symbolist (inspired by the mystical) expressionist art. In this respect, especially, *The Madonna of Excelsior* is a profoundly performative text. Most of the chapters in the novel take descriptions of actual paintings by

Claerhout as their point of departure and then recreate the paintings in language stylistically approximate to them. Some of these paintings are examples of plastic expressionism, others of symbolist expressionism, but in all cases they are set in dialogic relation to episodes in Mda's fictional narrative. The iconic narrative world is translated into a verbal one, which is retranslated again into an iconic one, as Mda creates an African literary expressionism, combined in this novel with documentary realism to produce his most remarkably hybridised text to date – one that belongs as much to autochthonous as to Western traditions of storytelling. The unfolding historical and fictional narratives of *The Madonna of Excelsior* are serially punctuated with variations on the motif of painting, to form a textual dialectic of visual and verbal art, and of paintings that are incorporated into prose and language that is painterly.

To select just a few examples: In Popi's description of the canvases of naked madonnas on easels in Claerhout's studio, for which Niki and the infant Popi had also modelled, one recognises a narrative equivalent of Claerhout's impasto painting technique, as detailed earlier in this chapter. In the description of each of the paintings in this series, the ground figure of the madonna is first verbally drawn, after which the qualifying language is applied directly, almost crudely, layer upon layer, in strongly outlined phrases and short sentences that stylistically combine distortion and rhythmic coherence, as all the individual variations on the figure of the madonna merge into a single, powerful emblematic image of the African mother and child:

All these madonnas
Madonnas all around. Exuding tenderness. Burnt umber mother in a blue shirt, squatting in a field of yellow ochre wheat. Burnt sienna baby wrapped in white lace resting between her thighs. Mother with a gaping mouth. Big oval eyes. Naked breast dangling above the baby's head. Flaky blue suggesting a halo. Unhampered bonding of mother and child and wheat.

Brown madonnas with big breasts. A naked Madonna lying on a bed of white flowers. Her eyes are closed and her lips are twisted. Her voluptuous thighs are wide open, ready to receive drops of rain. A black pubic forest hides her nakedness. Her breasts are full and her nipples are hard. Under her arm she carries a baby wrapped in white lace. A naked Madonna holds a naked child against a blue moon on a purple sky. The mother is kissing the back of the child's head. Another Madonna kneels, her head resting on the ground near the child in white lace, and her buttocks opening up to the sky. Ready to receive drops of rain. The fattest of the madonnas stands among red flowers, looking at yellow fields that cover large patches of the red and brown and green land, and that stretch for kilometres until they meet a blue and white sky. The madonna of the cosmos and sunflowers and open skies. Like all the others, she is naked. Tightly to her chest, she holds a baby wrapped in white lace.

After twenty-five years, these naked madonnas still live. (Mda 2002: 11) (see *Figure 6*; *Figure 7*; *Figure 8*; *Figure 9*; *Figure 10*)

Claerhout's symbolist expressionist painting, *Catcher of the Sun*, which gives the title to the series, is used by Mda to represent the drought in the eastern Free State, as perceived by the Afrikaner farmer, Johannes Smit, after he has raped the young Niki and becomes obsessed with her. The heavily outlined female figure in the painting is both strikingly contrasted to and merged with the blazing heat through her gesture of embracing the sun, the circular composition exerting a powerful attraction, while also being profoundly disturbing. Mda's reader is similarly drawn into the scene through the powerful, thickly applied verbal colour and the circularity of the textual composition, to become creatively involved in the image with its unsettling combination of threat and attraction:

She is holding the sun
She is holding the sun entwined in her arms. It is blazing red. With streaks of yellow. She is all impasto black and blue and yellow. The sun glows through her body, giving it patches of fluorescent red. She sits like a Buddha embracing the sun. She is wide awake, for night has passed. The whites of her eyes are milky white and the pupils are black like the night. Everything around her is fiery red. The sky is red. The ground is red. Rivers of white run on the red ground. Broad strokes.

She is dark and sinister. And beautiful. Under her impasto sun, plants are wilting. (Mda 2002: 25) (see *Figure 11*)

An anecdotal painting by Claerhout of village women carrying a sick child is translated by Mda into an impasto introduction to the young women of Excelsior meeting for an orgy in the barn with the white men of Excelsior. The entire scene is kept deliberately ordinary, almost banal in its repetitive detail, as if Mda, in his reinterpretation of the four figures, even more than Claerhout, might seem in his economical verbal brushstrokes to be preoccupied with the plastic rather than the symbolist possibilities of his composition. In the cumulative and emphatic ordinariness of these paragraphs, however, the essential humanity of this group of women begins to acquire a spiritual dimension, comparable to that in the original painting:

A barn full of moans
The one in front has big feet. Big brown feet with grey toenails. Five toes on each foot. An occasional departure from the trinity's norm. Feet and toes! She wears a grey knee-length dress and a grey beret. Her sad face is black and her eyes are cast down to the red ground. Her gaunt posture hides the fact that she is a leader. She leads four women in their prime. A woman in a red blanket and red slippers. A grey crocheted hat on a brown head. She has bedroom eyes, and she walks sideways. Her feet point in the direction from which she comes.

She is followed by the one who has thin legs. Grey legs without feet. The only one carrying a baby. There is a softness about her. Soft yellow blanket. Soft grey baby wrapped in a soft yellow blanket. The baby wears a soft grey woollen cap and the mother a soft grey beret. The mother is not really carrying the baby. The baby stands on the palm of her hand. The brown woman behind her holds out her open hand so that it can support the weight of the baby. The brown woman's bare feet point to where she is going. Forwards. She has only three toes. The last woman faces sideways, giving us her back. Giving us her bare heels. Her grey dress has a matching broad figure-belt. She wears a grey doek. Her black face is turned to the other women. She is looking in the direction they are all going. Her hands are raised to the heavens as if in supplication.

Five women sneaked into the barn. (Mda 2000: 51–52) (see *Figure 12*)

On the other hand, to introduce the chapter, 'Big eyes in the sky', where Niki gives birth to Popi, her child by Stephanus Cronje, Mda pointedly chooses a symbolist expressionist painting of the Nativity by Claerhout that owes perhaps as much to Chagall, or even to Raphael's madonnas with their attendant cherubs, as to the Flemish expressionists. Niki's suffering, the midwives' traditional medicines and the agony of the eventual delivery are all, however, much more realistically described in the novel than the scene in Claerhout's whimsical painting and the birth of Niki's beautiful 'Coloured' baby, unlike that of the infant Jesus, is destined to attract the rather more condemnatory gaze of Mda's white and black communities, as symbolised by the watching 'big eyes in the sky':

> A man in blue pants, blue shirt and red beret stands on the black roof of a skewed house one blue night. He lifts his arms to the heavens in a supplication that is reminiscent of the five women in their prime. The roof almost caves in from his weight. Wide-eyed heads appear in the blue and white and yellow sky. Milky-white eyes with pitch-black pupils staring at the man. Penetrating the house with their amazed gaze. Disembodied heads like twinkling stars in the blue night. White cosmos grows wild around the house.
>
> Bright eyes in the sky see everything. They see a newly-born baby wrapped in white linen. An intrusive star of Bethlehem has sneaked in through one of the two skewed windows and shines on the baby's body. It fills the room with light and yellowness. Two humans kneel on either side of the sleeping baby, hands clasped in prayer. One is a man in a blue suit and blue beret. The other is a woman in a blue nun's habit. The big star of Bethlehem suspends itself above her buttocks.
>
> It had not been easy for Niki, although this was a second child-bearing. (Mda 2002: 57) (see *Figure 13*)

And finally, Claerhout's painting of a village women's committee symbolises the insight that Popi comes to 30 years after the events in Excelsior. The painting of the four dignified women offers a final, symbolic variation on the earlier serial image of the women walking towards the barn, and simultaneously provides a final panel in the narrative cycle that began with the events in Excelsior in 1970. The painting symbolises a new millennium, a new country, and a new acceptance and celebration by Popi of her 'Colouredness' – or, as it is expressed by the collective narrative voice, speaking earlier for the wider nation, when it concludes: 'From the outrage of rape . . . our mothers gave birth to beautiful human beings.' (Mda 2002: 234)

> *From the sins of our mothers*
> The real new millennium has dawned. Four women with pointed breasts walk in single file. Their long necks carry their multicoloured heads with studied grace. Their hair is white with age, but their faces glow with youth. They do not lose their way, even though they undertake their journey with closed eyes. They walk straight and rigidly, their brown shoes hardly leaving the naphthol crimson ground. Their profiles foreground a white and yellow sky. The woman in front wears a green dress. Her face is pink and blue and green. She holds a bunch of white cosmos. The second woman wears a red dress. Her face is blue and orange. She holds a bunch of violet cosmos. The third woman wears a brown dress. Her face is blue. She carries a bunch of pink cosmos. The fourth woman wears a green dress. Her face is brown and pink. She holds a bunch of white cosmos.
>
> It was the time of the cosmos. And of the yellowness in the fields and the sandstone hills. Niki walked among the cosmos between the sunflower fields, collecting cow-dung in a sisal sack. (Mda 2002: 265) (see *Figure 14*)

Notes

1. See also the following reports in *The Friend*: 'Man up for immorality' (27 October 1970, 2); 'Appeal in morals case' (6 November 1970, 4); 'Brandfort man's sentence' (14 November 1970, 2); and 'Morals charge: Man on bail' (29 December 1970, 7).
2. For further accounts of the trial, see, for example, 'Immorality cases at Excelsior postponed', *The Friend* (20 November 1970, 3); 'Too many half-caste children in Excelsior, people said: IMMORALITY ACT WILL STAY, SAYS MINISTER', *The Friend* (3 February 1971, 1).

Works cited

Anstey, Gillian. 2001. 'Ways of writing: Interview with Zakes Mda'. *Sunday Times: Lifestyle*, 29 July, 12.

Claerhout, Frans. 1982. *Kromdraai*. Pretoria: Errol Marx Uitgewers.

———. 1983. *Catcher of the Sun*. Text by Leon Strydom. Cape Town: Tafelberg.

———. 1986. *Twee zoenen op één gesicht*. Roeselaere, Belgium: Drukkerij Huize Breughel.

Edwards, M.H.K. 1982. 'Frans Martin Claerhout'. In: Claerhout, Frans. *Kromdraai*. Pretoria: Errol Marx Uitgewers, vii–xii.

Hagstrum, Jean H. 1958. *The Sister Arts: The Tradition of Literary Pictorialism and English Poetry from Dryden to Gray*. Chicago: University of Chicago Press.

Hollander, John. 1998. 'Ecphrasis'. In: Kelly, Michael (ed.). *Encyclopedia of Aesthetics* Vol.2. New York: Oxford University Press, 86–89.

Jacobs, J.U. 2000. 'Zakes Mda and the (South) African Renaissance: Reading *She Plays with the Darkness*'. *English in Africa* 27(1): 55–74.

———. 2002. 'Zakes Mda's *The Heart of Redness*: The novel as *umngqokolo*'. *Kunapipi: South Africa Post-Apartheid* 24 (1 & 2): 224–36.

———. 2003. 'Singing in a split tone: Hybridising history in the novels of Zakes Mda'. In: Monti, Alessandro and John Douthwaite (eds.). *Migrating the Texts: Hybridity as a Postcolonial Literary Construct*. Torino: L'Harmattan Italia, 191–225.

Jonckheere, Karel. 1975. 'The artist of the Black Mountain'. In: *Frans Claerhout* (monograph produced for The Friends of Frans Claerhout). Tielt, Belgium: Drukkerij-Uitgeverij Lannoo, 37–40.

Kuijers, Arie. 1999. 'Frans Claerhout – perspektief en profiel: 'n oorskouing van sy bydrae met sy tagtigste verjaarsdag'. In: *Die Sonnevanger: Frans Claerhout – 80: 10-02-99-05-03-99*. Catalogue. Bloemfontein: Johannes Stegmann Art Gallery, University of the Orange Free State.

Mda, Zakes. 1993. *When People Play People: Development Communication through Theatre*. Johannesburg: Wits University Press; London: Zed.

———. 1995a. *Ways of Dying*. Cape Town: Oxford University Press.

———. 1995b. *She Plays with the Darkness*. Florida Hills: Vivlia.

————. 1997. 'Acceptance speech for the Olive Schreiner Prize (1997)'. *The English Academy Review* 14 (December): 279-81.

————. 2000. *The Heart of Redness*. Cape Town: Oxford University Press.

————. 2002. *The Madonna of Excelsior*. Cape Town: Oxford University Press.

Mervis, Margaret. 1998. 'Fiction for development: Zakes Mda's *Ways of Dying*'. *Current Writing: Text and Reception in Southern Africa* 10(1), April: 39-56.

Rock, Paul. 1975. 'Introducing Frans Claerhout'. In: *Frans Claerhout* (monograph produced for The Friends of Frans Claerhout). Tielt, Belgium: Drukkerij-Uitgeverij Lannoo, 29-35.

Schwager, Dirk and Dominique. 1994. *Claerhout: Artist and Priest*. Maseru: Visual Publications.

Scott, F.P. 1975. 'Introduction'. In: *Frans Claerhout* (monograph produced for The Friends of Frans Claerhout). Tielt, Belgium: Drukkerij-Uitgeverij Lannoo, 85-135.

Strydom, Leon. 1983. 'I heard no voice, that's certain. What makes one become a doctor, or a scientist? I don't know. I have no regrets and I'd do it all again'. In: Claerhout, Frans. *Catcher of the Sun*. Cape Town: Tafelberg, 7-23.

Temkin, Nicole. 2002. 'Imagining the past: Interview with Zakes Mda'. *Mail & Guardian: Friday*, 18-24 October, 3.

Van Wilderode, Anton. 1986. 'Frans Claerhout: "Een kind van twee moeders"'. In: Claerhout, Frans. *Twee zoenen op één gesicht*. Roeselaere, Belgium: Drukkerij Huize Breughel, 7.

15

Race, Satire and Post-Colonial Issues in The Madonna of Excelsior[1]

RALPH GOODMAN

IN *THE MADONNA OF EXCELSIOR*, Zakes Mda uses both post-colonial textual strategies and satire to 'decentre' South African whites by historicising their dominance and then ridiculing it. The novel deconstructs the discourse of apartheid by focusing on the Immorality Act, which forbade sexual acts across the colour line – miscegenation – on the grounds that the purported purity of the white race would be diminished and polluted by such contact. As the producer of a post-colonial text, Mda refuses to replace one set of binaries with another, but instead sets in motion a process of open-ended dialogue between the indignant patriarchalism of the South African state towards the existence of so-called mixed-race people on the one hand, and the subversive delight in creolisation taken by so many post-colonial texts, on the other hand. As Helen Tiffin remarks: 'Decolonization is process, not arrival; it invokes an ongoing dialectic between hegemonic centrist systems and peripheral subversion of them' (1987: 17). Post-colonial practice aims to dismantle polarised constructions of alterity and disrupt the stereotypical structures within which colonial discourse flourishes.

'[Homi K.] Bhaba has . . . asserted that the colonized is constructed within a disabling master discourse of colonialism which specifies a degenerate native population to justify its conquest and subsequent rule' (Ashcroft, Griffiths and Tiffin 1989: 178). The Immorality Act was an attempt at colonial eugenics, appearing to even-handedly deny any mingling of race, but covertly constructing black South Africans in particular as so degenerate that their genes had to be contained, lest they damage the fabric of society. The Immorality Act indicated how much whites projected their own felt inferiority onto black people and how crucial it was to the state to maintain the binary system it had established, attempting to naturalise it by labelling any breach of the system as abhorrent. The vigour (and ingenuity) with which these risibly permeable boundaries were policed were clear signs of the anxiety generated by any threat to the schizoid world which the apartheid regime inhabited.

Caliban knew well how to strike fear into the colonial heart when he threatened to people the island with little Calibans. Ania Loomba speaks of *The Tempest* as offering a 'sustained reflection upon the violence, the asymmetry, as well as the intimacy of the colonial encounter' (2002: 163). In *The Madonna of Excelsior* Mda, as he unwrites and rewrites the colonial text of black degeneracy in apartheid South Africa, demonstrates the applicability of Loomba's formulation, particularly with regard to the crushing intimacy of the colonial encounter. He makes apartheid the butt of his satire, enmeshing its creators in the web of their own discourse as he depicts white responsibility for depriving black people of agency. Yet he does not become collusive with colonial binary paradigms by merely reversing them and, in effect, allowing the structure of his discourse to be defined by them. Instead he sets up a dialectic that does not allow for absolute categories of oppression or collusion. According to Tiffin, post-colonial discourses are characteristically subversive. They 'offer fields of counter-discursive strategies to the dominant discourse. The operation of post-colonial counter-discourse is dynamic, not static: it does not seek to subvert the dominant with a view to taking its place, but to, in Wilson Harris's formulation, evolve textual strategies which continually "consume" their "own biases" at the same time as they expose and erode those of the dominant discourse' (1987: 18).

Mda's use of satire reinforces some of these qualities and this chapter will suggest that post-colonial practice – as evidenced by Mda in this novel – is closely allied to satiric practice. Both post-colonialism and satire are counter-discursive and dynamic in the way they operate. Mda's satire exposes the embedded colonial discourses imposed by apartheid so that satire and post-colonial practice converge in their subversive intent. Salman Rushdie is one of the textual practitioners of post-colonialism who advocates such subversion: 'I hope that all of us share the view that we can't simply use the language [English] in the way the British did; that it needs remaking for our own purposes . . . To conquer English may be to complete the process of making ourselves free' (1991: 17).

In terms of linguistic strategy, both satire and post-colonial practice can be seen as specific forms of what Mikhail Bakhtin calls dialogic, heteroglossic and 'parodic-travestying forms', to which he attributes particularly dynamic powers:

> They liberate the object from the power of language in which it had become entangled as if in a net; they destroy the homogenizing power of the direct word, destroying the thick walls that have imprisoned consciousness within its own discourse . . . Language is transformed from the absolute dogma it had been within the narrow framework of a sealed-off and impermeable monoglossia into a working hypothesis for comprehending and expressing reality. (1981: 60–61)

The effect of heteroglossia is the same as that of satire and post-colonialism: to create shifts in language, dissolve rigid categories and boundaries, and establish alternative worlds that interact in a dialogic way.

The following passage exemplifies Mda's simultaneous use of both post-colonial and satiric discourse in *The Madonna of Excelsior*:

> Sekatle – the rich business man who had now purchased a big house in town only two houses from Adam de Vries's English bungalow – adopted the Baipehi [landless squatters] and made himself their spokesman. He drove around the new settlement in his new Mercedes-Benz, making fiery speeches through a hand-held megaphone. He assured those who gathered around his car that the Movement would stand with them. The Movement had fought for liberation so that people could have roofs over their heads and bread and butter on their tables. The Movement would see to it that they were given title to the land they had already allocated themselves. The Movement would give them water and electricity and paved streets. The Movement. The Movement. (Mda 2002: 186)

Here Mda exploits ironies and contradictions, setting them off against one another in order to induce dialogism and liminal play into a previously static situation and thus foreground political exploitation. Mda focuses on Sekatle, using the disjunction between the intentions and the discourse of this former lackey of the apartheid system to satirise him. The passage exposes Sekatle as someone who has appropriated the discourse of 'the Movement' for his own ends and is using it to increase his constituency and consolidate his political power. Sekatle's discourse here is in strong contrast to the unspoken discourse of the Baipehi, their powerlessness stressed by their silence: their plight is conveyed to us indirectly, only through the narrator.

However, another level of interplay occurs between the apparently helpless position of the Baipehi and the fact that they are not entirely disempowered: as is clear from elsewhere in the text, they have managed to acquire a significant degree of agency by means of their indomitable spirit: 'They had constructed a number of shacks, about fifty or so, establishing instant homes. Tonight more than a hundred men, women and children were celebrating with songs and dances around the winter fire. Singing and dancing to a lone guitar' (Mda 2002: 185). Their determination to seize the agency they have been denied is emphasised by the name they have adopted: 'Baipehi' means 'those who have placed themselves'. Thus satire, traditionally a way of excoriating society for its evils, becomes in Mda's hands *also* a way of celebrating the particular strengths of marginalised communities.

But, however much satire and post-colonialism make common cause, they are not identical in at least one important sense. Satire does not, in general, operate from a specific moral or political agenda, preferring instead to give itself the flexibility to criticise any party, group or class. Mda's satire operates firmly within this tradition, retaining the right to satirise both white and black people across the board, but he deviates from the satiric paradigm by also being committed to a single serious purpose – that of post-colonial narrative. For David Theo Goldberg and Ato Quayson, the enabling pre-text of post-colonialism is 'the idea that post-colonialism is itself an ethical enterprise, pressing its claims in ways that other theories such as those of postmodernism and poststructuralism do not' (2002: xii). For Emily Bauman, post-colonial practice consists of a tension between what she calls 'an epistemological relativism' on the one hand, which exposes the discourses of colonialism and, on the other hand, 'a moral foundationalism', which justifies post-colonialism as 'politically necessary and progressive work' (1998: 79–80).

In *The Madonna of Excelsior*, Mda reveals moral foundationalism by (*inter alia*) making use of a first-person plural voice, which speaks sympathetically for black community values, though it is sometimes tinged with what seems to be an intrusion of Mda's own ironic vision. For example, in the following passage, Viliki, a former freedom-fighter and black politician in the new South Africa, has just emerged from a barbed interchange with an unlikely friend, Adam de Vries, a conservative Afrikaaner Nationalist lawyer, who claims the spurious honour of having tried to change the apartheid system from within. Mda's particular version of a Greek chorus then comments as follows:

> We watched Viliki walk out of Adam de Vries's office. We knew that whenever he was bored . . . he sauntered off to Adam de Vries's office in town. We wondered what it was that had drawn these two together . . .
>
> When the inquisitive quizzed him about it, Viliki would only say, 'He is a nice, guy, although a white man will always be a white man.' The likes of Tjaart Cronje and Johannes Smit said that Adam de Vries was Viliki's puppet . . . Otherwise what would an Afrikaaner lawyer have in common with an unschooled township boy? . . . We, on the other hand, were not bothered by these friendships. We put them down to the old love affair between black people and Afrikaners that the English found so irritating . . . The English, common wisdom stated, were hypocrites. They laughed with you, but immediately you turned they stabbed you in the back. The Afrikaner, on the other hand, was honest. When he hated you he showed you at once. He did not pretend to like you . . . When he smiled, you knew it was genuine . . . We never questioned what informed these generalizations. (Mda 2002: 222–23)

The complex texture of such interpolations offers information and commentary on events and attitudes, but also questions them. There is a strong sense of communal watchfulness and involvement, and there is also the airing of stock group attitudes, which are subjected to satire – or at least presented by Mda with an exaggerated air of innocence, which immediately undermines itself and declares that its intentions are subversive. Yet, as Mda challenges communal generalisations, he is simultaneously challenging the validity of his own narrative, by including himself in the 'we' whose views he is interrogating and by presenting a counter-discourse that insists on ontological slippages, rather than certainties.

However, there is another side to this text for, working against the elements of satiric playfulness, wit and irony in *The Madonna of Excelsior* is a deep, constantly repeated sombre note, which conveys the inescapable sadness left by racism in its wake. Black people do end up in political control of the town of Excelsior, yet possession of such power cannot exorcise the evils of apartheid overnight. What Mda shows in distressing personal detail are the psychological effects of racism on its victims. Although Niki is an intimate servant of a white family, the Cronjes, and takes a major role in the raising of their child, the social arrangements of the community constantly remind her not only of her difference, but also her inferiority: she may not eat at their table and she may not enter their church to worship. Mda describes with bland ferocity how, after she has perforce spent the entire service participating from the church gate, the town's lawyer, Adam de Vries, 'who always had a kind word for everyone', asks her whether she enjoyed the service, to which she replies, 'It was good, my baas' (Mda 2002: 31). Mda's anatomy of racism, rather than inveighing against injustice, confronts us instead with the tragic obliviousness which, on a personal and domestic level, marked the behaviour of most white South Africans at that time.

Continuing to turn the screw, Mda presents us soon after this with a scene in the butchery owned by the Cronjes, where Niki works to supplement her income. Niki is confronted by Cornelia Cronje during the ritual twice-daily weighing of all black employees 'to make sure they were not stealing her meat' (Mda 2002: 40). When Niki is found to be suspiciously overweight at the end of the day, Cornelia forces her to strip in public, but no meat is found on her person. ' "Magtig, Niki," said Madam Cornelia, "where did the kilo come from?" And she burst out laughing' (42). By the end of the novel, Niki has found a measure of redemption for her earlier life, but it is not unalloyed: 'Serenity rested on her shoulders like a heavy log' (209). The price paid for apartheid by black people is shown to be paralleled by that paid by whites in this novel, whose sensibilities it systematically erodes by offering them the false comforts of power and superior wealth. As Claire Pajaczowska and Lola Young say of whiteness: 'An identity based on power never has to develop consciousness of itself as responsible, it has no sense of its limits except as these are perceived in opposition to others' (1992: 202).

By the same token, the mass sexual exploitation of black women by white men that lies at the heart of the novel is made possible only by a process of marginalisation that the ruling race enforced, in the belief that it was mediating the natural order of things. Mda documents with unrelenting accuracy the coarsening of moral fibre and loss of basic human compassion in white people, which accompanied such exploitation. One of his most telling comments on the South African situation – both past and future – lies in the two parallel and heavily sardonic statements which frame his narrative: 'All these things flow from the sins of our mothers' (Mda 2002: 1) and 'from the sins of our mothers all these things flow' (268). This ominously uncompromising echo of the biblical idea that 'the sins of the fathers shall be visited upon the sons' stresses the embedded nature of the disempowerment caused by apartheid, in the course of which black people – in this text, black women, in particular – were scapegoats. In a bitterly satirical echo of the Western patriarchal values espoused by apartheid society, Mda exposes the way in which responsibility was denied and displaced in that era, in precisely the way that the white society of Excelsior managed to deflect responsibility for its guilt onto the black women involved. As Mda has the Reverend François Bornman reported as saying in a parodic illustration of this point: 'The devil had sent black women to tempt him and to move him away from the path of righteousness' (87). Faye Harrison, in drawing attention to the dynamics occurring within racist societies, foregrounds the term 'race' as primarily a constructed one: 'From the vantage points of the subordinate segments of racially stratified societies, the orderliness, lawfulness, and "natural" guise of structured racial inequalities are often experienced as profoundly problematic assaults against their dignity, life chances, and human rights. For them, "race" is frequently experienced as a form of symbolic as well as materialized violence' (2002: 146).

Institutionalised racial violence of a more personal and covert kind is equally damaging, as *The Madonna of Excelsior* shows. In South Africa, as elsewhere, invisible racism (invisible to the offender, that is) has often been perpetuated by those who fail to examine their own assumptions about otherness. Michelle Brattain demonstrates how the unexamined nature of whiteness in the southern United States allowed white people to naturalise whiteness and thus permit its implications to escape interrogation (2001: 7, 14). The extent to which racist ideologies occlude any awareness of structured racial inequalities from the perpetrators themselves is demonstrated in the deathbed scene between Tjaart and Popi at the end of Mda's novel:

> 'I have a little present for you,' he said, giving her a container of Immac hair remover. 'It is a cream that will make your legs smooth.'
>
> For a moment, anger flashed across Popi's face. Her hand did not move to take the insensitive gift from his shaking hand. But when she saw the earnestness of his face, she took it and said, 'I don't shave my legs, Tjaart.'
>
> 'You are a beautiful woman, Popi. Very beautiful. That cream is going to enhance the beauty of your long legs,' he said.
>
> Popi smiled and whispered, 'I do not shave my legs, Tjaart.'
>
> 'But you must,' cried Tjaart. 'You are a lady. A beautiful lady.'
>
> Popi was blushing all over. No one outside Niki and Viliki had ever called her beautiful before. At least, not to her face. Apparently she never knew how we used to gossip about her beauty. Grudgingly praising it despite our public denunciation of her being a boesman.
>
> 'Lizette de Vries told me that progressive women don't shave their legs,' she said. 'Not even their armpits.'
>
> 'Lizette de Vries is an old fart,' he responded, chuckling at his own joke again.
>
> 'I'll take the cream, Tjaart, because in my culture they say it is rude to refuse a present. But I will never use it. I love my body the way it is.' (Mda 2002: 263)

Popi is fighting to remain compassionate and patient, while asserting her own value, in contradiction of apartheid values. Tjaart, in the midst of his apparently kind and flattering gift, persists in defining her in terms of both gendered and racial power relations. His kindness is flawed by his deeply seated obliviousness: he fails to appreciate the inherent human value of both women and black people and he is unaware of the assumptions that have led to this. Like every other white person in the novel, he lacks the courage to acknowledge that the way in which he defines himself is dependent on defining black people as inferior – an effect of 'the deep-seated nature of racist socialization' (Tuckwell 2002: 123). Mda here creates the painful irony of a reconciliation scene that fails to create reconciliation between Tjaart and Popi, even though they are united because they share a father and look so much alike (Mda 2002: 264) – facts which, under other circumstances, might have made for real reconciliation. Their inability, even at Tjaart's deathbed, to acknowledge and exploit their common parentage for mutual healing dramatises the damage of apartheid, gathering the sadness of the text to a head. Here and elsewhere in the text, racist exclusionary practices and structures focus the reader on the power relations on which institutionalised racism depends. Mda's analysis of this problem highlights the axiom expressed by Kenan Malik: 'We do not define races because biological data compels us to do so. Rather, society begins with an a priori division of humanity into different races for which it subsequently finds a rationale in certain physical characteristics . . . The clue to the importance of race in Western thought, therefore, lies not in biology but in society' (1996: 5).

The Madonna of Excelsior suggests how the different 'racial' communities in South Africa became intertwined in a particularly static way, usually for worse, rather than for better. Mda shows how the marginalisation of black people, combined with their economic dependence on whites, resulted in black people gaining employment at the price of satisfying white needs for dominance. 'The self cannot come into being without the other . . . self and other are inextricably co-dependent' (Shildrick 2002: 104).

Yet Mda's focus in this text is also on the complexity and shifting quality of contemporary South African society, reflecting and challenging both current and past discourses. He creates new configurations of relationships that are renegotiable, rather than permanently fixed in colonial binary form. Mda does what Tiffin speaks of in another context, offering a 'post-colonial counter-discourse which is perpetually conscious of its own ideologically constructed subject position and speaks ironically from within it' (1987: 27). In *The Madonna of Excelsior* the slippages, counter-discourse and creolisation are constellated in Mda's handling of the issues of race. He reveals how much of racial identity is socially constructed, but he also shows how the apparently certain outward signs of race can be equally unstable. Loomba, too, puts the word 'race' under erasure:

> Precisely those features which are most commonly taken as evidence of racial difference (such as skin colour), are the most fragile from an evolutionary standpoint, which is to say that they are the quickest to mutate as a result of any sexual mingling. Perhaps that is why skin colour produced so much anxiety in Shakespeare's time: the assertion that it signified a deeper human essence was always challenged by its uncanny ability either to vanish or to show up in unwelcome ways. (2002: 3)

The way in which Mda sets out to create discursive fissures in the apartheid narrative of institutionalised racism is highlighted by the following commentary on Popi, Niki's daughter. She is one of many children born as a result of white and black people contravening the Immorality Act – a scenario which lies at the heart of the novel:

> We had witnessed Popi's emergence from the battering of two years before without a dent on her willowy body. We had watched her blossom into a woman of exceptional poise, with the dimples of Niki's [her mother] maidenhood. Her beauty had even erased the thoughts that used to nag us about her being a boesman . . . And we did not recall them every time we saw her. Perhaps our eyes were getting used to her. As they were getting used to others like her . . . Whenever we saw Popi, we praised her beauty and forgot our old gibes that she was a boesman. We lamented the fact that we never saw her smile. That a permanent frown marred her otherwise beautiful face. That her dimples were wasted without a smile. Perhaps we had forgotten that we had stolen her smiles. (Mda 2002: 168)

In comparison to the earlier passage concerning Viliki and Adam de Vries, the African/Greek chorus is weaker and less certain of itself here, apparently because the communal consciousness is more self-conscious. Popi's beauty is praised and the communal voice speaks of what was seen, but there is a lack of real involvement and a certain amount of discomfort about their past behaviour. Mda suggests how the community, having adopted aspects of colonial discourse, is unable to subvert or recuperate the term 'boesman', which still remains embedded in apartheid structures. As a result, the strength of community involvement has turned to helpless witness, unable or even unwilling to offer help, and this is reflected in the self-doubt of the last sentence in the excerpt above. Such loss of communal direction is inseparable from damage inflicted on both language and identity, and John Thieme's formulation about classic English realism can be usefully applied to the discourse of apartheid which, likewise, was 'a mode offering the illusion of a transparent representation of a social world, while obscuring the fact that the social reality it purports to represent is linguistically constructed' (2001: 54). Mda's novel, as it uses both postmodernism and satire to strip the veneer from the Potemkin-like village appearance of racism, shows how damaging a lack of awareness of the linguistic constructedness of 'reality' can be to the social fabric of society.

From a satirical perspective, Mda is interrogating the black community through the terms they use and the implicit judgements they make: the use of the word 'boesman' is unthinking on their part, as is the demeaning talk of 'getting used to' Popi 'and others like her'. A post-colonial view, by contrast, might focus instead on the fractured nature of the community that has been disempowered because it has been constructed, linguistically, in an oppressive way. According to Gayatri Spivak, because of 'the narrow epistemic violence of imperialism . . . the subaltern has no history and cannot speak' (1993: 82–83), meaning presumably, 'cannot speak *with agency*'. Shakespeare's Caliban *does* speak: 'You taught me language; and my profit on't/ Is, I know how to curse' (*The Tempest*, Act I, scene 2, lines 365–67). However, in so far as most of his energies – linguistic and otherwise – are directed towards cursing and plotting against Prospero, Caliban is prevented from developing his abilities in other directions.

Colonial epistemologies curtail agency, but they may also provoke unwitting collusion: the curse word 'boesman' is perpetuated here by those who are also trapped in colonial discourse, but do not bear the outward configuration of miscegenation/creolisation as Popi does. Here, as elsewhere in Mda's novel, the post-colonial goal is to redefine identity as open-ended, denying the existence – and the discursive usefulness – of stable, unitary signification and offering instead a complex of ambivalent discourses. Above all, *The Madonna of Excelsior* is an exposé of the evils that arise in a society in which 'race' is used as the primary and official marker of identity.

Stuart Hall speaks of identity as follows: 'Identity is not as transparent or unproblematic as we think. Perhaps instead of thinking of identity as an already accomplished fact, which the new cultural practices then represent, we should think, instead, of identity as a "production" which is never complete, always in process, and always constituted within, not outside, representation' (1994: 392). A major strategy in Mda's destabilisation of the colonial discourse of identity is his use of magic realism, specifically the pattern of his novel that introduces each chapter with either a reference to or description of a Frans Claerhout painting, or a passage written in Claerhout-type painterly prose, exploiting the non-realist, Chagall-like qualities of Claerhout's work to repeatedly pull the ontological rug out from under the reader. Related to this – and also occurring predominantly at the beginning of each chapter – is Mda's deliberate confusion of identity by, for example, exploiting descriptions of Claerhout's figures of people in unusual colours such as blue or red, his showing a nun as pregnant or his painting a madonna and child with the same face, and which are used to initiate the point at issue in each chapter. Mda's creolised, playful and satirical answer to the enforcement of racial categories in the past is to fragment and muddle as many human categories as possible, thus suggesting that identity is in fact complex, unpredictable and not, as the practice of apartheid suggested, related to mere surface appearances. As Donald Moore, Jake Kosek and Anand Pandian suggest: 'Cultural identities provide the very means by which we craft our futures. The politics of the possible is shaped profoundly by the ways in which we imagine our communities of affinity and our places of belonging' (2003: 42). Mda's novel focuses a great deal on issues of identity, by his imaginative creation denying and frustrating the forces in South Africa that previously enforced identity in terms of rigid categories. However, *The Madonna of Excelsior* also has a very sober side, not offering a utopian vision, but instead painting a picture of society in which issues of identity will not easily be resolved because destructive forces of the past will, for the foreseeable future, have life and influence through their linguistic persistence.

Earlier in this chapter, reference was made to Bahktin's preference for dialogic, heteroglossic textual forms that serve to liberate the subject from the power of hegemonic language, destroying 'the thick walls that . . . imprison consciousness within its own discourse' and turning language into a 'working hypothesis' for re-presentation (1981: 60–61). These elements of provisionality are shared by both satiric and post-colonial discourse. However, satire is relatively detached, with an agenda that is oblique – a marginalised form that capitalises on its marginality. Theoretical texts on satire reflect its lack of overt agendas: such texts are descriptive and analytic, but do not take firm positions over satire, its practice and purpose, since satiric practice is so idiosyncratic and evasive. Above all, in satiric theory, there is very little of the overt commitment and, often, controversy that mark post-colonial theory.

Post-colonial strategies, on the other hand, are essentially ethically and politically driven, even when such goals are not openly stated: they strive to challenge attitudes and structures that perpetuate inequality within societies. Many post-colonial theorists continuously reflect on the nature of their targets and their strategies, resulting in the kind of robust interaction that satiric theory lacks. This reflects the difference between the embedded marginality of satire and the more flexible and complex stance of post-colonialism towards marginality.

Satire is useful to Mda on the occasions when he requires that kind of detachment, though Mda's post-colonial practice is also akin to the most ferocious kind of satire, in that it gives no quarter, but grapples relentlessly with the results of colonialism in South Africa. It does so without rancour, but with a serious commitment to both deconstruction and reconstruction, in line with Tiffin's view that good post-colonial practice works by 'refusing, realigning, deconstructing the "master narrative" of western history [while] recapturing notions of self from "other" and investigating that destructive binarism itself' (1998: 179).

Note

1. This chapter is an extended version of my article, 'De-scribing the centre' (Goodman 2004). Both are part of a project, funded by the National Research Foundation (NRF), which is investigating post-1994 forms of South African transitional literature.

Works cited

Ashcroft, Bill, Gareth Griffiths and Helen Tiffin. 1989. *The Empire Writes Back: Theory and Practice in Post-Colonial Literatures*. London: Routledge.

Bakhtin, M.M. 1981. *The Dialogic Imagination: Four Essays by M.M. Bakhtin*. Translated by Caryl Emerson and Michael Holquist; edited by Michael Holquist. Austin: University of Texas Press.

Bauman, Emily. 1998. 'Re-dressing colonial discourse: Postcolonial theory and the humanist project'. *Critical Quarterly* 40(3): 79–89.

Brattain, Michelle. 2001. *Politics of Whiteness: Race, Workers, and Culture in the Modern South*. Princeton: Princeton University Press.

Goldberg, David Theo and Ato Quayson (eds.). 2002. *Relocating Postcolonialism*. Oxford: Blackwell.

Goodman, Ralph. 2004. 'De-scribing the centre: Satiric and postcolonial strategies in *The Madonna of Excelsior*'. *Journal of Literary Studies* 20(1/2): 62–70.

Hall, Stuart. 1994. 'Cultural identity and diaspora'. In: Williams, Patrick and Laura Chrisman (eds.). *Colonial Discourse and Post-Colonial Theory: A Reader*. New York: Columbia University Press, 392–403.

Harrison, Faye V. 2002. 'Unraveling "race" for the twenty-first century'. In: MacClancy, Jeremy (ed.). *Exotic No More: Anthropology on the Front Lines*. Chicago: University of Chicago Press, 145–66.

Loomba, Ania. 2002. *Shakespeare, Race, and Colonialism*. Oxford: Oxford University Press.

Malik, K. 1996. *The Meaning of Race: Race, History and Culture in Western Society*. London: Macmillan.

Mda, Zakes. 2002. *The Madonna of Excelsior*. Cape Town: Oxford University Press.

Moore, Donald S., Jake Kosek and Anand Pandian. 2003. 'The cultural politics of race and nature: Terrains of power and practice'. In: Moore, Donald S., Jake Kosek and Anand Pandian (eds.). *Race, Nature, and the Politics of Difference*. Durham: Duke University Press, 1–70.

Pajaczowska, Claire and Lola Young. 1992. 'Racism, representation, psychoanalysis'. In: Donald, James and Ali Rattansi (eds.). *'Race', Culture and Difference*. London: Sage, 198–219.

Rushdie, Salman. 1991. *Imaginary Homelands: Essays and Criticism, 1981–1991*. New York: Viking.

Shakespeare, William. 1984. *The Tempest*. The Arden Shakespeare. Edited by Frank Kermode. London: Methuen & Co.

Shildrick, Margit. 2002. *Embodying the Monster: Encounters with the Vulnerable Self*. London: Sage.

Spivak, Gayatri Chakravorty. 1993. 'Can the subaltern speak?' In: Williams, Patrick and Laura Chrisman (eds.). *Colonial Discourse and Postcolonial Theory: A Reader*. New York: Harvester Wheatsheaf, 66–111.

Thieme, John. 2001. *Postcolonial Con-texts: Writing back to the Canon*. London: Continuum.

Tiffin, Helen. 1987. 'Post-colonial literatures and counter-discourse'. *Kunapipi* 9(3): 17–34.

———. 1988. 'Post-colonialism, post-modernism and the rehabilitation of post-colonial history'. *Journal of Commonwealth Literature* 23(1): 169–81.

Tuckwell, Gill. 2002. *Racial Identity, White Counsellors and Therapists*. Buckingham: Open University Press.

16

Narrating Transformative Possibilities

The Collective Voice in The Madonna of Excelsior

N.S. ZULU

THIS CHAPTER EXAMINES the narrative voice in Zakes Mda's novel, *The Madonna of Excelsior* (2002), focusing on what it says about the crossing of boundaries and identities to foster transformation. Narrative voice can be defined as the voice of 'the narrator' or 'the speaker of a text' (Rimmon-Kenan 1983: 87). Paul Cobley simply calls it 'the voice of the poet or narrator' (2001: 104). Voice in narration, according to H. Porter Abbot, 'is a question of who it is we "hear" doing the narrating' (2002: 64). The voice we hear narrating in *The Madonna of Excelsior* can be identified as a collective one, speaking for a community.

A first reading of *The Madonna of Excelsior* might give one the deceptive impression that its collective narrative voice is monolithic and inward-looking, in so far as it speaks on behalf of the whole black community in South Africa, and specifically the community of Mahlatswetsa, the township near Excelsior. In addition, the narrative voice might also seem to be speaking against the white community of Excelsior during the heyday of apartheid and after its downfall, using a binary discourse in which the oppressed versus the oppressing subjects are put into distinct categories. However, a closer reading of the novel reveals that its collective voice is an outward-looking, omniscient one that is complex and multiple, self-critical and self-mocking, ironic and satirical. It is also a voice that subverts notions of racial and political homogeneity during and after apartheid. The voice offers corrective but de-totalising post-apartheid alternatives that dismantle past social and ideological categories and foster nation-building. The collective voice is therefore transformative.

The omniscient 'we' narrator is homodiegetically involved in the events being narrated. This is similar in some ways to the collective voice that the reader hears in Mda's earlier novel, *Ways of Dying*; however, the collective voice in *Ways of Dying* is far less complex:

> ...we live our lives together as one. We know everything about everybody. We even know things that happen when we are not there; things that happen behind people's closed doors deep in the middle of the night. We are the all-seeing eye of the village gossip. When in our orature the storyteller begins the story, 'They say it once happened...', we are the 'they'. No individual owns any story. The community is the owner of the story, and it can tell it the way it deems fit. We would not be needing to justify the collective voice that tells this story if you had not wondered how we become so omniscient... (Mda 1995a: 8)

In *Ways of Dying* the collective voice is at the level of 'the village gossip' ('They say'), whereas in *The Madonna of Excelsior* the collective voice presents the experiences of all those who were affected in one way or another by the social conflict in the polarised zones of apartheid. Consequently, the collective voice seems to demand the reader's involvement in the process of challenging his/her assumptions, as well as those of the novel and the author. Ralph Goodman argues that by using the collective voice in *The Madonna of Excelsior*, 'Mda challenges communal generalisations [as] he is simultaneously challenging the validity of his own narrative, by including himself in the "we" whose views he is interrogating, and by presenting a counter-discourse which insists on ontological slippages rather than certainties' (2004: 67).

The communal narrator has had first-hand experience of the essentialist cultural representations that divided South African society as a consequence of the legalised racial segregation that prevailed and thrived because of the 'Hertzog Native and Land bills' (Khunyeli 1994: 4), pillars of apartheid legislation that were amended from time to time to become more stringent in their control of racial identities. Essentialism, as we are reminded by Bill Ashcroft, Gareth Griffiths and Helen Tiffin, 'is the assumption that groups, categories or classes of objects have one or several defining features exclusive to all members of the category . . . In the analysis of culture it is a (generally implicit) assumption that individuals share an essential cultural identity' (1998: 77).

The collective voice parodies the essentialism of apartheid. In the novel, this manifests itself in fixed and stereotypical representations of social reality. For example, Adam de Vries's party in Excelsior is a typical Afrikaner event: there are 'boys who [are] playing with a rugby ball, practising throws that might see them being picked for Haak Vrystaat, or even the Springboks, in later years' (Mda 2002: 6) and the atmosphere is dominated by 'boeremusiek of the concertina' (7) with 'liedjies' and 'volkspele'. Some of the Afrikaner women are caricatured as 'voluminous'. All the people at the party are Calvinist Christians of the 'local Dutch Reformed Church', who believe in the creed of Dr J.G. Strydom, the prime minister of South Africa from 1954 to 1958, whose name is commemorated in the marble panel at the door of the church: '*As a Calvinist people we Afrikaners have, in accordance with our faith in the Word of God, developed a policy condemning all equality and mongrelisation between White and Black. God's Word teaches us, after all, that He willed into being separate nations, colours and languages*' (29–30; italics in original).

Because of this religious belief in separateness, black people live in Mahlatswetsa and white Afrikaners live in the town itself. Although not explicitly stated in the novel, the reader knows that there is a distance between the lives of black and white people. The poor blacks in the novel supply cheap labour to 'very prosperous' (Mda 2002: 7) Afrikaners, who ensure, through the enforcement of segregation and the denunciation of equality, that black domestic servants such as Niki wait outside the gates of the white masters' churches to look after their children. What is ironic about the Calvinist Christianity of the Dutch Reformed Church in Excelsior is that the white people, on rejoining their servants waiting outside, ask them whether they enjoyed the service. Adam de Vries, for instance, asks Niki, 'Did you enjoy the service?' and she responds, 'It was good, my baas' (31). Similarly, Stephanus Cronje asks, 'It was a beautiful service, wasn't it?' Niki agrees, 'It was very beautiful' and Madam Cornelia continues, 'We are grateful you agreed to look after Tjaart even though it's a Sunday' (32).

The situation in Excelsior illustrates how apartheid constructed boundaries between town and township, white and black, in trying to maintain the assumptions of the white self as 'civilised' and the other as 'primitive'. Bill Ashcroft points out that 'profound in the development of modernity was the construction of a boundary between civilised self and primitive other' (2001: 165). The strict apartheid laws were designed to regulate and organise cultural activities in fixed boundaries and identities. The Population Registration Act categorised people into ethnic and racial groups; the Mixed Amenities Act enforced separate public facilities; the Group Areas Act legislated where blacks and whites were to live and established barren homelands, inhospitable townships and towns with empty spaces in between; and the Immorality Act prohibited marriage between black and white people, so as not to pollute the pureness of the white race.

In its way, the collective voice mocks apartheid essentialisms and the racist maintenance of the boundaries between black and white. Parodying the Immorality Act, the novel singles out a group of conservative but sexually depraved Afrikaner men in Excelsior. Johannes Smit is representative of the hypocrisy of apartheid's policy of condemning 'mongrelisation between White and Black' that is enshrined in the Immorality Act. He is ridiculed in the novel as a perverted 'squat hairy gorilla' (Mda 2002: 15), with 'hairy buttocks' (17), a 'hirsute man with a beer belly' (15). Smit also symbolises the Afrikaner male's view of immorality as a pastime: he waylays black girls in the open veld and rapes them, as he rapes Niki. To Smit and his Afrikaner friends, such rape is 'great sport', a 'game' (15).

In this context, the collective voice of the novel satirises the Afrikaner masculinity that regards black girls as 'quarry' (Mda 2002: 74) to be hunted down and raped. As a regular player of this 'harrowing game' (15), Smit's lust for black women is public knowledge, despite his being the provincial leader of the 'ultra-right-wing Herstigte Nasionale Party' (88). The reader learns that in some instances, 'quarry' became permanent sexual partners, often swapped during group sex amid heavy drinking. The fact that a woman is taken as prey debases her as an 'animal-like, degenerate and stupid figure' (Lockett 1988:

21). Furthermore, as Dorothy Driver points out, since the frontier times, black women have 'often provid[ed] young white men with their sex education and even function[ed] as "second wives"' (1988: 15). It is also as an organiser of the sex orgies with black women that take place in his barn that Johannes Smit represents the double standards of the Immorality Act. He is an elder of a church that condemns immorality and mongrelisation, yet the community of Mahlatswetsa location recognises him as the man who seduces girls with 'bank notes' (Mda 2002: 15) to obtain other black girls for his 'pastime'.

The collective voice exposes the ironies of apartheid xenophobia and targets the double standards of all those who enforced it. Klein-Jan Lombard represents the apartheid officials who arrested and prosecuted the contraveners of the Immorality Act, yet he and his father, Groot-Jan Lombard, are players of this game. As a police officer and prosecutor, the magistrate asks him to recuse himself from prosecuting his own father. Tjaart Cronje represents the officials who overzealously lead the war against miscegenation, having been brainwashed by their fathers and grandfathers against black people, whom they see as terrorists and communists. The reader, however, suspects that Tjaart himself probably lost his virginity sleeping with a black woman. His 'horsey-horsey' games with his black nanny, Niki, are anything but innocent. Niki eventually stops carrying him on her back because whenever he was on her back, it 'induced an erection and [he] worked himself up with unseemly rhythmic movements' (Mda 2002: 9). In addition, the narrator reveals that, young as he was, Tjaart knew about the common practice of sleeping with black women because when his mother strip-searches Niki, his lust for her becomes obvious: 'Niki's triangular pubes loomed large in Tjaart Cronje's imagination. Threatening the pleasures of the future . . . He knew already that it was the tradition of Afrikaner boys of the Free State platteland to go through devirgination rites by capturing and consuming the forbidden quarry that lurked beneath their nannies' pink overall' (42).

The collective voice satirises the 'cannibalistic zeal' of Afrikaners in prosecuting their fellow Afrikaners for the 'pastime' of immorality:

It was the Golden Age of Immorality in the Free State. Immorality was a pastime. It had always been popular even before laws were enacted in Parliament to curb it. It became a pastime the very day explorers' ships

weighed anchor at the Cape Peninsula centuries ago, and saw the yellow
body parts of the Khoikhoi women. But what we were seeing during
the Golden Age was like a plague. In various platteland towns Afrikaner
magistrates were sitting at the benches, listening to salacious details,
and concealing painful erections under their black magisterial gowns.
Afrikaners prosecuting fellow Afrikaners with cannibalistic zeal.
Afrikaners sending fellow Afrikaners to serve terms of imprisonment.
All because of black body parts. (Mda 2002: 93–94)

The collective voice of the novel also derides the hypocrisy of the Dutch
Reformed Church and its Calvinist theology, as represented by Reverend
Francois Bornman, pastor of the Church in Excelsior. Bornman's preaching
supports the laws against miscegenation: 'We knew of him as a man of God
who preached obedience to His laws. Laws against adultery and miscegenation'
(Mda 2002: 75). Yet, at the same time, he shared in the 'great sport', the sexual
activities satirised in the novel as 'harrowing games' (15), 'partners-swapping
orgies', 'escapades' and 'wicked pleasures' (78). Bornman is one of the Excelsior
19 accused, who represent the rotten core of male Afrikaner lust, men who go
as far as to establish rules for their partner-swapping games. When these rules
are not observed, they accuse one another of 'obviously becoming
unsportsmanly' (53), behaving like 'selfish boy[s]' (54) wanting to have 'the
sole ownership' (53) of their partners.

The irony is that when the Afrikaner men are caught in their 'immoral
pastime', they hire the services of someone who has been guilty of the same
crime to defend them. Adam de Vries, who knows very well that they are guilty
as charged, denies that they have done anything wrong. According to him,
'these men are innocent. They have been framed by the blacks' (Mda 2002:
75). Subsequently, the court case is seen as a 'black conspiracy'. Assuming the
reader's familiarity with the miscegenation story of the Excelsior 19, the all-
knowing narrator ridicules the one-sidedness of the trial: 'All these things flow
from the sins of our mothers' (1). The greatest irony, of course, is that in court
Adam de Vries argues that the Reverend Francois Bornman and his friends
are innocent men who have been framed by the blacks, despite Bornman's
confession of guilt to him and other elders of the Dutch Reformed Church:

The devil had sent black women to tempt him and to move him away from the path of righteousness. The devil had always used the black female to tempt the Afrikaner. It was a battle that was raging within individual Afrikaner men. A battle between lust and loathing. A battle that the Afrikaner must win. The devil made the Afrikaner to covertly covet the black woman while publicly detesting her. (Mda 2002: 87)

Even the perverted Johannes Smit is said to be a 'good person who had been led astray by the devil in the guise of black women' (Mda 2002: 88). The narrative voice elaborates satirically on this belief in the intervention of the devil in the lives of the men of Excelsior:

The elders of the church were right. The devil was on the loose in the Free State platteland. Grabbing upstanding volk by their genitalia and dragging them along a path strewn with the body parts of black women. Parts that had an existence independent of the women attached to them. Parts that were capable of sending even the most devout citizen into bouts of frenzied lust. (Mda 2002: 89)

Such 'innocent' exaggerations have subversive intentions. To highlight the failure of the Immorality Act to regulate sexual activity between races, the novel confirms that, despite the publicity around the Excelsior 19 case, 'miscegenation had continued unabated' (Mda 2002: 115). The reader learns that the Seller of Songs, Viliki's lover and Maria's daughter, who is younger than Popi, was 'born several years post-Excelsior 19' (196) and is said to be the 'spitting image of Reverend Francois Bornman' (196). The blame, however, falls on Maria, the black woman, who had continued with her escapades with white men. She is represented as the temptress who continued to spread 'her body parts before the path of the dominee' (196). Driver argues that black women in the colonial and apartheid eras, like 'prostitutes who were seen as a safety valve for public morality', acted 'as vehicles or decoys for the kind of male lust that was not deemed suitable for their white counterparts' (1988: 15). According to Cecily Lockett, the alluring black woman is portrayed as a 'sexual temptress, often attractive . . . she becomes a destroyer figure, for by consorting with her the white man faces the danger of prosecution under the Immorality Act and, as a convicted criminal, his life and that of his family is destroyed . . . It is the black woman, and equally the law itself, which function as instruments of destruction' (1988: 29).

In its parody of the religious notion that Afrikaner men contravened the Immorality Act because black women tempted them to do so, the collective voice in Mda's novel provides the motif of the 'sins of our mothers' from the very first sentence – 'All these things flow from the sins of our mothers' (Mda 2002: 1) – to the last: 'From the sins of our mothers all these things flow' (268).

The collective voice also parodies the hegemonic feminism perpetuated by cultures of apartheid modernity. Hegemonic feminism during and after apartheid was based on the premise that there are rich white women who own the means of social production and thus wield enormous socio-economic power to oppress black women and other people who do not own the means of social production. The novel demonstrates that hegemonic feminism in apartheid South Africa was historically linked to class and race, as in the humiliation and subjugation of poor, black women, such as Niki, by richer, white women. For instance, at her butchery, Madam Cronje weighs black women in the morning and in the evening when they leave because she believes them to be thieves. She does not see anything wrong with stripping Niki naked in front of black and white men, children and Niki's female fellow workers. Throughout her humiliation, Niki is silent, yet her silence seems to valorise the alternative: treatment with dignity and decency. The narrative voice directs the reader to the oppression of one woman by another as the motive for Niki's subsequent behaviour: 'Anger was slowly simmering in Niki. A storm was brewing. Quietly. Calmly. Behind her serene demeanour she hid dark motives of vengeance. Woman to woman. We wondered why she did not resign from Excelsior Slaghuis after being humiliated like that. But she knew something we did not know. She was biding her time . . . she was nursing an ungodly grudge' (Mda 2002: 42). Her 'ungodly grudge' eventually leads her to sleep with Madam Cronje's husband, Stephanus Cronje who, having seen Niki naked, was 'seized by the fiend of lust' (41). Whilst Stephanus Cronje plans to make her 'padkos – my provision for the road' (49), thinking that she is 'ready and willing' (50), Niki is in fact exacting revenge. She sees him not as her boss or her lover, but as 'Madam Cornelia's husband. And he was inside her. She was gobbling up Madam Cornelia's husband, with the emphasis on *Madam*. And she had him entirely in her power. Chewing him to pieces' (50; emphasis in original). In this manner, the collective voice gives Niki agency as an individual who can intentionally resist subjugation.

Niki's 'place' under apartheid and African patriarchy appears to be that of the black woman suffering a double oppression as the subaltern female who occupies the lowest social position and is denied the capacity and possibility of moving to the highest social strata. The emphasis on the black woman as a mute, sad, pathetic and passive victim of colonial and male domination, who 'speaks' through her silences, is problematic in the sense that she is perpetually cast as the absolute other. Thus, with Gayatri Spivak, the reader asks: 'Can the subaltern speak?' (1988: 294) and concludes that of course she can and must speak. As Stephane Ibinga points out, 'silence can be adopted by people in a repressive political and/or patriarchal system to shun reprisal' (2005: 2). However, the presentation of the black woman as suffering double oppression highlights the white woman's collusion and complicity with patriarchy and apartheid, and simultaneously promotes liberating practices and ideals. By rejecting the representational system of the form of feminism that embraces the oppression of one woman by the other, the novel seems to be advocating a post-colonial feminism, which questions patriarchal subjugation in terms of detotalising, diversifying and denaturalising assumptions within social, political and historical contexts. Such a form of post-colonial feminism 'addresses how gender colludes with race, national origin, and class in women's oppression and how women participate in and resist their own oppression and the oppression of other women' (Richards 2000: viii).

In the second part of *The Madonna of Excelsior*, the collective voice speaks of liberating choices and possibilities. The novel provides a transformative space, which is introduced in Chapter 21 by an account of the liberation of political prisoners and the unbanning of political organisations in South Africa. The signs of transformation in the Excelsior camp are realised when Adam de Vries revises his past generalisations that 'all black people were bad' (Mda 2002: 150) and concludes that, like the moderate Sekatle, 'the majority of black people were good people', but a few of them, like Viliki, were communists and terrorists and therefore bad. Yet, after a longer interaction with Viliki, he notes that Viliki 'used to be a dedicated community builder' (251). This recognition and their subsequent friendship symbolise the hybridisation of cultures on a personal level. When asked why De Vries is his friend, Viliki responds that De Vries 'is a nice guy' (222). De Vries feels comfortable about being an African and boasts that, 'long before anyone else called themselves African, my people called themselves Afrikaners. Africans' (252).

Viliki leads transformation in the Mahlatswetsa township. As a freedom-fighter and 'communist', he shocks his sister Popi when he sends her to bank his money at the Afrikaner bank, Volkskas. It is also evident that the money is from an Afrikaner sponsor. She finds the connections between the Afrikaner bank and the Movement unthinkable. Viliki tells Popi that the political landscape is transforming: 'We [the Movement] are reaching a settlement with the Afrikaners. Next year we have a general election. April next year. We shall be liberated and we shall be one people with the Afrikaners. That is what the Movement stands for. One South African nation' (Mda 2002: 153). Moreover, Volkskas is itself transforming. In the bank, Popi realises that there are no longer two lines, 'a slow long queue for blacks and a quick short one for whites. One queue, now, for all the colours of the rainbow' (153).

The collective voice sees Adam de Vries's nation-building scheme, the Excelsior Development Trust, as an attempt to close the economic gap between white and black people. Its main aim is for 'Afrikaner farmers to support emerging black farmers' (Mda 2002: 254), but its secondary aim is self-serving: 'There were some benefits in getting into partnership with black farmers. Some affirmative action contracts and tenders would surely come his way, in the name of his protégés' (254). Nevertheless, the Trust provides a common contact zone for working together. Despite some scepticism from black and white people, it receives support from both sides and creates a powerful transformative space that enables blacks and whites to collaborate on nation-building projects. In this sense, the collective voice promotes hybridisation in the transforming South Africa by offering transcultural modes of representation, which are reciprocal transferences of culture. Such transmissions of culture operate in contact zones, or the in-between spaces, sometimes referred to as liminal zones.

These in-between spaces are 'social spaces where disparate cultures meet, clash and grapple with each other, often in highly asymmetrical relations of dominance and subordination – like colonialism, slavery, or their aftermath as they are lived across the globe' (Ashcroft, Griffiths and Tiffin 1998: 233).

Furthermore, the collective voice recognises the greater freedom of some of those who were formerly operating within the confines of the Movement, as is the case with Viliki and his sister Popi. Viliki becomes free to be self-critical now that he is no longer a member of the Movement and its councillor. He lashes out at the black man's culture of entitlement since attaining his freedom. He is deeply worried about the dirt that he sees in black people's gardens and yards, including his own. Post-apartheid black people, he observes, seem to expect the government to clean their yards while they sit down and wait. They also do not work, but expect the government to feed them. 'Is that what freedom means to us?' (Mda 2002: 253), he asks. Referring to his perennial war with Sekatle, Viliki lambastes Sekatle's corruption. He is also disgusted by the fact that the masses see the sell-outs of the past as the liberators of today, the 'new Mandela[s]' (189), while the true liberators are branded as sell-outs. Yet Viliki's freedom from the collective psyche of the people of Mahlatswetsa and their power struggles, from the acrimonious debates of the chamber, and from the totalising politics of the Movement symbolises greater individual freedom. Having attained such freedom, he moves from place to place with his wife, the Seller of Songs. They are said to have the

> freedom to immerse themselves in each other to their hearts' content. The two of them alone under the big sky. Away from the petty world of Excelsior, and particularly Mahlatswetsa Location. Away from the politics and the power struggles. He was free at last and didn't have any obligations to anyone. He had never thought it would be possible to enjoy so much freedom, without any cares in the world. (Mda 2002: 246)

Like Viliki, Popi 'took it as a blessing that she was no longer a member of the Movement' (Mda 2002: 212) and she 'felt free' (213). Her freedom and confidence affect the way the Mahlatswetsa community looks at her; formerly denigrated as a 'boesman', a 'hotnot', a 'bastard' or a 'coloured', she is now admired by the community, as the collective voice says: 'Apparently she never knew how we used to gossip about her beauty' (266).

Popi's quest for liberation is triggered by an obsession with two paintings that to her capture something about her history as a Coloured person. She has only a vague idea about the events of the Excelsior 19 case. People are always whispering in her presence, which makes her feel that they know more about her than she does herself. She had never enquired about her history from her mother, who in turn had never told her because she felt guilty. Popi, suspecting that the priest knows this history and had captured it in his paintings of the naked madonnas, visits 'the trinity' in Thaba Nchu to uncover her history. The visit to Thaba Nchu is said to have drained her of 'all negative feelings' (Mda 2002: 238); 'she felt she had been healed of a deadly ailment she could not really describe' and her anger was 'replaced by a great feeling of exhilaration. There was no room for anger and bitterness in her anymore . . . Anger had dissipated and left a void.' For instance, Popi becomes 'very busy admiring herself in the mirror' (238), but her mother feels she is overdoing it: ' "It is a beautiful thing to love yourself, Popi," said Niki. "But don't you think you are overdoing it now? Preening yourself in front of the mirror all day long?" "I am making up for lost time, Niki," giggled Popi' (266).

The collective voice evidently fosters a new notion of the 'coloured' as embodied by Popi. Her positive character change celebrates being Coloured as part of the beauty of the rainbow nation: 'From the outrage of rape (that's what we called it in our post-apartheid euphoria), our mothers gave birth to beautiful human beings. As *beautiful* as the Seller of Songs, who could *create beautiful things*. As *beautiful as Popi*, who could not create, but who knew how to *love beautiful creations*' (Mda 2002: 234; emphasis added). Similarly, the collective voice liberates Niki from her perpetual anger. She is changed by seeing Popi's acceptance of herself as a Coloured person:

'Oh, Popi!' cried Niki. 'I am so happy that at last you are so free of shame about being coloured that you can even make a joke about it.'

'My shame went away with my anger, Niki,' said Popi quietly.

'You are free, Popi, and you have made me free too. For a long time, I felt that I had failed you . . . that I had made you coloured!

Every time they mocked and insulted you, it ate my heart and increased my guilt.' (Mda 2002: 260)

In addition, the collective voice of the novel offers possibilities of change in parcels of wisdom as we hear the voice of Mda as writer and social critic sometimes intruding into the narrative voices of the story to persuade the reader to accept his views. Thus, the reader is influenced by both Mda's narration and by his attitudes towards the social issues of post-apartheid South Africa. Mda sees literature as having a transformative and reconciliatory potential in the post-apartheid order, as he asserts in his article, 'Theater and Reconciliation in South Africa': 'Arts have a role to play in transformation . . . Whether we like it or not, the artists will always respond to the prevailing political and social conditions because they select their material from society. Politics is part of their intimate daily experience, and for better or for worse, politics feature in their work' (1995b: 38).

Breaking in upon the narrative voices of the story, the voice of Mda teaches the society that is coming to grips with bridging apartheid's divisions that those who do not want to go beyond past boundaries will be caught up in self-pity, anger and self-destruction, because 'vengeance had a habit of bouncing against the wall, like a ricocheting bullet, and hitting the originator. Look what had happened to Niki when she filled her loins with vengeance! It was because of that vengeance that Popi was now a prisoner of the perpetual doek on her head, of blue eyes and of hairy legs' (Mda 2002: 143).

The destructive nature of anger and vengeance is epitomised by Madam Cronje, Tjaart Cronje and Johannes Smit. While Tjaart Cronje and Johannes Smit later lament that they have been sold out by their elders, Madam Cronje is angry that her husband was 'taken' by Niki: 'Poor Stephanus. She silently cursed the woman who had led him to his demise. She wondered what had happened to Niki. The traitor who had seduced her husband. She blamed her *for everything*' (Mda 2002: 150; emphasis added). Madam Cronje hates Popi 'for being a smoother, delicate and more beautiful version of Tjaart' (150). She calls her a 'bastard' and 'Niki's coloured brat' (150). Because of her antagonism towards Niki, Viliki and Popi specifically, she hates black people in general as if they, too, were responsible for taking away her husband. Her resentment infects her son Tjaart; she teaches him to hate black people as if they had taken away his father. The adult Tjaart becomes a 'right-winger' (199) and joins the conservative Afrikaner group that despises black people and he represents their views in the novel. In the municipal chamber, he rails about the 'failure of the "affirmative action people" to govern the town in a civilised manner' (187), while he ironically emphasises that 'I do not hate black people' (188).

The narrative voice draws attention to how Tjaart lives with racial anger that is inculcated and nurtured by his lonely and frustrated mother, and reinforced by the tradition of the voortrekker patriarchs. His racial hatred motivates him to open fire on a group of black demonstrators who are on their way to town. To him, a bullet is the only language they will understand: 'One could not reason with these people' (Mda 2002: 157). According to Pumla Gobodo-Madikizela in her book, *A Human Being Died that Night: A Story of Forgiveness*, behaviour such as killing the 'other' without conscience can be understood in terms of the social psychology of intergroup relations, which explains 'how individuals, through self-identification with the groups to which they belong, are drawn into violent behaviour against people defined as the "other". The construction of "otherness" is an essential step on the path towards the destruction of victims' (2003: 154). The collective voice explains that Tjaart's racist anger reveals his bitter personality, influenced and corrupted by apartheid ideology. As a soldier, he carried out orders that continually involved defending his group against what is depicted as a communist and terrorist enemy (129, 148). However, when this time comes to an end, he is even more angry and bitter because he has been coached and praised by his patriarchal order, and encouraged in terms of remuneration, promotion and power, to unleash legalised violence on blacks. In the process, evil grips and destroys his conscience; no wonder, then, that he refuses to accept the reality of the different new order.

Jacomina, who has watched Tjaart gradually being destroyed by his anger and resentment, eventually advises him to change: 'Maybe it is better for all of us to be part of this new South Africa' (Mda 2002: 254). This is the collective voice of Afrikaner people who want to change and so advise their fellow Afrikaners that the new South Africa has become the liminal contact zone for cultural contestations and transgressions that foster positive social change. It has become the transformative space for all to come to terms with the realities of a new and free society. The contact zone enables negative past cultural identities to be broken down.

Another wisdom that the collective voice seems to teach the Afrikaner people who resist inhabiting this liminal space is that they isolate themselves at their peril and that it is useless to harbour eternal racial hatred. The collective voice seems to be saying that those who still prefer to remain in the old South Africa, wallowing in their anger and lamenting their betrayal by their fellow white brothers and leaders, the way Tjaart Cronje and Johannes Smit do, should instead embrace the challenges of the new democracy. Furthermore, the collective voice questions, through Viliki, why Afrikaners such as Tjaart Cronje and Johannes Smit, who were privileged by apartheid, should be so angry, compared to black people who suffered under that system: 'Were people like Viliki, Popi and Niki not the ones who should be angry? Were they not entitled even to a shred of anger? Why should the Afrikaner hoard all the anger?' (Mda 2002: 225). Perhaps the answer is that they have not yet come to terms with the loss of their social, political and economic power, despite having defended it for a long time at all costs and with all their might. Yet, there are those, like Reverend Bornman, who realise that political change is inevitable: 'We all regret the past and yet are fearful of the future' (257). It is the voice of Adam de Vries that expresses the ultimate wisdom to those who resist change: ' "It is people like you, Gys, who take away all hope from these young people," said Adam de Vries. "You plant in their minds the false notion that Afrikaners are now the oppressed people" ' (258). Having been persuaded to embrace change by Adam de Vries, Johannes Smit represents the members of the old order who come to realise that clinging to racial antagonism is destructive. He joins Adam de Vries's Development Trust and 'declare[s] a truce' (261) with his old enemy, Niki.

Tjaart Cronje, however, left with his mother in their old South Africa, feels the ultimate betrayal. He does not make a secret of his anger. His people have been sold out by their leaders, he laments. Tjaart becomes almost insane and sick because he 'fought wars on behalf of Adam de Vries, whose generation never died at the border nor faced petrol bombs in the townships. Now he has made an about-turn, taking many good Afrikaners with him' (Mda 2002: 255). Yet Tjaart, too, eventually sees that reconciliation, at least with Popi, his half sister, is necessary, confirming Niki's prediction that 'one day Tjaart will understand that he must love you' (199). In order to initiate the process of coming to terms with having a Coloured sister, Tjaart sends Johannes Smit to call Popi because 'he wants to make peace' with her (260). He acknowledges, for the first time, that Stephanus Cronje was their father, and he acknowledges her beauty: 'You are a beautiful woman, Popi. Very beautiful' (263). Here, the Coloured person, despised by whites as a product of miscegenation, which was represented by Popi's struggle in the first half of the novel, is finally liberated from the burden of white anger and self-hatred.

However, Niki and Popi realise that Tjaart is still angry and that he continues to feel the need to retaliate. The ageing matriarch, Cornelia Cronje, is also unable to reconcile herself to her situation and joins him in his lament and in loneliness. It could still be because of his mother's infectious anger that Tjaart eventually fails to say 'sorry' to Popi, although his primary intention is obviously to make peace with her: '"I wonder what is eating him," Popi whispered to Niki. "Anger," Niki whispered back. "It is as I told you, Popi. Anger does eat the owner"' (Mda 2002: 263). Perhaps this is the ultimate wisdom that the collective voice of the novel offers to people such as Tjaart who fail to embrace the challenges of the new South Africa. These two lines sum up their fate: 'It is terrible to see him like this' (256) and 'it is sad to see him like this' (257).

Works cited

Abbot, H. Porter. 2002. *Narrative*. Cambridge: Cambridge University Press.

Ashcroft, Bill. 2001. *Postcolonial Transformation*. London: Routledge.

Ashcroft, Bill, Gareth Griffiths and Helen Tiffin. 1998. *Key Concepts in Post-colonial Studies*. London: Routledge.

Cobley, Paul. 2001. *Narrative*. London: Routledge.

Driver, Dorothy. 1988. '"Woman" as sign in the South African colonial enterprise'. *Journal of Literary Studies* 4(1): 3–20.

Gobodo-Madikizela, Pumla. 2003. *A Human Being Died that Night: A Story of Forgiveness*. Cape Town: David Philip.

Goodman, Ralph. 2004. 'De-scribing the centre: Satiric and postcolonial strategies in *The Madonna of Excelsior*'. *Journal of Literary Studies* 20(1/2): 62–70.

Ibinga, Stephane Serge. 2005. 'The politics of silence in Zakes Mda's *She Plays with the Darkness*'. Paper presented at the Nordic Africa Institute Conference on 'Writing African Women: Poetics of Politics of African Gender Research', University of the Western Cape, 19–22 January.

Khunyeli, Thabo Benjamin. 1994. 'The portrayal of history by African writers in *Bantu World*, 1932–1936'. Unpublished Master's thesis. Pietermaritzburg: University of Natal.

Lockett, Cecily. 1988. 'The black woman in South African English literature'. *Journal of Literary Studies* 4(1): 21–37.

Mda, Zakes. 1995a. *Ways of Dying*. Cape Town: Oxford University Press.

———. 1995b. 'Theater and reconciliation in South Africa'. *Theater* 25(3): 38–45.

———. 2002. *The Madonna of Excelsior*. Cape Town: Oxford University Press.

Richards, Constance S. 2000. *On the Winds and Waves of Imagination: Transnational Feminism and Literature*. New York: Garland.

Rimmon-Kenan, Shlomith. 1983. *Narrative Fiction: Contemporary Poetics*. London: Methuen.

Spivak, Gayatri Chakravorty. 1988. 'Can the subaltern speak?' In: Nelson, Cary and Lawrence Grossberg (eds.). *Marxism and the Interpretation of Culture*. London: Macmillan, 271–313.

17

Whales, Clones and Two Ecological Novels

The Whale Caller *and Jane Rosenthal's* Souvenir

WENDY WOODWARD

Introduction

SINCE THE POLITICAL transition of 1990–94, South African literature has barely begun to engage with more expansive subjects than those pertaining to apartheid histories. For David Attwell and Barbara Harlow, even as post-apartheid literature has addressed the 'larger predicament' of 'national reconstruction' (2000: 3), 'the future has little future' and reflections on the past have predominated (4). The two novels discussed in this chapter, Zakes Mda's *The Whale Caller* (2005) and Jane Rosenthal's *Souvenir* (2004), represent a major shift in post-apartheid literature. While these novels acknowledge aspects of national transformation, they locate South Africa within the global ecological predicament, in which the deterioration of nature and climate change threaten the sustainable future of the planet.

Both novels foreground the interactions and interconnections between human culture and the material environment, with paramount concerns for the future of ecological systems. *The Whale Caller* narrates an ecocentric relationship between a human being and what Val Plumwood calls an 'earth other' (1993: 137–40). *Souvenir* is more specifically concerned with the destructive repercussions of global warming for ecosystems and their inhabitants in South Africa in 2070. Both novels might be regarded as comedic, in terms of Joseph Meeker's definition (1972), because of their underlying concerns to promote positive, healthy relationships between humans and the earth and its inhabitants. *Souvenir* imagines adaptability and endurance even on a planet 'in a state of possibly terminal turbulence and flux' (Rosenthal 2004: 114) with Souvenir becoming a mother and surviving for many years, in spite of being a clone. *The Whale Caller* represents a relationship of loving biosociality between a human being and a whale, but is, ultimately, a cautionary tale. The novel ends violently and tragically, with the beached Sharisha euthanised and Saluni, the Whale Caller's human love, murdered by the Bored Twins, who have no respect for the sentience of reptiles or insects.

In *The Heart of Redness* (2000) Mda has already expressed ecological concerns in representations of sustainable development, corporate and state abuse of the land and the rural poor. Relationships between human beings and other animals, as well as birds, are interconnected with traditional spirituality and folktales (see Woodward 2003), aspects of which reappear in *The Whale Caller*. The novel is set in contemporary Hermanus and the eponymous protagonist is a wise fool who engages musically with Sharisha, a Southern Right Whale. He is never named beyond his vocation of calling whales; his pursuit has elements of the magical as he communicates passionately with the largest mammal on the planet. But the narrative does not have nature or an animal as an active healing force to 'right the disturbed equilibrium of society', which A.C. Jordan considers an essential element of folktales (1973: 218). Nor is the Whale Caller a heroic figure who triumphs over evil through his own courage, who conforms to social norms and who defines his own identity (see Jordan 1973: 192). Unmotivated by any dualistic quest, he is semi-nomadic and socially marginalised, with his identity defined by his love for Sharisha, the whale. Mda critiques modernity's treatment of nature as spectacle in ecotourism, or as a resource in perlemoen (abalone) poaching or whale hunting. Yet the novel is never overburdened by didacticism or polemic,[1] nor is the Whale Caller himself represented as one-dimensionally good. He is a complex character, struggling for survival and love, attempting, not always successfully, to live without Cartesian notions of dominion over nature.

Rosenthal's *Souvenir*, more so than *The Whale Caller*, has the earth itself as a central agent in the narrative. By 2070, the planet has been rendered a tenuous home, a place of unpredictable and deadly weather, with tsunamis caused by the melting of the ice caps of Antarctica destroying coastal cities and environments. The earth is agentive with its own dramas and dangers, which threaten the main human characters, Souvenir and Obed Will Obenbara, who becomes her lover. Cloning is the central ethical issue and overpopulation is no longer a challenge after the HIV/AIDS pandemic. Souvenir herself is, however, questionably 'human', as she is a barbiclone, engineered to function as a 'sextoy' and a 'household skivvy' (Rosenthal 2004: 6). In her self-reflexive struggle, she attempts to overcome this identity and redefine herself, travelling on her own in a dirigible to service the water-pump windmills and wind-power generators, on which the farming communities are dependent for energy.

Despite its futuristic setting and its imagining of a post-racialised South Africa, *Souvenir* does not wholly fit with Donna Haraway's notion of science fiction; while it is to some extent 'concerned with the interpenetration of boundaries between problematic selves and unexpected others', it does not consider, literally, 'the exploration of possible worlds in a context structured by transnational technoscience' (Haraway 1992: 300). The future South Africa does not constitute a new 'world' and, like Mda, Rosenthal does not empower science with changing the planet, either positively or negatively. Instead, the novel tends to represent a sometimes idealised, wholesome, (pre-)colonial, rural past.

Both Mda and Rosenthal are concerned with the history and politics of nature, depicting it as an intertwined nature-culture. At the opening of *The Whale Caller* Mda has the indigenous Khoikhoi dancing for joy, in the Whale Caller's imagination, around a beached whale, so thrilled are they at the prospect of products from its body. But nature may not always be balanced and they weep at the tragedy and waste of mass beachings and feel critical of Tsiqwa, 'He Who Tells His Stories in Heaven', for this excess (Mda 2005: 2). The indigenes' response to nature does not constitute a desire for seamless connections between humans and other animals. As Jane Carruthers reminds us, 'the oft-repeated notion that pre-colonial societies were idyllically living as the first ecologists in complete harmony with nature, needs . . . to be questioned' (2003: 12). For Mda, what is implicitly lacking in Khoikhoi relationships with whales, even as they use whale skeletons for their houses and baleen for the roofs, is that they cannot account mythically for these mammals as the Australian Aborigines do in their story of Whale Man (Mda 2005: 138–40).

The predominant response to nature in Western culture has been to other nature as lesser than the human and to regard it as a resource to be utilised. Both Mda and Rosenthal represent their respective primary locations, Hermanus and the Karoo, as sites metonymic of a planet that is ecologically threatened as a result of such Cartesian dualistic thinking. Both critique practices in which nature does not have intrinsic value (see Soper 1995: 6) but is judged instrumentally at great cost to the earth and its future sustainability. In *The Whale Caller*, Mda gives ample evidence of the human assumption of dominion over nature, exemplified in the condoning of the mass slaughter of whales in St Helena Bay in 1785, an event that left 'fumes of death that [still] permeated the air' (2005: 13). In *Souvenir*, we see the catastrophic results of such othering of nature. As a result of global warming, the South African interior has become a desert and the coastline transformed. Nature is, to all effects, defunct: humans, animals, insects and food are all genetically modified and/or cloned. Rosenthal's characters are passionate about butterflies, donkeys and roses, as they long for the nature of the past, even if it was cultivated, as a sanctuary within which to escape the difficulties of the present.

Environmental philosopher Val Plumwood urges conceptual caution when we challenge the mechanistic worldview's instrumentalising of nature, for we might too easily set up other dualisms, such as in the 'respiritualisation' of nature. She proposes: 'We should aim to find cultural ways to recognize and celebrate the play of intentionality and agency in the world (and for regaining sensitivity to the particularity and agency of place especially), but preferably ways which do not show disrespect for the otherness of nature by inscribing that agency with the cast of the conscious human mind' (1993: 136). To conceptualise seamless kinship between the human self and nature, or an 'earth other', is to colonise or appropriate nature by not valuing the latter's autonomy. The solution, Plumwood argues, is to recognise both continuities and differences between human and nature, a feat that demands what Verena Conley terms 'new modes of knowing' (2004: 163).

One way in which the authors in this discussion have their characters demonstrate such new epistemologies is through their ecological sensibilities. Plumwood identifies what she calls 'an ecological self', which is a 'relational self, one which includes the goal of the flourishing of earth others and the earth community among its own primary ends' (1993: 154). When we meet the Whale Caller, living in a Wendy house in Hermanus on his old-age pension, his whole adult life has been legislated by his desire to communicate with whales. In the past, he eschewed the acquisition of material possessions, becoming an itinerant fisherman, travelling up the west coast from his home in Hermanus, perfecting the art of whale calling with kelp horns. In *Souvenir*, Obed Will most obviously is concerned with 'earth others'' well-being. As State Lepidopterist, he travels modestly with donkeys to research the number of extant cloned and old gene butterflies. Souvenir's 'ecological self' initially finds expression in her botanical response to the environment, in her historical interest in roses, for example, but as she traverses the Karoo in her dirigible, she develops connections with non-human animals.

'Becoming-animal' in *The Whale Caller*

For years, the Whale Caller was a student of the whales' music: in his life on the west coast, 'he spent every second when he was not sleeping or eking out a living . . . listening to the songs of the southern right, the humpback and the Bryde's whales, and learning to reproduce them with his horn' (Mda 2005: 9). His aim was to converse with whales in intersubjective ways, for in developing a mutuality and kinship with them, he and the whales are transformed, their identities deconstructed. At the same time, the experience is spatialised for him as he 'lives inside the songs of the whales. It is soothing inside the song with fresh aromas that heal. He remembers telling Saluni once . . . that it is never night inside a song' (129).

The Whale Caller has a special, although not entirely exclusive relationship with Sharisha, a Southern Right Whale. Sharisha is his beloved. He knows the callosities on her face, which resemble the Three Sisters, koppies in the Karoo; he recognises her whale acrobatics and takes pride in the whiteness of her baleen, which is evidence that she is not infested with lice. Naming a whale may suggest some human desire to tame her wildness, yet Sharisha appears to be beyond such categorisation and when the Whale Caller obsesses about the need to revert to the original name of the town, Hermanuspietersfontein, it is made clear that 'the southern rights don't bother with the politics of naming' (Mda 2005: 15).

Gilles Deleuze and Felix Guattari's notion of 'de-territorialising identity', as opposed to the shoring up of a master consciousness within an apparently stable and separate ego, could also be regarded as part of an ecological self. Their concept of 'becoming-animal' is a useful one in relation to the Whale Caller and Sharisha. In its 'in-between' performance 'becoming-animal' goes beyond dualism and the human/nature opposition (see Urpeth 2004: 101), incorporating an ontological de-territorialisation and what James Urpeth terms 'a radical order of immanence' (102). For Deleuze and Guattari, the musician has a particular ability to 'become-animal at the same time as the animal becomes what [he or she] willed, at the deepest level of their concord with Nature' (2004: 95). The process or performance is reciprocal, for 'music is not the privilege of human beings; the universe, the cosmos, is made up of refrains; the question in music is that of a power of de-territorialisation permeating nature, animals, the elements, and deserts as much as human beings.' When Mda has the man and the whale make music together, desire and affect are involved, important aspects of 'becoming-animal'. The Whale Caller, preferring his intimacy with the whales to be private, is 'not a showman but a lover' (Mda 2005: 12).

Mda represents a reciprocal relationship between a human and the largest mammal on the planet that is both mythical and real. Occupying an ecological niche that is transoceanic and therefore transnational, whales are not companion species to humans, but the Whale Caller undermines the separation between species with Sharisha. Communication is possible because Sharisha is not just a massively different body, which would render her utterly other, but because she has a face, which substantiates her sentience and character, rendering her an ethical subject. She has a 'well-shaped bonnet that [the Whale Caller] knows so well, sitting gracefully on the whale's snout. White like salt . . . He blows his horn even harder and the whale opens its mouth wide displaying white baleen . . . It is a smile that the Whale Caller knows so well. Sharisha's surf-white smile' (Mda 2005: 36).

Emmanuel Levinas admits, with some reluctance, that 'one cannot entirely refuse the gaze of the animal. It is via the face that one understands, for example, a dog', but when questioned whether one has to have 'the possibility of speech to be a "face" in the ethical sense', he demurs: 'I cannot say at what moment you have the right to be called "face". The human face is completely different and only afterwards do we discover the face of an animal. I don't know if a snake has a face' (2004: 49).[2]

The Whale Caller has no Levinasian reservations about Sharisha's face, or about extending ethical considerations to non-human mammals.[3] He emulates Jacques Derrida, rather, who responds phenomenologically to the animal gaze of his domestic cat with the sense of being addressed and of being *seen seen by the animal*' (Derrida 2002: 382; italics in original).[4] Contradictorily though, the Whale Caller's passionate love for Sharisha imposes his desires, saddling her with another identity from her natural one, or, in Plumwood's phrase 'inscribing [her] agency with the cast of the conscious human mind' (1993: 136). Rather than visiting Hermanus once every three years in the whales' natural cycle, she comes annually and the Whale Caller boasts: '"Sharisha cannot live for three years without me"' (Mda 2005: 4). She mates in summer, instead of in winter, in the southern hemisphere, and although she gives birth in the geographically appropriate Hermanus, with the Whale Caller observing the process like a proud father, she subsequently stays all year round, rather than continuing her migration. Even in her singing, Sharisha's own agency has been displaced, as the Whale Caller has taught her to emulate the more complex and lyrical Humpback Whale songs.

In denying her separateness, as well as the difference between him and his beloved Sharisha, the Whale Caller unwittingly appropriates her identity and later, tragically, her life. To define the other only in relation to the (human) self, is to 'incorporate' and relationally define her and 'the qualities attributed or perceived are those which reflect the master's desires, needs and lacks' (Plumwood 1993: 52). In his human relationships, the Whale Caller does not, however, exhibit a master consciousness socially or, more intimately, in his sexuality with Saluni. Furthermore, he does not define Saluni instrumentally in a process of objectification, nor does he stereotype or homogenise her, both 'corollaries' of incorporation (see Plumwood 1993: 52–55).

In addition, as I have suggested above, he de-territorialises his own identity in relation to those of the whales when he makes music with them. If in 'becoming-animal', the Whale Caller sexualises his relationship with Sharisha, Mda's representation of this is skilfully ambiguous: to what extent the reader is to judge the Whale Caller's behaviour as excessive or grotesque is not always clear. At times, Mda seems to have it both ways: if the Whale Caller approximates a jester in his tuxedo and with his musical antics, he is also a celebrant in a sacred ritual. He longs for Sharisha when she is away, calling her 'the leviathan with a whore's heart' (Mda 2005: 3), but when she returns to Hermanus, their connection is reaffirmed in a 'mating ritual' (36). Sharisha's intentionality has to be taken into account as man and whale together occupy an ontological threshold: she performs her mating dance, while the Whale Caller breathes 'more and more heavily' until an orgasmic finale for both when 'his horn ejaculates sounds that rise from deep staccatos to high-pitched wails. Sharisha emits a very deep hollow sound. A prolonged pained bellow.'

After Sharisha's submarine mating with whales, to which the Whale Caller responds with feelings of jealousy and betrayal and a certainty that she was 'ravaged' although, again, her intentionality here is evident, man and whale have another 'mating dance' (Mda 2005: 57). Sharisha 'lock[s] [him] tightly in her embrace' (58) in a ritual that continues through the night, with spectators aware of 'the ecstasy of the man and his whale':

> Deep in the night the wails of his horn could be heard, sometimes sounding like a muted cornet and at others like a *Last Post* bugle, and then picking up again in the fast-paced scatting of a demented jazz singer. In the cool breeze of the night, and with the absence of spectators, the dance became even more frenzied. His horn penetrated deep into every aperture of the whale's body, as if in search of a soul in the middle of all the blubber. (Mda 2005: 59)

The dance is a mutual one and the next day, Sharisha and the kelp horn 'groan deeply like out-of-tune tubas' (Mda 2005: 59).

If, as Deleuze and Guattari suggest, 'becoming-animal replaces subjectivity' (2004: 100), both human and whale inhabit a liminal space beyond subject and object. The Whale Caller is not intent on taming Sharisha here, as together they engage in what Gary Snyder defines as 'wild' behaviour: 'artless, free, spontaneous, unconditioned. Expressive, physical, openly sexual, ecstatic' (1990: 10). That the Whale Caller might be making attempts to reach Sharisha's soul is indicative of the sacred ceremony that is being enacted, although the narrator never specifies that whales do have souls.[5]

For Saluni this ceremony is risible and she accuses him of shaming himself and her (Mda 2005: 60). Initially the 'village drunk' (19), Saluni is a 'glorious celebrant of worldliness' (69) and 'a transgressor of all that he holds sacred' (68). While she regards the Whale Caller as the 'love of her life', she feels trapped within 'the eternal triangle – man, woman and whale' (73) and rages that her rival 'that stupid *fish* has castrated' him (67; italics in original), yet Mda also suggests a number of parallels between Saluni and Sharisha, which undermine Saluni's sense of difference from the whale. When Saluni nearly drowns in buffeting waves, for example, the Whale Caller berates himself that 'not all women are at home in the sea' (70).

Her character provides a sceptical contrast to any high seriousness or self-important spirituality that creeps into the Whale Caller's vocation. In addition, in a parody of Christian confession and penance, the Whale Caller confesses to a mysterious Mr Yodd who lives in a grotto near the sea, and who later appears to be a rock rabbit. A travestied stand-in for God, Mr Yodd's laughter invariably leads to the Whale Caller's self-mortification. Contradicting a more ecologically congruent immanence or embodied spirituality, the Whale Caller, in subscribing to this code of guilt and self-abasement, enacts his attachment to a Christian universe's 'sense of separation and loss' (Allen 1996: 244).

Ecological concerns in *Souvenir*

In Rosenthal's *Souvenir*, no single animal is assigned the stature of the whale as in Mda's novel. Rosenthal's strategy, instead, is to represent different ecological aspects (including animals) of South Africa in 2070. In addition, Aunt Jem's journal or 'book-companion' from the turn of the twenty-first century provides some historical ecological context. The environmental changes brought about by colonialism are multifarious (Griffiths 1997: 1–16), but it does not necessarily follow that the ecological effects of colonialism should always be negative. Rosenthal celebrates colonialism's botanical diversity and satirises as misplaced the political correctness of officialdom's draconian laws to eradicate all aliens. In Rosenthal's view, the Invasive Alien Species Act, for example, would have legislated that a 'venerable old willow' (Rosenthal 2004: 9) on a Karoo farm should be cut down.

Aunt Jem is a participant in propagating aliens: she travels to 'smous[e] roses in the Karoo' (Rosenthal 2004: 26) and, as a 'land artist', plants (alien) hedges and trees on many farms. In order to 'soothe [a farmer's wife's] tree-craving heart', she designs an avenue of flowering gums, the seedlings of which have sprouted prolifically. She writes, ironically: '*So who are we to argue when God or someone sends such bounty? Is God keeping track of indigenous species or is this hoohah all a great joke to him? Perhaps he has a squad of angels on my tail making notes of the botanical mayhem*' (41; italics in original).

When Souvie (as Souvenir is called) travels through the same environment 70 years later, servicing wind turbines, she attempts to track Aunt Jem's achievements. At Molenrivier 'some zealot' (Rosenthal 2004: 135) from the Alien Eradication programme had obliterated the roses Aunt Jem had planted and the apple trees had died in the heat. On the farm Springfontein, however, Souvie locates a 70-year-old hedge of Felicite and Perpetue roses, the delight of bees and with its 'gloomy interior, smelling, even in the heat, of damp leaf mould and earth' (30), a welcome contrast to the heat. The hedge conveys to Souvie a sense of survival against the odds of heat and cold, so much so that its endurance leaves her 'impressed, even a little intimidated'.

Aunt Jem, with her botanical and artistic skills, functions as a benevolent guiding spirit for Souvie in her ecologically threatened existence. The former's creation not only attests to her ability to predict the rose hedge's longevity, but could be metonymic of Souvie's own ability to survive within a generally hostile environment. Souvie's name itself comes from the rose, Souvenir de la Malmaison, which Aunt Jem had given to her sister, Souvie's non-biological grandmother, who refused to countenance that the name meant 'remembrance of a bad house' (Rosenthal 2004: 19), insisting instead that it must have meant 'madhouse' (19), from the Afrikaans word '*mal*' (mad).

If Aunt Jem is a benevolent harbinger from the past, Obed William Obenbara, who becomes Souvie's partner, exhibits nostalgia for the days of colonial exploration and scientific amateurism in the best meaning of the word, as one who loves what he does. He models himself on explorers of the seventeenth and eighteenth centuries, regarding himself as a 'gentleman-adventurer of scientific bent' (Rosenthal 2004: 35), although Souvie notes, with some irony, that even as a 'devoted retro traveller' (95), he has a visiphone. Fittingly,

Obed Will prefers to research the whereabouts of uncloned butterflies, although the prevalence of cloned butterflies is also significant: 'He could try to establish how many previously tropical species had made their way to this area, where they could now survive because of the generally raised temperatures . . . Many had been bought for weddings and other celebrations and had naturalised around water sources, surviving the cold spells because of resistant genes spliced into them by the commercial butterfly companies . . .' (112). Rosenthal's ecological pointers here, not only about climate change, but also the deformation of nature itself through cloning, are disturbing.

That Rosenthal has Obed Will study such fragility underscores the tenuous survival of the planet. At the same time, the reader becomes acquainted with descriptions and classifications of butterflies in their terminal beauty, with Souvie, as focaliser, observing his work: 'On the table was a handsome black and yellow butterfly, held down on its side, its wings folded up from its furry body, and, as she watched, the number 42 was written on the wing . . .' (Rosenthal 2004: 37). The butterflies are not only metonyms for the demise of pristine nature, however, but creatures with sentience that seem aware of being caged: 'The butterflies . . . clung to the wire mesh with their tiny claws. Some walked up the gauze then fluttered down. Others merely sat, faintly quivering, their wings folded up, their red numbers showing' (38). Souvie considers, momentarily, releasing them, but Obed Will tells her they will be released before dark.

Without asking the reader, sentimentally, to inhabit the insect's consciousness or state of mind, Rosenthal skilfully represents them as embodied in a way that is redolent of Ted Hughes's representation of the jaguar, a poem noted by J.M. Coetzee's Elizabeth Costello for its 'bodying forth' of the animal (Coetzee 1999: 53). For Costello, it is the kinaesthetic embodiment of the animal that conveys its life; she proposes an awareness of 'fullness, embodiedness, the sensation of being' (33) and suggests that Hughes 'shows us how to bring the living body into being within ourselves' (53).

Rosenthal conveys a strong sense of the butterflies' beings. Although she describes them collectively, each butterfly has an individual life, as well as intentionality. Philosopher Raimond Gaita is adamant that 'speculation about the inner life of insects plays no part, and should play no part, in the pity we sometimes feel for them' (2004: 122), yet he proposes that it is through attributing some agency to insects that we can pity them. In Rosenthal's suggestion that these insects have both an individual and collective teleology or life goal, these butterflies are reminiscent of poet Ruth Miller's representation of a praying mantis ('Mantis' in Miller 1990: 52), but in contrast to what Elizabeth Costello calls a Platonic ecological vision where 'actual role players, as long as they are self-renewing' (Coetzee 1999: 54) are unimportant. In Costello's critique of this vision, it is 'the great complex dance with the earth and the weather' within different aspects of nature that signifies.

This interaction between life and weather obtains in animal husbandry in *Souvenir*: because of endemic hurricanes, animals are rarely farmed. Where they do exist, a return to indigenous breeds has made them more able to withstand the heat. Short-haired sheep and goats have replaced the heavily fleeced merinos, Afrikander and Nguni cattle – the colonially imported breeds. Tourists at Molenrivier pay for the privilege of viewing the old gene Brahman and Nguni cattle, 'priceless beasts' (Rosenthal 2004: 135), which are herded into underground stables at the threat of a windstorm.

None of these beasts, however, is named nor represented with any extended individuality. Souvie as focaliser is very aware of the 'bodiliness' of animals, but at the same time, they provide nurturance and a naturalness, even in their exotic and unusual identities. Souvie is comforted by the 'great warm body' of a cow that she escorts to safety because of the impending storm: 'Braver than with the donkeys, she had laid her arm across her great, gentle shoulders, taking strength from her. Turning her head, the cow had seemed to lean toward her, sensing that the wind was coming up again' (Rosenthal 2004: 136–37).

Jane Desmond's analysis of the 'consumption of radical bodily difference' (1999: 144) when tourists watch animals is not applicable here. Subject to this bovine gaze, Souvie is very aware of being addressed by the cow, and yet what Derrida refers to as the 'absolute alterity' (2002: 380) of the animal is challenged by the continuities between the woman and the cow, who are both sentient beings in danger from the weather. The cow's putative empathy for the woman also underscores their similarities and denotes an animal, acting as a helpmeet to a human, displaying an almost telepathic compassion (see Irigaray 2004).

Luce Irigaray (2004) and Gaita (2004) stress the unknowability of animals, while Haraway locates them in a liminal space, which is neither nature nor culture (1992: 332). To Souvie, Obed Will's draught donkeys are imbued with mystery, yet she also connects with them, while respecting their separateness:

> [Grooming the donkeys] made her feel tranquil, as though the pleasure the donkey felt was running back into her, as though she herself was being stroked and brushed all over. She finished the donkey she was working on and gave her a carrot, scratching her rough mane as she did so, although she did not quite dare to lay her face against her neck . . . She felt that although they knew her now, they had not become such close friends. (Rosenthal 2004: 114)

These donkeys are not named, apart from Dolfie (and Magda at Springfontein has Harriet who can count up to two), but they are sentient, responsive and have developed a strong donkey culture in which they 'talk to each other' (Rosenthal 2004: 84) and 'greet other donkeys' at the market (65) where they appear 'to be enjoying the passing parade'.

They are 'pure-bred Old Donkeys' (Rosenthal 2004: 60), rather than cloned, as they can be traced to Obed Will's Tswana relatives on subsistence farms who 'believed they knew how to breed good donkeys without having to pay good money for fancy doctored sperm. They just let the donkeys get on with it in the age old way' (61). Rosenthal stresses the ethical aspects, as well as the unnaturalness of a process that takes control of gene pools. Fifty years before, Cape Town's city 'authorities' had spliced baboons with Labrador dogs in an attempt to render the former more tractable. But the experiment had failed; the baboons became more belligerent, possibly because they were spliced with human genes.

Cloning is, of course, a development from and a manifestation of a mechanistic view of nature that has 'the other as an alien object or thing' (Plumwood 1993: 137). Cloning goes further by creating what then may become alien or other, enacting a hubristic desire for control of the planet, valuing science over nature and natural processes. In Rosenthal's novel, in the year 2070, cloning has become the paramount ethical issue, while, at the same time, 'in progressive and educated circles [it was frowned upon] to comment on genetic issues' (2004: 60). Yet scientific practice merits criticism for its cloning, which duplicates conservative social constructions of the human and non-human animal. Rosenthal dramatises the disorder and chaos that may ensue from unchecked cloning through her representation of the violent Van der Bijl family, who are involved in baboon experimentation and cloning. Their unnaturalness is compounded by their (proto)cannibalism, for not only do they eat baboons themselves, but they also feed this primate meat to the caged baboons. They threaten Obed Will, his workers, Adam and Solomon, and the donkeys whose DNA they could use for cloning. Ultimately when they slash and mutilate the donkeys, however, they seem imbued with a motiveless malignity, rather than any desire for tissue.

They bring to the Sutherland Market their monstrous creation, which others call the 'badass', half baboon and half donkey, a splicing of genes that Souvie thinks is 'not biologically or scientifically possible' (Rosenthal 2004: 80). The size and shape of a donkey, it has the head and canines of a baboon: 'More ass than ape it hardly seemed real . . . more like some mythological creature from some ancient cosmology' (68). A symbol of their power as scientists, the badass is commodified and displayed for its difference. The grotesque creature is not cognisant of the stir that it causes as a 'monster' (68), but looks back at the spectators 'with an air of friendly innocence' (68). Just what kind of selfhood is possible for this beastly Frankenstein is a moot point; curiously, given the horror that the onlookers project onto it, it does not embody violence, but a kind of detachment from its own identity.

When her friends discuss the Van der Bijls' modus operandi, Souvie, as a clone herself, not only feels 'confused' and 'contaminated', but also wonders if she is implicated in the 'revulsion' they convey. Even the adoring ten-year-old twins see her as 'a big doll, someone to play with' (Rosenthal 2004: 6). As a duplicate of the 'ideal woman from the early years of the century' (4), Souvie and other barbiclones have been cloned for their use-value in an extension of the management of farm animals and she is well aware of 'the obscenely confining way some people looked at her, the usual expectations' (23). She has nightmares of the gaze of 'mirror reflections of herself' (6) and labours under 'the taint of enslavement' (14).

Yet Souvie's subjectivity is as paradoxical as that of the badass, which contradicts the spectators' notions of its grotesque nature. While her identity has been entirely appropriated and instrumentalised, she has the self-reflexivity to challenge expectations of her, possibly because 'some streak of persistence [was carried along] from those hardy boere-settler women' (Rosenthal 2004: 166) in her genes. Brought up by adoptive parents who treated her like a normal child, her name Souvenir or 'remembrance' underscores her lack of uniqueness, her duplication of an original. Mara, her non-biological mother, accedes to the name as 'in a way [she] is a relic of the settler past' (19). Souvie herself attempts to accept her basic DNA, while changing her appearance and 'get[ting on] with her own inner life' (24).

Souvie longs for the 'desolation' of the Karoo, as though searching for a wilderness with its 'independence of the human' (Plumwood 1993: 161), a place where she hopes to escape her categorisation and redefine herself.[6] Her developing relationship with Obed Will is testy, for he has stereotyped notions of barbiclones that threaten to legislate their friendship, until her behaviour disabuses him. Ironically, given his initial prejudice, it is her status as an Energy People worker that provides him with safety when he is threatened by the Van der Bijls and it is her expertise in flying the dirigible that enables their safe passage, avoiding the worst of the windstorms caused by the cold tsunami.

In spite of the unfolding romance between Souvie and Obed Will, the ending of the novel foregrounds, rather than rendering as lesser, the ecological drama, with the earth as an intentional subject responding to the imbalances of global warming. The final scenes of the novel represent the devastation caused by a tsunami to a particular area of coast near Nature's Valley. Here the 'Canute faction', early environmentalists who 'believed some effort to save the planet Earth was at least worth a try' (Rosenthal 2004: 150), had been disregarded in favour of the dyke builders, 'with their swaggering and insincere parody of environmental concern' (150). The latter, with their scientism in league with global capitalism, were conveniently supported by both the Department of Environmental Affairs and the Department of Tourism. (The representation of a partnership between government and global capital indifferent to ecological systems echoes Mda's satire of proposed developments on the Wild Coast in *The Heart of Redness*.)

In an extensive casino built on the headland, bets are taken on the local consequences of the severing of part of the ice shelf in Western Antarctica from 'the land that had held it for ten thousand years' (Rosenthal 2004: 160). The representation of this unnatural event is apocalyptic, as with 'a sound no human had ever heard, millions of tons of ice fell slowly into the southern ocean, sinking into the turgid sea' (160). As a result, first a 'wind wave' hits the South African coast, then the wave itself. The casino wave-watchers, who have taken no heed of evacuation warnings and remained in order to bet on the tsunami devastation, die either in the initial wind shock or in the wave itself, the size of which is 'beyond heartstopping belief' (163). They die, quite literally, because they could not hear the ecological warnings in relation to climate change. Souvie and Obed Will, who are lodged some way inland in the official hostelry with rescue workers, survive.

Souvenir ends with some hope. Souvie is pregnant, in spite of being a clone, and the extended family community bonds around them. The Epilogue brings a felicitous closure to the denouement and when Obed Will is an old man, 'snow began to fall once again on the Roggeveld and lay metres deep on the Ouberg Pass' (Rosenthal 2004: 177). Rosenthal seems to suggest that some redemption is possible, climatically. Perhaps an ecological lesson was learnt from the tsunami. Certainly, scientism does not proffer solutions in the lives of the characters and the drama of the earth and climate change remains.

Ecological tragedy in *The Whale Caller*

Conversely, the ending Mda scripts for the Whale Caller, Sharisha and Saluni is tragic. The humans have just returned from an extended journey on foot, Saluni having blinded herself in the eclipse, in order, the Whale Caller understands, to get him away from his beloved whale and to lead him into the 'wilderness'. As soon as they return home (with Saluni's sight now restored), he retreats to the sea to seek the companionship of Sharisha, 'she who never calls him names or yells at him' (Mda 2005: 196). Spurned by Saluni, due to a misunderstanding, and not expecting Sharisha because it is winter, he intends to blow his horn until he dies, becoming one with the earth, and he fantasises that Sharisha will be his sole mourner. Sharisha hears him, however, and comes, not only to save him, but because of her own desire for the sound of the kelp horn. Unable to differentiate between deep and shallow water because of the blackness of the sea after storms and high waves have inundated Hermanus, Sharisha beaches herself.

What follows is a pantomime of would-be rescuers, politicians trying to get mileage out of the event and the Whale Caller is ostracised from the proceedings. Finally, because Sharisha cannot be dislodged from the sand and she is suffering, she is dynamited. The Whale Caller remains immobilised, too close to the whale, so that the 'blubber rains on him' and 'he is completely larded with it' (Mda 2005: 205). The watching Saluni, in her magical thinking, is full of regret, believing she is to blame, but she leaves to visit the Bored Twins where she gets drunk. First they lock her into the cellar and then when she hurtles out, planning to return to the Whale Caller with love, they worry that she will harm herself so they stone her – until she dies.

In the meantime, the Whale Caller plays a song for Saluni, but when she does not arrive, he attempts to visit Mr Yodd in the hope that the rock rabbit will laugh at him, only to find that the grotto has been obliterated by the sea. In his tragic circumstances, the Whale Caller reflects on his state of being: 'All he needs is mortification . . . Mortification becomes him' (Mda 2005: 209–10) and he then leaves the town, wearing a sandwich board stating: 'I am the Hermanus Penitent' and intending to 'walk from town to town flogging himself with shame' (210).

In a novel replete with humour, the darkness of the ending comes as a shock. Yet because the Bored Twins have always enacted violence against nature, torturing frogs, snakes and insects, the psychopathology of their murder of Saluni has been prepared for. Similarly, because the relationship between the Whale Caller and Saluni has always held the tension of his passion for Sharisha, their estrangement develops over time. If Mda does not permit them to reconnect, it is unlikely that a reconciliation would have lasted. In the representation of the Whale Caller himself, perhaps Mda is stressing his fatal flaw, his neediness for Sharisha, which finally leads to her death. Longing always for his mother, he has the whale in all her oceanic bliss as a substitute. To consider need only as negative, however, is, as Gaita argues, a distortion: 'The need we have – often unfathomable – of other human beings is partly what conditions and yields to us our sense of their preciousness. The same is true of our relations to animals . . . Humbled acknowledgement of our need is our best protection against foolish condescension to both human beings and animals' (2004: 17). Certainly the Whale Caller never condescends to the whales, regarding them always as fellow musicians, and to deny that Sharisha expresses her autonomy in approaching too close to the Whale Caller would be to condescend to her as a mere object of seduction.

When in his grief, the Whale Caller tells her calf to go, as he 'must not enslave the young one with his kelp horn' (Mda 2005: 209), he perhaps overstates his power. Still, Mda does seem to suggest that the Whale Caller denied Sharisha's difference and her teleology so that she ended up, inappropriately and fatally, on the land, which is his element. Another aspect of the tragedy that locates the relationship between human and whale more broadly is the fact that Sharisha misjudged the depth of the water because of the recent storm. If the excessive nature of this storm that flooded the town can be attributed to global warming, it suggests that connections between humans and 'earth others' cannot flourish on a planet that is out of balance because of human blindness.

The abilities of the Whale Caller himself are deficient through no fault of his own. When Sharisha has beached herself, he tries to summon up the powers of the Whale Man in Australian Aboriginal tradition. After whales had been enticed to the shore, the Whale Man of the Ramindjeri clan would sing the females and young out of the shallow waters and back to the safety of the deep sea. The Whale Caller 'prays for the powers' of this Strong Man, but 'his voice cannot be heard for the plea for her life is uttered only inside him . . . He beams [his messages] out in vain . . . He can never acquire the powers of those whose totem is [the whale] Kondoli nga:tji' (Mda 2005: 200). In despair, he puts faith in 'the experts from Cape Town' who 'will surely save' Sharisha.

Surely the most profound tragedy can be ascribed to the lack (due to colonialism) of an indigenous ecological tradition that can save 'earth others', as well as ourselves. Denied any spiritual abilities that could sustain relationships with 'earth others' in ways that can promote their survival, human beings, such as the Whale Caller, can only put a misplaced faith into scientism, mistakenly relying on experts whose only solution is sometimes to destroy those beings who are already under threat. Because the scientists cannot countenance whale subjectivities or emotions, they cannot interpret the anxiety of Sharisha's calf hovering close to her dying mother as anything more than a curiousness that they attribute, homogenisingly, to all Southern Right Whales.

Tragically, the Whale Caller takes responsibility for the faults of Western dualistic thinking onto his shoulders, quite literally, in the form of the sandwich board that he wears proclaiming 'I am the Hermanus Penitent' (Mda 2006: 210). Devoid of any sustaining beliefs that may offer hope or ecological connections, his only recourse is to a religion of self-mortification and shame. Saluni had considered him as 'a flagellant at heart' (108); that he imagines Mr Yodd, a rock rabbit, as his confessor suggests that his shame emanates from a self-sacrificial perception of human relationships with nature. As a human being, he, too, is culpable. Mda's message is astringent.

The apocalypse in the Whale Caller's universe can only foreshadow the ecological devastation that Rosenthal imagines for both the nation and the planet. Mda and Rosenthal have not scripted folktales in which the planet can be healed. They have challenged their readers to deal with ecological realities that cannot be wished away by fictionalising them.

Notes

1. See *All Over Creation* (Ozeki 2003) for an ecological novel in which the narrative is overwhelmed by didacticism.
2. Snakes, potentially, can be differentiated within their species: a zoologist in a research unit told me that she prefers caring for pythons as they 'have faces, more like dogs'.
3. When Marcus Bullock suggests that 'there is no part of an animal that does not look back at us' (2002: 101), his emphasis differs from that of Levinas. He stresses the continuities one has with the animal as a 'life' and 'an existence', but also his/her unknowability.
4. David Wood misses the point when he complains that communing with a domestic cat is never going to solve the ecological crisis of the planet (2004: 143). Surely what he denigrates as 'an adventure in difference' *is* the point, for if the predominant master consciousness shifted from its assumption of control over nature, the ecological crisis could be better addressed.
5. Compare with J.M. Coetzee's character, Elizabeth Costello, who maintains 'To be alive is to be a living soul. An animal – and we are all animals – is an embodied soul' (Coetzee 1999: 33).

6. Strictly speaking, of course, the Karoo is not a wilderness; its desertification is largely
   caused by human intervention in the form of overgrazing (see Archer 2003).

Works cited

Allen, Paula Gunn. 1996. 'The sacred hoop: A contemporary perspective'. In: Glotfelty, Cheryl
   and Harold Fromm (eds.). *The Ecocriticism Reader: Landmarks in Literary Ecology*. Athens,
   GA: University of Georgia Press, 241-63.

Archer, Sean. 2003 (2002). 'Technology and ecology in the Karoo: A century of windmills,
   wire and changing farming practice'. In: Dovers, Stephen, Ruth Edgecombe and Bill
   Guest (eds.). *South Africa's Environmental History: Cases and Comparisons*. Athens, OH:
   Ohio University Press; Cape Town: David Philip, 112-38.

Attwell, David and Barbara Harlow. 2000. 'Introduction: South African fiction after apartheid'.
   Special Issue South African Fiction after Apartheid: Modern Fiction Studies 46(1) Spring: 1-9.

Bullock, Marcus. 2002. 'Watching eyes, seeing dreams, knowing lives'. In: Rothfels, Nigel
   (ed.). *Representing Animals*. Bloomington: Indiana University Press, 99-118.

Carruthers, Jane. 2003 (2002). 'Introduction: Environmental history in southern Africa: An
   overview'. In: Dovers, Stephen, Ruth Edgecombe and Bill Guest (eds.). *South Africa's
   Environmental History: Cases and Comparisons*. Athens, OH: Ohio University Press; Cape
   Town: David Philip, 3-15.

Conley, Verena. 2004. 'Manly values: Luc Ferry's ethical philosophy'. In: Calarco, Matthew
   and Peter Atterton (eds.). *Animal Philosophy: Essential Readings in Continental Thought*.
   London: Continuum, 157-63.

Coetzee, J.M. 1999. *The Lives of Animals*. Edited by Amy Gutmann. The University Center
   for Human Values Series. Princeton, NJ: Princeton University Press.

Deleuze, Gilles and Felix Guattari. 2004. 'Becoming-animal'. In: Calarco, Matthew and Peter
   Atterton (eds.). *Animal Philosophy: Essential Readings in Continental Thought*. London:
   Continuum, 87-100.

Derrida, Jacques. 2002. 'The animal that therefore I am (more to follow)'. Translated by
   David Willis. *Critical Inquiry* 28 (Winter): 369-418.

Desmond, Jane. 1999. *Staging Tourism: Bodies on Display from Waikiki to Sea World*. Chicago:
   Chicago University Press.

Gaita, Raimond. 2004 (2002). *The Philosopher's Dog*. London: Routledge.

Griffiths, Tom. 1997. 'Introduction. Ecology and empire: Towards an Australian history of
   the world'. In: Griffiths, Tom and Libby Robin (eds.). *Ecology and Empire: Environmental
   History of Settler Societies*. Edinburgh: Keele University Press; Pietermaritzburg: University
   of Natal Press, 1-16.

Haraway, Donna. 1992. 'The promises of monsters: A regenerative politics for inappropriate/d
   others'. In: Grossberg, Lawrence, Cary Nelson and Paula A. Treichler (eds.). *Cultural
   Studies*. London: Routledge, 295-337.

Irigaray, Luce. 2004. 'Animal compassion'. In: Calarco, Matthew and Peter Atterton (eds.). *Animal Philosophy: Essential Readings in Continental Thought*. London: Continuum, 195–201.

Jordan, A.C. 1973. *Tales from Southern Africa*. Translated and retold by A.C. Jordan. Berkeley: University of California Press.

Levinas, Emmanuel. 2004. 'The name of a dog, or natural rights'. In: Calarco, Matthew and Peter Atterton (eds.). *Animal Philosophy: Essential Readings in Continental Thought*. London: Continuum, 47–50.

Mda, Zakes. 2000. *The Heart of Redness*. Cape Town: Oxford University Press.

———. 2005. *The Whale Caller*. Johannesburg: Penguin.

Meeker, Joseph W. 1972. *The Comedy of Survival: Studies in Literary Ecology*. New York: Scribner's Sons.

Miller, Ruth. 1990. *Poems, Prose, Plays*. Edited and introduced by Lionel Abrahams. Cape Town: Carrefour.

Ozeki, Ruth L. 2003. *All Over Creation*. London: Picador.

Plumwood, Val. 1993. *Feminism and the Mastery of Nature*. London: Routledge.

Rosenthal, Jane. 2004. *Souvenir*. The Crags: Bromponie Press.

Snyder, Gary. 1990. *The Practice of the Wild*. Berkeley: North Point Press.

Soper, Kate. 1995. *What is Nature?* Oxford: Blackwell.

Urpeth, James. 2004. 'Animal becomings'. In: Calarco, Matthew and Peter Atterton (eds.). *Animal Philosophy: Essential Readings in Continental Thought*. London: Continuum, 101–10.

Wood, David. 2004. 'Thinking with cats'. In: Calarco, Matthew and Peter Atterton (eds.). *Animal Philosophy: Essential Readings in Continental Thought*. London: Continuum, 129–44.

Woodward, Wendy. 2003. ' "Jim comes from Jo'burg": Regionalised identities and social comedy in Zakes Mda's *The Heart of Redness*'. *Current Writing* 15(2): 173–85.

18

Ways of Writing

Zakes Mda's Self-Reflexive Art in Cion

J.U. JACOBS AND DAVID BELL

ZAKES MDA'S SIXTH novel, *Cion* (2007), shares the same twin discursive features of his earlier novels: a distinct historiographic element and a marked performative quality. Mda's novels generally tend to derive their main narrative thrust (their emplotment) from a historical narrative: the back stories of Toloki and his 'homegirl' Noria in *Ways of Dying*; the history of coups and military governments in Lesotho from 1970 to 1994 in *She Plays with the Darkness*; the story of Nongqawuse and the Xhosa cattle killings of 1856–57 in *The Heart of Redness*; and the Immorality Act scandals in Excelsior in 1970 in *The Madonna of Excelsior*. Parallel with the historical narrative in each novel is a contemporary one, which comprises, usually within a love story, a thinly plotted disquisition on culture, society and politics: *Ways of Dying* provides an essay on death and political violence in South Africa in the transitional period immediately before the advent of democracy in 1994; *She Plays with the Darkness* analyses traditional, rural and spiritual values and ways of life in southern Africa – as opposed to contemporary urban, materialistic ones; *The Heart of Redness* fictionally stages a debate between traditionalist and progressive Xhosa factions on issues of culture, sustainable development and globalisation in present-day South Africa; and *The Madonna of Excelsior* examines various cultural, racial and political adjustments to life in post-apartheid South Africa. Mda's historical narratives unfold in a dialogue, or counterpoint, between their past and present strands. His fifth novel, *The Whale Caller*, provides an exception to this general tendency, however. While the story is, almost didactically, concerned with the Southern Right Whales that visit the coast of Hermanus in the Western Cape annually and with the town's tourist industry, the narrative unfolds mainly in the present and raises its larger social, economic and metaphysical questions together with the development of the love triangle between the Whale Caller, Saluni and the whale, Sharisha.

The historiographic discourse in Mda's fiction is combined with a second, more expressive one. The dialogue between past and present in the novels is usually mediated through some form of cultural or artistic performance, which is not only explicitly identified in the novel, but also – and more importantly – *enacted* by the narrative. This performative writing may be seen in the manner in which Noria's inspirational singing and Toloki's professional mourning give the text of *Ways of Dying* its lyrical quality, the manner in which both the traditional and urbanised songs and dances of the Basotho help to shape the narrative rhythms of *She Plays with the Darkness*, the manner in which *umngqokolo*, the split-tone singing of the Xhosa people, enables the simultaneous unfolding of the past and the present narratives in *The Heart of Redness*, and the way in which the Flemish expressionist paintings of Frans Claerhout are stylistically mimicked by the prose in *The Madonna of Excelsior*. In this respect, *The Whale Caller* is no exception: the narrative derives its main momentum from the erotically charged, ritualised exchanges between the Whale Caller and Sharisha as she responds to his dancing and kelp-horn serenades with her own repertoire of whale songs and performances.

This discursive blending of history and performance in Mda's fiction is continued in *Cion*. The historical narrative deals with slavery in the United States in the nineteenth century and the contemporary story provides a thinly fictionalised reflection on African-American and Native American, and also South African, culture and the politics of identity. In the performative discourse with which this historical discourse is combined, however, Mda's latest novel not only self-consciously engages with various forms of cultural and artistic expression, but through them also – and especially – self-reflexively performs and flaunts its fictionality, the status of its author and its protagonist, and the processes through which the text has been produced, as well as those through which it is received. Whereas in the earlier novels, Mda experiments with various ways of writing fiction, *Cion*, with its self-conscious commentary on its own status as fiction (see Waugh 1984: 93), is his most overtly metafictional novel to date, self-reflexively foregrounding as its subject writing *about* ways of writing.

That Mda regards both history and fiction as porous genres is apparent from the outset of *Cion*. In the acknowledgements, he pays tribute to, among others, the writers and historians who have provided him with the background material for his novel: Keith P. Griffler (*Frontline of Freedom*, 2004), Jacqueline L. Tobin and Raymond G. Dobard (*Hidden in Full View*, 2000) and J.A. Rogers (*Sex and Race*, 1942). There is no prefatory disclaimer to the effect that the novel is a work of fiction and its events and characters imaginary. The omission is understandable: Mda especially thanks Barbara Parsons and Irene Flowers of the Kilvert Community Centre in Kilvert, Athens county, Ohio, where the novel is set, and Terry Gilkey, keeper of the cemetery records in Athens, Ohio, for having assisted him with the oral and recorded history – only to have them then cross over from the ontological realm that they inhabit on the acknowledgements page to become, in the course of the narrative, 'fictional' characters in the novel who contribute to the development of the main character, Toloki.

The merging of reality with fiction is equally evident in the range of intertextual references in *Cion* through which the narrative texture is enriched. Characters and events from the real world, as well as from the world of fiction, are alluded to without any differentiation between these disparate sources. Mda introduces into his fictional plot the figure of the actual Virginian lawyer, George Fitzhugh, author of *Sociology for the South* and proponent of the view that 'slavery was a natural and rightful condition of society' (Mda 2007: 167), but his view is premised on class, rather than race. On another occasion, the intolerance of a fundamentalist Christian preacher is compared to the ayatollah who issued the fatwa against Salman Rushdie for his alleged blasphemies against the Prophet in *The Satanic Verses*. And as part of Mda's historical plot in *Cion*, in an episode that is an obvious literary allusion to the metafictional ending of Gabriel García Márquez's novel, *One Hundred Years of Solitude*, the character Niall Quigley finds himself reading the story of his own life encrypted in a scroll that he has bought from his own former slave. Quigley's discovery that the scroll contains not only the story of his life right up to the present time, including his 'reading about himself reading the scroll' (172), but probably also the story of his future, has its hypotextual source in *One Hundred Years of Solitude* in Aureliano's deciphering of Melquíades' prophetic parchments, on which are encoded the histories of the Buendías and of Macondo, including the story of Aureliano's own origin and of his immediate past, up to the prophecy of his deciphering the last page of the parchment in anticipation of the date and circumstances of his death – in effect, reading to its conclusion the novel in which he is a character (see Márquez 1978: 334–36).

Cion can perhaps best be described as a work of historiographic metafiction, in which, to quote Linda Hutcheon, 'the notion that history's problem is verification, while fiction's is veracity' (1988: 112) is confused. The respective 'truth' values and 'authenticity' of history and of fiction are contrasted and complicated through the combination of historiography with metafiction and their mutual influence. Both fiction and history are exposed as narrative genres, their productions as constructs, and the line between them blurred (see 113).

The narrative events in *Cion*, beginning on 30 October 2004 and ending a year later on 31 October 2005, are framed by the actual Court Street Halloween parade in Athens, Ohio, into which Mda has introduced the fictional Toloki, the professional mourner from his first novel, *Ways of Dying*. Mda's protagonist in *Cion* has now crossed over various ontological divides: between the work in which he had his original being and this new fictional context, and from a world of fiction into one that is historically 'real'. (The inclusion of the Court Street Halloween parade in *Cion* recalls the framing function of both the actual Ficksburg Cherry Festival in *The Madonna of Excelsior* and the Kalfiefees whale festival in Hermanus in *The Whale Caller*). Halloween goes back to Celtic and Anglo-Saxon times when, at the end of summer and the eve of a new year, it was also 'the occasion for one of the ancient fire festivals when huge bonfires were set on hilltops to frighten away evil spirits' (*Encyclopaedia Britannica, Micropaedia* IV: 862). In medieval times, it remained a holy or hallowed evening, the eve of All Saints' Day on 1 November. Toloki reminds the reader that this 'is also the day of the disembodied spirits of those who died last year. They come back in search of living bodies to possess for next year. That is their only chance of an afterlife' (Mda 2007: 266). What had its origins in a religious ritual to mediate the physical and spiritual worlds has, however, in modern times become essentially a secular performance of pranks by children. As Toloki remarks: 'The Court Street creatures, of course, do not have in their minds the Celtic roots of the feast as they prance around, even though their ghoulishness is reminiscent of the original Celts. It was a look that was meant to frighten the disembodied spirits away so that they fail to take possession of any living man, woman or child.' Although the Court Street Halloween procession is now, generally speaking, a form of carnival, with its performative principle of public spectacle and rule of riotous subversion of the social order, it is, more pertinently, an occasion for self-fictionalisation, for self-concealment and self-projection as the masked revellers present themselves as grotesque impersonations of, amongst others, various US cultural icons and political ogres, from Paris Hilton, Yoko Ono and Maharishi Mahesh Yogi to Vice-President Dick Cheney and Defence Secretary Donald Rumsfeld. The actual historical figures are parodied, undermined through exaggeration and reduced to sharing the streets with those other larger-than-life US beings, Superman, Spiderman and Batman.

Within the carnivalesque frame of the Court Street Halloween procession in the novel, another historico-fictional performance takes place with similar, self-conscious exaggeration and a comparable blurring of the realms of the real and the unreal: the self-reflexive relationship between the fictional Toloki and his implied author, Zakes Mda, that lies at the heart of the performative metafictionality of the novel. Mda, the creator of Toloki, is somewhat esoterically referred to throughout by Toloki as the 'sciolist': the novelist as neither scientist nor sociologist, but as 'sciolist', a superficial pretender of knowledge. And as Mda's fictional offspring, Toloki becomes not his 'scion' or descendant, but merely the eponymous 'cion', the word referring, in its Middle English spelling without an 's', to a twig, runner or offshoot, a cutting for grafting. The metafictional discourse in the novel is centred on the figures of the 'cion' and the 'sciolist' and the relationship between them that emerges in the narrative. (In his review of *Cion*, Chris Dunton points out that in the *Concise Oxford Dictionary*, '(s)cion' is the entry immediately following 'sciolist' (2007)).

In *Cion*, Toloki may perhaps best be understood in terms of Thomas Docherty's argument that in contemporary fiction, the conceptual notion of a stable, autonomous 'character' is replaced by a 'process of characterisation':

'Rather than being clearly delineated centres around which we can orient ourselves and our attitudes, [characters] become fragmentary or evanescent. The stability of "character" is replaced with the more mobile "subject" [. . . and] in some cases, instead of characters we seem to have fragmentary "instances of subjectivity" ' (1983: xiv–xv). Such fragmentation involves the reader, Docherty says: instead of the author being the source of meaning for the text, this responsibility becomes shared between the writer and the reader, who is obliged to inform the subjectivity of these mobile subjects in a collaborative dialogue with the fiction.

Toloki's self-awareness as a contemporary fictional construct is clear from the way he advertises his fictionality from the outset. He begins by telling the reader directly that he was 'conjured . . . into existence a decade or so before' (Mda 2007: 2) by the sciolist in Durham, England and, after his birth as a fictional being in South Africa, later transported back to Durham at the suggestion of a Shakespearean professor at Ohio University, only to be 'abandoned' again in Durham. When the sciolist later brings him to Athens, Ohio and he finds himself caught up in the Halloween procession, he introduces himself to the young American Obed Quigley via Mda's novel, *Ways of Dying*, as 'Toloki the Professional Mourner' (12). When Obed asks whether *Ways of Dying* is a 'manual on how to die', Toloki replies: 'No. The story of my life . . . We are indeed all from stories. Every one of us. All humanity" (123). Later on in the narrative, Toloki again directly addresses those of his readers who are familiar with his back story as 'those of you who know me from *Ways of Dying*' (117) and who remember his fondness for raw onion and Swiss roll. At one stage, he also distinguishes between his US and South African readerships, when he speaks about the lack of free, independent media in the United States, which, he says, 'will certainly amaze those who are following my story from South Africa' (132).

At the more conventional end of the fictional spectrum, the relationship between Toloki and the implied author Mda is that of conventional character and author, with Toloki a virtual mouthpiece for his creator when he transparently offers information and opinions about a host of topics ranging from the invasion and bombing of Iraq to the origins of tap dancing and the medicinal properties of sassafras tea.

Towards the postmodernist end of the spectrum, however, the relationship between Toloki and his creator is more existentialist, rather than essentialist, and becomes one of increasing tension and antagonism as the cion deliberately distances himself from the sciolist. The novel opens with Toloki dismissively saying: 'The sciolist has delusions of Godness' (Mda 2007: 1), and then going on further to undermine his author's omnipotence in an unflattering description of the sciolist, who physically resembles Mda himself: 'His belly hangs out like an apron' (8). From the outset, Toloki rejects the sciolist as insane and he returns throughout the narrative to this figure of compromised authority and questionable judgement. At times, he ironically defers to the sciolist – 'He brought me here [to Athens]; he will have to provide the answers' (9) – while at other times, the tension between the dependence of the over-determined traditional character on his author and the independence of the indeterminate postmodern fictional subject erupts into open antagonism: 'I have to go somewhere too. I have no idea where. Damn that sciolist!' Toloki expostulates in frustration at one point (15). Later on, Toloki rhetorically asks his reader whether the sciolist perhaps resents 'the independence and the freedom to determine the course of [his] life' that Toloki has gained in the village of Kilvert where the Quigleys live: 'Is he taking vengeance on me for having lost myself in the lives of the living and momentarily forgetting my mission in life: to mourn the dead and to search for ways of mourning?' (83). Toloki questions the competence of the sciolist as orchestrator of not only those narrative events that he features in, but also those that he is given to narrate. The sciolist's insistence on a predetermined role for Toloki eventually loses momentum, however – as Toloki puts it: 'The sciolist nagged me until he got tired: *Toloki, you are a professional mourner. You have a vocation to fulfil . . .* That voice has since gone silent' (150; emphasis in original). Finally, the figures of 'character' and 'author' devolve into two interactive subjectivities in the narrative, similarly limited in their understanding and agency and similarly contingent in the fictional and real worlds that they inhabit.

Mda's narrative engages with the contemporary history of the year that Toloki spends with the Quigley family in Kilvert and signals the major national and international events: the US election of 2 November 2004 that saw George W. Bush re-elected as president; the anti-war sentiment after the US-led invasion of Iraq; the court martial of Lynndie England for abuse of Iraqi prisoners in Abu Ghraib; the Asian tsunami disaster – and to add a bit of local South African interest to his US narrative, there is even a reference to the South African gambling resort magnate Sol Kerzner and his casinos in Native American reservations in Connecticut. It is, however, in its engagement with the nineteenth-century history of slavery in the United States, for which it is heavily indebted to its sources, that Mda's text again derives its main narrative thrust. Through the story of the ancestral slave woman, the Abyssinian Queen, and her two sons, the half-brothers Abednego and Nicodemus, their flight to freedom in 1838 and the subsequent killing of Nicodemus, and the story of the slave-dealing Irishman Niall Quigley who is himself tricked into slavery, Mda's novel provides a comprehensive account of the whole business of slave-breeding in the United States in the first half of the nineteenth century. The discourse around slave-breeding is presented in relation to David Fairfield, referred to as 'The Owner', and Fairfield Farms, whose sole business was breeding slaves and whose 'whole machinery was geared for the smooth and fast production of children, who were then sold when they reached fifteen' (Mda 2007: 35). Slaves as livestock, slave-breeding as a long-term investment, with the stock needing 'many years to mature and be ready for the market' (91), the rotation of studs over the female slaves in the breeding bays, the goal of breeding mulatto children, the dangers of inbreeding, the separation into house slaves and field slaves – the whole obscenity of slavery is presented in the novel, together with its paradoxes. White slavery continued at Fairfield Farms into the 1840s, despite its supposed end soon after the Revolutionary War, so that white women could be mated with pitch-black black studs to produce mulattos 'who looked mulatto rather than white' (51). Because of the large-scale breeding taking place on the plantation and there being not enough white men to service black women, it became 'easier and more cost-effective to hold white women in bondage than to employ white studs' (51). And if it was true that white slaveholders rented out their white girls who were unproductive to bordellos in the neighbouring cities, the narrative points out that it was no less true that there were a number of wealthy free black people in Virginia and Maryland who owned slaves, and that some of these black slaveholders were 'happy to keep white women both as slaves and concubines' (157). Mda's text rehearses the whole drama around slavery and its fugitives – the operation of the Underground Railroad with its conductors and stations and supportive abolitionists – and he identifies all the main role-players in pursuit of escaped slaves, including slave traders, slave chasers with their dogs, slave stealers and bounty hunters.

The planned and unplanned consequence of this racial engineering – mixed racial and cultural identity – is foregrounded in the novel. Toloki remarks that Obed Quigley 'would have been classified as a coloured in my country' (Mda 2007: 12). Obed and his mother Ruth frequently return to the question of the cultural identity resulting from their slave past. Ruth says of the Kilvert community: 'We don't belong to nobody. Our race of people is different from any race of people that ever lived on earth' (28). Obed echoes this sense of not belonging anywhere: 'White people hate us because we ain't white enough. Black people hate us too. They call us high yella niggers.' Ruth later gives a more positive interpretation to their Coloured identity when she tells Toloki, 'We're everybody' (55), and this is again echoed by her son when he tells Toloki that they are referred to by others as 'WIN people': 'We don't call ourselves that. Other folks do. Know why? 'Cause we got three bloods in all of us . . . We got the White blood and the Indian blood and the Negro blood. Get it? WIN people' (62). Ruth and her husband Mahlon are 'both descendants of African-Americans, Native Americans and Caucasian Americans who intermarried . . . They are all part of the inbreeding that has happened over the decades in Kilvert' (135), from when fugitive slaves first found refuge among the Native American tribes (Shawnee, Cherokee, Powhatan) and many of them intermarried with the Native Americans and with the Irish immigrants who had also sought sanctuary in Tabler Town, as Kilvert was formerly known. Obed and his mother may both be confused about the exact Native American ancestry that they lay claim to – Shawnee or Cherokee or even Navajo – but for Obed the finer distinctions are irrelevant: 'Shawnee . . . Navajo . . . same difference 'cause they all Indians . . . and I am a freakin' Indian' (120). His mother puts it more pragmatically to Toloki when he points out the fact that they all have strong Native American features: 'Ain't no pure Indians any more. Them pure Indians was all bred out. Like whites will be all bred out. That's what scares them most' (58). Ironically, Toloki comes to realise, the racial and cultural uncertainty of these people results from their having shifted from suppressing their Africanness and Indianness and celebrating instead their white ancestry during the days of oppression, to now wanting to reclaim all three heritages as a source of pride and uniqueness: 'But they no longer remember who they were, on the African and Native American side' (238).

Significantly, this debate about racial and cultural mixing is mediated through Toloki, whose own racial purity is problematised from the beginning when Ruth remarks that he does not look like an African and says, 'You're yella', prompting him to explain to his readers: 'Perhaps it is necessary to account for myself for having what she considers an unusual complexion for an African. I try to explain to her that there are strong possibilities that my ancestry is a Khoikhoi one, which is the case for many Southern Sotho and Nguni people in South Africa' (Mda 2007: 25).

In the present-day narrative chronotope of 2004–05, Toloki's South African perspective is brought to bear on the theme of cultural continuity and discontinuity, especially as regards African and African-American traditions. Some ancient African cultural traditions have survived only in the African diaspora, whereas others are purely inventions of the diaspora. As Toloki puts it:

> I have observed that people of African descent in America often create African heritages that no one in Africa knows about. There are some who are descendants of kings and queens who existed only in the collective imagination of their oppressed progenitors. I also know there are many rituals and traditions long dead on the mother continent, that were preserved and transformed and enriched by the slaves to suit their new lives in America. (Mda 2007: 119)

Not only does Mda use his hybrid protagonist, Toloki, to mediate the African-American cultural hybridity of the Kilvert community, but the novel itself, with its discursive mix of history and metafiction, is the hybrid vehicle for Mda's fictional discussion of cultural mixture, change and innovation. As in his earlier novels, various traditional and innovative artistic forms are described and also *performed* by the narrative itself. The most important of these in *Cion* is the tradition of quilt-making in Kilvert and in particular the reverence for old quilts that 'embody the life of the family' (Mda 2007: 30) and are carriers of memories. The traditional Irish Chain and African designs bring with them the 'peculiar . . . smell of history' (30) and the African design, which supposedly originated with the Abyssinian Queen in the 1830s, represented not simply 'beauty for its own sake' (48), but was encoded with secret messages that provided guidelines for fugitive slaves. The various traditional quilt designs (Drunkard's Path, North Star, Shoofly, Monkey Wrench, Bow Tie, Crossroads, Log Cabin, Wagon Wheel, Flying Geese) were codes, perhaps not literally mapping the way to freedom, but nevertheless serving an important function. In the words of the Underground Railroad conductor Birdman to the fugitive Nicodemus, quilts

> bound the individuals into a cohesive force, and reminded them of their duty to freedom . . . Quilts were like sayings . . . they were like adages and proverbs learnt from the elders and were effective in jolting the people's memory and in recording the values of the community for present and future generations. Quilt designs did not map out the actual route to the Promised Land but helped the seekers to remember those things that were important in their lives. They did the same work as spirituals. Like the stories the storytellers and the griots of the old continent told whose rhymes and rhythms forced people never to forget them and the history they contained, the patterns and the colours and designs and ties and stitches of quilts were mnemonic. (Mda 2007: 109–10)

In the lore of quilts in Kilvert, the tradition of expressive textiles that spoke secret languages to the initiated can be traced back via the Abyssinian Queen to the 'old continent' (Mda 2007: 48), Africa. Toloki finds such a belief that quilting is a development of an African tradition acceptable:

> since in the motherland (which is what the descendants of slaves fondly call Africa) there were many examples of art that spoke. Particularly fabrics and beadwork and even lids of pots. They did not only adorn or cover our nakedness or our food. They transmitted messages in a practical way. They spoke about the status of the wearer or user; about

love life, life's journeys, life's transitions, emotional states, aspirations, protest, even pet peeves. Why wouldn't the African carry on with the tradition of talking fabrics in the new world? (Mda 2007: 142–43)

There is, furthermore, a South African analogue for the quilts, Toloki says, in the slogans and songs that were chanted and sung during apartheid. The songs might not have expressed anything that wasn't already known, nor did they provide any particularly new insights about how to overcome apartheid, but they did give people courage and 'created a spirit of oneness and camaraderie' (Mda 2007: 143) among them. People drew strength from the songs and were resolved to fight against apartheid 'to the bitter end'. In this respect, the quilts served a similar function for the slaves in the United States – as did their spirituals: 'They contained folk wisdom. They invigorated memory.'

The different attitudes towards tradition are represented by Ruth Quigley and her daughter, Orpah. Ruth is an uncompromising traditionalist who, despite her poverty, is only prepared to reproduce the ancestral designs, which do not sell at the farmers' market. People see in them, Toloki says, 'wonderful craftsmanship but no artistic vision' (Mda 2007: 211). Artistic vision is precisely what Orpah's quilts, with their original designs and stitched-on collages of found objects, embody, which Ruth resolutely destroys. Toloki recognises that Orpah is 'the founder of her own tradition' (130); she is engaged, like others, in turning pieces that have established cultural significance 'into works of art that make statements about their world today'. The same may be said of Mda's innovative art of fiction in *Cion* which, drawing on African and US cultural roots and traditional forms, provides a creative textual collage that makes a statement about the contemporary world and the role of the writer within it.

Orpah's drawings and her quilt-making, like her sitar playing, through which she manages to make the Asian instrument 'speak a new language' (Mda 2007: 146), form part of the intricate pattern of artistic performances, each of which provides a *mise en abyme* for the main subject of Mda's novel, which is a metafictional concern with ways of writing. To a lesser extent, Obed's dabbling in African and Native American shamanism, and to a far greater extent, their father Mahlon Quigley's performances together with his daughter, are part of this pattern. Mahlon continues into Orpah's adulthood an elaborate nightly ritual of not only telling, but later also performing in costume, stories derived from collective memory and from his own invention, which she co-creates by either developing them in tandem with him or completing them in paintings. Mahlon's performance as a 'medium man' (246), drawing on ancient sources, rehearsing established cultural traditions and creating new ones, provides an embedded metaphor in Toloki's narrative for his own role as a 'medium man' in his conception of himself as fictional subject and professional mourner – which in turn serves as an embedded metaphor in the novel for Mda's role as a 'medium man' in his conception of himself as custodian and innovator of the art of fiction.

Toloki, a 'votary of [his] own Order of Professional Mourners' (Mda 2007: 2), had fallen into a rut in South Africa: the violent deaths that he used to mourn during the transitional political upheavals made way for what seems to Toloki to be boringly similar deaths resulting from the HIV/AIDS pandemic. Feeling himself contaminated by the conspiracy of lies around AIDS and his 'once revered howls and whines' (3) now lacking sincerity, he developed a new practice of studying the headstones of graves in cemeteries and imagining the deaths of the people buried there. Mourning thus acquired a dimension of fictionalisation, as Toloki says: 'The richness of re-creating deaths lies in the fact that you first have to re-create the lives of the deceased before they died' (5). Disillusioned by his discovery that he had not invented the art of mourning for compensation after all, but that there were ancient traditions of professional mourning in other cultures, he resolved to become 'an itinerant mourner' (4), his 'aim to travel the world in search of mourning' and his stay in Ohio marking, he tells Obed, 'the first leg of a long journey' (13–14). He is, Toloki says, 'no longer the simple professional mourner of yesteryear' (61) – just as, one may add, he is no longer the simple fictional character of yesteryear.

When he joins Obed at the grave of Niall Quigley, Obed's Irish forefather who eventually accepted himself and lived as an African, Toloki teaches him new mourning wails, combining what Obed describes as the sounds of a coyote with 'groans and moans and sacred chants of [his] own invention' (Mda 2007: 152). Obed joins in the innovative performance and, in Toloki's words, 'together we are able to muster a two-part harmony at one time, and a call-and-response at another. Our mourning transports us to another place; another realm;

another time.' Toloki's first collaborative mourning combines his howling with African and US song traditions, a new, hybrid form in the context of a hybrid culture.

The manner in which Toloki serves as a *mise en abyme* for Mda's self-reflexiveness in this text can be seen in the development of his professional mourning from autonomous to collaborative performance. At the funeral of a young boy who was killed, Toloki's harrowing whimpering and moaning are blended with the voices of the minister conducting the service and of Obed, citing various sources from the Bible to give legitimacy to Toloki's performance. Toloki's mourning, together with the account he provides of the function of the Nurse in the African funeral tradition to narrate the death of the deceased, dramatises the double discursive strands of performance and historiography in Mda's novel. At the memorial service for Margaret Tobias, Obed's white grandmother who was committed to a mental hospital by her family for having married a Coloured man, Toloki wishes for the first time in his mourning career to perform, 'to dance to [his] wails' (Mda 2007: 263). He incorporates some of the movements that he had seen the 'medium man' Mahlon perform through the window and Toloki's 'whole performance routine, except for the sounds, is informed by his routine'.

The full significance of Toloki's innovations in his tradition of professional mourning for Mda's metafictional discourse becomes clearer when Toloki begins his mourning collaboration with Orpah, who takes charge and choreographs their routine. Orpah sees herself 'as the manager and artistic director of this whole enterprise' and incorporates into the opening routine Obed's speech at the young boy's funeral 'about the ineptness of human beings in handling grief and the necessity of professional mourning in bringing back aplomb and dignity to the art of grieving' (Mda 2007: 268). The sciolist also comes to Toloki's – and his reader's – assistance with a letter he received from a Professor William Edwards with information about mourners and mourning: Mourning 'was a kind of legitimation . . . It signified the fact that an individual had a worth which may not have been acknowledged in the ordinary patterns of social relations' (270). (Arguably, the novel offers a similar form of legitimation of the worth of the otherwise unacknowledged individual life.) As the creative ensemble of Orpah and Toloki develops into his sewing quilts as an interpretation of her sitar-inspired designs and her changing her tunes in line with his newly invented sounds of mourning, their work becomes a source of *jouissance*, 'an expression of joy. Joy that was not dressed with anything to make it valid. Naked joy' (271). In collaboration with Orpah, Toloki develops from mere professional mourner to true performer – and a performer, moreover, who comes to understand through innovation not only the basis of his own expressive art, but also the roots of a literary tradition:

> After all, the roots of tragedy lie in mourning. I am talking here of tragedy on the stage. For the ancient Greeks dramatic tragedy was a ritual that took the songs of professional mourners at funerals to the levels of performance. It gave the dead a voice since the corpses could not utter a sound any more. Like actors who steal the voices of those who cannot speak for themselves, professional mourners are hypocrites who weep for those who never belonged to them in the first place. Through Orpah's direction the hypocrisy of the actor and of the professional mourner converged. And the movements that resulted from that union were intense and stirring. (Mda 2007: 271–72)

In this *mise en abyme*, Toloki, the fictional subject in Mda's novel, can be seen as speaking for his author's acknowledgement of the ventriloquism and vicarious experience of life in professional mourning out of which Greek tragedy, and eventually his own theatre pieces and works of fiction, have developed.

Toloki concludes his narrative by declaring his final separation from his author. Together with Orpah, he looks forward to their future as itinerant mourners in search for mourning and to 'the performances and exhibitions with which [they will] dazzle the bereaved' (Mda 2007: 286). Before coming to Kilvert, Toloki says, he 'found the present a very lonely place to be', having before 'lived only in the past and in the future'. Hopefully, they will discover how to live in the present – and they 'will do so without the aid of the sciolist' whom they have left behind with his 'rambling narratives' in Athens, Ohio. The final words in the dialogue between cion and sciolist are given by Mda to his creation, Toloki, whom he sets free through the very act of being rejected by his professional mourner:

The sciolist is in the God business. And like all Gods he lives his life vicariously through his creations. Like all Gods he demands love from his creations. That's why he creates them in the first place . . . so they can shower him with love . . . so they can worship him and praise him . . . so that they can bribe him with offerings. Creation is therefore a self-centred act.

I need my independence from him. (Mda 2007: 286)[1]

It is with this fictional conundrum that Mda concludes his novel, as Toloki, in obedience to the slave's duty to freedom, makes his escape from the fictional world of Zakes Mda.

Note

1. In an interview in *Tinhouse* (http://www.tinhouse.com/mag/back_issues/archive/issues/issue_20/interview.html, accessed 12 October 2008), Mda actually uses the words: 'When I write a novel I am in the God business.' He has also elaborated on this idea in an interview with Venu Naidoo: 'The world that I was writing about was the world that I created . . . I am the God of that world, so I can make things happen the way I want them to happen.' (Naidoo 1997: 250).

Works cited

Docherty, Thomas. 1983. *Reading (Absent) Character: Towards a Theory of Characterisation in Fiction*. Oxford: Oxford University Press.

Dunton, Chris. 2007. 'A small village in Ohio forms the backdrop for Mda's sixth and best novel'. *Sunday Independent*, 15 July.

Hutcheon, Linda. 1988. *A Poetics of Postmodernism: History, Theory, Fiction*. New York: Routledge.

Márquez, Gabriel García. 1978. *One Hundred Years of Solitude*. London: Picador.

Naidoo, Venu. 1997. 'Interview with Zakes Mda'. *Alternation* 4(1): 247–61.

Mda, Zakes. 2007. *Cion*. Johannesburg: Penguin.

Waugh, Patricia. 1984. *Metafiction: The Theory and Practice of Self-Conscious Fiction*. London: Methuen.

Works of Zakes Mda

A Select Bibliography

Fiction

1995a. *She Plays with the Darkness: A Novel.* Florida Hills, South Africa: Vivlia (Trenton, NJ: Africa World Press, 1999).

1995b. *Ways of Dying.* Cape Town: Oxford University Press (New York: Picador, 2002).

1997. *Melville 67: A Novella for Youth.* Florida Hills, South Africa: Vivlia.

2000. *The Heart of Redness.* Cape Town: Oxford University Press (New York: Farrar, Straus, and Giroux, 2002).

2002. *The Madonna of Excelsior.* Cape Town: Oxford University Press (New York: Farrar, Straus, and Giroux, 2004).

2005. *The Whale Caller.* Johannesburg: Penguin.

2007. *Cion.* Johannesburg: Penguin.

Drama

1979. *Dark Voices Ring. Sketsh* (Winter): 29–34.

1979–80. *The Hill. Scenaria* 16 (November–January), a six-page insert between pages 48 and 49 and *Scenaria* 17 (January–March 1980), an eight-page insert between pages 48 and 49.

1980. *We Shall Sing for the Fatherland and Other Plays.* Johannesburg: Ravan (*Dead End; Dark Voices Ring*).

1990. *The Plays of Zakes Mda.* Introduction by Andrew Horn. Johannesburg: Ravan (*Dead End; We Shall Sing for the Fatherland; Dark Voices Ring; The Hill; The Road*).

1992a. *Kalamazoo!* Unpublished.

1992b. *The Dying Screams of the Moon.* Unpublished.

1993a. *And the Girls in Their Sunday Dresses: Four Works.* Introduction by Bhekizizwe

Peterson. Johannesburg: Wits University Press (*Joys of War; And the Girls in Their Sunday Dresses; Banned; The Final Dance*).

1993b. *We Shall Sing for the Fatherland*. Johannesburg: Ravan.

1995. *Broken Dreams*. Script. Johannesburg: Market Theatre Laboratory.

1996. *Four Plays*. Compiled and introduced by Zakes Mda. Florida Hills, South Africa: Vivlia (*So What's New* by Fatima Dike; *Umongikazi* by Maishe Maponya; *The Nun's Romantic Story* by Zakes Mda; *Member of Society* by Makwedini Mtsaka).

1997. *Dankie Auntie*. In: Granqvist, Raul and Jürgen Martini (eds.). *Preserving the Landscape of the Imagination: Children's Literature in Africa*. Special series of *Matatu: Journal for African Culture and Society* 17-18: 145-75. Amsterdam: Rodopi.

1998. *Let Us Play*. Compiled and introduced by Zakes Mda. Florida Hills, South Africa: Vivlia (*Love Letters* by Zakes Mda; *Kweku Ananse* by Walter Chakela; *The Extras* by Hilton Swemmer).

1999. *The Day of the Two Suns: The Trial of the Xhosa Prophetess Nongqawuswe*. Video recording. Johannesburg: Film Resource Unit; SABC2 Television (*Saints, Sinners and Settlers* series; script by Zakes Mda).

2002. *Fools, Bells, and the Habit of Eating: Three Satires*. Introduction by Rob Amato. Johannesburg: Wits University Press (*The Mother of All Eating; You Fool, How Can the Sky Fall?; The Bells of Amersfoort*).

Poetry

1977. 'Dance of the Ghosts', 'A Sad Song', 'Sad Times'. In: Fleischer, Tony (ed.). *New South African Writing (PEN)*. Hillbrow, Johannesburg: Lorton, 12-19.

1980. 'Birth of a People'. *Staffrider* 3(1): 17.

1986. *Bits of Debris: The Poetry of Zakes Mda*. Graphics by Alpheus Mosenye. Maseru, Lesotho: Thapama Books.

1992a. 'Bloodless Philosophies', 'In the Arms of Loving Fire', and 'My Desolate Kinsman'. *Staffrider* 10(3): 12-13.

1992b. 'Blossoms and Butterflies'. In: Kromberg, Steve and James Ogude (eds.). *Soho Square V*. London: Bloomsbury, 102-03.

1996a. 'Mamane'. In: de Kock, Leon and Ian Tromp (eds.). *The Heart in Exile: South African Poetry in English 1990-1995*. Johannesburg: Penguin, 227-28.

1996b. 'Slaughtered Gods' and 'Uninspired Graffiti'. *Staffrider* 12(1): 70-71.

Scholarly works

1983. 'Commitment and writing in theatre: The South African experience'. *The Classic* 2 (1): 13-15.

1984. 'Extracts'. In: Daymond, M.J., J.U. Jacobs and Margaret Lenta (eds.). *Momentum: On Recent South African Writing.* Pietermaritzburg: University of Natal Press, 295–97.

1987. 'The utilization of theatre as a medium for development communication: An examination of the Lesotho experience'. Ph.D. thesis. Cape Town: University of Cape Town.

1989. 'Marotholi Travelling Theatre: Towards an alternative perspective of development'. In: Ngara, Emmanuel and Andrew Morrison (eds.). *Literature, Language and the Nation.* Proceedings of the second general conference of the Association of University Teachers of Literature and Language (ATOLL) held at the University of Zimbabwe, 24–28 August, 1987. Harare: ATOLL, in association with Baobab Books: 113–19.

1990a. 'Marotholi Travelling Theatre: Towards an alternative perspective of development'. *Journal of Southern African Studies* 16(2): 352–58. Reprinted in 1994 in: Gunner, Liz (ed.). *Politics and Performance: Theatre, Poetry and Song in Southern Africa.* Johannesburg: Wits University Press: 203–10.

1990b. 'When people play people'. *African Kora* July/October: 3–4.

1993. *When People Play People: Development Communication through Theatre.* Johannesburg: Wits University Press; London: Zed Books.

1994a. 'Another theatre of the absurd'. In: Breitinger, Eckhard (ed.). *Theatre and Performance in Africa: Intercultural Perspectives (Bayreuth African Studies* 31: Yearbook of the Association for the Study of the New Literatures in English, Band 4). Bayreuth: University of Bayreuth, 105–12.

1994b. 'Learning from the ancient wisdom of Africa: In the creation and distribution of messages'. *Current Writing* 6 (2): 139–50.

1995a. 'Culture in the process of reconciliation in South Africa – Truth and Reconciliation Commission'. Paper presented at Seminar No.9, Centre for the Study of Violence and Reconciliation, Johannesburg. http://www.csvr.org.za/index.php?option=com_content&task=view&id=717&Itemid=191, accessed 26 September 2008.

1995b. 'Theater and reconciliation in South Africa'. *Theater* 25(3): 38–45.

1996a. 'Introduction'. In: Mda, Zakes (ed.). *Four Plays.* Florida Hills, South Africa: Vivlia, i–xxvi.

1996b. 'Politics and the theatre: Current trends in South Africa'. In: Davis, Geoffrey V. and Anne Fuchs (eds.). *Theatre and Change in South Africa.* Amsterdam: Harwood Academic, 193–218.

1997a. 'Acceptance speech for the Olive Schreiner Prize, 1997'. *The English Academy Review* 14: 279–81.

1997b. 'Theatre for children in South Africa'. In: Granqvist, Raoul and Jürgen Martini (eds.). *Preserving the Landscape of Imagination: Children's Literature in Africa*. Special series of *Matatu: Journal for African Culture and Society* 17–18. Amsterdam: Rodopi, 137–44.

1998a. 'Acceptance speech for the Thomas Pringle Award for Reviews, 1998'. *The English Academy Review* 15: 356–58.

1998b. 'Current trends in theatre for development in South Africa'. In: Attridge, Derek and Rosemary Jolly (eds.). *Writing South Africa: Literature, Apartheid and Democracy, 1970–1995*. Cambridge: Cambridge University Press, 257–64.

1999. 'Mourning for a town that didn't have to die'. In: Macfarlane, David (ed.). *The Mail & Guardian Bedside Book, 1999: A New Selection of Superb Journalism from Africa's Best Read*. Johannesburg: Mail & Guardian Books, 74–81.

2000. 'Then and now in a Free State town'. In: Macfarlane, David (ed.). *The Mail & Guardian Bedside Book, 2000: A Selection of Journalism from Africa's Best Read*. Johannesburg: Mail & Guardian Books, 11–16.

2001. 'Steve Biko's children'. Second Steve Biko Memorial Lecture. http://www.sbf.org.za/index.htm?sbf_prog_1_txt2b.htm~main, accessed 6 August 2007.

2002a. 'Introduction'. In: Kani, John. *Nothing but the Truth*. Johannesburg: Wits University Press, v–ix.

2002b. 'South African theatre in an era of reconciliation'. In: Harding, Frances (ed.). *The Performance Arts in Africa: A Reader*. London: Routledge, 279–89.

2006. 'South African theatre in an era of reconciliation'. In: Arndt, Susan and Katrin Berndt (eds.). *Words and Worlds: African Writing, Literature, and Society: A Commemorative Publication in Honour of Eckhard Breitinger*. Trenton, NJ: Africa World Press, 79–90.

Interviews

Anon. 2001. ' "I see stories everywhere": Interview with Zakes Mda'. *Internet: Africultures* (40): 17. http://www.africultures.com/anglais/articles_anglais/40mda.htm, accessed 26 September 2008.

Austen, Benjamin. 2005. 'An interview with Zakes Mda'. *nat creole* magazine. http://www.natcreole.com/features.htm#title1, Part i, accessed 16 December 2005; Part ii, accessed 19 January 2006.

Galgut, Damon. 2005. 'In conversation with Zakes Mda'. *The ABSA/LitNet Chain*

Interview. LitNet 19 July. http://www.litnet.co.za/chain/damon_galgut_vs_zakes_ mda.asp, accessed 19 January 2006.

Holloway, Myles. 1988. 'An interview with Zakes Mda'. *South African Theatre Journal* 2(2): 81–88.

Horne, Andrew. 1980. 'An interview with Zakes Mda'. *BBC Arts and Africa* 316: 1–5.

Kachuba, John B. 2005. 'An interview with Zakes Mda'. *Tin House* 20. http://www.tin house.com/issues/issue_20/interview.html, accessed 14 September 2005.

Mbele, Maggie. 1989. 'Profile: Putting people first: Interview with Zakes Mda'. *Tribute* 13 November: 62–64.

Mongo-Mboussa, Boniface. 2000. 'Interview with Zakess [Zakes] Mda: South Africa'. *Internet: Africultures* 24. http://www.africultures.com/anglais/articles_anglais/int_ mda.htm, accessed 26 September 2008.

Naidoo, Venu. 1997. 'Interview with Zakes Mda'. *Alternation* 4(1): 247–61.

Nuttall, Sarah and Cheryl-Ann Michael. 2000. 'African Renaissance: Interviews with Sikhumbuzo Mngadi, Tony Parr, Rhoda Kadalie, Zakes Mda, and Darryl Accone'. In: Nuttall, Sarah and Cheryl-Ann Michael (eds.). *Senses of Culture: South African Cultural Studies*. Cape Town: Oxford University Press, 107–26.

Rapola, Zacharia. 1996. 'Of life & art'. *Tribute* May: 54–56.

Salter, Denis.1997. ' "When people play people" in (post) apartheid South Africa: The theories and practices of Zakes Mda'. *The Brecht Yearbook* 22: 283–303.

Solberg, Rolf. 1999. 'Zakes Mda'. In: Solberg, Rolf. *Alternative Theatre in South Africa: Talks with Prime Movers since the 1970s*. Pietermaritzburg: Hadeda Books, 31–40.

Wachtel, Eleanor. 2000. 'Writers and company, with Eleanor Wachtel'. Toronto: CBC Radio Arts and Entertainment. 8 audio cassettes.

Wark, Julie. 2005. 'Interview with Zakes Mda'. *Studia Africana: Revista Interuniversitària d'estudis Africans* (Barcelona) 16: 109–23.

Weber, Rebeca L. 2004. 'Q&A: Zakes Mda'. *The Africana* 25 May. http:// www.africana.com, accessed 14 September 2005.

Williams, Elly. 2005. 'An interview with Zakes Mda'. *The Missouri Review* 28 (2): 62–79.

Critical Writings on Zakes Mda

A Select Bibliography

Amato, Rob. 2002. 'Introduction'. In: Mda, Zakes. *Fools, Bells, and the Habit of Eating: Three Satires*. Johannesburg: Wits University Press, v–xxi.

Attwell, David. 2005a. 'Introduction'. In: Attwell, David. *Rewriting Modernity: Studies in Black South African Literary History*. Pietermaritzburg: University of KwaZulu-Natal Press, 1–26.

———. 2005b. 'The experimental turn: Experimentalism in contemporary fiction'. In: Attwell, David. *Rewriting Modernity: Studies in Black South African Literary History*. Pietermaritzburg: University of KwaZulu-Natal Press, 169–204.

Austen, Benjamin. 2005. 'The pen or the gun: Zakes Mda and the post-apartheid novel'. *Harper's Magazine* February: 85–89.

Barnard, Rita. 2004. 'On laughter, the grotesque, and the South African transition: Zakes Mda's *Ways of Dying*'. *Novel* 37(3): 277–302.

———. 2006. 'The place of beauty: Reflections on Elaine Scarry and Zakes Mda'. In: Nuttall, Sarah and Henrietta Rose-Innes (eds.). *Beautiful Ugly: African and Diaspora Aesthetics*. Durham, NC: Duke University Press; Cape Town: Kwela, 102–21.

———. 2007. 'The location of post-apartheid culture'. In: Barnard, Rita. *Apartheid and Beyond: South African Writers and the Politics of Place*. New York: Oxford University Press, 147–74.

Bell, David. 2003. 'The persistent presence of the past in contemporary writing in South Africa'. *Current Writing* 15(1): 63–73.

———. 2006. 'The teller of tales: Zakes Mda and the storifying of post-apartheid South Africa'. In: Davis, Geoffrey V. (ed.). *Literatur in Wissenschaft und Unterricht*. 39(2/3): 157–75.

————. 2007. 'The intimate presence of death in the novels of Zakes Mda: Necrophilic worlds and traditional belief'. In: Rönning, Anne Holden and Lene Johannessen (eds.). *Readings of the Particular: The Postcolonial in the Postnational*. Amsterdam: Rodopi: 93–106.

Blumberg, Marcia Shirley. 1996. 'En-gendering voice, staging intervention: Constructions of women in contemporary South African theatre'. Ph.D. thesis. Toronto: York University.

Cloete, Nettie and Richard Ndwayamato Madadzhe. 2007. 'Zakes Mda: Shifting female identities in *The Heart of Redness*'. *English Academy Review* 24: 37–50.

Cosser, Michael. 1991. 'Dramatic discourse in the foreground of *The Hill*'. *South African Theatre Journal* 5(2): 66–79.

Courau, Rogier Philippe. 2004. 'Re-imagining community histories in the South African fiction of Zakes Mda'. Master's thesis. Durban: University of KwaZulu-Natal.

————. 2005. 'Reading transnational histories: The representation of the Afrikaner in Zakes Mda's *The Madonna of Excelsior*'. *Scrutiny2: Special Issue: Transnationalism and African Literature* 10(2): 103–15.

Devant, Teresa. 1993. 'Zakes Mda: A director's view'. In: Mda, Zakes. *And the Girls in Their Sunday Dresses: Four Works*. Johannesburg: Wits University Press, xxv–xxviii.

Duggan, Carolyn. 1997a. 'Gabbling like a thing most brutish: The postcolonial writer and language, with reference to the earlier plays of Zakes Mda'. *South African Theatre Journal* 11(1/2): 109–32.

————. 1997b. 'Things of darkness: Character construction in the earlier plays of Zakes Mda'. *Alternation* 4(1): 27–44.

————. 1999. 'Strategies in staging: Theatre technique in the plays of Zakes Mda'. In: Banham, Martin, James Gibbs and Femi Osofisan (eds.). *African Theatre in Development (African Theatre 1)*. Oxford: James Currey, 1–12.

Farred, Grant. 2000. 'Mourning the postapartheid state already? The poetics of loss in Zakes Mda's *Ways of Dying*'. *Modern Fiction Studies: South African Fiction after Apartheid* 46(1): 183–206.

Feldbruegge, Astrid. 2004. 'The representation of hybridity in Zakes Mda's *The Heart of Redness*'. Master's thesis. Leipzig: Institute of English Studies, University of Leipzig.

Flockemann, Miki. 2004. 'Traumas and transformations: Fictions which play with what "they say", by Zakes Mda and Lindsey Collen'. *Journal of Literary Studies* 20(3/4): 248–64.

Gohrisch, Jana. 2006. 'Cultural exchange and the representation of history in postcolonial literature'. *European Journal of English Studies* 10(3): 231-47.

Goodman, Ralph. 2004. 'De-scribing the centre: Satiric and postcolonial strategies in *The Madonna of Excelsior*'. *Journal of Literary Studies* 20(1/2): 62-70.

Gorak, Jan. 1989. 'Nothing to root for: Zakes Mda and South African resistance theatre'. *Theatre Journal* 41(4): 478-91.

Gräbe, Ina. 1998. 'Real and imagined space in Zakes Mda's *Ways of Dying*'. *Anglo Files* 106 (April): 63-66.

Hagemann, Michael Eric. 2005. 'Humour as a postcolonial strategy in Zakes Mda's novel, *The Heart of Redness*'. Master's thesis. Bellville: University of the Western Cape.

Holloway, Myles Kenton. 1988. 'Zakes Mda's plays: The art of the text in the context of politics'. Master's thesis. Durban: University of Natal.

————. 1989a. 'Discordant voices of a lived reality: Zakes Mda's *The Hill*'. *South African Theatre Journal* 3(2): 33-50.

————. 1989b. 'Social commentary and artistic mediation in Zakes Mda's early plays'. *The English Academy Review* 6: 28-41.

Holloway, Myles, Deidre Byrne and Michael Titlestad. 2001. 'The politics of reading [and] writing'. In: Holloway, Myles, Deidre Byrne and Michael Titlestad. *Love, Power and Meaning*. Cape Town: Oxford University Press, 271-337.

Horn, Andrew. 1986. 'South African theater: Ideology and rebellion'. *Research in African Literatures* 17(2): 211-33.

————. 1990. 'People are being murdered here: An introduction to the theatre of Zakes Mda'. In: Mda, Zakes. *The Plays of Zakes Mda*. Johannesburg: Ravan Press, vii-liv.

Jacobs, Anthony. 2005. 'Flying in the face of convention: *The Heart of Redness* as rehabilitative of the South African pastoral literary tradition through the frame of universal myth'. Master's thesis. Bellville: University of the Western Cape.

Jacobs, J.U. 2000. 'Zakes Mda and the (South) African Renaissance: Reading *She Plays with the Darkness*'. *English in Africa* 27(1): 55-74.

————. 2002. 'Zakes Mda's *The Heart of Redness*: The novel as *umngqokolo*'. *Kunapipi: Special Issue: South Africa Post-Apartheid* 24(1/2): 224-36.

————. 2003. ' "Singing in a split tone": Hybridising history in the novels of Zakes Mda'. In: Monti, Alessandro and John Douthwaite (eds.). *Migrating the Texts: Hybridity as a Postcolonial Literary Construct*. Turin: L'Harmattan Italia.

John, Philip. 2003. 'Verowering in *Duiwelskloof* (1998) en *The Heart of Redness* (2000):

Implikasies van ons siening van die verlede vir ons toekoms'. *Stilet* 15(1): 284–301.

Kerr, David. 1996. 'African theories of African theatre'. *South African Theatre Journal* 10 (1): 3–23.

Koyana, Siphokazi. 2003. 'Qholorha and the dialogism of place in Zakes Mda's *The Heart of Redness*'. *Current Writing* 15(1): 51–62.

Litkie, Celeste Avril. 2003. 'Selected black African dramatists south of the Zambezi'. Ph.D. thesis. Stellenbosch: University of Stellenbosch.

Liu, Yao-Kun. 2003. 'Zakes Mda's *We Shall Sing for the Fatherland*: An illustration of African life using European dramatic modes'. *English in Africa* 30(1): 123–34.

Lloyd, David. 2001. 'The modernization of redness'. *Scrutiny2* 6(2): 34–39.

Lombardozzi, Letizia Maria. 2002. 'Gender on the frontline: A comparative study of the female voice in selected plays of Athol Fugard and Zakes Mda'. Master's thesis. Westville: University of Durban-Westville.

Lombardozzi, Litzi. 2005. 'Harmony of voice: Women characters in the plays of Zakes Mda'. *English in Africa* 32(2): 213–26.

Mazibuko, Nokuthula. 2005. 'Silence and violence in *She Plays with the Darkness*'. *Scrutiny2: Special Issue: Transnationalism and African Literature* 10(2): 93–102.

Mervis, Margaret. 1998. 'Fiction for development: Zakes Mda's *Ways of Dying*'. *Current Writing* 10(1): 39–56.

Mngadi, Sikhumbuzo. 2005. 'Some thoughts on black male homosexualities in South African writing: Zakes Mda's *The Hill* and Kaizer Nyatsumba's *In Happiness and in Sorrow*'. *English in Africa* 32(2): 155–68.

Moslund, Sten Pultz. 2003. *Making Use of History in New South African Fiction: An Analysis of the Purposes of Historical Perspectives in Three Post-apartheid Novels*. Copenhagen: Museum Tusculanum Press, University of Copenhagen.

Naidoo, Venugopaul. 1998. 'Magic realism in Zakes Mda's *Ways of Dying* (1995) and *She Plays with the Darkness* (1995)'. Ph.D. thesis. Westville: University of Durban-Westville.

Panday, Sunitha. 2004. 'Singing for the fatherland: Four South African protest plays'. Master's thesis. Durban: University of KwaZulu-Natal.

Peeters, Erik. 2007. 'The accidental activist: Reading Zakes Mda's *The Heart of Redness* as a parody of the disappointed African intellectual'. *Internet: Postamble* 3(2): 30–43.

Peterson, Bhekizizwe. 1993. 'Introduction'. In: Mda, Zakes. *And the Girls in Their Sunday Dresses: Four Works*. Johannesburg: Wits University Press, vii–xxiv.

————. 2000. 'Zakes Mda: 6 October 1948–'. In: Scanlon, Paul A. (ed.). *South African Writers (Dictionary of Literary Biography, v.225)*. Farmington Hills, MI: The Gale Group, 257–69.

Pheto, Rakgomo. 2002. 'Perspectives of tragedy in black South African drama: An analysis of selected plays by Zakes Mda, Mbongeni Ngema and Maishe Maponya'. Master's thesis. Potchefstroom: Potchefstroom University for Christian Higher Education.

Ruden, S. 1998. 'Thoughts on Mda, Ndebele and black South African writing at the millennium'. *The Iowa Review* 28(2): 155–66.

Samin, Richard. 2000a. ' "Burdens of rage and grief": Reconciliation in post-apartheid fiction'. *Commonwealth Essays and Studies* 23(1): 19–26.

————. 2000b. 'Marginality and history in Zakes Mda's *Ways of Dying*'. *Anglophonia/ Caliban* 7: 189–99.

Schauffer, Dennis and Mahendra Raghunath. 1999. *Zakes Mda: A Profile*. Westville: ASOKA.

Sewlall, Harry. 2003. 'Deconstructing empire in Joseph Conrad and Zakes Mda'. *Journal of Literary Studies* 19(3/4): 331–44.

————. 2007. ' "Portmanteau biota" and ecofeminist interventions in Zakes Mda's *The Heart of Redness*'. *Journal of Literary Studies: Special Issue: Ecocriticism/Ekokritiek Part 2* 23(4): 374–89.

Solberg, Rolf. 1999. 'Introduction'. In: Solberg, Rolf. *Alternative Theatre in South Africa: Talks with Prime Movers since the 1970s*. Pietermaritzburg: Hadeda Books, 1–30.

Steinmeyer, Elke. 2003. 'Chanting the song of sorrow: Threnody in Homer and Zakes Mda'. *Current Writing* 15(2): 156–72.

Titlestad, Michael and Mike Kissack. 2003. ' "The foot does not sniff": Imagining the post-"anti"-apartheid intellectual'. *Journal of Literary Studies* 19 (3/4): 255–70.

Twalo, Thembinkosi Gladden. 2001. 'The subversion of nationalist politics in Zakes Mda's *Ways of Dying*'. Master's thesis. Johannesburg: University of the Witwatersrand.

Uwah, Chijioke Macdonald. 1998. 'A sceptical dramatist in the South African political context: A study of Zakes Mda's use of symbolism and satire'. Master's thesis. Bloemfontein: University of the Orange Free State.

Uwah, Chijioke. 2003. 'The theme of political betrayal in the plays of Zakes Mda'. *English in Africa* 30(1): 135–44.

————. 2004. 'Theatre as social critique in the South African political context: The plays of Zakes Mda'. *Acta Academica* 36 (1): 84–100.

Uwah, Chijioke and Roy Muller. 2003. 'The development of dramatic symbolism and satire in the plays of Zakes Mda and the realities of South Africa's political situation'. *Acta Academica* 35(1): 154-66.

Van Vuuren, Sonja. 2004. 'South African satire: A study of Zakes Mda's *The Madonna of Excelsior*'. Master's thesis. Stellenbosch: University of Stellenbosch.

Van Wyk, Johan. 1997. 'Catastrophe and beauty: *Ways of Dying*, Zakes Mda's novel of the transition'. *Literator* 18(3): 79-90.

Vital, Anthony. 2005. 'Situating ecology in recent South African fiction: J.M. Coetzee's *The Lives of Animals* and Zakes Mda's *The Heart of Redness*'. *Journal of Southern African Studies* 31 (2): 297-313.

Walder, Dennis. 1998. 'Spinning out the present: Narrative, gender, and the politics of South African theatre'. In: Attridge, Derek and Rosemary Jolly (eds.). *Writing South Africa: Literature, Apartheid and Democracy, 1970-1995*. Cambridge: Cambridge University Press, 204-20.

Wenzel, Marita. 2003. 'Appropriating space and transcending boundaries in *The Africa House* by Christina Lamb and *Ways of Dying* by Zakes Mda'. *Journal of Literary Studies* 19(3/4): 316-30.

Woodward, Wendy. 2003. '"Jim comes from Jo'burg": Regionalised identities and social comedy in Zakes Mda's *The Heart of Redness*'. *Current Writing* 15(2): 173-85.

————. 2005. 'Laughing back at the kingfisher: Zakes Mda's *The Heart of Redness* and postcolonial humour'. In: Reichl, Susanne and Mark Stein (eds.). *Cheeky Fictions: Laughter and the Postcolonial*. Amsterdam: Rodopi, 287-99.

————. 2007a. 'Postcolonial ecologies and the gaze of animals: Reading some contemporary Southern African narratives'. *Journal of Literary Studies* 19(3/4): 290-315.

————. 2007b. 'The killing (off) of animals in some southern African fiction, or, "Why does every animal story have to be sad?"' *Journal of Literary Studies Special Issue: Ecocriticism/Ekokritiek Part 1* 23(3): 293-313.

Notes on Contributors

David Bell (Ph.D. Umeå University) is a freelance translator and independent researcher. His research interests include British working-class writing of the 1930s and contemporary South African fiction. His publications include *Ardent Propaganda: Miners' Novels and Class Conflict, 1929–1939* (1995); *Latitude 63° North* (ed. 2002), and *Joseph Conrad's 'Nigger of the Narcissus': A Dialogue Seminar* (ed. 2002). He recently co-edited, with Gerald Porter, a volume of essays called *Riots in Literature* (2008).

Rogier Courau obtained his Master's degree from the University of KwaZulu-Natal, with a dissertation on the novels of Zakes Mda, and his Ph.D. was on black South African intellectual histories and writings in the first part of the twentieth century. He was a doctoral fellow in African literature at the University's Centre for African Literary Studies in Pietermaritzburg and has also been a visiting researcher at the Interdepartmental Program in Afro-American Studies at the University of California, Los Angeles. He is currently lecturing in the Department of English Literature at the University of the Witwatersrand.

Hilary P. Dannenberg is Professor of English Studies and Anglophone Literatures at the University of Bayreuth in Germany. She has a Ph.D. in German Literature from the University of Cardiff and a higher doctorate (*Habilitation*) in English Literature from the University of Freiburg. She has published articles on American and British film and television, narrative theory, post-colonial Anglophone literatures and British fiction. Her book, *Coincidence and Counterfactuality: Plotting Time and Space in Narrative Fiction*, was published in 2008.

Carolyn Duggan completed a Ph.D. on the early plays of Zakes Mda at the National University of Ireland, Cork, where she currently lectures in drama in the English Department. She is artistic director of the Thinking Image Theatre Company and works professionally as a director and actor in Ireland.

Grant Farred is Professor of Africana Studies and English at Cornell University. He is the author of several books, most recently, *Midfielder's Moment: Coloured Literature and Culture in Contemporary South Africa* (1999), *What's My Name? Black Vernacular Intellectuals* (2003), *Phantom Calls: Race and the Globalization of the NBA* (2006) and *Long Distance Love: A Passion for Football* (2008). He is the general editor of the journal *South Atlantic Quarterly*.

Gail Fincham is head of the Department of English at the University of Cape Town. She has edited, co-edited and contributed to three volumes on Joseph Conrad: *Under Postcolonial Eyes: Joseph Conrad after Empire* (1996), *Conrad at the Millennium* (2001) and *Conrad in Africa* (2002). She has also contributed chapters to *Conrad: Voice, Sequence, History, Genre* (2008) and *J.M. Coetzee and the Aesthetics of Place* (forthcoming). With Jeremy Hawthorn and Jakob Lothe, she co-edited *Literary Landscapes from Modernism to Postcolonialism* (2008).

Ralph Goodman teaches in the English Department at the University of Stellenbosch. His current research areas include South African cityscapes, South African society in transformation, truth and reconciliation, parodic-travestying texts in post-1994 South African literature, and liminality and boundary issues.

Shane Graham is Assistant Professor of English at Utah State University and formerly a Mellon post-doctoral fellow at the University of the Witwatersrand. His book, *South African Literature after the Truth Commission: Mapping Loss*, is forthcoming and his essays have appeared in journals such as *Studies in the Novel, Modern Fiction Studies, Theatre Research International, Safundi, Research in African Literatures* and *Scrutiny2*.

J.U. Jacobs (Ph.D. Columbia University) is Senior Professor of English and Fellow of the University of KwaZulu-Natal in Durban. He has published extensively on South African and post-colonial fiction and autobiography; his most recent, co-edited book was *a.k.a. Breyten Breytenbach: Critical Approaches to his Writings and Paintings* (2004). His current research projects are on diasporic identities in contemporary South African fiction and the use of paintings in post-colonial novels.

Mike Kissack teaches in the School of Education at the University of the Witwatersrand. His main research areas are in the development of courses in the humanities in the post-apartheid curriculum, with a particular focus on the future of literary and historical studies. His recent publications include essays in *Postcolonial Studies*, *English in Africa* and *Religion and Theology: A Journal of Contemporary Religious Discourse*, all of which are co-authored with Michael Titlestad.

T. Spreelin MacDonald is a Ph.D. student of African Literature and Performance Studies at Ohio University's School of Interdisciplinary Arts. His research concerns South African cultural studies, publics and the intersections of literature and performance.

Nokuthula Mazibuko obtained a Ph.D. on the novels of Zakes Mda from the University of the Witwatersrand. She has taught at the Universities of Cape Town and Witwatersrand. For e.tv, the SABC and ZIFF, she wrote and directed *Lady Was a Mshoza*, *The Gift of Song* and *The Spirit of No Surrender*. She also directed two documentary films on South African writers for the series *Mantswe a Bonono*. She has published two novellas for youth, *In the Fast Lane* and *A Mozambican Summer*, as well as a collective biography, *Spring Offensive*.

Sally-Ann Murray is an award-winning poet and Associate Professor in the Department of English at the University of KwaZulu-Natal in Durban. Her current research is on forms of South African art, with publications that explore the work of Ivan Vladislavić Willem Boshoff and Leora Farber.

Meg Samuelson is Senior Lecturer in the English Department at the University of Stellenbosch. She has published a number of articles on southern African literature and culture, as well as *Remembering the Nation, Dismembering Women? Stories of the South African Transition* (2007), and co-edited *Nobody Ever Said Aids: Poems and Stories from Southern Africa* (2004).

Harry Sewlall obtained his Ph.D. on the early works of Joseph Conrad. He has published journal articles and book chapters on a wide range of subjects – from Zakes Mda and Ngugi wa Thiong'o to George Orwell, Fyodor Dostoevsky and Joseph Conrad – in South African publications, as well as abroad. He is an Associate Professor at North-West University (Mafikeng Campus).

Michael Titlestad is Associate Professor of Literary Studies at the University of the Witwatersrand and has recently been seconded to the Wits Institute for Social and Economic Research (WISER). He has published in the field of post-colonial literary and jazz studies, and is the author of *Making the Changes: Jazz in South African Literature and Reportage* (2004). He is currently engaged in writing a collection of essays on the literary representation of shipwrecks from the late 1700s to the present.

Christopher Warnes is Lecturer in Postcolonial and Related Literatures and Fellow of St John's College, University of Cambridge. He previously taught at the University of Stellenbosch in South Africa. His book, *Magical Realism and the Postcolonial Novel: Between Faith and Irreverence*, is forthcoming in 2009.

Wendy Woodward is Professor in the English Department at the University of the Western Cape, where she teaches post-colonial literature, literature and ecologies, and creative writing. Her book, *The Animal Gaze in Southern African Narratives*, was published in 2008. *Love, Hades and Other Animals* (2008) is her most recent poetry collection.

N.S. Zulu is Professor of African Languages at the University of Stellenbosch. He writes poems, short stories and novels in Sesotho, and has published articles and books on these genres. His first novel, *Nonyana ya tshepo*, won first prize in the Kagiso-FNB Literary Awards (1996–97) for a novel written in Sesotho. His latest Sesotho novel is *O titimetse*. His current research is on cultural translation in literary texts.

Index